Table of conte

This book is dedicated to all the haters who told me I couldn't do it, and laughed when I said I'm into astrology.

More importantly, this book is dedicated to my sister Amy, as a present on her 34th birthday, and my nephew Eli, for having an eclipse on his very first.

Testimonials

Britney Utecht
  I knew Matt for several years before he got into astrology. After he guessed my birth time to the exact minute I had him read the natal chart for my toddler as well. He scarily predicted my son's issue with croup and TWICE forecasted the week the flare ups would occur. Then one day he told me I would be getting a phone call from my younger brother's estranged ex-wife and sure enough, forty-five minutes later my phone rang with her screaming on the end. From his column in the Betty Pages to my personal horoscope I truly enjoy reading his writing.

Rikka Johnson
  Matt and I played softball for a decade before he introduced me to astrology. My first major question was about my marriage and if I was headed for divorce. He honestly replied "Yes" and sure enough the relationship fell through. About a year later he told me I would be finding a new job and boyfriend. I had sincere doubts but, as predicted, both came true during the week he told me and I love both my job and my man! Matt is a wonderful astrologer whose work is truly an inspiration.

Eric Arps
  Matt was one of my best friends since the eighth grade and when he came to me wanting to predict my future with the stars I told him he was full of s*!$. He force fed me this astrology stuff and to my dismay he was actually right. His first prediction came true, so did his second, and eventually he told me when my wife would get pregnant. Today, as much as I want to punch him in the

2

head, he's actually spot on and I even ask him when to align my children's birthday and time.

Matt Simon

I knew Matt back in high school playing basketball on the playground and working at the same telemarketing firm for a bit. We lost contact after graduation when I moved to California but when he asked for some help I extended my hand. The horoscopes he wrote for my wife and daughter were accurate and very well written and my personal report definitely helped open my eyes. His predictions are yet to be determined but given his track record I eagerly anticipate his forecast. This book is a wonderful asset for anyone interested in astrology whether you're educated on the subject or not.

My Introduction

I slapped my dick on Oprah Winfrey's front door. No I didn't have sex with the big O. Nor, did I have sex with her door. I did, however, whip out my pecker and mushroom stamp the hinge side on one of the doors for her Hawaiian ranch house. How I accomplished such a feat doesn't need to be too publicized, but it's there, my personal stamp of approval somewhere on her front door. Deep down, I'm nothing but a wild assed yahoo who enjoys drinking beer, smoking pot, and fist fights just like every other good hearted Christian American. I've been abducted by aliens since I was three, talking to ghosts since I was ten, and harassing law enforcement since nineteen. Take one look at me and you'll never guess I'm passionate about astrology. It took a very harsh and dysfunctional life leading me down many paths and I suppose I wouldn't have it any other way. The intention of this book isn't a boohoo woe is me tale about my horrible life but hopefully an inspiration either spiritually or intellectually. I only bring up my past to emphasize the desolation astrology guided me out of. My goal is to teach others the basics of astrology and a little of the spirituality which helped me deal with depression, mental illness, and suicidal despair. Some of my experiences are written in this book although most are not. I'm a no bullshit guy who didn't think for one second the planets had any influence on us humans. When it came to astrology I was like most any other random person. I knew I was an Aries and had a primitive knowledge about what that meant. I understood on an astronomical level that the Sun appears in different constellations as we revolve and that the Moon followed suit, but that was it.

If you don't believe in astrology that's fine, neither did I. Religion or spirituality had nothing to do with my interest either. I picked up an introductory book determined to teach myself the Moon phases hoping to become a better fisherman. Everything I read touched me so personally and helped explain my less fortunate life that I became infatuated and couldn't stop. Never once had anything opened my mind or soul like the stars had. I grew up in a Lutheran church and had my own radical opinions about religion but nothing prepared me for this. The more I studied the more I found how influential astrology once was. Now that my eyes are opening I can see how all the major religions around the world have an astrological basis to them. Islam, Judaism, and even those crazy Christians are entrenched in the cosmos without even knowing it. Read this book and just take what you want and leave the rest. I've been rescued by the stars and if you want to learn how I did it, this was my path. Your journey and destination will definitely be different, but if you've come this far you obviously have an interest which shouldn't be suppressed. Whatever your motives, I hope you find as much comfort as I did, and realize your place amongst the universe.

My dysfunctional path

At six years old my life was that of any normal child. I lived in a small town called Ferndale in the most Pacific Northwest corner of Washington State. My father was a stone mason who worked on the potlines at an aluminum plant while my mother was a part time secretary at the local courthouse and library. Until I was eight everything seemed to fall in line with the American dream and then my dad starting acting extremely different. There were nights when he wouldn't come home from work until the wee hours of the morning without any explanation. He would go out with his friends not telling us where he was or what he was doing. I would fall asleep crying myself senseless not knowing where my daddy was. After a while we found out he had developed a horrible addiction to cocaine and was spending all his time and money entrenched in drugs. After a long battle in and out of multiple rehabilitation facilities, my mother inevitably had to divorce him. I understood more than most youngsters would, and the fact my father only moved a short distance away definitely helped ease the transition. Eventually his disease would cost him his job forcing him to move into an apartment with my grandpa and uncle and go to work with them. One day my grandfather had a heart attack on the job site and suddenly died right in the arms of my father. This catastrophe sent my father and uncles packing to Jackson Hole, Wyoming in search of steadier work. I was entering the sixth grade when all this mayhem occurred and, even though I didn't notice it at the time, my father's absence was greatly impacting my life. I know I'm not the only person to have their dad take off, but usually when a kid's father figure disappears like mine did there's an uncle, grandpa, or other family member who steps up and fills in. Not for me. All my family members lived thousands of miles away and completely ignored me.

Middle school skipped by with the usual teenage boy problems. I was misbehaving and regularly given after school detention for my pre-teen shenanigans. Once high school started I realized the emergency contact sheet the school sent home had a slot for the other guardian's signature in case the parents weren't together. Halfway through my freshman year after my mother signed her spot I would sign my father's name into the second slot so his signature was in my writing. Sometime during the second semester I began skipping school every day and writing my own excuse notes. At the end of my first year I had missed my math class twenty-five times during a ninety day semester. My sophomore, junior, and senior, years skipped by miserably, hitting rock bottom as a junior. I didn't have many friends. Most people teased me. I was the fat, funny looking poor kid who nobody really liked. I found a few friends as a member of the good old FFA and I definitely have some great memories to help ease the trouble but there was definitely more bad than good. For every wonderful memory I have there are four horrible ones with it. Most of my time was spent tucked away in my room playing video games, talking to the voices. Eventually my loneliness and isolation led me into suicidal depression. Near the end of my junior year I decided to take a handful of sleeping pills and drink a bottle of Nyquil. Obviously my attempt failed and the drugs only made me exceptionally sick. While throwing up like there's no tomorrow, my mind processed more thoughts about life than you could imagine. After passing out not knowing if I was going to wake up I finally came to the next morning with an adjusted outlook on life.

The rest of high school was spent not caring about any sort of responsibility, and after five years I graduated as a super senior and embarked out into society. Community college was my first destination which ended up as futile as high school. Because I was poor, I qualified for government grants and my schooling was free. This made it much easier for me to blow off class just like before. The fact my best friend lived a stoners throw away from the campus gave me a definite reason to skip class and smoke some pot. I sometimes wonder what life would be like if he hadn't lived there. After getting three V's and two incomplete grades my funding was taken away and I was forced into the working world. I was working at a fast food restaurant still living with my mother and at twenty I moved into my first house with one of my best friends. His parents owned an extravagant woodshop and because I was basically family, they gave me a job.

Eventually my thirtieth birthday rolled around and my life completely changed.

On May 26th 2012 I spent my first night on the wild streets of Bellingham, Washington sleeping in my bright and shiny ambulance. It had been an interesting turn of events leading me to such a scenario but there I was, overlooking the bay in a beautiful section of town called Fairhaven. Getting there hadn't been easy and the snowball effect actually started when one of my best friends bought an old ambulance off some dude from Craigslist. He owned it for a couple years but I definitely had my share of the crazy stories. Eventually my little putter car broke down and he told me it was for sale. Without hesitation it was mine and that's still the best 2000 dollars I've ever spent. My magnificent purchase occurred in February and my original plan was to make it livable and move to Vegas. I intended to umpire softball and work in restaurants for a couple years, have a little fun, then move back. It took me a couple months to put in cabinets, hardwood floors, and make a couple other minor adjustments but by my birthday in mid April my ambulance was habitable.

My thirtieth birthday was one of the worst days of my life. Despite the wild happiness of my ambulance I was slowly drifting into a deep pit of depression. Sitting at the bar by myself I had one friend that hadn't completely ditched me. He didn't remember it was my birthday and apologized through text a little but once I asked him to hang out he stopped responding completely. Nothing could describe the utter despair I felt. There I was. Thirty years old with no friends, no family, and never once had anyone showed me more positive attention than negative. Not my parents, not my family, and never once had I ever had a girlfriend. The last time I felt like this was a dozen years ago when I tried to kill myself. Somewhat sobbing as I finished my beer I decided this was finally it. I had a gun at home and no reason to live. Trudging the half mile walk home time passed incredibly quickly and to this day I'm

8

still surprised I'm alive. After getting to my place the little .22 rifle was already next to my bedside I truly believed this was going to be the end. A couple bong hits later the barrel was pressed against my forehead but as my finger reached for the trigger an unknown voice told me not to do it. Whether it was the voice of God or not doesn't matter. It said "Don't kill yourself and I'll give you something reasonable." I replied fine, I want to get fired and collect unemployment for the summer while I live in my ambulance. There was no response and four days later I got my wish.

Before my birthday I took a week vacation for some personal reflection. My fateful night was a Saturday, and when I returned to work on Monday my attitude had definitely changed. Sure enough the boss was having a bad day and after shrugging my shoulders at him a couple times I was sent packing. After a few weeks of red tape and paper filing and my unemployment checks came rolling in. At 350 dollars a week I made the equivalent of twelve bucks and hour at forty hours per week. Pretty easy to live off that. Insurance was cheap, my ambulance was paid off, and my cell phone cost twenty bucks a month. Other than a significant pot habit and basic living needs I had no bills of any kind. Craigslist provided a great opportunity to make some under the table cash and every once in a while I would do some odd moving or landscaping job. Those five months my life was the most carefree and spiritually enlightening time of my life. Of course Thoreau's classic Walden was my number on reading priority, and I was delighted to learn one of his frequently visited places was called Fairhaven as well. Haitian Voodoo and of course a little witchcraft was next on my list, but after some gnarly spirit stuff I needed to shun it aside for a while. Winter was approaching and I had no idea what was in store for me.

It was October of 2012. Unemployment was still paying me regularly and the odd jobs were becoming few and far between. The temperature but more importantly the sunlight was decreasing a little each day and by December I was living in utter cold and darkness. The heater in my ambulance was really good but it was connected to the entire engine radiator system so I had to have the ambulance running for it to work. Many nights were spent shivering myself to sleep. The coldest I can remember waking up was seventeen before the wind chill, and lord knows how many times my bong water froze at night. That little .22 rifle I kept was once again looking very enticing. One especially cold night I was overlooking the water thinking about ending it again. I was barefoot for some reason and as I fiddled around with the gun I proceeded to take aim at my little toe. Pablo Picasso came to mind, and it may sound weird but when I called to him he answered me. I said "Pablo, why did you cut off your ear?" He replied "Cause I knew I didn't need it anymore." "Really," I said. "That sounds odd." Then he burst out laughing and said. "You dumb mother fucker. I didn't cut off my ear. Van Gogh did." I chuckled at myself and simply unloaded a few bullets into the poster I had on my wall. Don't worry I knew what I was shooting into.

After a miserable three months I was living in a state of psychological doldrums. My friends had pretty much given up on me. Not once during the frigid cold snap did anyone call to check in on me. Nobody cared enough to think about me when it was below freezing and I was all alone in the dark. It was the middle of February and I could feel the light making a difference on my soul and brain. Then I was meddling through the spiritual section at the local library and saw a basic astrology book. Fishing was the first thing that came to mind, and I figured if I could determine how they migrated to the tide cycles I would catch more fish. Because the Moon influences the tides so much I wanted to correlate the two and start slanging some salmon. The book I chose intrigued me so spiritually I wanted more. Astrology helped explain my difficult life and upbringing. After diligently teaching myself the basic's I was ready for something more advanced. As I stared at the selection of books at the library Alan Oken's Complete Guide to Astrology started talking to me. After looking at Mr. Oken's natal chart I was astonished to see how similar we were. Three times in thirty days is how fast I read that book, and it completely changed my life. I was hooked. Astrology was now embedded in

10

my cosmic soul.

By 2014 I had been entrenched in natal astrology for a year and began my interest in predictive. When I when up to my best buddy Eric and told him he was going to get in a car crash near the middle of January. He told me I was full of shit and just shook his head like usual. To his damnedest surprise he was rear ended by a random driver near the day I had forecasted. With a little more interest he asked me to look ahead the world softball he was going to in Vegas. After looking at his chart I said he was going to get into a fist fight on such and such a date and time. Once again I was right. There he was, on the day I predicted sitting in the casino. Because he was too intoxicated they asked him to leave. I say that again. A casino in Las Vegas told my buddy he was too drunk to be in their establishment. He told them no and after a good scuffle he was escorted to the local jail. Fourteen hours after my astrological estimate.

These two predictions were just the tip of the iceberg. Random coffee baristas were my astrological guinea pigs and I was able to tell them when they would be finding a new job, and once I was able to figure out when one of them would be getting proposed to. In 2015 I realized the worst prediction you could think of. Seeing what was in store for me on my mundane birthday of June 15th I saw on June 15th of 2016 I was in store for a horrific event possibly involving the death of a family member. My grandmother was the first person I thought of and sure enough that fateful day rolled around. Sitting in the coffee shop like usual my premonition struck me like a rock. Over the previous nine months my grandmother and I developed a much deeper relationship. Never once had she ever had a driver's license and she was slowly deteriorating making it difficult to walk. I was keeping groceries in her fridge and stopping be once or even twice a day to check in, get something to eat, and socialize for a while. As I rang her doorbell that morning there was no answer. That didn't surprise me because it was sunny and at 10:00 in the morning on sunny days she was rarely home. My mother lived less than a mile up the street and I went there for a quick snack. She was worried about Nana

11

and told me to check on her. I told her I would in a couple hours and if she was so worried she should go check herself. Sure enough I showed up a little while later following in an ambulance with the lights flashing and sirens blaring. My mother's car was in the parking lot and I knew what was going on. Running up the stairs expecting the worst I got exactly what I anticipated. There she was, my Nana's lifeless blue body, being futility zapped by the paramedic's defibrillator. I was third in line discovering the body and although it was difficult at first I know deep everyone dies and Nana went out instantly and painlessly, sitting in her favorite chair watching television and the cars go by.

Over the few years I've been studying this craft there are more reasons than I can list for my belief in astrology. Read the yearly farmer's almanac and you'll be astonished at all the planet conjunctions and Moon phases. It's been around for more than 200 years for a reason. The more and more I follow the stars the more and more proof I get. My absolute favorite prediction is by far the incarnation of my little nephew Eli. On January 18th of 2016 I told my younger sister she would be having a baby around January 18th of 2017. Three months before she was pregnant I was able to give her a date and sure enough, her due date was January 22nd but she didn't have him until the 31st. My attempts at fishing have been as unproductive as it ever has. My first two tries resulted in me snapping my pole within fifteen minutes and throwing a bunch of gear into the river. After giving up for a couple seasons I hit the river again and saw more fish activity than ever. I've never caught anything more than a good buzz and a few Irish salmon (just a stick) but I definitely find more schools of fish. Now that you've read a little about my path to astrology it's time for you to begin yours. If you're an already knowledgeable astrologer you can skip straight to the interpretations and if you're brand new then simply continue on.

Getting started

Reading a natal chart is a lot easier than it looks. Once you get past the funny signs and symbols the puzzle clears up tremendously. The first step is acquiring your birth chart and the aide of technology has made that extremely simple. Several websites provide free chart generating services everyone can easily access. I use www.alabe.com, but other sites such as astrotheme.com or astro.com are also very popular. If you can figure out how, Astrotheme.com will even provide you with a list of your personal aspects. Creating a chart by hand is very time consuming and you'll have to consult an ephemeris, which I don't teach you how to use. As long as you have your birthday, time, and the city you were born in any of these sources can give you what you need.

Once you've acquired your chart you'll see a circle divided up into twelve sections with some unusual symbols around the outside. Those glyphs on the outside are the constellations and planets at their relative position for the time provided. Think of the circle as an upside down compass. East is on the left, up is the South, right is the West and down is the North. This is because from our vantage point the Sun is in the South. Each planet rises from the East on the left and continues to rise until it contacts the mid-heaven, then sets in the West. Two of the intersecting lines are usually bolder than the rest. The top half of the circle represents the sky overhead at the time selected. The bolder lines are very important divisions in your chart. One line is horizontal and the other is somewhat vertical. The horizontal line never moves but the vertical line most definitely does. On the left of this stationary line is the point called your ascendant or rising sign. As the Earth rotates, each constellation crosses this point in a span of about twenty-four hours. It's a very simple concept, one rotation equals one day. The vertical line represents the Earth's axis and usually has an arrow on the upper point. That arrow is called the mid-heaven, which is described more later on.

13

In the middle of the circle will be series of blue, red, and green lines. Blue lines are the sextiles and trines. Red lines are the Square, oppositions, sesquiquadrate. Green lines are the quincunx and semi-sextile. Their purpose is to show you which planets are within a given orb of influence. After your Sun, Moon and rising signs the aspects are the personality traits making you who you are.

Once you've acquired your natal chart here are the first few steps I use when interpreting.
1. Look at the ascendant and the relationship with the Sun. Whether good or bad this indicates how easily you integrate your spirit into your personality.
2. Look at the relationship between the ascendant and Moon. Whether good or bad this indicates how easily you integrate your emotions into your personality.
3. Look at the relationship between the Sun and Moon. This indicates how well you integrate your emotions and spirit.
4. Look at the sign of ascendant and the relationship to its ruling planet. This planet is your ruling planet.
5. Look at the relationship between the ruling planet to the Sun and Moon.

The planets

The Sun

  The Sun is only referred to as a planet for simplicity sake. It's one of the luminaries and the source of all energy driving human life. As the ruler of our solar system he governs many things. Every astrologer compares it to a battery and I am no different. Both natally and progressively, he charges our spirit, vitality, and will to live. His condition shows the nature of your human spirit and how easily you express it. Good aspects will make you pleasant and wonderful, while bad aspects indicate difficult energy. It may be difficulty recognizing the energy, difficulty accepting the energy, or the difficulty expressing the energy. This is the inner vitality trying to individualize itself through the human ego. Along with the ascendant, the Sun is the most important point in the natal chart. A lot can be told about someone by its condition alone. Bad aspects to your ascendant show difficulty recognizing the energy. Bad aspects to the Sun create bad energy coming from within. His alignment with your rising sign shows how easy you integrate the spirit within and the personality displayed. A disgruntled Sun in good aspect with your ascendant might be a horrible person being able to do horrible things easily. Alone, his basic nature he is to individualize the ego and establish himself as different or and more outstanding than his peers. House placement will show where you best direct yourself, and the sign will show the manner you do so. I call un-aspected Sun indicates the characteristic called "The light's are on, but no one's home syndrome." No aspects to your Sun indicates it can't direct the energy anywhere.

The Moon
        The Moon is the third most important part of the natal chart. She's the subconscious side of humanity and the cosmic partner to the Sun. Along with Venus she influences our femininity and nurturing emotions. Her condition will show your relationships towards women, especially your mother. Ruling the sign of Cancer, she has crablike claws which can be quite vicious when crossed. Taurus is her exalting sign and if you could take those claws and put a bull's attitude behind them you have the powers of the Moon. She fluctuates like the tides she controls, and is always changing her mind. Your unconscious habits and emotional reactions are her domain. Nostalgia and fond memories of the past are her resting place with tradition playing a large part as well. Her purpose is to provide comforting emotions like a mother to a child. This is not a dominant planet and her relationship with the others is much more important than the Sun's relationship with them. The Sun can function alone. The Moon cannot. She requires the light of the Sun in order for her beauty to shine. House placement will

15

show where your mind is always dreaming to and your place of retreat when severely distressed. She's as predictable as a hurricane, and by no means does logic or reason have anything to do with her thinking. She's total emotion. As the Sun's opposite, herd instinct drives her towards others because numbers provide her safety. When properly aligned there's nothing she can't help accomplish.

Mercury

Mercury is the smallest planet in our solar system and named after the wing footed Roman messenger who traveled at lightning speed. He rules intelligence, motor skills, and the nervous system. He's also in control of our communication skills and functions best in Gemini along with Virgo. His condition represents how fast you can intake and process information presented before you. I compare him to the processor of a computer. At roughly 36,000,000 miles away he's the closest planet to our Sun and takes only eighty-eight days to complete one revolution. He's never the main attraction, but the ultimate side-kick. His wit is uncanny and matched by none. Math, music, and science are all areas of expertise, but this little bugger can also be the annoying little child asking questions at every turn. Quickness and agility are a necessity because the smart-ass mouth he possesses is always instigating trouble. He loves childish pranks and irresponsible antics. While most of his characteristics are displayed intellectually, his physical influence isn't nearly as dominate. He's a lot like a squirrel, bouncing from branch to branch with the sharpest of motions. "Monkey see monkey do" is his general philosophy which makes learning by observing a snap.

Venus

Venus is the second planet from the Sun and often called Earth's sister planet. She rotates backwards and at a snail's pace. It takes her longer to spin on her axis then to revolve around the Sun. One rotation takes nearly 243 Earth days while a revolution takes 224. Taurus and Libra are her ruling signs, and being exalted in

Pisces she's the definition of beauty and grace. Describing Venus as a feminine planet I mean it in the very sense of the word. From womanly charm to female emotion her, along with the Moon, give us nurturing motherly compassion. This influence can be seen in your clothes, hairstyle, and even your voice. She's a very demanding and diva like planet that enjoys stirring up commotion. This lady makes mountains out of molehills unless she's the one at fault, and unlike Neptune who represents compassion for all humanity, Venus is only affectionate towards a select chosen few. Most likely the ones who shower her with the most extravagant gifts. Whether it be romantic, professional, or plutonic, her condition and house placement will show what you provide and what you will need to work on in order function within your relationships. Partnership is her number one priority and she's obliviously lost unless she's found a dedicated companion. She attracts possessions and is highly materialistic always requiring balance from someone else. Known as the lesser benefic, she brings us all the wonderful material stuff we love.

Mars

Mars is the fiery red planet who's known for aggression, determination, and energy. Not like the spiritual energy produced by the Sun, but the desire to take that spirit and go do something with it. Many times Mars is the bully who attacks weaker because he knows he can dominate easily. Only about twice the size of our Moon, he's the little short guy ready to drop everything and fight anyone who crosses his path. His mode of establishing dominance is usually by force. He's known as the Lesser Malefic, and his selfish ways aren't usually pleasant. Establishing your personal ego is the task he's been assigned and he does it by any means necessary. Battles are won because Mars refuses to concede in defeat, despite whatever the odds may be. Poor aspects will make you timid or mean, while positive aspects allow you to direct your energy into productive outlets. Possibly even more than the Sun, he's the epitome of masculinity and is the opposite attraction to Venus. Like Mercury and Venus he rules two signs. The bold pioneer Aries is his first sign of domain and the deadly sexual sign of Scorpio is his second. As best friend with the greater malefic Saturn, and he's exalted in Saturn's ruling sign of Capricorn, lacking any caring emotion. This planet is only concerned about one thing, himself. Negative aspect with other planets can indicate catastrophic accidents or illnesses. They can also produce extreme violence and hostility. His condition, along with much more important Venus, will show how well you get along with others.

Jupiter

Jupiter is the largest planet in our solar system and known to astrologer's as the greater benefic. He's the planet of higher spiritual thinking, expansion of human life, and the eternal optimist. He's as flamboyant as he is arrogant and is the wonderful teacher who's full of enthusiasm. No one sets higher expectations and nothing good is ever enough. It's like eating a gallon of ice cream. The first little bit was great but the final three spoonfuls aren't too pleasing. He stimulates growth spiritually and physically, sometimes needing harsh circumstances in order to make his point. He provides relief in disparity and saves you from the pits of hell. Picture Santa Claus as a planet. Religion or advanced forms of education and philosophy are his favorite topics, and he loves projects where the potential is limitless. He never believes in failure or rejection. This jolly giant has unachievable aspirations where moderation is a thing of the past. Hard work isn't for him because everything comes naturally and this sometimes becomes a problem. Because he can look past the negativity sometimes he's too forgiving and passive when he needs to be a tough ass. Sagittarius best expresses his spirituality while Pisces best displays his compassion. Cancer may be his sign of exaltation, but Jupiter produces great things in every sign, just in different ways. His position in your chart will show where you experience the most luck and feel the most spiritually comfortable. He's the greater benefic who gives us the grandest of grand philosophies.

18

Saturn

Saturn is the farthest of the personal planets and also the most distant planet known to astrologers until the discovery of Uranus. His general philosophies are responsibility, structure, stability, and sound reasoning, along with many others. He's the least flamboyant of any in the solar system, and prefers to be left al alone. The grinchiest Grinch of all time isn't as cold hearted as this planet. There's little room for emotion with his logic, and he doesn't care about your feelings when teaching you a lesson. It's definitely a masculine influence that represents your father figures and relationships with men. Capricorn is his most comfortable sign, and before Uranus he was in charge of Aquarius. He can be known to cause depression, emotional detachment, and fear or refusal of change. This is the brilliant and dedicated scientist who spends hundreds of hours proving himself wrong. Then after most would give up, an unexpected discovery from a totally different area finally opens his mind and allows the invention to succeed. Bad aspects, especially from Mars, can cause anger management along with anxiety problems. Because of his slow speed, house Saturn's house placement is more important than the closer planets. Where ever Saturn is placed in your charts will show where you need the most stability, and his condition will indicate how easily you express it.

Uranus

Uranus is barely, and I mean barely, on occasion, and under great conditions, visible to the naked eye. It's also the first in line of the generational planets and wasn't discovered until the later 1700's. At eighty-four years a cycle, it's the only generational planet you have a chance of completing once. This particular planet causes eccentricity, originality, rebelliousness, individuality, innovativeness, and the desire to break completely free from the standard norm. It adds a colorful fuel to the fire stirred up from the personal planets. He's the screaming yahoo on street corner hollering the end is near and the devil is among us. There's no

19

other rebel more inspired to die for the cause. He's an instantaneous outburst that no one can control. Any aspects with other planets are only important when in a close orb. Alignments must be closer than five degrees and grow exponentially in power as they become exact. This unconventional genius hates being told how to think and will discover gun powder while trying to invent the light bulb. Negative influences represent total anarchy and fanaticism. Not necessarily malefic like Saturn and Mars, but a close number three. Distinguishing oneself as a separate individual in a proper manner will be requires or you'll turn to a life of crime to gain attention. He's associated with the sign of Aquarius and ruler of the eleventh house. The house this planet occupies will show where you strive to be the most unique and independent.

Neptune

Neptune is second in line of the generational planets and wasn't discovered until 1846. This planet represents total compassion and oneness with all. It's the mystic magician, distorted painter, and dramatic actor. Like the other two generation planets Neptune's expressions are displayed through Venus, Mars, and the closer friends of the solar system. Close orbs of aspect are required to fully experience these delusions. The reason Neptune is so good at what it does is because he can escape reality and enter the other realms of the universe. He is pure psychicism and wonder. Extreme influences make you oblivious to fraud and deceit. In no way does this planet provide stability or structure. This is the color, style, and glamour of whatever is being built. Just as your interests may be music, theater, or art, it can be drugs and alcohol as well. Depression and ultimate sadness make are Ultimate compassion and understanding for all. The dynamics of Neptune instill the spirit to fulfill social obligations in the most ego-denying way. The dreamland of Pisces is the most comfortable sign and water is definitely the most satisfying element. Relationships with Venus or the Moon will stimulate emotion and sympathy. Bad aspects will dissolve and structure the planets are trying to create. All and all it's the essence of your imagination.

Pluto

Each of the generational planets represents the ultimate something. Uranus is ultimate independence, Neptune is ultimate compassion, and Pluto is ultimate obsession. This can be obsession about something good or something bad. Jealousy, possessiveness, even violence are associated with this distant dwarf. Like Uranus and Neptune, Pluto expresses itself through the other planets and directs the infatuation through them. Being the farthest planet in our solar system not much is known about Pluto. After first discovered by Clyde Tombaugh in Flagstaff, Arizona in 1930, we have barely scratched the surface of Pluto's capabilities. He's compared to Shiva the Hindu god of destruction, and in my personal experiences I couldn't agree more. Pluto is the intensifying catalyst working like gasoline on a fire. He can resurrect you from hell, but first you have to go there. Massive transformations and changes through catastrophic events are the way Pluto works, much like the phoenix rising from the ashes. There's no room for B.S. here. Demands of the inevitable are met through the evolving social structures catalyzed by the forces of Pluto. He prefers a subtle approach with an explosively magnificent ending. None of the energies of Pluto dictate any one area of life. Very similar to Neptune his roots are deeply imbedded in your subconscious mind. No matter what though, Pluto has an inner lust for complete consumption of any and all resources. Pluto follows suit with Mars by ruling Aries and Scorpio alongside him.

Ascendant/rising sign

By definition, your ascendant is the degree of the constellation rising due East at the time you were born. Time and position on Earth both affect this point making that information vitally important. Often called the rising sign, this is arguably the most important point in the natal chart. The Sun represents your spiritual energy burning within. The Moon represents your emotions and subconscious. Your rising sign is the combination of both into a physical entity. It's more like a second Sun sign than

21

Moon sign, and quite often people relate to the traits of their rising sign more than their Sun. This point is that the Sun and Moon are trying to establish and express as different. No matter what, it's the beginning of the first house and is just as important progressively as natally. Good aspects from other planets allow you to use their energies efficiently, while obviously bad aspects will make things difficult. Like the Sun you can get a good idea of a person's overall character by their rising sign. If no planets are in aspect with your rising sign then the Sun takes over as ruler, and you probably have lots of trouble finding yourself. Some people never do. Whichever planets are in aspect will be more powerful and influential in your chart. Those in line will be your strengths and weaknesses.

Mid-heaven

Like the eclipse node, the mid-heaven isn't an actual entity you can go out and see. It's the invisible point in the sky where the planets begin their decent along the horizon. Picture an arc from East to West representing the path each planet takes while rising and setting each day. The mid-heaven is the very top of that arc, indicating several important things in your chart. Similar to the ascendant, its position changes based on what time and place you were born in. A person who was born in the Northern hemisphere with the twentieth degree of Gemini rising will have a different mid-heaven than someone born below the equator with the identical rising sign. Personally, it represents the style and manner in which you express your ego to the public. Behind your big three this is the fourth or fifth most important point in your chart. If you ever want to make someone mad look at their mid-heaven and tell them that's what they're not. Tell a Taurus they don't work hard, or an Aquarius they're not smart, or a Virgo their facts are wrong. No matter what, this point is the beginning of your tenth house. Your occupation is directly dictated by this and if you're not happy with your job it's because you're not following your mid-heaven. Or, you have horrible aspects natally and you'll never be happy at work. In my opinion this is a more important point progressively than natally. Transiting planets over this part of your chart always

22

stimulate action in the business area of your life.

North/South Nodes:
     The eclipse nodes aren't an actual physical entity we can see with our eyes. There's the North node and the opposite south. Astronomically, it represents is the point in our ecliptic where the Sun and Moon cross paths. Picture two hula hoops representing the path of the Sun and Moon around the Earth. The nodes are where the hoops intersect and we experience a solar or lunar eclipse. This is by far the most karmic point in your chart in your natal chart it, and shows where your soul is trying to go and what it's needing to learn in your life. Your North node indicates where you're going and the South shows where you feel most comfortable and are somewhat stuck in from previous lives. Extensive books are written about this point alone and it's best just to recognize it as a second Jupiter like planet. It teaches you philosophical lessons by whatever sign and house placement you have in your chart. The sign it's in displays the style your soul is learning, and house placement shows the manner you will learn your philosophies.

Dignitaries
     Each of the planets has a set of signs which increases or restricts their energy. Given the names ruling and exalting, these are the two signs the planet will operate best in, while the sign of detriment will oppose the rule and the falling signs sits across from the exalting. The only argument you will get from me about dignitaries is about the planet Uranus. I fell that planet is exalted in Gemini and treat it as such. Most astrologers accept Scorpio as the standard exaltation of the planet but I strongly disagree. I feel the intellect and other properties of Gemini are much more associated with the energies of Uranus. Given the relative newness of the generational planets I don't think astrologers can make an educated decision for many years. I definitely agree with the standard Neptune and Pluto rulerships astrologers have given them, but Uranus is different.

Planet	Rulership	Detriment	Exaltation	Fall
Sun	Leo	Aquarius	Aries	Libra
Moon	Cancer	Capricorn	Taurus	Scorpio
Mercury	Gemini/Virgo	Sagittarius/Pisces	Aquarius	Leo
Venus	Taurus/Libra	Scorpio/Aries	Pisces	Virgo
Mars	Aries/Scorpio	Libra/Taurus	Capricorn	Cancer
Jupiter	Sagittarius/Pisces	Gemini/Virgo	Cancer	Capricorn
Saturn	Capricorn/Aquarius	Cancer/Leo	Libra	Aries
Uranus	Aquarius	Leo	Gemini	Sagittarius
Neptune	Pisces	Virgo	Leo	Aquarius
Pluto	Aries/Scorpio	Libra/Taurus	Pisces	Virgo

The signs

Name-Mode-Element-Symbol

Aries-Cardinal-Fire-Ram
Taurus-Fixed-Earth-Bull
Gemini-Mutable-Air-Twins
Cancer-Cardinal-Water-Crab
Leo-Fixed-Fire-Lion
Virgo-Mutable-Earth-Fair Maiden
Libra-Cardinal-Air-Scales
Scorpio-Fixed-Water-Scorpion
Sagittarius-Mutable-Spirit-Centaur
Capricorn-Cardinal-Earth- Mountain Goat
Aquarius-Fixed-Air-Water Bearer
Pisces-Mutable-Water-Fish

The Elements
Fire-Masculine-Spirit, Inspiration, Assertiveness
Earth- Feminine- Strength, Determination, Possessions, (material, spiritual, and philosophical)
Air-Masculine- Intelligence, Nervous system, curiousness

Water- Feminine- Emotions, Habits, Unconscious actions

Asteroids

There are thousands of asteroids in our solar system and a few have been deemed important. Chiron, Ceres, Pallas, Vesta, Athena, and Juno have weaseled their way into chart interpretation, and although I suppose they may provide some insight, I don't use them for any natal or progressive readings.

The Vertex

The vertex is defined as the angle where the western most point of your natal chart crosses the vertical prime. Personally I have no idea how to calculate this and never use it in chart reading. I don't think it's meaningless, just not necessary. Avoid any confusion and ignore the vertex.

Part of Fortune

Like the nodes and vertex, the part of fortune isn't an actual physical entity we can get a telescope and see. It's a somewhat unknown subject in Western astrology, but very popular in Arabic. You don't need to know much about the part of fortune to be a good astrologer. I've had a lot of success shunning this point completely. I feel this point is more important the asteroids or vertex, but it is still just as unnecessary.

Retrograde/Direct motion

All the planets revolve in a in a counter clockwise direction. Everything begins at 0 degrees Aries progressing upwards finally ending at the 29th degree of Pisces. When a planet appears to be moving backwards from 29 degrees towards 0 it is said to be in retrograde motion. This happens because the Earth has revolved to the farther side of the Sun making the other planets appear to progress in the opposite direction. Planets being in retrograde definitely have an impact on your natal chart which is hard to describe. This makes the planets have to work ten times harder to accomplish the tasks at hand. It's comparable to the boss being away and the managers trying to run the company. You have an idea of what needs to be done but you don't want to piss off the higher ups by doing something wrong.

Aspects
What is an aspect? The term aspect has been given to the distance between one point on your chart is to another. Because not all aspects are exactly aligned there is a term called "orb of influence" which describes the distance needed for each aspect to be more dominant in your chart. These orbs fluctuate dramatically and every astrologer has their own set of criteria when assessing the orb. Like everything the sign and house placement will increase or decrease the strength of each aspect.

Major aspects
Conjunction- 0 separation- 10 degree orb- same sign
Sextile- 10 degree orb- two signs away
Square- 8 degree orb- three signs away
Trine- 8 degree orb- four signs away
Quincunx/Inconjunct - 5 degree orb- five signs away
Opposite- 8 degree orb- six signs away

Say your Sun is in the 15th degree of Aries. You would look at the 15th degree in each of the following signs for the exact aspect.
Sextile 60 degrees- Gemini/Aquarius
Square 90 degrees- Cancer/Capricorn
Trine- 120 degrees Leo/Sagittarius
Quincunx/Inconjunct- 150 degrees Virgo/Scorpio
Opposite- 180 degrees Libra

Applying and separating aspects should be an easy concept to grasp. The faster moving planet is the one which determines either or. Say the Sun is in the 15th degree of Aries again. Mercury in the 10th degree of Aries will be considered 5 degrees applying. Mercury in the 20th degree will be considered 5 degrees separating. Once more the Sun is in the 15th degree of Aries. Mars in the 10th degree would make the Sun 5 degrees separating while Mars in the 20th would make the Sun 5 degrees applying. An applying aspect is exponentially more powerful than a separating. Of course there is a special orb for each planet I and I consider faster moving planets to have a larger orb. For the Sun and Moon I use 12 degrees applying and 10 degrees separating. For the generational planets I only use a 5 degree orb, and moderate Jupiter and Saturn I use an 8 degree orb.

Speed of the planets
Ascendant/rising sign
Moon
Mercury
Venus
Sun
Mars
Jupiter
Eclipse node
Saturn
Uranus
Neptune
Pluto

Aspect interpretations

Conjunction

1 Corinthians 15:40-41
There are also celestial bodies and terrestrial bodies, but the glory of the celestial is one, and the glory of the terrestrial is another. There is one glory of the Sun, another glory of the Moon and another glory of the stars, and one star differs from another in glory.

The conjunction is when two planets occupy the same degree of the same sign in the ecliptic. It's the most powerful aspect in astrology and whether they admit it or not, conjunctions will be very prevalent in an individual's personality. These aspects will be the ones that distinguish your ego and help you establish a sense of direction. Orbs of influence differ extremely from planet to planet. I use a twelve degree orb with the Sun and Moon. Mercury, Venus, Mars, Jupiter, and Saturn have an eight degree orb while Uranus, Neptune and Pluto have a five. Sign and house placement can both expand and restrict these orbs. Planets in their ruling signs get three degree expansion, but only a two degree restriction in a less comfortable sign. When interpreting a natal chart begin with the conjunctions. After the Sun, Moon, and rising sign, these will give you a good idea of the person's most prominent characteristics.

Sun conjunct ascendant

Your ascendant is the most important point in your chart, and the Sun, the most influential of luminaries or planets. When aligned in the same sign and degree this makes you a powder keg of energy just waiting to explode. You're aggressive and dominant in nature, forcefully projecting your opinions. You take on the traits of the sign the fullest and your Moon is definitely less dominant. If someone doesn't agree with you, more assertiveness is used. It's extremely difficult to apologize because this is an admission you were wrong. Your direct and straight forward attitude can get you ahead in the business and professional world, but it's also going to cause you to lose many casual acquaintances. If you're not careful your high self confidence level will eventually turn into egotism and conceitedness. If the Sun is positioned in your first house the desire for control and authority will dictate many of your actions. While, if it is in the twelfth house you will have a more philosophical, compassionate, and imaginative personality. You make decisions quickly and decisively. Sometimes you're right and things go properly, but when you fail, it's pretty horrific. By itself this aspect produces high spirits, but doesn't indicate stresses or pleasures. More or less, it simply

28

energizes everything touching it, allowing the other energies to flow. A couple squares or oppositions from Mars, Uranus or Saturn are the worst, but won't completely wreck you. If there are three or more harsh aspects then expect strenuous consequences.
Conversely, if you have all good aspects modifying this you're just rainbows and sunshine. Whichever sign this may be in, the ruling planet and its condition will need to be analyzed in order for a proper assessment. If you care to follow up in advanced day to day astrology you'll find when planets progress over this point is when you experience the significant events in your life, especially when it's a Saturn transit.

Sun conjunct Moon

A conjunction between the Sun and Moon indicates a new Moon, is one of the best aspects someone can have. It basically integrates the spiritual essence of the Sun with the emotional properties of the Moon allowing you to understand your feelings. The only problem will be if several other planets are in significantly bad aspect. More often than not, this alignment eases all those harsher energies. Any squares or oppositions will only give you a direction in life. Usually, it shows your acceptance of whatever situation is in front of you. Your temperament is generally calm, unaffected by conflicting influences of others, and you basically maintain your own beliefs. Your balance between emotional and logical reasoning leads to more rational decisions which eventually turn into success. This ability makes it easy to set attainable goals well within your resources and abilities. Success comes naturally because you don't over exert energy into useless endeavors, and you generally learn from your first mistake, sometimes even the blunders of others. No one is allowed to interfere with your personal affairs, nor do you care to interfere with the affairs of others. You establish firm boundaries because this keeps others at an arm length and prevents them from invading your space. This is one of the more introverted base structures for other planets to build on. Squares and oppositions from or Venus, Mars, or Saturn will cause your timidness to severely afflict your

29

life. Although you should be well grounded, house placement and other alignment can mess this up real quick. House positioning is important because it show where you will emotionally retreat to when everything goes awry.

Sun conjunct Mercury

Because Mercury is so close to the Sun it can be separated by only twenty-eight degrees, making every notch closer increasingly critical. The only major aspect which can be formed is the conjunction, and according to Nostradamus, is second only to an eclipse in power. A good general rule is Mercury should be as far away as possible, and in a different sign. The Sun in conjunction with Mercury shows you're extremely subjective in your views, which you express forcefully. Others get irritated because you refuse to listen and acknowledge their ideas and opinions are just as valid as yours. You're usually ego centered and your interests generally relate to matters involving yourself. Not only will you be the first to start a conversation, you also feel a need to have the final word because you want to leave a lasting impression. In your haste to be first, you make decisions quickly and often prematurely. You don't always get the facts before making an opinion and will have to apologize for jumping to conclusions early. It isn't easy for you to say you're sorry because it's the admission of a mistake and you hate being wrong. No alignment can make you more talkative, so learn to shut up. You can observe a lot by listening and the sooner you learn this lesson the better. You love to give orders and will respond negatively to those who oppose you. Sharp tongued and very quick witted you're a brilliant speaker. You can think and process information faster than most, much faster. When closely aligned as such you take on the characteristics of your Sun sign prominently. Basically, you think you can say whatever you want, to whom ever you want to.

Sun conjunct Venus

The conjunction between the Sun and Venus represents a

30

strongly developed and highly passionate love nature. Although it may not be apparent to the casual observer, your desire to be accepted and loved is matched by none other. Although you're very social and friendly compromise is difficult, simply because you don't want to appear weak. Once she gets going nothing can be as over dramatic as Venus, and if you're Sun is in one of the fire signs, you can expect some blazes. You especially want to be recognized as a substantial individual who offers many important values, ideas, and views. Unfortunately, Venus is known for being social, graceful, and beautiful, not intelligent. Hopefully you have some brain power from elsewhere. I personally consider Venus the air head of the solar system, and accept any arguments against it. Her positioning shows where anyone is the most ditzy and oblivious. Intelligence aside, you succeed through your social alliances and personal contacts. You know how to get a group of people to function properly. Art, music, and theater, are all areas you can excel in. You'll enthusiastically join a conversation even if you know little about the subject, allowing yourself to become more informed about something new. At its worst this makes you over demanding and expectant of things you don't deserve. You sometimes pompously presume your mere presence is enough to merit everyone's attention. The other major difficulty is your complete obliviousness and the inability to see how your behavior affects your situation. You constantly falling in love and you're a romanticist at heart being swayed by a simple display of affection.

Sun conjunct Mars

You desire to assert your will and establish control over others. Power and authority are very important to you. Determined to attain both, this drives you towards whatever you set your mind to. Whether positive or negative, a conjunction between the Sun and Mars makes you aggressive and assertive. Compromising is impossible with you, and you refuse to submit to anyone. You believe life would be better if everyone just thought and acted like you. In many cases you presume superiority which causes others to see you as conceited. Your lack of consideration can be

31

detrimental to your career. When someone finally does stand up, questioning your authority or intelligence, it's a clash of titans. Athleticism and recklessness are also caused by this conjunction. Extreme sports will attract your attention and you shouldn't ignore it. Auto racing, rock climbing, or skydiving can be some interesting hobbies for you. You're the ultimate competitor, and when you don't succeed, you're the ultimate sore loser. Several times you may just take your ball and go home. Be careful when using machinery and dangerous objects, your tendency to move fast and not pay attention could prove unfortunate. Be careful when Uranus eventually transits over this alignment. It will always indicate a serious injure affection you somehow.

Sun conjunct Jupiter

A conjunction between the Sun and Jupiter is always positive. In all actuality you're the most gigantic spirit on Earth who wants to get noticed by everyone. This makes you extremely out going and flamboyant, thinking you're the ultimate rock star. Everything about you needs to be bigger, better, and more noticeable than everyone around you. My best comparison is the Sun being a car stereo and Jupiter is the biggest amplifier money can buy. Any aspects from other planets will be highly charged and prominent in your personality. Your biggest downfall is you rarely act in moderation, and don't always know when to stop. Significant health problems are caused by too much drinking, eating, and sleeping. Learn moderation and you can spend your extra money on home projects instead of bar tabs. If Mars is negatively involved you may be excessively competitive, and possibly very violent. Many of your disappointments arise from over inflated expectations placed upon yourself and others. Spirituality is a big thing with Jupiter, and to you it's more important to live a full life, rich with experiences. You can be generous to a fault. No one with a tale of woe will be turned away empty handed. This is one reason you may have difficulty saving money.

Sun conjunct Saturn

The Sun conjunct Saturn shows you're serious, cautious, and overly reserved. Saturn is the stabilizing force teaching us wisdom and accountability. You're capable of handling more responsibility than others, and resent it when they expect you to bear their workload. You matured early and probably had a strict upbringing where you were disciplined harsher than most children. The discipline you received from your father may cause you to become angry and resentful, especially if your Moon is poorly positioned as well. If your father was abusive the traumas you endure haunt you into your adult years. Professional counseling may be needed to relieve the psychological tensions. Until you realize nothing can be done about the past, the downward spiral eventually leads to chaos and destruction. Many times you don't get along with your father because you're extremely like him. If you're fortunate enough to have a loving and caring father the bonds are unbreakable. In romance you choose a partner who's responsible and respectable. The position you attain within the community will be important to you, and you should seek public office. Your greatest problem is you tend to react negatively to minor setbacks and become bitter. Try to establish goals which can be met within the near future. Don't get into a rut when challenges no longer seem as exciting as they were when you started them. You learn many of your lessons from your father. Whether it be through his successes or failures. Physical ailments such as ulcers and digestive problems are caused by all the undue stress you place on yourself.

Sun conjunct Uranus

Energetic and eccentric, you're quite an odd ball when you have a conjunction between the Sun and Uranus in your natal chart. You move freely around your environment and are very comfortable with new and exciting situations. Life will be filled with unusual circumstances and experiences, many times finding yourself in the wrong place at the wrong time. Don't be surprised

33

by encounters with law enforcement or city government. The drum you march to doesn't play their kind of music. Even if you ask nicely they won't use pink fuzzy handcuffs when they arrest you. Personal freedom is more important than anything, and you will react instantly, sometimes violently, when it's threatened. Living the normal bland lifestyle is not for you. You need constant excitement from many different sources in order to be happy. You can be extremely inventive, creating something where there was once nothing. Although you're open to different personalities, you're also very impatient and intolerant of inadequacies when you have to work with them directly. Be careful not to judge others harsher than you judge yourself. You can be extremely inflexible with your views and opinions. Uranus is the epitome of rebellion, and the wild revolutionary buried inside will need to find a proper outlet. Consider a career in politics or social activism.

Sun conjunct Neptune

Hazy, spiritual, and dreamy are the first three words I use to describe the Sun conjoined with Neptune. There are definitely modifying influences from other planets, and if this is dominant, it only inspires creativity. As with everything there are many different possibilities, but for this alignment the discrepancy between the two is exceptionally large. First, you may find it difficult to assert yourself against those who are obviously stronger or more talented. Conversely, you may have deluded visions of self-grandeur and think entirely too much of yourself. If Mars or Jupiter are involved the latter description is more probable. Your self-confidence takes a hit because you feel your competitors are as good as you are. Aggressive people will try desperately to cover them up, while the timid will use them to their fullest advantage. Don't underestimate your abilities and talents by conceding to any presumed authority. If you can channel your energy into music, art, or writing you can find great success. You have a highly active subconscious and will experience many waking nights with vivid dreams. Sometimes your dreams will be extremely difficult to separate from reality. This is aspect is very sympathetic towards social disparity, and economic injustice tears at your heart. If you have driver aspects from elsewhere you may begin your own non-profit organization. Professionally, you can find much success in fields of medicine, social work, or care giving. A short attention span may cause excessive daydreaming and trouble in school as a youngster. As a child your school teachers were usually on your case to pay attention and quit distracting the class. This wasn't because you were misbehaving you just weren't interested in what the teacher was teaching. This is sometimes like a deer caught in the headlights. When something unknown is immediately upon you the reaction time is delayed and you get smacked.

Sun conjunct Pluto

The conjunction of the Sun to Pluto indicates you're a total extremist and highly passionate about everything you do. Your likes and dislikes are intense, with acting in moderation extremely difficult. House position will indicate where you place and waste most of your energy. Pluto is an obsessive control freak and positions of authority attract you. Pressure tactics are by all means necessary. When negatively influenced this means you become extremely unethical and even violent. Everything, especially direct competition, is met immediately even with the risk of significant loss. You're willing to lose something just to prove you're a force to be reckoned with. Don't cut your nose off just to spite your face. Pluto is a lot like throwing gasoline on an already existing fire. The Hindu destroyer God Shiva is closely related to Pluto for a reason. You have immense power to recover from catastrophic events, but unfortunately this means catastrophic events must occur. There's a lot which can become of this energy when influenced by the other planets. The Moon will intensify your emotional state, and Mars influences your aggression. A talented astrologer can easily tell how each planet will individually respond. Your desire to pursue deeper and farther than anyone else can lead you into interesting careers. Whatever you do you want to be the best and brightest star. Advanced areas of law, medicine, and especially psychology will prove most fulfilling.

35

Moon conjunct ascendant

You have a very compassionate and charming personality when the Moon is conjunct your. All too often you extend a hand of generosity towards an undeserving individual and get taken for. Be informed because not all sob stories are true and educated guesses turn out better than shots in the dark. When your Moon is placed close to your ascendant this makes you very much like your mother. Her emotions, characteristics, and probably even her appearance are similar to yours. Because of the intense emotions towards her, the relationship you develop as a child will play a dramatic role in your life. You may even need to seek professional help in order to cope with the grief and psychological stress. If you're lucky enough to have at least a semi functional relationship with her then the bond will be unbreakable. Sign is especially important because the Moon is so easily influenced. If this is a water sign you retain weight easy and your excess pounds will just have to be accepted. Along with sign house placement will be vital as well. A first house placement will make you more emotionally expressing outwardly, while the twelfth house will make you reclusive and need to get away more often. All by itself there is no aspect more compassionate. This can relieve stresses of a few harsh energies, but anything more than three will be too many to handle alone. At its best this allows you to see your emotional side and express your feelings accurately.

Moon conjunct Mercury

A conjunction between the Moon and Mercury bestows you with a sympathetic, good hearted nature. There are only a handful of what I call "teddy bear" alignments, and this is one. Because of your natural compassion you attract many friends seeking advice or a shoulder to cry on. You have an unconscious need to communicate issues and express your emotions freely. Consider child psychology or therapy as a career. Also try avoiding casual gossip where you reveal more than you care to, as this is how rumors start. Sometimes you forget the walls have ears and little

36

birdies talk around a bar counter. Alcohol should be consumed in moderation as it can turn you into a blundering cry baby clinging on to the arm of your comrades. Other times you're going to be an emotional tornado, destroying everything in your path. As with every Moon alignment this affects the relationship with your mother. Generally, this makes you talk and express yourself exactly like her. She's also your main source of sympathy when distressed. If the relationship is estranged this is a major source for resentments. This is an easily modified alignment and the importance of other planetary influence cannot be stressed enough. All by itself this shows you desperately desire her contact. The most major malfunction is your inability to separate emotions from intellect. You generally act upon how your feeling and not what reality dictates you should. Then your delusions catch up, and the malfunction occurs. This usually indicates a mental breakdown sometime throughout your lifetime, probably when Saturn is progressing poorly.

Moon conjunct Venus

Lucky for you this is one of the kindest most compassionate alignments in astrology. You wish to express the nurturing qualities of the Moon throughout all your relationships. You're pretty much in love with love, and must learn to control your attractions. Emotional bonds are the most important thing in the world, and you constantly seek new contacts. When intrigued by someone you're not one to sit around and wait for them to make the first introductions. You're more inclined to walk up and spark the conversation. Venus is very refined, and sometimes a priss. Make sure not to become arrogant and rude towards those less fortunate. Although your compassionate to the needs of others, your personal space needs to be kept clean and they can take their grimy dirt elsewhere. Not one for arguments you try and avoid situations where violence or fighting are likely. Some males, by especially Females born with this trait are very much like their mother and will have difficulties separating themselves from her. It is very possible for you to become too nice and get taken advantage of. You have a subconscious desire to fit in with the crowd and can get caught up with the wrong people very easily. You desire to please everyone around you and frequently take on too many projects of others. It's difficult to say no to those you love and can be kind of a pushover at times. You're fond of fine art, food, and music, and the presentation is just as important as the event itself. A slice of pizza can be a romantic date if it's wrapped up with a candle light table and soft music. If you become "too nice" to people, others will think you're up to something and have ulterior motives to your generosity. Remain courteous and polite just don't over extend yourself to them.

Moon conjunct Mars

The conjunction of the Moon and Mars creates emotional turbulence and anxiety. The aggression of Mars and passiveness of the Moon do not mesh well together. Because of your over active imagination you spend too much time mulling over personal attacks that were never made. On many occasions you verbally abuse others because you have taken something out of context. You get caught up in your own life so much you fail to realize just how much your words and actions have on other people. Your feelings are strong and in constant upheaval. Anyone who approaches you aggressively is met with instant retaliation. You instantly put them in their place letting them know their role and where they stand in the situation. You desperately want to establish close relationships, but you just don't know how to handle yourself when you finally do. This conjunction doesn't indicate a certain professional field, but it most certainly indicates trouble with your coworkers. Once you realize not everyone is out to get you or your things, you can settle down in complete peace of mind. You will require lots of personal soul searching and meditation for you to do so. In competition you hate to lose and can be an extremely sore loser. Crying after a loss will happen more frequently than you admit, even if the emotions aren't shown to other people. You will also have to thicken your skin when it comes to criticism. Accept constructive criticism with a grain of salt and then get on with your business. If this is not accomplished you can expect multiple job changes because your attitude will get you terminated very quickly.

Moon conjunct Jupiter

When conjoined with Jupiter, the nurturing qualities and emotions of the Moon are immensely expanded. You're very caring, but usually only towards the select few close to you. Jupiter enlarges everything it touches and the ebbing flow of emotions produced by the Moon doesn't always handle this well. Along with the tender qualities you possess, there are also crabby claws at the end of your hands. You can be inadvertently snappish and rude towards the wrong people when emotionally distressed. The natural reactions of the Moon are always based on feelings, not facts. However, more often than not this balances out the handful of bad aspects everyone has, and it's going to take several negative influences to turn this aspect sour. At their best these two give you an infinite amount of spiritual knowledge. You unconsciously possess many of the secrets locked away in the universe, and have a psychic calling to them. Not always organized religion, but higher realms of philosophy or spirituality will provide you with great psychological relief. There are things out there greater than humans and you know this. Whether you accept it or not there are guiding forces in your life showing you the path to enlightenment. Deep down your heart is as big as the Sun and you become attached to everything easily.

Moon conjunct Saturn

We all have close ties to our father, and no one is ever unaffected by either of their parents. This aspect shows the condition of the emotional bond you have with your father. The aspects from Mars, Venus, and especially the Sun will determine whether the intensity is good or bad. All alone this is a great alignment which helps stabilize the relationship. Whether positive or negative you're greatly impacted by the relationship with him and, this bond is so close because in many ways you're just like them. You think like him, behave like him, and probably even look

39

like him. The house these two are located in will be the best way
for you two to bond. Saturn is a very shy planet which makes you
cautious too an extreme. The house these two are in will also show
where you feel you must be the most organizes. This will be
especially problematic if in your sixth or twelfth house, along with
being placed in the sign of Virgo. It takes you a while to warm up,
and when if you do it isn't entirely. Only several emotionally
bonding events can truly unveil who you are. This is also going to
give you an emotional attachment to all your work and school
environment. Either the office or the classroom needs to feel like
home to you. Professionally, you take your job seriously and
probably need to lighten up. When this alignment is functioning
properly it instills a sense of responsibility in the back of your
head. The worst overall effects lie somewhere between depression
and fatigue.

Moon conjunct Uranus

Of all possible Moon aspects, this particular alignment is the
most spontaneous and unpredictable. You're a very unique
individual attracting people as different as you. For the most part
this aspect is highly unstable and erratic. Nothing out there
produces as intense emotional fluctuations, so get ready for some
tail spins. A trine or sextile from your ascendant generally shows
you handle the variations much easier than those with squares or
oppositions. Too many other planets bearing down on this point
will make you a psychological cluster f*ck. That's the simplest
way I can describe this. When there aren't other planets involved
you're provided with a high energy level and lots of unique
qualities. Because the Moon is one of the most personal planets
conjunctions with her are considerable profound. House placement
will show which area of life you experience the most unusual
difficulties. The emotional state of the Moon is already in limbo
even before Uranus becomes involved. His rebellious nature can
cause you to act out against whatever you're taught. Once is
energies are embedded into your subconscious you become the
ultimate revolutionary who must change society to their every

whim.

Moon conjunct Neptune

You're psychic, imaginative, and emotional, when the Moon is conjoining Neptune. These are two easily swayed planets which will definitely be influenced by the other planets. The biggest confliction is the confusing emotional states they put you in. This pretty much places you into a constant delusional dreamland where it's difficult to determine reality. You naturally absorb the emotions of others and can project yours onto them. You're attracted to others with serious issues wishing to help all in need. Many times you'll extend your hand of generosity and then become angry when you're taken advantage of. The imagination you possess is so vivid while at work your attention span is short because you're off in fantasy land. If you stay doing the same thing for hours on end it will drive you crazy. Setting your own pace and hours can be helpful if that's an option for you. If not, you will probably be fired for being late, lazy, or dawdling at least once or twice in your life. Vivid dreams and psychic visions are also effects of this aspect. Be very careful when you get bad feelings about people, you will find out you're right more often than not. Sign and house placement will add significant power to this aspect. If this takes place in the fourth, eighth, or twelfth your abilities will be profound.

Moon conjunct Pluto

This aspect causes you to get passionately lost in all your emotions. Rather than waste your time in useless and casual relationships, you wish to have close personal contacts with everyone you meet. Many times this causes you to cross personal boundaries into the affairs of others. Once told to mind your own business, you get offended, and the ensuing arguments begin. Because you become so emotionally attached to possessions, obsession sets in and can't control your life. As you reach your teenage and early adult years if you choose to fill any emotional voids with drugs or alcohol you will most definitely develop an

41

addiction. Those voids can cause deep depression, especially if Mars or Saturn is negatively involved. Because of your desire to have all emotional needs met you're constantly re-evaluating your partner. This will make it very difficult for your spouse to live with you. When all your needs are not met you become depressed, then create problems where none exist. Both of these planets have a significant effect on the unconscious human mind, and it will be vital you realize your unconscious habits from an objective outsider's view. These unseen reactions are the snowball beginning to fall at the top of a hill. Then only when things become cataclysmic will you finally change. Especially if this means admitting you're wrong. Once you finally do fall in love it's forever. No one who's let into your life is ever forgotten.

Mercury conjunct ascendant

Quick, agile, and clever are three cliché terms describing Mercury. Conjunctions with your ascendant are the most powerful way planets can emphasize these affects on your personality. Here the childlike qualities of Mercury make you talkative, and energetic, enjoying pranks or jokes as well. You're curiosity will get the best of you and remember humans don't have nine lives. Much of your conversation is about you or your beliefs. This isn't because your conceited it's just when there is silence you think you need to talk. It doesn't matter where the teacher sits you you're going to talk anyway. If heavily afflicted, you can be quite immature and never truly grow up. This isn't to say you can't possess responsibility, but if you do it's being produced elsewhere. You're too smart for your own good and enjoy causing mischief with it. The little laws you break are the constant conundrum causing you to spend your resources on court fines and traffic tickets. Do this too much and at forty years old you'll be living in a van down by the river. Life has to be in constant movement and yes, spinning in circles is considered constant movement. Language, math, and science are all areas you can excel in.

Mercury conjunct Venus

When the extremely swift moving planet Mercury conjoins Venus, you're incredibly social and love talking to random people. Telling others your opinions and ideas are usually the beginning points of most your conversations. All alone there will be nothing bad but an occasional "shut the hell up" will be thrown at your direction. You're a rock star singer even if it's only in your shower or car. Full volume on the radio can turn you into a Grammy winning artist. The softness of your eyes and caring tone in your voice entices others to warm up to you. Unless you smoke a bunch of cigarettes or methamphetamine, then you'll be a haggard old bag. When working in groups you're an excellent communicator and statistician. Consider being the treasurer of whatever social group you're a part of. You could find enjoyment in public speaking or the dramatic arts. Having close contact with the public is important and journalism should be considered as a career. Cleverness in devising schemes for improving your financial conditions will be a strong point. You have the uncanny ability to use your childish charm to get other to do what you want. Relationship wise you will need a partner as talkative as you. This is because your constant chatter will grind their nerves until they pack up and leave.

Mercury conjunct Mars

This aspect makes you talkative and verbally aggressive. Your temper is usually short and when others make remarks about you, your reaction is instantaneous. You're assertive and determined to make your presence known by forcing your opinions onto others. Your sharp tongue and inflated bravado will cause many issues between you and your associates. In a heated debate you will even say things you don't believe in, just to get under the skin of your opponent. When directed properly this energy can be very productive. Law, politics, and the military are all careers you may find success in. There is a lot of energy running through your body and it can be very difficult to handle at times. Because your mind is active and eager to experience new things, you tend to think about too many issues at once. Even when you try and focus

43

on one thing, in the back of your mind you are thinking about something else. As a result nervousness, high anxiety, and hyper activity are all associated with this aspect. Meditation in your own quiet space will be necessary to relieve your psychological tensions.

Mercury conjunct Jupiter

The conjunction of Mercury and Jupiter is one of the most intellectually expanding aspects in astrology. Nothing can inspire intelligence and higher forms of philosophy like the combination of these two. Just where you direct your aptitude is up to you. You're very bombastic and usually the first to approach someone wasting no time introducing yourself. Despite your age you still possess childlike philosophies and if you can grow them properly this makes you an excellent candidate for a youth pastor or sports coordinator. It's easy to take your ideas and express them into words that others can understand. Teaching is another profession you should consider pursuing. When Saturn is positively involved chances are you get into business or higher education. The negative parts of this aspect are the complete inability to focus on one thing for very long. You're an expert at making people think you're smarter than you are and when put to the test you fail miserably. Maintain intellectual honesty and you'll go far Unfortunately this can make you an arrogant know it all as well. You can be very opinionated and will need to realize that not everyone shares your views. When you forcefully disagree with someone they in turn see it as conceitedness. Your exceptionally curious nature will make life very interesting. As a child anything with flashing lights, bells, or whistles, fascinated you. Still into adult hood all these things are interesting. If you choose to use your intelligence productively eventually, you will develop an interest into religion, philosophy, or higher spirituality. If you were not raised in a religious sect you will eventually seek out and find one, but not necessarily one of dogmatic tradition. It's your open mindedness that will take you far in life.

44

Mercury conjunct Saturn

Conjunctions between these two are difficult to describe because it's an intellectual aspect. All alone it indicates that you're smart, curious, and can solve problems all by yourself. A lot depends on which planet is dominant. If Saturn's properties are stronger then you accept responsibility as a child, and mature at an earlier age. However, if Mercury's properties are more prominent then you will be completely irresponsible and reject all your social obligations. The sign and house will determine which is better. If you chose to use this by getting involved with drugs or gangs you will be a very good criminal, and probably spend most of your adult life behind bars. Once you figure out a positive ambition to pursue, then the sky is the limit. You naturally understand your position in life and readily accept it. Success is attained through your ability to work within the limits of not only your capabilities, but resources as well. Not everyone is blessed with all the opportunities to succeed. Even if you were born into poverty you're able to use all your limited resources efficiently and effectively. You're a good conversationalist and an even better listener, as long as the person talking is interesting and educated. Understanding that there is a lot to learn from others you will usually keep opinion's to yourself, until you have enough knowledge to form an accurate one. Professions in architecture, engineering, or research and development can prove very interesting and profitable for you.

Mercury conjunct Uranus

This can be one of the most interesting aspects in astrology. Uranus is the planet of rebellion and revolution. When put in contact with the childlike, but still brilliant characteristics of Mercury, the possible outcomes are endless. At its best you possess genius caliber brain power and if you can direct your abilities into science or technology your final projects will be innovative and leading its field. If you get the irresponsible and immature side of Mercury then you will reject your requirements completely and take off and leave. Your personality is quite electric and you're

45

kind of an oddball with their own eccentric ways. Not many planetary alignments can stimulate your curiosity like this one. One of your best traits is your natural fascination and understanding of everything. You can figure how something works simply by looking at it then taking it apart. If you put your projects back together then Saturn is involved. There's pretty much no subject too complicated or complex for you. Because you realize you're so different from others, you desire to stand out amongst your peers and colleagues. Excited about things that are unusual you're drawn to people from all walks of life. You have a keen intellect that can process information faster than most. You're extremely talkative and can engage yourself in deep conversations and philosophies.

Mercury conjunct Neptune

With this planetary alignment your imagination and fantasy life are in constant overdrive. Too much time is spent in dreamland, but when you focus your creative talents the work your product considerably better than most. Art, music, and theater, will interest you, possibly to the point of a professional career. The reason for this inspiration is you have a direct connection with the mystical and magical realm of Neptune. Neptune is ultimate reality where all is one. Whether sleeping during the day or night your dreams are often interpreted as reality. Very often it will be difficult to discern fact from fiction. As you grow older your psychic abilities will increase if you allow them to. Your gut instinct will usually be right. Most times you ignore this and just do whatever you want. If negatively aspect by other planets you can be a downright liar. Bending the truth and frequently telling little white lies is the most likely scenario. It will be the denial of your responsibilities and emotional realities that will lead you towards a path of addiction and alcoholism.

Mercury conjunct Pluto

Mercury in the same degree as Pluto gives you the ability and desire to probe deep into whatever you choose. This alignment boosts your intellectual capacities and makes you smart in your own special way. You look past face values, and the inner secrets or functions are what you desire. This conjunction will make you possessive and obsessive, never letting anything just casually slip by, whether it be possessions or philosophies. You remember everything and usually everyone associated with it. As you receive and interpret all your surroundings you do so like a detective, slowly piecing everything together. As you evaluate everything precisely and cautiously, using your psychic senses will reveal the untold secrets before the actual clues. Sometimes people will only tell you part of the story and you can detect the outcome beforehand. You curious about almost everything spiritual and occult like. Possibly going to extremes gathering all the knowledge and information you can get. You will also possess a talent for asserting yourself persuasively, convincing others to follow your path. This generally isn't a brash alignment where you enjoy telling people all you know. Rather it turns you into a better listener when the person is educated on a subject. Because Pluto revolves so slowly this alignment can be in only a few signs. For those born with this in Scorpio you should consider medicine and especially human psychology as a career. The relationship this is forming with your ascendant is vital when determining influence. House placement will show you where you are the most intellectually obsessed.

Venus conjunct ascendant

Venus conjoined with your ascendant makes you charming, beautiful, and socially graceful. You love the public's attention and have many friends along with acquaintances. Deep down you desperately want everyone to like and accept you, causing you to become dependent on the approval of others. This in turn, causes you to sway from one viewpoint to the next depending on the opinion of the crowd. This doesn't mean you change your beliefs completely, you just won't overly object when your opinion is different. It's easy for you to identify your positive qualities and use them to your advantage. Beneath your soft and friendly exterior down inside you are calculating the benefits and advantages of all your social contacts. Not to say you use people, although when negatively aspected you can be conniving and manipulative, using others solely for your own gainful purposes. Although you're generally well behaved, when you don't get what you want you become aggressive and demanding. Venus can most definitely throw a good hissy fit from time to time. If this occurs in the signs of Taurus or Libra then the effects of Venus couldn't be stronger, and her progressions should be noted for any future prediction.

Venus conjunct Mars

Venus and Mars aligned in the same sign and degree is simply a keg of gunpowder waiting to explode. I call it Adolf Hitler aspect because he had this alignment prominent in his chart, and it's definitely not to be trifled with. You generally think you can go around doing whatever you want, whenever you want to. Mars can't handle the femininity of Venus and over reacts with aggression. You act with a macho bravado because deep down you're just a sensitive sissy. The sign this occurs in is indescribably important. Conjunctions between Venus and Mars produce an intense and burning passion to express yourself at all times. You're always willing to interrupt to state your opinions, and many people will find you pushy and irritating. This is a frustrating aspect that adds lots of tensions to your chart. The difficulties you experience with the opposite sex are caused by your unwillingness to allow your partner to take charge. You are also attracted to individuals who are aggressive and abrasive as you are. This aspect can be a relationship killer. The dominant force churning within you is always trying to gain recognition and push its way into the world, never wanting to make concessions. When you choose your friends you do so indiscriminately. Athletic competition and exercise will be vital in maintaining a healthy lifestyle. You are too much of a busy body to abhor anything which keeps you indoors and unable to have the social contacts you deeply desire.

48

Venus conjunct Jupiter

Jupiter is known as the greater benefic and Venus is known as the lesser, thus making their conjunction nothing but peaches and rainbow. At least that's the theory. This aspect shows you're extremely kind and generous to everyone, making you an easy target for con artists. Avoid being too friendly to those you don't know very well as they're more likely to be fraudulent and deceptive. The sign and house placement is key because they determine which planet is more dominant. If Venus is in charge you're going to be more beautiful and emotional, whereas Jupiter will make you large and smart. You're generally self-indulgent with your material possessions, and get quite upset when someone touches your things. In childhood you probably had trouble sharing your toys with your siblings. You can be stunningly beautiful if this conjunction is in good aspect with your ascendant, and may very well have a beautiful singing voice. But unfortunately the opposite is true as well. If it isn't harmoniously involved with your rising sign you may be fat and ugly. Regardless of size and figure you're still gorgeous on the inside. Remember if a story is too tall to really believe, it probably is.

Venus conjunct Saturn

When Venus and Saturn are positioned like this you feel you always have to make concessions in order to get what you want. Neither of these planets is known for being aggressive so hopefully you get that elsewhere. This can be a humbling alignment where you feel inadequate in all your relationships. Because you're able to see the tiny areas the relationship can improve any positive emotions sometimes take a back seat. Instead of focusing on what needs to be changed you're going to need to relax and let things happen gracefully. Generally speaking you desire to be in a committed relationship where stability is a priority. You know how to get the most of every relationship you possess, and all your friends must serve a purpose. Business management is possible because of your ability to be social at work. It's much easier for you to warm up to strangers when you're forced to work with them. More often than not this shows a positive relationship with your father. Any negativity is because you're exactly like him an just can't get along with yourself. This relationship can be easily influenced from other planets. Aspects from wild planets like Uranus or Mars will indicate a harsh upbringing where he may have been abusive. Other planets generally enforce the positive characteristics of this alignment. Your major malfunction is you feel unless you're the one to make adjustments the relationship won't develop properly. This is because you delusionally think you can organize every part of every relationship. When aspecting with other planets, or placed in the second house, this can lead to an obsession with cleaning and hoarding. Success in the professional world will be found in areas where you can set your own pace within a certain set of guidelines and deadlines. Architectural design or engineering could be two areas where you can find interest and success. When you find a profession you will stick with it, more than likely with the same company.

Venus conjunct Uranus

The conjunction between Venus and Uranus usually indicates you're extremely social and possess a sparkling personality. Your flamboyant zest for life requires you to be free and unrestricted from any boundaries. You're fascinated by human encounters and seek contacts with as many different people as you can meet. From saint to sinner, everyone has an interesting life story and you enjoy all of them, the more unusual the better. Even though you're comfortable with short social acquaintances you don't always let others into your close circle. Not everyone is honest and you must be aware not to get taken advantage of. Even in your romantic relationships you seek the exceptionally unique. Your partner must set themselves separate from their peers and establish their own personality. Intelligence and common sense are also qualities you value in a partner. In no way are you interested in a door mat who allows you to walk all over them. Because of the difficulties in establishing a permanent relationship it will be better to put off marriage until you're settled down in life and have made it on your own. You can be quite the party animal and if you're not careful you will get carried away all too often. Romantically you're going to need someone completely different than most. I believe this may also increase your romantic interest in people of the same gender.

Venus conjunct Neptune

When Venus is conjunct Neptune you're a dreamy and imaginative romanticist who is constantly falling in love. Whether it's with another human or the cute fuzzy dog walking down the street, your fluttering emotions tumble over and over again. You can be vulnerable to deception and will have to look intently into everything you do. Although the famines, disease, and wars, disturb you if there isn't fire elsewhere in your chart you will just sit and watch, until it affects you directly. You're a lover of the finer things in life and must have a beautiful home decorated with unique artwork from throughout the world. With an occasional picture of loved ones, you would rather have voodoo masks, unique pottery, or paintings hanging on your walls. Traveling to strange far off places will spark your creative abilities. If you choose to unlock them your creative potential is endless. Because you desire everything around you to be functional, you overlook serious issues with your loved ones. If drug and alcohol use plagues your family then you will need to make sure you do not become an enabler. The absolute worst part of this will be the confusion in your love life. You don't know just what you desire out of a relationship and then have no clue how to achieve it. Spirituality is probably the missing ingredient when forming a close personal bond. Choose someone who can expand your philosophies and perceptions towards religion.

Venus conjunct Pluto

With this aspect in your chart you experience recurring crisis on all your relationships. This is because you're constantly pursuing ultimate fulfillment in every personal contact. You're

51

attracted to a wide variety of individuals, and love immersing yourself in their lives. You're possessive of your current love interest, but the attention is easily distracted by someone you think can provide a deeper relationship. When you become emotionally involved with someone you demand they show it with tokens of affection. The gifts you receive reassure you that you are cared for and loved. Since you're willing to make such major concessions you feel it's only fair others do as well. One major pitfall is the illusion there is a perfect partner for you. You desire someone who can fill all your physical, emotional, and spiritual needs, and actually think there is someone who can meet all the high standards set for your partner. This is simply not true and you need to just move along. No single alignments guarantee how someone will act, but I'll bet you a dollar you're obsessive and possessive when you partner shows interest elsewhere. You're the type of person who stares at an ex jealously when you see them out having fun without you. No one is ever let go once they have made an impact in your life. Even ten years later you might not remember what they said, but you remember how they made you feel.

Mars conjunct ascendant
        Mars is the planet of attitude and aggression and there had better be some other planets balancing this aspect out. All alone is gives you an endless amount of energy, just nowhere to direct it. The aspects formed will show where you need to focus your attention and resources. Positive alignments allow you to use your energy efficiently and direct your ambitions into positive outlets. Poor afflictions cause you to become angry at the world for no particular reason Of course sign will be the most important factor because your ascendant is the most influential point in your entire chart. The aggression Mars inspires is meant to stimulate action. Part of the reason you get things done is because you know what you want, then go get it. It's also because you're an ego maniac who loves being better than others. Competition allows you to show off your stuff and athletics will need to play a role in your life. It's vital you find a physical outlet for your energy. Your

biggest hang up is when you overly assert your opinions to those who are considerably more timid than you. The overly assertive way you project your opinions will drive those who are timid away. Mars suffers from short man's disease, and always thinks everything is a fight. You never back down from a challenge especially when you know you can dominate easily. If you're not careful your ego will get punched in the mouth when you're drunk at the bar. The best benefit is your ability to work longer hours at more strenuous tasks.

Mars conjunct Jupiter

When these two planets align by conjunction, you're hard headed, even harder working, and determined to succeed like none other. You definitely feel your ego, and your self-confidence will need to be kept in check. Once you make a decision you stick with it until completion. When opposed you have no problem asserting yourself properly. Because you're generally straightforward and direct others often form wrong opinions of you. Many times you won't care whose toes you have to step on in order to get what you want. To you that's just the nature of competition. You possess an extremely addictive and obsessive nature and do nothing in moderation. Drugs, gambling, or work, may take over and control your life. Getting intently focused on one thing prevents you from attending to other needs. Latter in marriage your partner may start to feel isolated when you have so many responsibilities and fail to acknowledge them. This can make you extremely athletic and competitive. Negative aspects with poor house placement can make you angry and violent. The expansive properties of Jupiter can intensify the aggressions of Mars, causing more and more tensions. You may also be exceptionally athletic and competitive.

Mars conjunct Saturn

I compare every Mars and Saturn alignment with a car's racing engine. This particular aspect is like a gas pedal controlling the flow of the throttle. If the vehicle isn't in gear the throttle becomes extremely sensitive to a change in pressure, and responds dramatically. Once you find an outlet and put yourself in gear there's nothing you can't accomplish. Conversely, if no outlet is found the engine eventually explodes. These two planets are known as the Malefics for a reason, and it isn't usually pleasant. House placement is extremely important because it will indicate where you experience the most sensitivity and aggravation. Unfortunately, many astrologers would say this is a top five most difficult alignment to handle. If there's more than two harsher aspects involved, you're going to need help. When faced with severe trauma, you become emotionally cautious and reserved, as well extremely nervous about past experiences. Possibly when you parents disciplined you it made you feel unloved. Maybe, they were neglectful and you still desire their attention. Many of these tensions will be because you over dramatize the negativity and none of the positivity. The overly cynical events in your younger life will cause a residual sensitivity to criticism and ridicule. Romantic fulfillment will come from relationships with older more responsible individuals. Many times life will seem like a giant rain cloud, it will be difficult for you to see the light through the clouds. It will be very important for you not to dwell on the past. Not letting go of negative experiences in life will produce depression and high anxiety.

Mars conjunct Uranus
        Uranus is the closest of the generational planets and when Mars conjoins it this isn't a pleasant experience. Alone by itself this makes you erratic, hyperactive, and argumentative. The rebellious spirit of Uranus is only invigorated my Mars, and you must be your own unique individual. It will make you overly anxious and creating all sorts of nervous problems. You possess a strong will which desires to be completely free from any restrictions. Other people's boundaries are usually of no use to you and you're going to do what you want any way. Injuries and accident are always to be expected. The excess energy causes you to be careless while being reckless with the consequences usually painful and expensive. Every time someone tells you not to do

54

something you do it simply to be contrary. Always being rebellious creates a direct confliction with authority. You break the law, get in trouble, then react uncontrollably when restrained and placed into handcuffs. If you can't set the rules and parameters you're simply not going to play the game. If there isn't any excitement, then you will create it. As you grow into your older years you will have to learn that society is stabilized by rules and codes of conduct. If you can't learn to follow these rules then it will lead you down a path of jails, institutions, or death. Although there is mostly stressful energy produced by this aspect, life isn't entirely bad. The innovative thinking abilities you possess will give you an advantage over others. Your brain works naturally quicker than others and if you can focus this energy productively it will be your greatest asset. As you aggressively trample over people you will have to realize that sometimes you have to accept no as an answer. Usually the taker and not the giver pay attention to how you treat others. You may need their assistance sometime down the road.

Mars conjunct Neptune

In my opinion the conjunction between Mars and Neptune is one of the top ten most difficult aspects to have. It's not in the top five, but definitely six thru ten. The greatest problem is your inability to realize which dreams and visions shouldn't be acted upon. Neptune gives you a vivid imagination and brilliant creativity when thinking bad thoughts, while Mars produces an instant reaction to those delusions. The house placement between these two is vitally important. Whichever area of your chart these two are located will be where you experience the most utter confusion. Neptune is all for everyone and Mars is all for myself. Obviously these energies naturally conflict. You don't always see the consequences of your actions, becoming angered when the results are negative. The most major malfunction is your inability to see burdens you place on yourself and others. This aspect requires positive influences from elsewhere to gain stabilization. You have sudden outbursts of intense anger and during your deluded state of thinking behave inappropriately. Afterwards you don't apologize because you can't recognize when you're wrong. This doesn't mean only doom and gloom is produced, but again it's in my top ten most difficult for a reason. Your imagination is vivid and you probably wake up in the night, confused about the reality of your dreams. Sometimes they are even psychic. You fit into groups because it's easy for you to take on whatever qualities needed to blend with the crowd. If you hang out with the wrong crowd you will end up the worst of them. If this conjunction takes place in the twelfth house then mental disorders will need to be addressed.

Mars conjunct Pluto

This conjunction indicates you stop at nothing to get what you want, and it takes catastrophic obstacles to prevent you from achieving your goal. Every conjunction involving Mars is very difficult to handle because they directly affect your ego drive. This particular aspect can make you obsessively possessive, and jealous. Many mistakes will be made because you allow your bad attitude to influence good judgment. If someone tells you something is impossible or against your best interest, you still do it no matter how harmful or counterproductive. Then, you're stuck in a rut, finding it difficult to pull yourself out. Unfortunately this also produces a natural attraction to the seedier areas of life. If you get caught up in drugs, gangs, or violence, chances are you will be a career criminal, spending most of your time locked up. If positively influenced from elsewhere this alignment will provide you with endless amounts of determination. The best description is highly volatile with volcanic explosiveness. In relationships you are usually the aggressor, with no problem taking control of any situation. Be aware that if this aspect takes place in the twelfth house a serious mental illness is likely probably not until your later years though.

Jupiter conjunct ascendant

The absolute worst possibility when Jupiter is aligned with your ascendant is that you're fat and lazy. Being big boned won't be a problem unless you ignore your health completely. If you can follow a healthy and honest diet you find you can maintain weight easily. Other than that, it will take a significant amount of bad aspects to make you a sourpuss. Jupiter near the same degree as your ascendant gives you endless bounds of enthusiasm and optimism. To you, anything worth doing is worth over doing, and you have a tendency to go overboard in everything you participate in. You do this believing your excess will turn out for the better in the long run. When this doesn't happen you suffer major disappointment. Worrying about tomorrow is for suckers, and so is dwelling on the past. To you upsets are just minor inconveniences and are easily handled. Unless aspected poorly by other planets you will never stay down for too long. If Jupiter is positioned in your first house this will make you larger physically, if it is placed in the twelfth house you will be an intellectual giant. Your biggest problem will be maintaining a conservative and serious lifestyle. Learning to live within your means will be a difficult task that you may never learn. If Mercury is positively aligned then you're exceptionally smart. If it's poorly positioned then you're going to have to learn work hard in order for success.

Jupiter conjunct Saturn

Because Jupiter and Saturn are the two slowest of the personal planets, their alignments don't occur frequently and are exceptionally powerful. Sometimes referred to as the grand conjunction, this formation occurs once about every nineteen years and the sign along with house placement is vital when interpreting its influence. Although the expansive properties of Jupiter and the restrictive elements of Saturn are usually counterproductive, when properly aspected by other planets, these two giants function with monumental results. Once you find your niche, this energy gives you endless amounts of inspiration and determination to pursue your goals. Several times this indicates you happen to be in the right place at the right time and your wise decisions end up in success. As you slowly grow and mature into adulthood this aspect allows you to use you experiences throughout life to teach you

57

responsibility and perseverance. You naturally understand that nothing will be given to you for free, and your success is a direct result of the work you're willing to put into something. One negative part of this aspect is that it can make you an obsessive control freak. Others may think of you as stern and bull headed because of the forceful way you project your opinions towards them. It's usually true. This aspect can provide the better of two worlds. The expansive, indulgent, playfulness of Jupiter can be experienced, while the responsible, calculating, restrictive energies of Saturn can level out your over excessiveness. Naturally, just like every other aspect if you has negative influences from other planets this can act as a catalyst for destruction. At worst you take on too much responsibility and fail because your expectations are too high.

Jupiter conjunct Uranus

A conjunction between Jupiter and Uranus doesn't occur very often and they usually indicate high expectations about yourself and the future. The spiritual philosophies of Jupiter make religion or higher forms of consciousness a very important factor in your life. Many secrets of the universe a locked away in your subconscious and they reveal themselves as need be. You're basically a spiritual giant. You possess keen insight when developing your talents and how to use them efficiently. Jupiter never believes in failure, only in minor hiccups along the way. Obstacles are met with a reliance on the greater forces guiding you along. You respect knowledge and pay close attention to those you feel more educated and intelligent. Any conjunction with Uranus is going to produce some form of difficulties. You may have psychological disorders, high anxiety, or severe drug addiction. Jupiter expands everything it touches, and Uranus is just flipping crazy. With this planetary combination you may be a ticking time bomb, just waiting to explode on an unexpected victim. Normal religious concepts are generally of no interest to you. You have strong beliefs about the universe and the afterlife which require massive amounts of proof before you change your mind. Your progressive thinking causes you to feel there is always room for advancement and everything must evolve in order to survive. You may experience crazy forms of luck and find money comes from unexpected ways from highly unusual sources. Be careful of obsessive indulgence and consume everything in moderation.

Jupiter conjunct Neptune

Alignments between Jupiter and one of the generational planets occur infrequently and require assistance from elsewhere for energy. All alone this produces intense visions and philosophical inspirations. It also instills you with confusion and laziness. Your imagination and creativity are matched by none, and an outlet of music, art, or theater will be needed. Hard work causing you to sweat is generally for someone else, and if it isn't yard work beautifying your home you rarely work out. The thought of exercise may intrigue you, but halfway through you generally give up. You naturally understand it's the little things making the difference, and will put forth the effort needed to succeed. You pay attention to the smaller sometimes insignificant intricacies knowing they're the difference between average to good, and from good to great. Your interest in beauty and art will inspire you to create things which are pleasant to look at. If you're a female you may be interested in fashion and jewelry design. If you're male then architecture, construction, or engineering may spark you curiosity. If Venus is involved this will make you very good looking and beautiful. Your imagination runs so deep that many times you won't accept it. Psychic abilities and intuition are abilities we all possess and these planets aligning like this will give you some. Like any other muscle in the human body, it can be exercised and developed. If you choose you can open your mind into different realms of the universe you experience it like none other. Drugs that make you hallucinate and enter different states of consciousness can have negative and positive effects. Use them carefully and in moderation.

Jupiter conjunct Pluto

When Jupiter and Pluto are positioned like this you're constantly seeking ultimate knowledge and definite truth. You constantly enjoy life to the fullest and will have to learn moderation sometime during your life. The personal drive within you is strong, and can direct your path into a great many things. Very rarely will you think failure is possible or your opinions inaccurate. You always try to get the most out of everything you do or possess, and this can lead to extreme hoarding along with intense obsessions. This aspect doesn't determine what you will obsess about, just the tendency to do so. House placement will indicate where the most passions and jealousy will take place. In professional affairs you will need an occupation where there advancement is limitless. Areas of law, politics, or psychology will be a good way to direct your interests. You might be extreme risk taker, not always seeing the disadvantages of doing so. Close alignments from Mars will make you a spectacular athlete, and you should be one for a profession. Remember great rewards can often mean great failures when things don't go according to plan. If your ego still remains in the way of your personal and professional relationships you will never be happy. Be careful not to exaggerate and over emphasize your abilities and opportunities, as this will lead to conceitedness and arrogance.

Saturn conjunct ascendant

The most powerful way to feel the energy of a planet is to have it conjoined with your ascendant. This particular alignment allows the conservative, well disciplined, and determined properties of Saturn influence you greatly. You generally stay within the rules of your game and expect others to do so as well. Because of Saturn's reserved characteristics it will be difficult to assert yourself all the time. There is absolutely no logic in physical combat according to Saturn. If you ever do have a violent altercation it's only after all options are exhausted and there is no other choice. This isn't because you're a pushover, you just wait till the most opportune moment to strike and many times wait too long. You're shy about your feelings, and very slow to completely open up to someone. Saturn is always stuck in rigid familiarity and hates straying from its well-worn path. Methods that are tried and true always prove more effective than the obscure or abstract. Part of this is because you're insecure about yourself and your feelings. Since no one is perfect, you see your character flaws and assume that others do as well. It will be through your experiences in life which causes you to mature out of this. As you progressively succeed you will accept your adequacies and slowly feel comfortable in your own skin. Best of all, it's easy for you to use all your resources efficiently. You can get the most out of everything and everyone.

Saturn conjunct Uranus

The conjunction of Saturn and Uranus is one of the most power aspects someone can have. It affects a whole generation of people born during a year and a half span once every thirty five years or so. Because it affects society on such a massive level the personal characteristics are difficult to single out. It basically shows rebellious reform within all levels of society. Last occurring from 1987- 1989 it won't align like this again until 2032. The degree of each planet is just as critical as house placement. Activities which require pinpoint precision and calculations will suit you well. Probably pool, bowling, or darts. Saturn is the supreme leader of responsibility and when positively influenced you're abilities in business and politics. Negative afflictions will make you think responsibility is a total burden. No matter how positive or negative the desire, you usually accomplish whatever you set your mind to. House placement becomes so important because it will direct you to your most natural ambitions. Your desire for personal freedom is great, and you react immediately. The positions of Mars will indicate if this reaction is violent. It's going to be extremely difficult to work with others when you're not in charge. You have to work for yourself at some point in time in order to prove this to no one but yourself. If it was meant to be then you will succeed. Sometimes this indicates an incredibly unusual relationship with your father or a male parental figure. It

61

can also show you have a job that is extremely different than most. This is definitely one of the harsher aspects planets can form, and if there isn't cooling influences elsewhere your anger issues will need serious work. If you're not careful you become so intently focused on one single thing the failure to recognize your mistakes instigates havoc in everything you do.

Saturn conjunct Neptune

Saturn and Neptune are two of the slower moving planets, making aspects between them mildly generational. This particular one indicates you protect yourself by not trusting situations or individuals which are unfamiliar. Although you're gullible at times, you're not going to be deceived for very long, partially because you're extremely psychic. If there are other aspects from the Moon, Sun, or Mercury you will experiences extremely vivid, and sometimes disturbing, dreams. The generation experiencing this alignment will go through a major restructuring of religion, politics, and medicine. This is most definitely not a lighthearted aspect and should be taken quite seriously. Although potent, one of the planets needs to have a relationship with the ascendant. The cosmically expansive properties of Neptune don't handle the narrow minded or restrictive issues of Saturn very well. Our imagination and sub consciousness are extremely influenced by Neptune and when Saturn becomes involved it's nearly impossible to get out of your own head. Most of your personal problems will be because you're clinging on to something dysfunctional that needs to be ridden of. Wars and upheaval stemming from land, resource, and political control will run amuck. The "Up yours" attitude this aspect will produce some of the most rebellious and influential world leaders to come along in centuries. You never accept anything at face value and inquire about the validity of everything you are presented with. House placement and aspects from other planets will be extremely influential and can change the outcome of this one easily.

Saturn conjunct Pluto

Saturn is the slowest of the personal planets, and Pluto is the slowest of all, making their alignments infrequent, and exceptionally powerful. Pending retrogrades, this alignment occurs only once every thirty-eight years or so. Previously in 1982 while in the sign of Libra, this monumental formation will occur again in 2020 in the sign of Capricorn. Pluto is going to test your fortitude at every turn, and if you're not up for a significant challenge then don't try working for yourself. You need to work alone with your own set of obligations, but sometimes the unseen stresses of self employment take their toll on your psyche. So many people are influenced by this aspect that it's useless trying to describe each individual characteristic. You can endure more than most and will be tested to the extremes. The generations who experience these hardships must overcome horrible atrocities created by the previous generation. Extremely secretive about your thoughts, plans, and desires, you never want others to know more than you do. Life is a constant competition and you realize that you need all the advantages you can get. Producing qualities of leadership and authority the world will see the rise of many powerful leaders, dictators, and governmental revolutionaries. Despite all your abilities for authority many times you are forced into a profession before you realize what you really want to do. When you do set in somewhere professionally if there is no room for advancement into authority you will grow restless and leave. It can also indicate the ultimate obsessions with your job and career.

Uranus conjunct ascendant

Aspects to Uranus are always interesting, especially this one. No other alignment will allow the rebelliousness of Uranus to flow through your veins stronger than the conjunction to your ascendant. You're always a unique individual marching to the beat of a different drum. Your potential for innovative greatness is dependent on how you handle your excess energy. This planet's natural instinct is to throw away the rule book and break out onto its own path. Left alone this makes you erratic and eccentric. Like owning sixteen cats type crazy. Venus will inspire style, Mercury your brain, and the other planets undoubtedly cast their special influence also. This aspect doesn't indicate any particular characteristic other than just plain weird. You're the crazy Thomas Edison who invents Kool-Aid while trying to discover gun powder. If others try to control you the natural response is to pack up and leave. Your innovative and brilliantly intelligent mind will need to find an intellectual interest. If Uranus is in your first house you will have a more forceful personality, while if you have it in your twelfth house you will be more of a head case, possibly with mental illness. This most definitely produces a high strung nervousness. Anxiety disorders are all too possible, especially with harsh alignments involving Saturn or Mars. If no proper outlet is found you spin around in circles until your energy level is completely depleted. Many times this will indicate a very unusual upbringing in your early years. Unfortunately this can also mean an unusual illness or brain injury as a youngster.

Uranus conjunct Neptune

At about once every 170 years, the alignment of Uranus and Neptune occurs less frequently than all but one, the conjunction of Neptune to Pluto. This will be a generation breaking down almost every form of social, religious, and government structure we have. The vastness of this revolutionary rebellion will be unprecedented in all human history. Because this involves two of the generational planets it's more of a building block for other planets to structure around. It provides a beautiful starting point. Occurring in the earliest stages of Capricorn back in the 1820's, then again farther into the sign during 1990's sign only assumptions can be made. Judging by the American industrial revolution during the 1800's I believe this indicates another revolution only with computers overtaking mechanics. There will need to be individuals inspired to think and create these advancements. Everyone born from 1989 until 1997 has this in their chart, and are the only people with this aspect for almost two centuries. Reforms in religion, government, and environmental control will spark many wars and conflicts. This generation will also be the ones that begin the long term clean-up of our environment and bring natural medicines into the forefront. They will incorporate science into religion and discover ghosts along with space aliens.

Uranus conjunct Pluto
(1847-1854) (1961-1969)

Conjunctions between generational planets have a global revolutionary affect. Occurring over a hundred years apart this is no ordinary alignment and won't occur again until past 2100 Because of the duration of this aspect house placement as well as the relationship to the ascendant will determine how much each individual handles the energy. This alignment can be primarily defined by the hippie revolution of the 1960's. A time when science, religion, and more importantly world politics received an overhaul. Some were free spirits, refusing to be restrained by government forces. Others were sticklers for the rules, and had to enforce their authority. People will go take great measures and go to extremes in order to gain or preserve their freedom. During the 1800's the world experienced the third round of the French revolution and the American civil war shortly after that. Then in the 1960's there was the conflict in Vietnam with the rise of communism and the ignition of the cold war. I can only guess and imagine what will happen around the year 2100 AD when this happens again. I'm gonna be a ghost or 112 years old, so I don't really care. Not only does this bring social revolutions to the forefront, it will also bring massive technological and spiritual revolutions as well. The technological world will intertwine into the spiritual realm and open doors into existence never thought possible. As we recognize the meaninglessness and insignificance of human life on Earth as we evolve into more cosmical entities the awesome magnificence of the universe will reveal itself when we are ready for it.

Neptune conjunct ascendant

All generational planets need a close alignment to your ascendant in order to be influential. The conjunction is the most powerful there is. Not necessarily organized religion, but spirituality will be very important to you. Other than possibly Venus or the Moon, Neptune is the most delusional planet in the solar system. You're extremely sensitive, and intuitively pick up on the unconscious emotions of others. This can make you a wonderful counselor or social worker. The atrocities taking place around the world make a profound impact on you, and you desperately wish to help. Neptune instills ultimate compassion and healing. The fact of the matter is that you are psychic, very psychic. You only have a loose grip on reality and love living in fantasy. Despite your immense psychic ability you don't always accept things for the way they are. Even though you know the truth you don't readily accept it and can turn a blind eye to any problem. If others fail to live up to your expectations you give them the benefit of the doubt while inside you're deeply saddened. Being overly generous towards the undeserving can be your downfall. You're so willing to help others that you give what you can't afford to those who don't really need it. Because our see everything as one collective in nature, humans, animals, and even plants have their proper place in the universe. Although you are exceptionally sensitive to the environmental conditions around you there will need to be external driving forces to get you up and moving.

Neptune conjunct Pluto

This is the most infrequent alignment in all astrology. The last time these two were in the same sign and degree was in 1893, and I can't tell you when it will happen again. Those born with this played a major part in creating the tensions resulting in WW1 and then the rise of the Nazis igniting WW2.

Pluto conjunct ascendant

The most powerful way for a planet to express itself is through a conjunction with your ascendant. This is especially true for the generational planets like distant Pluto. The condition Pluto is in will be indescribably important when making an assessment.

All too often this far off warrior is compared to the Hindu destroyer god Shiva. When the other planets are harshly aligning with this you have nearly unbearable catastrophes constantly shattering your life. The purpose of Pluto is to provide you with insurmountable amounts of energy to cope with disaster. Rebuilding after annihilation is what Pluto does. It's the unfortunate truth we all must deal with. Obsession will always be used describing Pluto, and the house placement of the aligning planets will show where you're the most possessed. You tend to get what you want and don't really care what it takes to get it. Despite any obstacles in your path, the mountain you need to overcome will be conquered and the reward reaped to the fullest. The influence from Pluto into your subconscious is strong, and can put you in touch with artistic abilities. If this aspect is on the twelfth house side you will have a much stronger connection to the darker realm of spirituality and the underworld. While in the first house you will be a power tripping control freak. If this is in Scorpio you are the very meaning of psychic and if it were the 1500's you would be burned at the stake as a witch.

Sextile

Colossians 2:16
So let no one judge you in food or in drink, or regarding a festival or a new Moon or Sabbaths.

The separation of sixty degrees is known as the sextile and arguably the best aspect in astrology. Along with the trine, a sextile allows the energies of the planets involved to flow in good accord. Usually, this indicates a pleasant companionship and you understand how to use the planets energy efficiently. However, if the planets have significant problems elsewhere, this shows negative feelings are what is being transferred between the pair. Like everything else, the sign and condition of the planets are what is important. The orb if influence I use is quite different than most astrologers. I use a six degree apply orb and a twelve degree separating. Reason being, at seventy-two degrees you reach the lesser known but still extremely powerful quintile. The six degree separating orb of the sextile, combined with the six degree applying orb I use for the quintile it's easier to just say twelve degrees separating from the sextile, with a little "no man's land" around six to eight.

Sun sextile ascendant.

The sextile between the Sun and your ascendant is one of the best relationships for the two. This alignment allows whatever energies being produced by the other planets to express themselves easily. Granted, if the other planets are in poor condition, this aspect does a little to soothe the difficulty, but usually just lets the negative energy to prevail. Conversely, if you have all pleasant aspects this can make you think life is a cake walk and you just casually get by. All by itself, you're generally happy and optimistic, with the ability to keep your spirits high. These are two of the most important point in your natal chart and their condition is an over good indicator of your personality. You take on all the prominent traits of both signs, especially the rising sign. Opinions are very easy for you to express, and you have a sense of suave finesse about yourself. You feel like everyone can be a friend, and usually look upon people with kindness regardless of their appearance. Be advised that some people need their space, and you shouldn't force yourself upon them as they may become nervous and overly cautious about your intentions. You're generally a high spirited individual who can functionally get along with just about anyone. More importantly you're comfortable with yourself and possess the ability to find the niche of society you fit in.

Sun sextile Moon

This is one of the most helpful aspects in all of astrology. Sextiles indicate positive energy and a balanced accord between the two planets involved. When those planets are the Sun, your

68

spirit, and the Moon, your emotional subconscious, their integrated synergy is very useful. In layman terms this means you accept yourself and others. Unless horribly afflicted by other planets, mainly Mars and Saturn, this eases the tension from other alignments. Your affable nature attracts many friends along your path, and you generally associate with those who follow the law. You're guilty of a few minor misdemeanors, but no serious felonies. Sometimes this is also an indicator your parents remain married until one passes. When the situation calls for emotion you respond properly, and when you need to separate feelings from logic, you do so fluidly as well. After a short breather and analyzing the situation from a different point of view, problems are tackled in a reasonable fashion. You possess a plethora of creative ideas, and your imagination can make you a great artist or musician. Remembering the traumas and the mistakes made in the past, there is no desire to return to where you have come from when your past is dysfunctional. As anticipated this is a fabulous alignment to soothe the harsher aspects from any of the other planets.

Sun sextile Mars

A sextile between your Sun and Mars gives you an abundant amount of energy and personal drive. You articulately express how you're feeling, and won't be shy when disagreeing with someone. This brashness will eventually drive wedges between your friends, colleagues, and family members. You enjoy sports and athletics, even if team events are not your thing. Exercise and activity will be crucial in maintaining a balance between your nervousness and high energy level. Migraines and extreme irritability will be the result of lacking exercise. Although you can be dominant and pushy at times but still relate to people in a polished way which can work effectively within the business or political realm. When you accept responsibility there's nothing standing in the way of your goal. A sextile always shows positive energies flowing between the planets involved. Mars is the selfish and arrogant vagabond who only cares about themselves. Despite the usually pleasantness indicated by a sextile when Mars dominates too much you're just plain mean. For the most part thought, your ego is kept in check and you only blow up occasionally. This can also make you extremely athletic and competitive. It's your combative nature that allows you to defeat opponents while protection your own. Romantically, you must seek a partner who is gentler and calmer than you in order to compensate for your aggressiveness.

Sun sextile Jupiter

You're intelligent and curious, possessing a philosophical mind that is always absorbing information. Obtaining as much knowledge as you can through your various experiences, you desire to get out and see everything the world can offer. Your early conditioning trained you to strive for success and never accept failure. You succeed at whatever you do solely because you believe you can never fail. Any obstacles will be met head on and usually dealt with reasonably. If this aspect takes place in the fifth or ninth houses you can be extremely lucky in gambling or speculative matters. If Mars is involved you will be more naturally athletic than most. The negativities of this aspect and be as substantial as the positive ones. On the bad side, you can be lazy and arrogant. Jupiter is the king of extravagance, and you may think you're entitled to all the finer things in life. This attitude may induce you to spend money of recreation and frivolously impulsive purchases. Because of your gregarious and flamboyant nature others can see you as conceited or rude. If you project your confidence level too forcefully then expect these negative responses. When you do socialize make sure it is in a reasonable manner. You will most definitely get carried away from time to time, and it will be necessary for you to learn to follow a strict budget. Any involvement into drugs or alcohol will cause serious problems in your life. You possess a natural tendency to take everything to the extremes. Modesty, humbleness, and humility, are all virtues you will have difficulties learning.

Sun sextile Saturn

Just as the Moon and Venus affect the relationship we have with our mothers, the Sun and Saturn affect the relationship we have with our father. Sextiles usually mean there is a close, affectionate bond. Other than possibly the trine, this is the best possible relationship. You learn most of your life's lessons from whatever male role model you're influenced by, and if the relationship is poor and neglectful then expect some malfunction. It doesn't matter if it's an uncle, grandfather, or biological father you learn more from males than females. This is definitely a stabilizing aspect which can give you a good balance between what you can and can't do. Part of your success is you accept what you're not good at and can focus on productive projects. Unfortunately this can cause you to be overly cautious when in close competition. Because you follow the rules you expect your competitors to as well. If they don't you're the one screaming foul when they cheat. Saturn's properties of organization, precision, and responsibilities easily express themselves and you accept your duties readily. Saturn's house placement usually shows where you should direct your career. The Sun energizes your ambition and if you can find a positive outlet success usually follows.

Sun sextile Uranus

When the Sun and Uranus are aspecting each other like this you feel it's important to maintain in constant communication with everyone. This makes you talkative, energetic, and many times eccentric as well. Your spirit is entirely unique and must be expressed accordingly. You're eager about life and wish to share your personal experiences with everyone around you. Opinionated and outspoken, you're not afraid to stand up for what you believe in. Nor are you bound by the restrictions of what is accepted by society or tradition. This makes you a full time adventure seeker, wishing to do things not everyone has a chance to do. You find your greatest personal revelations and passions are experienced from traveling into other cultures and peoples. To you, life is always exciting and there's constantly something interesting to go do. If you choose to develop your innovative way of thinking areas

71

in technological research and development may interest you. It's easy for you to adapt into any profession you choose, and if negatively aspected by other planets you may sink into a job with no room for advancement and still be happy with it. This isn't a comforting aspect nor is it a bad aspect. It definitely shows originality and rebelliousness. The other planets will direct just where this attitude will go.

Sun sextile Neptune

The Sun sextile with Neptune indicates the awareness of your creative potential, but you still need a direction to use it. You understand your social responsibilities and that you need to be instrumental in relieving the suffering you observe. However, you prefer to leave the burden of work to someone with more energy. You're extremely sensitive and any rejection of your services hurts you deeply. This can cause some difficulty since it is so important for you to relate to others in a personal way. Your professional abilities are quite varied. Like a chameleon you can take on whatever characteristics needed in your occupation. Ideally your work should involve public related activities where you can use your creative abilities. Your imagination and creative talents could be exploited in writing or media in. You freely relate to many different people and are rarely shocked by the characters around you. It will necessary to watch someone suffer from time to time. When you can't realize how much you can actually help someone your personal resources are dwindled. Sometimes you intentionally accept the challenge others would avoid, thinking you can discover something hadn't. Despite the congenial nature of the sextile sometimes the Sun only charges the delusional thoughts. Be careful not to fall for far-fetched schemes or speculations. It's very easy for you fall for things that seem too good to be true.

Sun sextile Pluto

With a sextile between the Sun and Pluto in your chart you're strong willed and can accomplish anything you choose. The ability to see the bigger picture allows you to make decisions

72

which coincide with attaining your goals. Part of your success is you possess highly acute psychic senses and see things before they actually happen. You seem to read people very accurately from the moment you first meet them. If you pay attention to your gut instinct you find many times it's right. When negatively aspected by other planets, especially Mars or Saturn, this can indicate several hardships and mountains to climb before success is fully achieved. Because you're capable of handling extreme adversities the universe will constantly put you to the test. Chances are you will have to overcome massive calamities that other simply do not. When these unfortunate events do occur you are entirely ready to battle the issue head on. You can completely breakdown one failing system and replace it with a more functional one with relative ease. Fascinated with the mystical world, you find an interest in yoga, the occult, and maybe organized mainstream religion. More often than not, this indicates you know where to focus your obsessions. When you finally make a decision as what you want you simply go get it, despite whatever obstacles.

Moon sextile ascendant

Nine times out of ten a sextile to your rising sign is pleasantly tranquil, especially when the Moon is involved. Its basic nature allows you to integrate your emotions into your personality. You experience feelings as they were created to be, and express them accordingly. Don't forget this includes negative emotions, not just the positive one. Your love and generosity is matched by none other, the same with your anger and vengeance. You're extremely sensitive to what people say about you, and take words more dramatically than others. When people talk negatively you try to understand why they would say such things, and what their emotional charge behind it was. The melancholy attributes of the Moon make you feel others are not satisfied with your work and don't appreciate the effort you put forward. This is simply just not true. The fact is the only one unsatisfied is you. This will also intensifies the emotional bond with your mother. Her influence, whether good or bad, will be a dominant factor in your life. Many

73

times discipline coming from mom will be more profound and effective than from dad. This is definitely a soothing aspect which should ease the tensions produced by squares or oppositions elsewhere.

Moon sextile Mercury

This is a very pleasant aspect giving you a warm and thoughtful personality. It can soothe and comfort some of the negative aspects elsewhere in your chart. Basically, you absorb information emotionally, meaning you recognize how something makes you feel before realizing anything else. Remembering what someone said will be sometimes difficult, but you will never forget the way you felt, you're also more receptive to the tone and inflection people talk to you in. Words hurt and comfort you more than most. Mercury adds a childlike essence to your emotional side, and unfortunately causes you to act immaturely from time to time. Remember the old cliché curiosity killed the cat? Place that philosophy in the back of your head. Many times you will find yourself in bad relationships just because you're curious about that person. Once you realize how boring they truly are you move onto the next. It's generally your mind which is your worst enemy most of the time, and you're very sensitive to your thoughts. You love talking to your mother, and this can indicate your parents remain married. Be careful not to become complacent, and think everything is forever. It's also very easy for you to set problems aside and let others deal with them. Often this indicates a pleasant singing voice or at least a softer tone, depending on sigh of course. If this is fire and air your words a quick and decisive, while if it's Earth and air you're dealing with the nurturing side is more prevalent.

Moon sextile Venus

With the Moon forming a sextile towards Venus, this allows you to realize and make the proper compromises in order to maintain harmony in your relationships. Having a clear indication of what you want, it's easy to express your desires and form a rewarding partnership. Whether it's romantic or otherwise, you make concessions where necessary and expect others to do so as well. Falling in love is easy and simply put, you're in love with love, and must feel you're needed all the time. This can lead to several failed romances because you're addicted to the butterflies a new passion produces. You wish to experience all life has to offer, but must do so with your mate. Because you want to spend every waking minute with them sometimes they feel you're too clingy and possessive. You're socially charming and will most likely end up participating in many fund raisers or community events. The large group of acquaintances provides you with a sense of personal self-worth and securities. This is one of the harmonizing aspects which can smooth out any severe troubles produced by the other planets. At the worst this will make you completely and oblivious to your lovers faults, which can lead to abusive relationships.

Moon sextile Mars

The purpose of this alignment is for the Moon to soothe the anger and hostility of Mars. Unless placed in a fire sign, Luna's comforting nurture is calming and balances the aggression allowing you to direct your efforts into a proper outlet. The houses these two occupy are where you should focus that direction. Generally speaking this makes you a lover not a fighter. Although you may react emotionally it will take other negative aspects from other planets to make you physically violent. Sextiles are usually positive, but any alignment between these two adds volatility to your already unstable inner psyche. Even if you're usually calm you still have your days of complete unpredictability. This will probably occur when Mars makes a harsh alignment progressively. You never want to burn down a bridge. Even in a heated argument you still try to keep good relations with your opponent. Respect is earned by your ability to maintain a cool head when they themselves wouldn't have. This can lead to other more aggressive individuals taking advantage of you. Knowing you won't fight back much they can push you around sometimes trample over you. Occupations that put in close personal contact with the public will suit you perfectly. Refrain from eating because you're angry and try to leave business affairs at the office.

Moon sextile Jupiter

This is one of the most wonderful aspects possible. At its best it relieves many of the conflictions produced by harsher planetary alignments. Jupiter is known as the greater benefic which positively expands everything it touches. A sextile is arguably the best relationship there is and this counter balances your other issues. The basic nature of this contact is to increase your feelings of emotion. You experience love, joy, and happiness on a grander stage than the rest of us. Conversely, you also feel rage, hate, or anger more than others as well. The biggest issue you have is over emotionalizing a situation where rational thinking is needed. Despite all the positive effects this is definitely not a grounding alignment. Jupiter is enhancing your emotional complexity and sometimes you don't embrace the feelings. In fact it stimulates dreaminess, and if Venus is involved you're a total space case who constantly falls in love. If you can remain inspired by vivid dreams you can tap into the vast resources of your creative potential. Art, music, or theater will be great outlets for your creative expression. Careers in medicine of social work will prove most fulfilling. You're also going to retain weight as you get older. Diet will be very important in old age.

Moon sextile Saturn

The sextile between the Moon and Saturn allows you to see responsibilities clearly and apply them in a proper direction. Once you recognize the limits of your capabilities and resources you're very efficient in using then reasonably. The restrictive tendencies of Saturn will calm down any irrational aspects from planets elsewhere. Despite the general harmony of this aspect, one negative influence will be your inability to break free from any traumatic experiences. Although you're able to organize your emotions you still cling onto anything which has made an impact on your life. Emotional detachment is a main philosophy of Saturn, and the Moon is pure emotion. Obviously this is a direct confliction of interests. Each planet understands their feelings in a different way, yet they both seclude themselves when distressed. Both planets must get away by themselves in order to regain personal insight. Saturn takes much longer to warm up but eventually will. If you tend to be a recluse depression will definitely be an issue. At its worst this forces you to make sense of your emotions, which is impossible. Make sure to get a proper amount of social interaction. Locking yourself into your own little rabbit hole will never solve anything. At the end of the day this is still one of the best aspects you can have. Anything built upon this has proper structure and form. Of all the planets which can stabilize the Moon Saturn is the best.

Moon sextile Uranus

Anything involving Uranus adds excitement and eccentricity. In this case your emotions are harmoniously balanced with the influence of Uranus. The biggest problem, Uranus is highly volatile and completely unpredictable. Although the sextile is supposed to be a good alignment, the best relationship between the Moon and Uranus is none at all. Basically, the tighter any formation the crazier you are, and the more intense your nervousness or anxiety. The Moon fluctuates easily and is constantly seeking stability, which is never provided by Uranus. Fortunately this doesn't produce anything negative naturally. All alone this is a wonderful aspect which allows you to accept your unique personality. Individuality is something you pride yourself on, and you enjoy those who are rebellious as well. There is a lot of potential for creative brilliance, but you're going need more structure to form anything solid. Look to Saturn, Jupiter, or a tenth house placement for that needed base. Along with Neptune and Pluto, Uranus is a generational planet which requires a close alignment to your ascendant in order to release its most potent energies. Deep inside your mind is a calling to explore the distant realms of the universe. When anyone or anything restricts your freedom the rebellion is usually instantaneous. Even if you're generally the most mellow headed person every once in a while you flip out for no apparent reason. House placement is very important because it will show where you experience the most emotional instability caused by the most sudden of events.

Moon sextile Neptune

When the Moon and Neptune are in sextile you're extremely sensitive to your emotions and those of others around you. Not many aspects can reveal the universal secrets locked within the human subconscious but this one can. Your dreams appear as reality and you have a tendency to get lost in fantasyland. This aspect makes you caring and compassionate with you strive to show affection to everyone. The motherly properties of the Moon and the oneness for all produced by Neptune can make you and overly sensitive patsy. You're going to need to develop courage and confidence in order to get past this small road block. As you see the injustices taking place take place around the world you desperately want to help. Fascination into the mystical is the realm of Neptune and your interests into the occult. If you choose to direct this ability towards art, music, or poetry, you will find great success. Because you're so sensitive to the environmental surroundings you take on the emotions of the room intuitively. Psychic abilities allow you to read the emotions of people very well, although you may have difficulties identifying your own. This aspect will also make you emotionally connected with your mother. Despite the fact she can get under your skin sometimes, you will always need her around. After her passing you will have strange dreams and contacts with her.

Moon sextile Pluto

Your Moon in sextile to Pluto bestows you with and understanding of love greater and deeper than those around you. Whether good or bad, you experience intense periods of passion and your emotions are larger than life. This is a good indicator of your ability to overcome great obstacles through positive emotional contacts. Any sextiles with the Moon produce positive emotions somewhere. Look to the house placement of these planets as a place of retreat for personal solitude. Your unconscious curiosity into the unknown makes the mysteries and secretive fascinating. Because of this natural ability you would make a wonderful psychiatrist or counselor. If Mercury is positively involved consider pediatrics or elementary education. The reason you're so good at connecting with them is because you're extremely psychic and they feel comfortable opening up to you. You pick up on their unconscious signals and sympathize with their problems. The bad side is experienced by your total refusal to let go and forgive those who harmed you. Insults are never forgotten and sometimes the personal attacks and met with total annihilation. Once you explode an atomic bomb is set of and the closer the alignment the bigger the eruption. Nobody can mess with you and get away with it. It's easy for you to get carried away with the wrong crowd, and you should be very aware of mob mentality, as your generosity is easily preyed upon. Many times those who seemed to be your closest friends turn out to be nothing more than the predators feeding on your kindness. This will also give you a very emotional bond with your mother, especially if the Moon is placed in the first house. She will be your source of comfort and support, any neglect from her will be especially traumatizing.

Mercury sextile ascendant

Mercury in sextile to your ascendant makes you bright, energetic, and extremely curious. You have no problem vocalizing your opinions and will do so more than people care to hear. All your ideas are great in theory, but many times the actual work is for someone else. Unless Taurus or Saturn is involved, then you may be amazingly responsible and dedicated to success. Be cautious who you share your creations with, because if you're not careful when keeping ideas to yourself competitors may take credit which isn't theirs. Mercury aspects aren't usually projected physically except by talkativeness, speed, and agility. This is a great base structure for planets like Saturn or Uranus to inspire brilliance. As a child you probably said the darndest things at the darndest times, and learned to swear early. If Venus is involved you have a beautiful singing voice, or at least good public speaking skills. Part of the reason you're so difficult to teach is because the basic concepts of math, science, and reading come naturally. Then once you've advanced yourself ahead of your class you lose interest in the teacher. Unless you have a crush on them.

Mercury sextile Venus

Because Mercury and Venus are so close to the Sun they can only form two major aspects, the conjunction and sextile. A sextile is the better of the two, and this particular alignment gives you the gift of gab, but the ability to know when listening is just as important. The soothing tone in your voice entices people to warm up quickly, and you're probably a gifted singer. You're generally friendly to even the casual stranger, until you're taken for a fool. One of your biggest problems is you treat too many people like a close friend and assume they have your best interest in mind. Once they overstep personal boundaries either an argument ensues, or you bottle up the emotions creating other problems. Mercury alignments aren't always the most physically prominent aspects. Other than being short, quick, and talkative, they generally inspire intelligence, speed, and aptitude. Your ability to socialize allows you to work your way up the ranks into management. Romantically, you're attracted to someone who's not necessarily educated, but they can't stupid. You'll be a sucker for the way they talk to you. The houses these two occupy will show what areas of your life you enjoy talking about the most.

Mercury sextile Mars

With Mercury and Mars in this position you're restless intellect is only matched by your insatiable curiosity. Your mind will never rest until it has probed into all available information. When you don't get all the facts, the rash conclusion you come to is generally wrong. If someone questions your correctness the response may get hostile and possibly violent. You're usually an

80

honest and genuine person who will walk up to anyone and strike up a conversation. The mental agility and usually affable personality can allow success when working within groups, if you can control your ego. You recognize and accept your role readily, and will do your job with enthusiasm and energy. No task is too big or small for you. You're generally optimistic and naturally give people the benefit of the doubt, but once you're deceived you lash out like a lion. Communicating with others will be a strongpoint and you will find many friends seek your advice because of your ability to tell them like it is. House placement is what you like to talk about the most.

Mercury sextile Jupiter

Any aspect involving Jupiter is positive and this is one of the best. You're gifted with intelligence and learning ability, but because Mercury is so scatterbrained it's difficult to realize your potential. In turn, you often short change yourself by thinking you're not as capable as others. These spiraling consequences cause you to feel oppressed and underachieving. As you mature and realize your abilities these feelings of inadequacy will eventually dissolve away. You make sure to get the facts before you make a decision and stay as informed as you can. Other than arrogance about your intelligence there isn't much that can go wrong with this alignment. You have excellent logic and reasoning ability, but once again the constant analysis of Mercury gets in your way. Don't over think yourself and the short comings will be limited. Travel will bring you open your eyes and teach you many things about life. Education through travel will provide more useful than bookwork. Experiencing other culture broadens your horizons by allowing you to see outside your box. Your mind is philosophically inclined to the greater forces of the universe and religion or spirituality needs to be an important role in your life.

Mercury sextile Saturn

When these two planets are aligned like this you possess a good understanding of your limitations and capabilities. This aspect allows you to remain focused on a single goal or objective for long periods of time. You're usually well informed about many subjects, but mainly personal interests, which you're always willing to discuss with others. Backing up your statements with facts and statistics is more important than anything. Most people with this in their charts mature and accept responsibility earlier than most. You may have felt isolated and alone as a child. This is because you feel more comfortable around others who are older and more mature. Constantly learning, you're endlessly curious about how and why things work. The little intricacies of machines, computers, or sciences fascinate you and can keep your attention for hours. Your aptitude for precise calculations and statistics will make you an excellent engineer or architect. House placement will be a good indicator of where you seek to be the most knowledgeable. This alignment also eases the relations you have with your father. It's easy for you to open up to him by communicating your thoughts and feelings.

Mercury sextile Uranus

A sextile between these two planets usually indicates your intellectual ability is highly above average. Although you're impatient with ignorance, you're still reasonably tolerant of those who cannot think at your pace provided they show an effort to learn. You're extremely alert, curious, and can be a little high strung or on edge most of the time. Your happiest profession should allow you to use creative abilities and not be mentally confined. Uranus is the epitome of progressive thinking and you respect the past only for the lessons it has taught you. To be successful you need to develop self-discipline and persistence. If you don't understand something naturally your inclination is to find something you do pick up quick. Uranus has significant rebellion issues, and Mercury simply interjects these philosophies into your brain. Establish definite objectives and construct a positive plan for attaining your goals. You will have extreme difficulty winding down and relaxing. Your impatience and excitability will eventually lead to exhaustion, both physical and mental. More often than not this will show you excel in music, science, or technology.

Mercury sextile Neptune

This aspect shows your mind is in tune with Neptune, allowing your spiritual and psychic abilities to function properly. Your imaginative and creative abilities greatly exceed those around you, but there is no desire to accomplish any of them. All this aspect does, is allow you to think thinks up. The contemplative nature of Neptune allows you to cope with your problems reasonably. As you constantly search for knowledge, you're determined to gather as much information as you can before making a decision. Be careful when taking things at face value, as Neptune is easily deceived into believing things that are simply not true. Neptune is mystical and spiritual, with Mercury acting as a catalyst projecting these energies throughout your chart. In order to use your imagination and creative abilities properly it would be wise to seek higher forms of education. This doesn't necessarily mean a four year university, but a vocational school or art institute will allow you to refine your skills. Be careful if you choose to dabble in the darker realms of religion. This aspect puts you in close contact with it. Neither of these planets provides you with much ambition. Mercury is more of the side kick and Neptune just wanders around lost in the woods.

Mercury sextile Pluto

Mercury and Pluto in sextile usually indicates you have an intelligent mind and are capable of higher learning and complex studies. Areas of medicine or technological research and development will be great outlets for your advanced abilities. Your intuitive skills are greater than you can imagine, and you pick up the unbroadcasted signals projected by others. As you grow older and more aware of your capabilities you can learn to take advantage of it. Trusting your gut instinct is difficult sometimes and more often than not you will find it to be correct. When aspected by other planets you can be intently possessive and obsessive. Many times this indicates you become infatuated with something or someone and refuse to let it go. Once you do find a positive outlet you stop at nothing to become an expert, even if this means being the biggest gossip on the block. You probably develop a deep fascination into human psychology, or even the occult. Romantically this shows communication is vital in your relationship. You have to talk about everything and when your partner doesn't you feel there is something wrong. The positioning of Venus will be a good indicator of the intensity and direction of these desires.

Venus sextile ascendant

Venus in sextile with your ascendant is one of the most outgoing and social energies you could possess. This aspect indicates your desire to maintain a harmonious relationship with everyone you meet. You want to be friends with everyone and in turn make substantial concessions thinking it will win their approval. If you're not careful you may become a door mat, wasting your resources for the benefit of others. Hopefully you're the peace making type, and take the responsibility of getting everyone to cooperate during family gatherings. You should refrain from getting to close to business associates and co-workers. They may only want to take advantage of you and the romantic entanglement will cause great disruptions in your life. Venus is a planet of harmony and balance causing you to constantly feel things should be as such. It will be difficult to realize when things are turning sour and you may stay in a dysfunctional relationship merely to avoid a conflict. Generally, you're a sissy most of the time, and you need drive and aggression from elsewhere in your chart. You only mildly deviate from the law, and don't wish to cause many problems.

Venus sextile Mars

The relationship between Venus and Mars is vitally important in someone's chart. Of all the possibilities a sextile is the easiest to handle. This separation gives you a warm and affectionate nature which attracts many friends. Part of your success is the positive energy you exude entices others to make concessions to your ideas. Sometimes your ego gets in the way and not everyone will see it, but deep inside you're a caring individual. Your physical needs are considerable, and you find yourself happiest in a committed relationship. Because you must feel needed by another, relationships reinforce your personal self-worth by giving you a sense of emotional security. You're bold and courageous. The aggressive dominance of Mars and the feminine passiveness of Venus are in a harmonious balance. Life is a lot better when you're not naturally pissed off at it. You're able enjoy the most beautiful elements of life and should surround yourself with flowers or fine exotic works of art. You have a generally optimistic perspective and shouldn't stay mad too long. This is a wonderful building block for the other planets to structure around. It allows you to direct your energy into a positive outlet, which is usually visible to the public.

Venus sextile Jupiter

Alignments between Venus and Jupiter generally produce wonderful energy which mellow out harsher aspects elsewhere. This can make you the eternal optimist even when the outcome looks grim. You're out going and personable, making friends with anyone and fitting into many different social circles. House placement shows where your biggest difficulties will come from. Jupiter's position will show where you are the most arrogant and over inflated about yourself. Whereas, Venus, will indicate which relationships you have the grandest expectations. Although the sextile is one of the best possible alignments, it does cause higher than attainable expectations. No matter how hard you work to attain the goals of each house they never live up to your dreams. Artistically, this is a top five relationship. You see wonderful beauty in everything and can make chicken soup out of chicken poop. Jupiter's optimism is dispersed throughout all your relationships. Part of your romantic problem is once again, you think too big for your britches. Unless this is the only positive aspect you have, you can accept life on its terms once you realize where you need work. It's possible you get lucky in love and only death parts you once you finally say "I do." It may take several failed relationships, but once you find someone you can relate to spiritually the bond will be forever.

Venus sextile Saturn

Sextiles between these two planets gives you with a refined social charm and distinct sense of style. Your beauty and taste fit in perfectly along with your personality, and you always find your own niche of creativity. When it comes to design, color, or flair, everything has to flow and fit together precisely. The rainbow always has to go ROYGBIV with you. If you're wild and crazy, your clothes and possessions will reflect that. If you're calm and mellow your possessions will reflect that. Aspects between Venus and Saturn are only mild in a natal chart, and they merely show how you fit into the responsibility of your relationships. The sextile usually means you accept your duties and know how to fill your role in the partnership. Opening to strangers is only possible if you have one planet in a fire sign or fire house. Otherwise you tend to stick to acquaintances that will be useful in the future. Part of your success is the success of those you associate with, and your ability to make the best of your friendships. Although you have several good social contacts, there are only a few you consider close personal friends. Sometimes this indicates you have to assume family responsibility at an early age. By taking on extra household chores made you feel that your productivity was greatly appreciated, and it was. Perhaps you were born into poverty and had to help out financially.

Venus sextile Uranus

This sextile indicates your desire for relationships with different and unusual characters. You have a wide array of friends which range from vagabond to prince, and enjoy the strangest of strange. Any aspects with Uranus add difficulties with rebelliousness and erraticness. Venus places these tensions into your relationships. The house placement of this will show where your off beat interests are most profound. You usually find love affairs spark up randomly out of the blue, but only with someone who has a distinct character. This can definitely make you in love with love, like many other influences involving Venus. Anyone who doesn't possess their own sense of uniqueness is of no interest to you. When in a relationship you need to feel free to pursue your endeavors. Part of your partner's problem will be your flirtatious attitude towards former flames. Uranus is completely unpredictable and Venus is constantly seeking balance, making a natural confliction between the two. Just because a sextile is generally a positive aspect, the powers of Venus are easily swayed and this isn't always pleasant. If there are seriously negative aspects elsewhere this one isn't strong enough to hold its ground. Be very careful because aspects with Uranus can and will cause chaos everywhere. Creatively this is a great structure for your imagination to build around. Although you may not be able to make a living off of it your artwork may provide you with an extra source of income.

Venus sextile Neptune

This aspect blesses you with a creative imagination and a brilliant ability to express beauty and art. It's easy for you to take the ideas in your head and manifest them into the real world. Where others see the negative ugliness you can see the luster, and have a knack for making them appear better than they are. Ways to express your imagination and artistic abilities will come and go throughout your life, as one of the downsides to this, the inability to always see things through will be your stumbling block. In your mind the final product is polished, refined, and gorgeous, but in reality many of your ideas just never take flight. When things don't look like you had planned you simply make adjustment and try your best again. The inner romanticist within is extremely vulnerable and sometimes gullible. Because Venus is such a personal planet, and Neptune confuses everything it touches, these illusions trespass into your relationships. Because you actually believe there's the perfect someone who will sweep you off your feet many partners come and go. Unfortunately, you will have to go through several heartbreaks until you find that perfect someone. Even then you will still think the grass is greener elsewhere, and you can do better. Neither one of these planets is good at seeing things as they actually are. If you don't gather all the facts you will be taken for a sucker and lose your valuable resources.

Venus sextile Pluto

The sextile between Venus and Pluto provides you with a deeper understanding of love and beauty. It's easy to recognize emotional bonds require both parties make adjustments for it to function properly. Once your relationship is developed these changes become more fluid and occur naturally. Because you unconsciously know how love can develop over time, once you marry, it's usually forever. You're an intense lover and become so attached to people you endure serious abuse in order to keep things together. If you're not careful you can become entirely dependent on the resources of someone else. After you see where adjustments need to be made the concessions aren't always made fairly. After you realize where you have been taken advantage of you aren't always willing to stand your ground. You will need other influences giving you a backbone and courage. You're usually accurate evaluating others because you aren't deceived by their falsehoods. You may accept their little lies just so you don't start a commotion. The darker side of this aspect can make you snobbish and judgmental. Clothes and appearance is important to you. If someone doesn't care enough to take care of them self, neither will you. You still help those in need, but do so from a distance. When someone is truly in desperate you will never turn a blind shoulder, helping where ever you can. Once you see that someone is no longer in need you may continue to support them, make sure not to become a push over or enabler.

Mars sextile ascendant

A sextile with your ascendant is one of the best ways to get the positive qualities of Mars. Of course his condition is important, but all alone this aspect gives you large amounts of energy, strength, and determination. What this aspect displays is your ability to put large amounts of effort into some form of a project. Just what that project is will be determined by you. The worst problem is when you actively pursue all your goals at once. Consequently, the depletion of resources and energy causes you to become more hasty and rash when making decisions. It's nearly impossible to rest until all your physical energy is gone and you're nearing a breakdown. Not only does this alignment produce superior authority skills it also gives you athletic ability and endurance. This may even lead to a career in professional sports, whether it be team or individual activities. The aggressiveness of Mars can make you conceited and arrogant at times. Despite the general harmony of the sextile, if Mars is severely afflicted by other planets it causes you to become hostile and violent. Overall this is a good aspect to have. Although it doesn't balance out any negative energy it doesn't produce the stress that Mars is capable of. The sextile calms down the hotheaded ways of the little red planet.

Mars sextile Jupiter

Aspects between Mars and Jupiter are interesting because of all the things Jupiter can intensify. Exceptional intelligence, spirituality, athleticism, anger, aggression, and determination are all possible outcomes when these two align. The sextile will calm down the volatility of Mars, and Jupiter helps out as the king of all kindness. The effects of this alignment can mean many different things. If there are poor aspects from other planets or weak house placement, it can signify an uncontrollable and explosive temper, sometimes even violent. In no way does this mean everyone born under with this is violently angry, and there will need to be serious afflictions from elsewhere to manifest this. The sextile is one of the two best alignments, and usually produces positive energy. When Mercury becomes involved you may become a brilliant specialist in your chosen profession. It may not be directed towards athletics, but you're an extreme competitor and you hate losing. As a child you may have gotten a huge attitude every time you couldn't win easily. You set prestigious personal goals and take any necessary procedure to make sure your work is used efficiently. Early in life you realized you were smarter than most other kids and exploited it whenever you could. Asserting yourself under pressure is not a problem. Once you establish your beliefs you stand your ground if someone cares to challenge you. Not only are you quick to defend yourself and your loved ones but you are just as concerned with the wellbeing of others who cannot defend themselves. Many people will admire and respect you for this.

Mars sextile Saturn

When a sextile is formed between these two planets you have a well meshed integration of your brain and your brawn. Meaning you generally know where and how to direct your energy. There is a fluidly flowing force giving you determination and responsibility. It's important for you to get something right the first time and you're very disappointed when you don't. Most times you think before you act, and carefully plot out your course of action. Because of your precise actions, you generally accomplish what you get started on. This can also indicate your job is related to athletics, possibly even being the star athlete yourself. It's possible you remember everything and everyone. Your memory is one of your assets towards success. Friends will come to you because of your ability to sort things out and give an honest, responsible answer. You're driven to achieve prominence amongst your community. This aspect may guide you into a profession of law, business, or politics. Whichever group you socialize amongst you will be one of the organizers and leaders. When there is no distinct superior you fill the role naturally. Many times you lead by example and others follow suit.

Mars sextile Uranus

Despite the usually pleasant nature of the sextile, between

Mars and Uranus it doesn't matter. This still makes you restless, impatient, and very over anxious. You're constantly looking for outlets to subdue endless supplies of energy. When none are found you go create your own. Once you're firm in your opinions you're never hesitant to voice where you stand. Most times this shows extreme difficulty changing your mind. It's true that sextile are good aspects producing happier energy, but Mars didn't earn the name the lesser malefic for nothing. When you freak out you can do a lot of damage in thirty seconds. You act immediately and impatiently, often making rash decisions only getting you into trouble. It's best for you to avoid contacts with the law and other authority figures. When your freedom is jeopardized you respond instantly and sometimes violently. You work best in areas requiring originality and intellectual skills. Fields of research and development are going to be excellent outlet for your brilliance. An intellectual rebel you're quick to challenge old doctrines that have long outlived their usefulness. You demonstrate your concern for society by being highly active in community service programs and stirring up dissent to instigate necessary changes.

Mars sextile Neptune

The sextile between Mars and Neptune indicates you have an active imagination and fantasy life, which you get lost in it easily. You have vivid dreams which are hard to separate from reality, and daydreaming will be one of your worst enemies. If you give in to your illusions trouble will definitely ensue. From financial trouble to relationship woes, this aspect can cause confusion in whichever houses the planets occupy. Your main difficulty dealing with others is your tendency to give them the benefit of the doubt too often. Be careful when you're making long term commitments or decisions. Despite whatever your beliefs are, you'll be susceptible to fraud when you don't get all the details. Medicine, social work, and the finer arts will interest you and should be pursued as careers. If you can find a profession where your creative abilities and passion to help others are used and challenged you will find much success. You see beauty where others don't, and can create

91

beautiful art out of mere scraps or recycled garbage. You understand you have a social obligation, but just can't seem to find a way to pursue it. Your best fit will be in creative design and creating an area that is aesthetically pleasing. The worst effects of a Mars/Neptune alignment are the inability to see how your actions influence the future. Pay attention to what's in front of you and not what's in your mind and you'll over come this.

Mars sextile Pluto

The best aspect between Mars and Pluto is no aspect at all. Any alignment between the two will intensify your ego, and despite the generally good nature of the sextile the relationship with the other planets is still vitally important. All alone this sextile provides you with an understanding between what is right and wrong along with an interest into deeper spirituality. One of the major problems is that you get so caught up in your own beliefs that you refuse to listen the opinions of others. Deep down inside you see the negative side of society and you desperately want to change it. You're compassionate towards others and give the benefit of the doubt to those who are undeserving. Remember of all possible aspects the sextile is the best and it should be considered and asset to your personality. It will allow you to overcome serious adversity and help you deal with your major problems. The driving ambition produced by this should be directed to whatever houses the planets occupy. You become so obsessed once you immerse yourself into something that you forget other areas of your life. Psychically this intensifies your powers greatly. Vivid dreams will keep you awake at night because of their eerie accuracy foretelling the future. Pluto is meant to destroy and rebuild with Mars activating this energy. Even if you must face horrific experiences in life this aspect brings you up from the pits of disparity.

Jupiter sextile ascendant

Jupiter is known as the greater benefic, and a sextile from it is a wonderful aspect. Alignments with your ascendant are plain and simple, the closer they are in degree the more you take on the characteristics of that planet. Jupiter is the gregarious giant who's always full of high spirits and optimism, along with arrogance and attitude as well. The energy produced here gives you endless amounts enthusiasm and you outlook on life is usually bright. Even calamity strikes, you're always able see the light at the end of the tunnel. Coping is easy because you turn the obstacles in your life into positive learning experiences. Many times religious or spiritual ways help deal with your grief and emotions. Jupiter is the ultimate philosophical expansionist who continually finds new ways to develop his beliefs. Your only problem is directing the proper amount of energy into your projects. Because you think you can accomplish more than you're capable of, many times you bite off well more than you can chew. This isn't to say that you don't finish everything that you begin it's just your final results would have been better with less attention diverted elsewhere. Overall, this is a very good aspect to have in your chart. The positive energy produced by this can nullify most negative energies produced elsewhere. It generally means that once you find comfort is whatever path Earth has given you.

Jupiter sextile Saturn

The greatest asset with a sextile between Jupiter and Saturn is your extensive amount of knowledge and the ability to use it in an effective manner. Remember effective doesn't mean positive. You're intelligent, well informed, and generally set to the rules. You're extremely resourceful and usually responsible, sometimes to the point of excess, not being able to kick loose and just let go. You're in constant search of new endeavors that can expand or challenge your vast intellectual capabilities. As with everything, if you fail to develop your skills they will gradually slip away. There is always a little luck involved with your profession, you either know the right people, or are just in the right place and the right time. Higher learning interests you because you know smarter people are usually more successful than idiots, granted some idiots are in high ranking offices. House placement will be a key

93

determining factor when analyzing the deeper meaning of this aspect. Whichever houses the planets are placed in is where you will experience the biggest and most flamboyant part of your personality. These are the two slowest personal planets. Their alignments are semi generational, and other than the opposition or conjunction they occur at infrequent intervals.

Jupiter sextile Uranus

Aspects between Jupiter and Uranus are very special and will require the modifying influences to make an accurate judgment. Because Uranus is one of the generational planets, and Jupiter is a slower moving of the personal ones, the alignment they form with your ascendant will be a major determining factor. Jupiter expands everything it touches and Uranus adds creativity and ingenuity. You can be brilliantly smart and well aligned, or you can be a completely neurotic basket case. This can be quite a catalyst when forming aspects with other planets. This is an extremely spiritually uplifting aspect. You desire the ultimate form of philosophy and education and will go to great lengths to acquire it You generally have good foresight and see the need for proper planning. Whether your ambitions are directed towards positive or negative endeavors is up to you. It's easy for you to see everything needed to accomplish what you want. This is because you possess a natural understanding that knowledge in invaluable. The more you know the farther you will go is your motto. Although quite intelligent many times you will not use your vast intellectual capabilities. If you were raised in less fortunate conditions chances are you're forced into a life of responsibility and hard work. As you mature into your later years if you have not found a career path that allows you to live up to your potential than a career change will be necessary. The outgoing nature you possess causes you to always be on the move. If there is nothing to do, then you will make something to go do. Your innovation and inventive capabilities are off the chart. If you choose a career into the advanced sciences you will find much success in research and development. Eccentric and quirky, you seek to be your own unique individual. If someone

94

tells you that you can't do something you will try it just to see. Make sure you look before you leap. Rushing into things head on can cause more problems than it solves.

Jupiter sextile Neptune

Jupiter and Neptune are both extremely spiritual planets, and the sextile is the best relationship they can have. You posses an advanced knowledge of the universe and accept your spirituality along with the religions of others. Neptune is pure mysticism and magic, while Jupiter is universally expansive and philosophical. The only problem is although millions may be born during this alignment, only a handful of people get to experience the energy it inspires. Neptune is the middle of the generational planets and Jupiter is one of the slower personals. One of these planets is going to need to be forming a close aspect with your Sun or ascendant to release the potential. The masses without this prominent still feel the optimism and high spirits it produces. Whether it's a strictly dogmatic religion or your own crazy spiritual journey, higher philosophies play a great part of your life. The most basic concept of this sextile allows the energy between the two to flow freely. House placement is as equally important as sign because it indicates the two life areas you feel the most flamboyant, Jupiter, and most confused, Neptune. At its worst this over inflates your ego and you're completely oblivious to your arrogance.

Sometimes the expansion of Jupiter only heightens the sense of delusion caused by Neptune. Even if you recognize your social obligations, many times you will cast them aside for more pleasing endeavors. However, you will most definitely take action when you see a horrible atrocity take place. Not many have a heart as big as yours and you're generous and giving to an extreme. Although you're kind and compassionate, this aspect does not denote hard work. In fact it can cause the opposite. If you have other planets providing you with drive and determination you will make a wonderful employer. If you channel your subconscious properly you find yourself extremely psychic. Vivid dreams and prophetic intuitions are also produced by this aspect. As a child you probably had horrible nightmares keeping you awake at night.

Jupiter sextile Pluto

Because of their slow speeds, Jupiter and Pluto possess a very special relationship which is extremely spiritual. A sextile between these two is a phenomenal starting point for planets like Mars, Mercury, and Venus to build upon. This particular aspect enhances your intellectual powers, and produces a mind wishing to probe deeper into the deepest canyons. You love getting all the information you can about someone or something, and will go to great measures to attain such info. When you direct this energy properly you will find much success in outlets of medicine, law, or business. Whether it be a personal or professional interest you will seek opportunities in which the advancement is limitless. You put your all into everything you do and expect others to do so as well. This can lead into misguided obsessions and obscure behavior. You will actively seek out and explore many areas of the religious and philosophic. You're continually expanding your mind and consciousness, which will eventually lead you into a path of distinct spirituality. Even if your interests are low during childhood or adulthood, as you mature the powers of the universe will eventually attract you. If you decide to travel into the world of the paranormal and spiritual you will find your talents are profound.

Saturn sextile ascendant

Your ascendant is the most powerful point in your chart, and when planets are aligned with it their influences are usually prominent. This should provide stabilizing energy allowing you to grow up and accept responsibility easily. The key factor determining how this will affect you is going to be the condition of Saturn. If your Saturn is all messed up by harsh aspects this will cause you to have difficulties accepting your duties. If you're blessed with positive aspects influencing Saturn then maturation is a much smoother process. You see what you want and the process of obtaining it. Although sometimes referred to as the greater malefic, Saturn produces precise, reserved, and overly calculating energies. If you're talkative and outgoing it's only until you have warmed up to someone and have become comfortable in their presence, or Mercury is prominent for you as well. It's always difficult for you to break away from your chosen path and unless there are more inspirational aspects elsewhere, you can be kind of a grouch. Because you're so slow to warm up to people others may see you as kind of melancholy and cold.

You're very careful in how you express yourself, usually saying what you mean exactly how you mean it. You're in strictly disciplined in everything you do so you had better find positive outlets. Once you set your mind into something it's difficult for others to change your opinion. Although, because the sextile is a positive influence it will be easier for you to change your ways, but only when it's completely obvious you are in the wrong. Action will never take place until it you've precisely decided your objectives and determined your goal. Nothing you do is easy and you sometimes choose the more difficult method just to prove you could do it. You understand where you need to place your efforts and have the energy to handle large workloads. Business and law are professions that may interest you. This also establishes a strong emotional bond with your father. Any traumatic experiences will be exceptionally harmful and haunting. As you progress into your professional life this aspect gives you a desire to establish yourself amongst your peers. Even if you don't know who everyone is, you enjoy every one knowing who you are.

Saturn sextile Uranus

Those with this aspect in their charts have a sincere and deep respect for those who possess knowledge and use it well. An alignment between these two planets is seldom, and the relationship with your ascendant most definitely changes the influence. Occurring in the late seventies and early eighties, then again from 1995 until 1997 this will not happen again until 2024. Most aspects between Saturn and Uranus are difficult to handle, but the sextile is definitely the easiest. This can give you an uncanny ability in some unusual field. You possess universal knowledge and wisdom buried deep within your subconscious. This small generation will be extremely disciplined and self-sufficient. Many great things are expected to come from these brilliant individuals. Saturn is always a base structure to build upon, and personality traits aren't usually prominently displayed. It's the house placement, and relationship between the personal planets which will indicate just how this pans out. Mercury will indicate brain power, Venus will indicate relationship structure, and Mars will show determination and responsibility. Planets in sextile or trine will produce the positive qualities, while oppositions and squares indicate problems. The negative parts of this aspect are as massive as the positives. The only way to describe Uranus is crazy, just plain crazy and rebellious. Saturn is described as responsible and cautious, always wanting distinct organization. Obviously, this is a direct confliction between interests.

Saturn sextile Neptune

Because of the slow speeds these two planets travel at, their alignments are fairly generational and other modifiers will need to be referenced to make an adequate judgment. Last occurring during the middle of the 1990's, then again around 2020, and finishing the unusual cycle in 2031. After that you have to wait until the middle 2050's for it to align again. This particular positioning is quite fortunate as it allows you to see through the fraudulent claims of others, and make fair judgments despite what they say. Generally speaking, you need significant amounts of proof before you to change your viewpoint. Your perception to artistic detail is exceptionally keen, and there will be some wonderful artists come from this generation. The refinement to creativity some individuals possess will produce some of the most significant advancements in music, technology, and spirituality the evolution of mankind will be sped up tremendously. Ghosts and space aliens are soon to be discovered by these inquisitive scientists. You also understand we all have a responsibility to others, and not only need to help people, but protect Earth as well. The atrocities inflicted by mankind on itself abhor you. Those born with this will be responsible for cleaning up the mess that is created by the previous generation. You have a good understanding of what is right and wrong and can usually stay within the constraints of the law. This can also have negative traits as well. Because Neptune confuses everything it touches when aligned with Saturn you may have issues realizing your responsibilities and how to attain your goals. The relationship with your father is also greatly affected by this. Stay away from psychologically controlling drugs. Even if they are prescribed by a physician, you will have issues with chemical dependency once you try and stop. Neptune has issues accepting reality and when it's given a chance to escape it will run rampant. Even though you recognize this you are not motivated enough to start anything new. You are more apt to help another's cause then begin your own.

Saturn sextile Pluto

Saturn is the slowest of the personal planets and Pluto is the slowest of all. Their alignments occur very seldom and the power is immense. Hundreds of thousands of people across the globe are influenced and not everyone feels the magnitude. Because of this infrequency the relationship to your ascendant along with house placement will be especially significant. This aspect shows you realize the importance of careful planning and organization in order to reach to success. You're terrified to depend on chance, and if afflicted right you're an obsessed hypochondriac. You want things to go just how you planned, every single time. If failure occurs chances are you're completely devastated and the world comes crashing in. Experience will always be the most efficient instructor and if you don't understand this you're going to repeat the same mistakes over and over again. In turn, you may choose to do everything the hard way simply because it's tough and you want to prove your mighty strength. There is also a distinct philosophical side to this alignment. Whether it be a strict dogmatic religion or your own personal spirituality, higher philosophies and in depth thinking will interest you. Once you immerse yourself into something you do so completely. All the knowledge will never be enough, along with cocaine if you choose to do drugs. Whichever your choice, you will pursue it intensely and possibly become and expert. It would be a wise decision to pursue careers where there is no limit on advancement. Medicine, psychology, or architecture are all professions where your talents can be put to the test.

Uranus sextile ascendant

Uranus is the planet of total rebellion and when in sextile with your ascendant your personality shows it. This planet is completely unpredictable and totally unstable. Nothing you do has to make sense to anyone, not even yourself. Fortunately the sextile indicates you put these energies towards positive outlets. You hate being told how to think and can barely be restrained when told how to act. Early in life you realized you were different than of your peers, and tried to establish your own identity. When rejected, you simply went off and did your own thing alone. You were probably raised in a different environment than most, and your childhood was probably marked by several unexpected changes. Maybe you moved to a new city, a divorce, or possibly a death in your immediate family. Whatever your dysfunction, you possess a revolutionary mind which leads you to go down the path less traveled. It's the excitement of doing something new which inspires you. If your creativity and spirit were oppressed as a child you definitely rebelled. With a flair for the dramatic, you love it when others recognize you for your ideas and ingenuity. Professions in telecommunications and technology can prove to be very prosperous.

Uranus sextile Neptune

Uranus and Neptune are the first two of the three generational planets. Aspects between generational planets are just that, generational. They occur very rarely and affect everyone across the globe. The sextile being when one planet is sixty degrees from each other, this seldom alignment forms in uneven intervals. They were aligned like this back in the mid-sixties when Uranus was in Libra and Neptune was in Scorpio. In 2027 Uranus will be in Gemini while Neptune is in Aries. Coming in uneven intervals, the sextile must not be taken lightly. Fortunately for mankind this will inspire more positive energy than bad. There will be a great healing from unexpected advancements in technology and medicine. This generation will be extremely suspicious of the government and any forms of controlling authority. Societies will revolt and rebel in the most revolutionary of ways. Long standing forms of government will be forced to adapt or survival is grim. This alignment indicates significant changes within our societal structure. Connections between the human race and the spirit world expand tremendously as our minds and DNA evolves. As seen by the spiritual and social revolution within the hippie uprising during the sixties, the influence of these planets can cause the most unusual of circumstances. Just as we realize the horrific consequences produced by the opposition or squaring of these planets, the toll we have taken on our environment will have to be addressed. Occurring from 1850 until 1854 these people cleaned up the mess of the industrial revolution. Then again during the sixties the world governments were the revolutionary focal point. Individuals will be brilliant in ways humans have never seen. Art, music, and technology are all advanced in the most creative of ways. This is a very good base structure for the other planets to build around. The house Neptune occupies will be where you're the most creative and artistic, as well as confusion. While the house Uranus is positioned in is where you will be the most innovative, imaginative, and spontaneous.

Uranus sextile Pluto
(1942-1946) (1990-1997)
    Uranus and Pluto are two of the three generational planets. This is a very slow moving aspect which previously aligned from 1942 to 1946, then again in the 1990's, and won't align again until the 2080's. Because of this infrequency the relationship with your

101

ascendant is vitally important. The most basic description available is obsessively crazy. Pluto intensifies passions like gasoline on a fire, and Uranus can be described as electricity with water. The combustible possibilities are indescribable. For the most part you despise those who abuse their power and authority to oppress those less fortunate. Out of control government programs and private industry will experience a sudden and unexpected overhaul. Those born between 1990 until 1997 will forcefully object to the unjust treatment they are receiving. In many regions this will be violent. Civil wars, international wars, and environmental wars will completely plague the globe until those in this generation step up and repair the mistakes of generations past. On a personal level you have an uncanny ability to see falsehoods within your elected officials. Seeing through their lies and deception you detect their false hoods and demand they start telling the truth. Exceptionally rapid advancements in medicine and technology will mark this generation special. Breakthroughs in holistic and all natural healing processes will also lead this generation into the Age of Aquarius and bring about a new meaning to the term spirituality.

Neptune sextile ascendant

Neptune is a slow moving generational planet which gives you a vivid imagination and a greater sense of the universe. Because of its generational nature you need an aspect towards your ascendant to feel its powers. Fortunately the sextile is one of the easier alignments to handle. Neptune's biggest problem is it's very passive and non-confrontational. It's the master at creating confusion. All too often you project yourself in a way that's disorienting to others. The message your body language sends doesn't always match up with what you're saying and doing. This in turn causes the mass confusion with your associates. You're a dreamer and a romanticist at heart, and seeing all the injustices around the world, you truly wish to change them. Although you're likely to help out you are not likely to start something on your own. Neptune doesn't possess a backbone. Unless you have fire driving you from elsewhere you're more likely to just donate some time or money to a cause. Your fantasies are deeply ingrained into your reality. You would rather live in a world of dragons and castles, or aliens and spaceships. It's imperative you figure out which is dream and which isn't. Make sure you're not seeing a problem just because you need something to fix. Many times you perceive there to be issues where there is none. Neptune has a great ability to accept severe abuse until finally breaking or falling apart. If you're not careful you can be extremely delusional, and gullible. Always make sure to get all the facts before making major decisions in life. You will constantly regret your choices if you don't.

Neptune sextile Pluto

The sextile between the two outermost planets is generational which will last for over a hundred years. Beginning back in the 1940's we can only speculate what energies this will produce. Describing individual personality traits is relatively ridiculous.personality traits Although the planets will change signs throughout the sextile they will not completely break this aspect until the 2050's. House placement and relation to the ascendant will determine how much someone's personality is affected by this. During this alignment medicine and technology will start to recognize the advantages and powers of the natural world. The spirituality of the human race as a whole will be changed by these new, innovative technologies and practices. Throughout the globe more and more people will abandon old religious doctrines and turn to new and more progressive beliefs. There will be an increase of interest in astrology and the occult during this time. All natural healing techniques will be discovered and the old ones developed. Religious wars, hostile take over's, and possibly even first contact with extra-terrestrials is possible and highly likely. Because these planets were discovered so late, Neptune in 1846, and Pluto in 1930, astrologers don't really know what to expect from this.

Pluto sextile ascendant

Pluto is the most distant and slowest of the known planets.

Because of this, its effects are most potent when aligning with the ascendant and the exactness of degree is going to be important when analyzing the effects. When Pluto is in sextile with your ascendant, you understand how influential you are in the lives of other people, and also how you become affected by them. Because of this you can learn how to throw your weight around when it comes to getting things done. You willingly accept the challenges life faces you and never get down for too long when you aren't as successful as you had hoped. You never want competitors to get ahead you wait slowly, letting them make the first move. You have an intuition you should learn to trust more. Being highly psychic you can see things before they happen and pick up on the true intentions of those you encounter daily. You naturally understand things about the spirit world that most don't. There is more to life than meets the human eye and you know this. An interest into the occult and arcane will stimulate your mind into new philosophies on the religious and spiritual. Pluto always adds an obsession to something or someone. The sextile allows you to accept these energies and direct them into a proper outlet.

Square

Ezekiel 46:6
On the day of the new Moon your sacrifice shall be a young bull without blemish, six lambs and a ram, all without blemish

At ninety degrees separated planets reach the square and always remember "Be aware of the Square!" It's definitely the most difficult alignment planets can form, and generally indicates troubles and conflicting energies. Whichever planets are involved don't like each other and aren't willing to cooperate. I call them driving aspects because they stimulate enough hostile emotions for you to take action. These along with the conjunctions and oppositions are usually the most dominant aspects in someone's personality. Along with the problems they cause, their house position can show where you're the most dedicated and ambitious to succeed. Every person has one or two of the harsher aspects in their charts meant to provide some feistiness. Squares and oppositions are those aspects designed to do such.

Sun square Ascendant

This is a highly charged aspect which requires calming influences from elsewhere. As your spiritual battery, the Sun energizes you in a way that makes everything feel like a challenge. You're highly competitive and must always assert your dominance. Quite often you offend others without even knowing it. For some reason your actions are never convincingly sincere, even when you act with the best of intentions. The reason being, many times you come on too strong and others question your motives. Despite all your flattering words people always suspect your true inclination. You usually possess lots of energy, but very little direction. It's difficult for you to not get what you want, and you only compromise when all the other alternatives have been exhausted. Basically, there are problems integrating your spirit into your personality. You say one thing thinking it will win over one group, and act the opposite while different individuals are around. Chances are you constantly change your mind towards whatever the situation dictates. However, once you have gotten over your own ego, you will be able to function very well within groups. Everything in your life will seem difficult, even when it isn't. There is always turmoil and dissention somewhere in your life. Because there is resistance in everything you do, the obstacles you encounter will occur more often than most. Seeing your own personal character flaws and admitting your mistakes will be impossible and you will overlook them constantly.

Sun square Moon

This is one of the most problematic aspects in all of astrology. The basic root of the problem is your emotions are constantly conflicting with your spirit. It's very difficult for you to use your available resources effectively and efficiently. You bitterly resent it when you have to make concessions and even more vengeful you must make enormous adjustments to get what you want. It seems you never have quite enough education to get where you desire, and you're only half-hearted in acquiring the training to do so. Although you want the good life, sometimes you feel like that can never be achieved, thus causing depression and strife. Your negative response distorts the information you receive and makes it more difficult to learn from your experiences. The frustration you feel has inhibited you character development and is a problem in other areas including domestic matters, social relationships, emotional interests, and professional affairs. You must learn to bring your emotions and your will into line and subdue them with intellect and organization. You seem to think any response will satisfy your desire to achieve success and this isn't so. Results directly reflect actions. Proper action equals proper results. You must learn self-control when dealing with others and how to compromise properly. What you gain from your habitual actions is usually inadequate in the teaching process. You frequently forget the lessons you have learned through previous experiences. There's a natural chip on your shoulder that will cause issues within domestic relationships. You're argumentative and defensive, probably because of your emotional insecurity. This can be reversed if you will change your fighting attitude and become more compromising. You have a serious misalignment between what you want and what you are willing to do to get it. The possibility of realizing your dreams is in direct proportions to the investment and concessions you make. This basically puts a natural chip on your shoulder which makes you think everything is a competition.

Sun square Mars

This is a bad aspect and will need some emotional support from either Venus or the Moon to calm it down. Acting as the driving force behind your personality, this alignment pisses you off enough to get up and do something. All alone it makes you angry, hostile, and bitter. Basically your ego is mad all the time doesn't know how to express its spirit. This usually produces resentments and vengeance. Mars is extremely volatile and the Sun is the battery igniting all the planets energy. Unfortunately the square always represents major confliction. Especially when compounded by negative aspects from Saturn or Uranus, the pent up frustrations cause severe psychological destruction. Your tendency to dive into things head first, with little planning, causes many let downs and hang ups. One major factor is you're rarely afraid. Along with the agitated nature, courage is also produced. That's why when harmonized by the Moon or Jupiter this makes you quite productive. Remember no single aspect determines just how someone behaves. You feel there is nothing you can't handle, and no one can knock you down. This makes you especially susceptible to depression when you actually are defeated or broken. It will be difficult to make concessions to others, especially when they are in the wrong.   Exercise and physical activity is the only way to successfully vent your energy. This alignment makes you very competitive, athletic, and strong. Look into careers in sports, military, or a physically demanding job. No matter what you choose you'll never be happy until you're in control of your own destiny. Once you eventually discover it you'll calm down and mellow out. You tend to dominate over your competition and are a force to be reckoned with in any debate. Associates who don't know you personally may take this as arrogance, and most times it probably is. Patience is a virtue you will have to learn. You get really frustrated really quickly when things don't go as speedily as you think they should. This causes high blood pressure, migraine headaches, and intestinal problems.

Sun square Jupiter
    Very rarely do Jupiter alignments with the Sun produce negative energy, but this is the most difficult aspect between these two. Your biggest issue is the trouble identifying and accomplishing your dreams and higher aspirations. You possess significant amounts of creative talent, just no outlet to produce

107

something. You're not a half-hearted person and everyone knows it. A square between the Sun and Jupiter produces a complete lack of moderation in anything you do. It will be important for you to gain understanding when organizing priorities and goals. You tend to bite off more than you can chew and spend lots of time and resources skipping around from one project to the next. Consequently, you run out of time, money, and energy, becoming overly anxious about the situation. Quite often nothing lives up to your expectations. If you can maintain responsibility then success is unlimited. In several ways you wish to be a wheeler and dealer, and with negative aspects from Mars you can be quite conniving or seedy. If this aspect is connected to the eighth house you will have a dark fascination with the occult and possibly the Satanic. Although squares usually produce negative energy the benevolent nature is only magnified by the energy of the Sun and positive things are usually produced. If there aren't any serious problems elsewhere the optimism and enthusiasm are unrivaled. Jupiter is very arrogant and you're rarely intimidated by challenges enjoying tests of your abilities.

Sun square Saturn

Any astrologer who's knowledgeable about squares will tell you this is one of the worst. This represents a direct confliction between your spirit and your sense of responsibility. Your inner soul desperately wants to express itself through the means of the Sun sign, while Saturn indicates where you're supposedly grounded to reality. In your early years you had conflicts with your self-worth, and the relationship you had with your father was unfulfilling at best. Whether your parents divorced and he was placed out of the house, or business took him away, or he was there and completely inattentive. If Mars is closely involved this relationship may even be violent. As a child your instincts told you to instantly go on the defensive every time you perceived an attack. When someone unknowingly offends you the response isn't always mature and apologies are needed on your part. Rejection from others hurts you immensely. If your father was out of the picture early or, possibly even abusive, the emotional scarring will haunt you throughout your life. Professional psychiatric help can possibly be needed. Although it is difficult for you to open up to strangers, and objective third party will be of good use in dealing with your issues. Many times you cover up your psychological and emotional hang ups by immersing yourself in your work. The distraction from your inner most feelings is a welcome relief but still doesn't solve anything. Life will never be easy and chances are you have to start at the bottom no matter what profession you choose. This can be because you didn't have the educational opportunities that your colleagues have. Once you have obtained success all your insecurities will turn into self-assurances.

Sun square Uranus

Squares between planets are never a good sign, especially when it's the Sun and Uranus. You're going to need other aspects mellowing out the high strung and unpredictable energy of this alignment. The square between these two is one of the top ten most difficult aspects to handle. The energy produced shows you're intelligent but mostly undisciplined in your behavior. You're insistent on being allowed to do whatever you want, whenever you want, even if you know you're wrong. Many times you do the opposite just to instigate problems. Power struggles always occur because you hate being told what to do, especially when it's unclear who the person in charge is. Always wanting to be different you always need to express you opposing viewpoint, if only to simply ruffle the feathers of others. In order to succeed you will need to re-evaluate your attitudes about authority, giving concessions where need be. You're very sensitive to your ego and must recognize that others are the same way as well. Once you realize this you can build a firm setting for realizing your objectives. If you can remember that compromising will assure partial agreement for everyone there is no stopping you. There is a special wiring in your brain that allows you to think in ways others can't. At times you can be full of brilliant ideas which no one else can fathom.

109

Sun square Neptune

This is the most difficult aspect the Sun can make to
Neptune. This biggest issue caused is your inability to integrate
you spirituality into your individuality, along with your completely
distorted views of reality. Your ego understands the greater
universe out there, but it's difficult for you to pinpoint your beliefs.
Many times this indicates several attempts at religion before you
find something comfortable. More often than not this shows you
simply turn a blind eye to the mystical and religious. The
difficulties during your upbringing have made you extremely
sensitive to your inferiorities. If you were misunderstood by your
parents while trying to establish you own individuality you built up
unconscious barriers to protect yourself. Once you matured you
still grasped onto these negative feelings of self-doubt. It's difficult
to let go of the past and you use the former feelings of self-
uselessness as a driving force behind your success. As you grow
professionally start with activities which involve little
responsibility at first. You have to learn by experience and will
make many mistakes along the way if you act too hastily. Psychic
awareness and vivid dreams are commonly associated with this
aspect. If you can learn to trust your intuition more than your logic
than you will go far. You are naturally drawn to unstable and
unpredictable people, subconsciously thinking that you and you
alone can help them though their issues.

Sun square Pluto

One thing can be said about every aspect between the Sun
and Pluto, pure intensity. The square is generally the most difficult
to handle because it causes you to have serious issues getting over
your past and accepting fate. Chances are your life was
considerably more traumatic than others and this caused you to feel
like an outcast amongst your peers. Because of these horrific
experiences during youth, you allow the insecurities and negative
emotions to affect you well into your adult years. Once you can
find the courage to face the demons haunting you, the regenerative

powers of Pluto can be harnessed in full force. If there are negative aspects from Mars you can be very violent and uncontrollable. Talk things out with a professional counselor or psychologist if life starts to spin too far out of control. Since its discovery in 1930 astrologists are still trying analyzing the full capabilities of this distant planet. Several astrologers have linked Pluto with obsession, possessiveness, and jealousy. Self-control and moderation are two things which must be learned in order for personal growth and happiness. The houses occupied by the Sun and Pluto are where you will experience the most traumatic difficulties.

Moon square ascendant

When the Moon is squared with your ascendant, it initiates difficulty expressing how you feel to others. You're a victim of bad habits taught to you as a child which you carried into adulthood. Anything imprinted in your mind during your youth has a long lasting effect on you. Many times you become confused about how you feel and why you feel it. Then, not knowing how to display the emotion your loved ones suffer your wrath. Although deep down you're a caring individual many times you fail to show it properly. You offend many because of the straight forward, and sometimes tactless, way you confront people. When left alone, you have a long fuse and rarely show emotion, leading to people to think you don't care. If Mars or Uranus is involved then all bets are off. One of those two will make you a hot headed Tasmanian devil. Once you blow up everything is over and it's best to just let you wear yourself out. Be very careful to direct your anger and displeasure in the right direction. Very often you will lash out after being pushed too far on sever different things. You can be unintentionally sharp in the way you talk to others. Choose your words wisely young grasshopper they are more powerful than you think. If you're not careful you may fall into an abyss of alcoholism and drug abuse. Don't try to numb your emotions with drugs and alcohol this will undoubtedly turn into a significant problem.

Moon square Mercury

The Moon square with Mercury indicates you have difficulty making reasonable judgments and quick decisions. This is because your feelings are usually the driving force when coming to a conclusion. You ignore analyzing and assessing your troubles with a logical mindset and in turn the consequences are less than desirable. It isn't easy for you to stay completely rational or objective and you act quite immature at times. You may also have difficulty separating fact from fancy and unfairly assume people are criticizing you when it's not the case at all. Because of this you may get into several misunderstandings with many random people. You become preoccupied with trivial things and waste a lot of needless energy and effort on them. You dwell on your insecurities, constantly looking at what is wrong. Try to refocus your thoughts to something outside your own personal life. This distraction will provide an outlet for you excess energy. After you realize your short comings you can relate to people more easily. You communicate well with the people you know because you're past your insecurities and fears. It is quite different with those you don't know. You resent having to make allowances and adjustments for other people. You hold fast to your opinions and are defiant when anyone suggests you're mistaken. Chill out a little, it will be a lot less painful for you and also encourages others to be more sympathetic and understanding.

Moon square Venus

The square causes more relationships problems than any aspect in astrology. When it's between these two your life is made very difficult. Basically this shows your inability to integrate your emotions into your relationships. All your personal contacts seem to be in a state of constant crisis. You're apprehensive about forming close personal ties because of the responsibilities they bring. Once it falls apart the departure is easier to handle. These are both extremely personal planets and this is a horrible starting point for other planets. When there are negative influences from other places in your chart they allow the negative attitudes to seep into different areas of your life. Their house placement shows where most of your problems will come from. Venus habitually rejects any negativity by obliviously looking away. Be extremely cautious you don't tell yourself everything is ok when it isn't. You generally confuse the way you're feeling and act towards others inappropriately. The past clings like glue and the traumatic experiences still haunt you today. You will have an underlying difficulty with women, especially when one tries to interfere or criticize your personal life. Stay away from overly negative women because you easily pick up on their issues as if they were your own. It would be advisable to become independent as quickly as possible. As a parent the thought of your children moving away is your worst nightmare. You need the companionship of people who expect nothing from you except friendship. I personally think there is nothing good about this alignment, and I hope you have happy aspects from Jupiter to ease the tensions. The only positive characteristic is your ability to not care about hurting people. This helps you in the business realm by not giving your competitors a compassionate edge.

Moon square Mars

Unfortunately for you the Moon and Mars really don't get along even when aspecting each other positively. With the square being the most problematic of alignments, one can only deduce this causes serious emotional tensions. The Moon symbolizes your emotions and their stability. Mars provides energy, aggression, and the driving force behind everything you do. While it's sitting square you have difficulties identifying your emotions which cause unrest and instability. You encounter many obstacles developing personal relationships because you're generally unsure about how you feel. It's easy for you to misinterpret emotions then react inappropriately. You feel compromising any beliefs means someone is taking advantage of you. Because you're vulnerable and insecure you build walls of defense trying to keep everyone out. This is one of the alignments which doesn't produce much positivity. Like the Moon's square to Venus, when confronted you lash out emotionally and sometimes violently. Uncalled for eruptions create many unneeded issues in all your relationships, from plutonic to romantic. There will be times when you need to put your emotions aside and make a logical decision. This is difficult for you because you can't stop thinking about the repercussions of whatever action you choose. Emotionally driven to succeed you can tolerate long hours of work better than most. You have a dominant forceful personality and usually make a dramatic impact where ever you go. When you experience serious emotional strain you will become nauseous and sick to your stomach.

Moon square Jupiter

Squares with the Moon usually produce emotional turmoil and strife, and the one between her and Jupiter is no different. You regularly react with excessive emotion without making any intellectual assessments, basically acting without thinking. Because of this you frequently jump to conclusions which are wrong and have to retrace your steps making apologies. Your over generosity will be a downfall, and many times you find you're lacking funds for something important because you wasted money on useless junk, usually food, clothes, or drugs. You need to create, and strictly follow, a regiment which limits your financial expenditures and teaches you to accept responsibility for your actions. Once you do fall in line responsibly then you can achieve wonderful things. You are easily susceptible to gaining weight and must exercise regularly. This alignment causes constant over indulgence and moderation will have to be learned. Although squares are generally bad this one can produce more positive energy than most. Jupiter is known as the greater benefic and allows whatever it touches to function at a bigger potential. One problem you have is differentiating between your emotions and your intellect. Many times you get confused with what you want and how to get it. You become over committed too fast and then feel dejected when others won't reach your level of commitment. Deep down you truly care

114

about others and are so generous many times you go without so that another can have.

Moon square Saturn

The square between the Moon and Saturn is one of the worst in astrology. This makes it very difficult to let go of your past and anyone in it. You're constantly living in the depressing side of life and can't seem to see any light at the end of your tunnel. During your childhood years traumatic events plagued you. Eventually you became overcome with guilt any time you or someone else expressed disloyalty. Deep inside you're extremely attached to your childhood and the environment you were raised in. Moving away from home is nearly impossible and if you do so it's for work. Unless you accept your difficult past as your past, and forgive those who harmed you, the anger and resentments can destroy your life. Make sure you eat wholesome foods and try not to eat alone. This particular square induces loneliness and isolation. You may become obsessed with work, causing tensions and problems within your family life. Part of your problem is that emotions are difficult for you to express to others. It usually takes you a while to truly open up to others and rarely do so completely. Generally this indicates severe emotional issues with not only your mother but father as well. Most times this indicates your parents end up divorced. The lack of emotion you receive from them is especially traumatizing and professional counseling may possibly be needed.

Moon square Uranus

A square between the Moon and Uranus causes you to act emotionally impulsive and rash. There is a hair trigger when it comes to you and most people know it. You're an eccentric character, and fitting into any normal section of society just isn't for you. You make erratic decisions hastily then wonder where things went wrong. All your emotional reactions are instantaneous and usually misguided. When someone crosses you the reactionary outburst is quick, unexpected, and usually hot tempered. If the

115

planet Mars is involved in any way this reaction will probably be violent. In romance you must give your interests the same freedoms you enjoy. This will cause tensions in any relationship when boundaries are not set early. You desire to roam wherever may be the most pleasurable. Marriage will only succeed when you learn to compromise and give up some of your freedoms. You're emotionally unstable and can be quite a basket case. Several times throughout your life you will need to re-evaluate what you want and how to go about getting it. The realization the life is never perfect, and you never really get all you want will be the key to your happiness. There are very few alignments as difficult to predict as this one. House placement is key for this alignment because it will indicate the two houses you experience the most spontaneous catastrophes.

Moon square Neptune

The Moon squaring off with Neptune is one of the easier squares to handle. The biggest downfall is it makes you an overly sensitive sissy and very gullible. You're dreamy and imaginative, getting lost in your own fantasies frequently. Many times you have trouble deciphering what is the truth and what is false. An overly developed imagination is going to cause you to adjust reality into what you want to be true. The main problem is you're capable of creating a fictitious environment where you can retreat when in distress. Early in your childhood your parents didn't condition you for the competition of the outside world. Because of the lack of faith in yourself the fear competition causes you to cower away from those obviously more dominant. Your jaded view of people allows them to take advantage of your generosity. Be careful not to make close alliances with shady individuals, this will always prove to be extremely unfortunate. This is one of the aspects that is easily influenced from other planets. Because its fluctuations are extreme negative relationships are intensified and much more emotionally charged. Other planets are definitely going to influence this, and they had better be trines or sextiles. Oppositions or squares will cause you to carelessly float through life, without the ability to recognize your responsibilities.

Moon square Pluto

Squares between the Moon and Pluto usually produce a very difficult energy. Distraught emotional intensity is the most basic description. It's extremely troublesome to let go of your past and you cling to it obsessively. You're constantly dwelling on the negative emotions from your previous hardships. The problems you faced as a child makes you nervous about the future so you withdraw in defense. Until you can address these issues properly the obsessions, jealousy, and possessiveness of Pluto will definitely take over and control you actions. You spend too much time alone and when you do socialize you often force yourself amongst others. You're highly obsessive, sometimes to a psychotic level, and over indulge yourself in everything you do. Part of your apprehension is you're highly psychic and can see the motives of others intuitively. Unfortunately, this can make you very insecure about your emotions. When someone crosses you the reaction is usually instantaneous. You have an extreme fanaticism about the mystical and occult. Be very careful what you learn and how you use it, as it will be difficult to keep things in perspective. Both these planets are deeply rooted within the human subconscious and you should consider exploring it.

Mercury square ascendant

Squares involving Mercury usually produce difficulties within your nervous system or communication abilities. Chances are you have problems talking, listening, or behaving. This is a very modifiable aspect and the other planetary influences are important. There can be several effects of this alignment. First, you may have a speech impediment, like a stutter or stumble, or you talk with a soft, mumbling voice which others have trouble understanding. It's also possible your deaf or just plain don't listen to anyone. Most times this indicates troubles expressing what you're thinking or how you're feeling. Over anxiousness, nervousness, and paranoia are all indications of the negative part for trait. If you don't talk too much, you're spending most of your time listening and learning lots from it. When you are talkative, chances are you talk about the wrong things and say the least appropriate thing and the most inappropriate time. People react negatively to you because you project unseen signals to which confuse them. This in turn leads to the many breakdowns between you and your associates. Many times it's your inability to assert yourself confidently causing the miscommunication. It may also take you a while to learn to talk as a child. It's difficult for you to shut your mouth and open your ears to the advice of different opinions. Many times this indicates foot in mouth disease.

Mercury square Mars

A square between Mercury and Mars produces an enormous amount of mental energy, anxiety, and is usually difficult to handle. Although you possess the ability to handle stressful situations, the psychological after effects are very traumatic. You have very firm opinions and take offense when your views are not accepted. You're verbally vicious, and sometimes even violent. You're going to need to develop the ability to recognize when this is happening and learn some self-control. People may avoid getting into conversations with you because the length at which you talk. Your imagination is extremely active and you only need to apply it constructively. If you can realize others need to express themselves as much as you do many arguments will be avoided. You will face many obstacles in achieving your goals, and may feel you have road blocks most others don't. If you can accept the cards you've been dealt then you will realize your capabilities and. If you're wrong in an argument, admit it. When you're correct, say so diplomatically as not to create more tension.

Mercury square Jupiter

In general, squares produce discord and negative energy. This particular square indicates you're intelligent but lack the ability to direct your talents into something productive. Many times this means you enjoy childish games and have troubles accepting responsibility. Quite often this can also distort your perception between truth and reality. As you receive the signals projected by others your first initial response is usually wrong and you in turn send mixed signals back. Many times you misinterpret what people are actually trying to tell you. Once you come to your hastily made decision you find several errors made along the way. Despite the fact you know mistakes were made you rarely recognize where or how they happened. Consequently, you never learn from your first mistake. It isn't until you're completely broken will you learn your lesson. Arrogance, conceitedness, and thinking you should always start on top are not positive traits and you need to watch for this. If you were spoiled as a child once you grow into adulthood you feel more deserving than you actually are. Although this isn't a chart wrecker alone, when influenced by other destructive alignments explosions can happen. Not a completely bad aspect, this will also make you eager to learn as much as you can while you are interested in something. Your major malfunction is the fact you can't stay focused for very long. You will need this attribute from elsewhere in your chart.

Mercury square Saturn

A square between these two planets shows your early childhood upbringing will inhibit your creative and expressive abilities. It basically makes it difficult to accept your responsibilities and know how to get what you want in life. Sometimes you biggest problem is figuring out just what you want. Social obligations can usually take a back seat to fun and games and you need to figure out some direction. You become deadest in your ways and your traditional, sometimes old fashioned thinking restricts the ability to use your imagination. Once you get set into a certain line of thought it's extremely difficult to break away. If you were slow in school it wasn't necessarily because you aren't intelligent, you just take a long time to learn something. The work and effort needed to prove your aptitude just wasn't worth it. If you don't succeed quickly and with little effort you become discouraged and give up easier than most. This also restricts the limits of your creative and imaginative potential. Deep down you have insecurities about proving yourself to others. Because you don't want to admit somebody might be better than you, going off into individual endeavors is more your style. If you don't get over the fear of competition you will continually be passed up by others who are not. Many times this indicates problems listening to your father. If he smacked you as a child it was probably because you were mouthy and usually deserved it. When you don't say nice things you don't get nice results. Learn to choose your words wisely.

Mercury square Uranus

Aspects between Mercury and Uranus inspire ingenuity, creativeness, and brilliant innovation. The problem is you don't always use it in reasonable or responsible ways. Squares always indicate some form of difficulties, and the two houses these planets occupy will show where you have the most problems. You think in ways others don't, and if you can focus your attention long enough your brain will be your greatest ally. It's your ability to think quickly on your feet which allows you to excel through life. You strive to think independently, and when restrained you only resist more intensely. The eccentricity added to your intellect is what separates you from others. Your superiors will recognize this and place judgment on you, sometimes good, sometimes bad. Rebelliousness runs through your veins whether you accept it or not. It's easy for you to blow off the rules and openly object to whoever put them in place. This is a very good base aspect for horrible aspects to build on. The nervousness, high anxiety, and mental illnesses are all amplified tremendously when also aligning to this. Mars and Saturn will be especially devastating. If Venus is involved you can expect communication difficulties in all your relationships.

Mercury square Neptune

The square always indicates some sort of malfunctioning difficulty. Mercury in this position with Neptune creates problems

with your imagination, spirituality, and sense of responsibility. Despite the fact there are lots of grand ideas in your head the fleeting inspirations are too swift to manifest themselves. Just as you get into one project another pops up. It's like the artistic creator in you is boxed in and can't get out. Religion is an unusual subject for you. Although you feel there is a greater source of being out there you can't quite put your hand on it. It's very difficult to find your spiritual niche and you may never do. Many times this is because you weren't raised around religion and never developed any beliefs as a child. Despite the direct connection between you and the spirit world, you refuse to accept it. Sitting alone in a quiet, serene, environment, deep in meditation is the only way to properly find your religious path. By no means is this to be interpreted as a negative aspect. True, it adds tension but it can be easily modified by other planets. At its best it takes away any gullibility and you can see through the unclear motives of others. At its worst this will make you feel incapable and incompetent. The two houses these planets occupy will be where you experience the most confusing situations
.

Mercury square Pluto

When squared with the generational planet Pluto, tiny little Mercury has significant tensions placed upon it. You make great mountains of your burdens and become completely immersed in them. If your first option doesn't work out then you become depressed and pessimistic about the future. Power and control are both difficult for you to relinquish and chances are you obsess about them. Anything you can't completely dominate will be discarded according to your own will and desires. Despite the stresses caused by the square it also places you in tune with the psychic world and makes you extremely intuitive. You just don't accept it easily. Because of the generational influences of Pluto, close relationships with your ascendant will intensify the energies of this. Especially formations with Saturn, negative influences will make it very difficult for you to talk about your past and current problems. This can make you a ticking time bomb, waiting to explode. As an intense emotional release is inevitable, and you will eventually spill your guts out to a select chosen few. When Mars transits over one of these planets you will usually experiences headaches and fevers.

Venus square ascendant

This is usually an unpleasant aspect which makes you extremely sensitive to criticism and socially dysfunctional. It basically symbolizes your inability to integrate your personality into both society and your relationships. You don't know exactly where you want to fit in or who you want to be around. Eventually you get caught up in the wrong crowd and run around causing trouble. Because you can't figure out how to distinguish yourself you don't know what path you need to take to get somewhere. It's impossible to fit in with every group of every people and you will need to determine where you stand. This can show you go through several personality changes throughout your life. Remember Venus is one of the easiest planets to influence and her condition is crucial. Nothing will stop you from telling others what you're thinking, and this is why they think you're a bitch. The emotional clinginess makes it extremely difficult to let go of your past, and more importantly the people in it. All your traumatic events have an added dramatic emphasis causing you to believe there is no relief. The house Venus is stationed in is where you will place most your most passionate emotions and must feel the most complete relationship wise. You feel leaving home means you're turning your back and abandoning the past, thus letting your loved ones down. Squares are usually difficult aspects causing strain in our lives and this is no different. Issues with women are especially prominent with this, feelings of jealousy and vengeance will overtake your spirit from time to time. The most positive effect of this aspect is that you will maintain your beauty well into your elder years, provided you take care of your health. You will also be clean fairly organized person. You may have lots of possessions, but they are not strewn about. Neat and tidy pleases you greatly. Unfortunately this can make you completely oblivious to how your behavior actually affects the environment around you. Pay attention to your actions and the messages you unconsciously project. Sometimes it shows the total inability to refrain from overspending.

Venus square Mars

The square between Venus and Mars shows you're very difficult to get along with and expect others to make concessions to your needs and desires. It isn't easy for you to maintain long lasting relationships, whether romantic or otherwise. You have trouble compromising and constantly take what you think is yours leaving nothing for the rest. There aren't many aspects as bad as this one. When there are terrible influences from Saturn or Uranus then expect major catastrophes to constantly plague you. Chances are as you read this you don't accept it and think I'm full of junk. This just proves me correct. Mars and Venus are both personal planets with the sign and house placement determining which is more dominant. Whichever is inferior will have the most random flare ups as the planets progress. Your pent up hostilities are the result of personal insecurities and confusion about your abilities. Very rarely are you satisfied with yourself and your accomplishments. The unconscious resentment you possess towards women will make criticism from females considerably more offensive than from males. This leads to all sorts of problems within all relationships. Personal, professional, and romantic affairs will all create tension in your life. Sexual confusion, strife, and aggression are all produced by this less than fortunate aspect. If you can't find a problem to scream and yell about you create one, even if it means stepping on toes in the process. Finding an athletic outlet or some other form of organized competition will be key in relieving your aggression and pent up frustrations. If both these planets are in retrograde you're probably homosexual or have intense sexual fantasies.

Venus square Jupiter

Squares with Venus make you irritable and demanding. This

one can magnify that tendency exponentially. When these two planets are positioned like this it generally makes you irresponsible, careless, and self-indulgent as well. When things are pleasant and running smoothly you're gracious and sociable, but once life starts getting difficult, you become agitated and discourteous towards undeserving individuals. Quite often you recognize the proper adjustments needed then casually pass them along once you realize the work required. You're generous towards others only when you can see a personal gain from it. Someone you cannot benefit from will not receive random displays of attention or affection. You love attention and when ignored you may take desperate actions to attain it. It will be important to learn discipline and self-control at an early age. If these responsibilities are not instilled as a child then it will make it more and more difficult as you mature into adulthood. Your greatest asset with this is your ability to socialize and use your charm to your advantage. If you can learn to stop being so defensive and compromise by meeting others half way then it will be easy to use the negative energy produced by this productively. House positioning is important because it will show where you're the most arrogantly oblivious. This square also hinders your artistic expression. Although you have many hidden talents you refuse to accept them. For some reason your scared as to what doors they might open.

Venus square Saturn

Any square involving Venus is going to create constant tension somewhere in your relationship circle. This particular alignment affects the contacts you have within your career or education. Basically you don't get along with people at work. You're very uncooperative until you get your way and don't know how to express your emotions, assuming people psychically know how you're feeling. If there are too many other harsh aspects you're not a very nice person and should learn some courtesy. This aspect makes it difficult to open up and relate to others freely. Emotional expressions show signs of weakness and dependency. Saturn wants to do everything by itself and Venus is entirely reliant on others. In turn, this causes you to feel socially unaccepted and isolated from society. You're constantly on the defensive and unwilling to accept the responsibilities of forming a long lasting relationship. In your childhood years this usually indicates tensions in the relationship between your parents, especially your father. The conditioning you received as a child directly affects your life long into adulthood. Don't be afraid to seek professional counseling and help if the negative emotions become too difficult to handle. If your parents divorced you may have felt it was your fault and they didn't love you enough to stick it out. As you choose to isolate yourself the feelings of depression and disparity grow along with it. You need to learn how to be optimistic and hopeful about the future, not dwelling on the past. Not to be scared of this alignment, there are a few positive qualities produced by this. The attention you pay to the little details can make you an expert in your chosen field. Because you're so nit-picky about everything the final product you develop is usually better than the rest.

Venus square Uranus

The effects of Venus aligning with Uranus are interesting to say the least. You're very impressed by individuals who possess unusual and unique qualities or talents. Because you're an oddball yourself, anyone must be a little zany to make your inner circle. The biggest hang up here, you're utterly attracted to those outside your normal realm. Inside you can't seem to put your finger on what you desire in a partner and the opposite of yourself is the most appealing. You remain infatuated for only a little while, and become uninterested once a close bond starts to form. You do so in order to remain free of any restrictions complications. It's very difficult for you to accept the responsibility of belonging to one person. Although this fear or responsibility is unrealistic and inconsistent, it will plague you off and on throughout your life. You defy conventional thinking and show disdain towards those who fall within it. Complete refusal of tradition allows you to feel like your own individual with your own personality. It's easy for

125

you to win over friends, but you aren't exceptionally committed to them. Your social circle is so large there is just not enough time or resources for everyone. In your mind it's easy to confuse friendship with a romantic interest and may fall into many overdramatic relationships. It's impractical for you to expect others to give you your freedom and space without giving them their own as well. This will be the main source of all the difficulties within your personal and romantic relationships.

Venus square Neptune

This square causes your imagination to create extreme difficulties in all your relationships. You're completely deluded as to who you're attracted to, who's attracted to you, and how much you really love them. Neptune represents unconditional love, and Venus isn't too far behind. When they square off neither wants to fight and injure the other. It's basically just a shoving match waiting for someone to throw the first punch. Then something pushes one into the other and the brawl is on. The biggest problem, nobody knows why they're fighting. Deep down you seek ultimate fulfillment and see beauty everywhere but don't know how to attain it. You're not sure what you want to do and definitely not how to go about getting it. Many times you respond as if you were being threatened even when you are not. Instead of using rose colored glasses you just choose to put on blinders and not pay attention to the problem thinking it will casually go away. Coming to wrong conclusions and making accusations that aren't justifiable will also cause tensions in your life. As a result of this psychological stress you retreat into your own fantasy land where things aren't so bad. Running from your problems will get you nowhere. What you need to do is find an individual creative outlet where you can go in times of distress. You will have to discipline yourself in personal and romantic affairs. It's easy for you to fall for the wrong person maybe they are extremely dysfunctional or already taken. Either way, you will face multiple romantic disappointments before finding your happy mate.

Venus square Pluto

With Venus squaring Pluto you're constantly let down by the lack of fulfillment with your emotional life and it brings more difficulties than satisfaction. Every time you become romantically involved the relationship quickly falls short of expectations and eventually dissolves entirely. You desperately want to find that one person you feel completes you, yet everyone you meet never seems to live up to your standards. Reason being, your standards are too high. More often than not, what you want isn't necessarily what you need. This eventually leads you into a spiral of frustrations with your need for a permanent partnership. When you don't get what you want instead of coming out and blatantly saying what the problem is, you tend to try and send your message with subconscious signals having your body language do the talking for you. Just come out and communicate what is bothering you so others don't misinterpret your message and create more tensions. You may also sit around secretly criticizing every little thing wrong with others, neglecting your own personal inadequacies. At its worst this shows you stay in a failing marriage well past its termination date.

Mars square Ascendant

The square formed between Mars and your ascendant provides you with a fighting, competitive, and aggressive nature. You assert yourself constantly and have a drive to succeed like none other. This aspect also gives you athleticism and enjoyment for anything where you can prove your abilities. If this isn't calmed down by others planets you're probably violent and excessively combative. When offend you take instant action, and when aspected by Mercury you lash out verbally. This is generally a negative aspect which makes you enjoy being rude to others. Watching people become angry and defensive by your actions, you frequently provoke others into fighting. Sign and house placement will be very important in determining which direction this energy is influenced. You do this because you aren't very sure about your authority. Being the ultimate superior is very important to you. If

127

you do not find a profession where you can be your own boss and work at your own pace you'll never be happy. Until you do so you will move from job to job, by personal decision or the employers. The house this is in will be important because it will indicate where you're the most passionate to succeed.

Mars square Jupiter

This aspect indicates you need to learn how to use your abundant physical and intellectual attributes efficiently. You will spend large amounts of resources on useless and unproductive ideas or enterprises only to get lost in the chaos. Admiring and imitating those in authority doesn't mean you're qualified for the top, and if you fake success any inadequacies will eventually be exposed. Learning is only possible after making many mistakes. The square is usually the most difficult aspect in anyone's natal chart. This can be a very bad catalyst when aligning with other planets. Harsh aspects from Uranus or Saturn will prove devastating. House placement will be the key indicator of where your most troubles are. Mars shows where you're overly aggressive, and Jupiter will indicate where you're the most arrogant. Athletics and competition will be an important release of energy. The determined competitor in you makes it difficult to accept defeat graciously. You must always be victorious and Pluto can cause stooping to low levels when getting there. Your general disregard for safety and authority indicates either catastrophic injuries, jail time, or both. Any recklessness must find a proper outlet or psychological breakdowns begin. When the physical energies aren't released you unconsciously take out your anger towards others. Exercise is obviously the best option, but so are house chores requiring hard labor. Use your creative abilities and get into masonry and stonework.

Mars square Saturn

The square between Mars and Saturn is considered amongst the most difficult in all of astrology. This indicates your attitude takes drastic swings from aggression to depression and then back to aggression. You're greatly sensitive to criticism and think your opinions are the most golden of gold. You feel constantly on edge and that everything is a competition. Until you lose the chip on your shoulder and pay attention to how your behavior affects the situation will you finally calm down. Prayer, meditation, and quiet personal reflection will ease your psychological tensions greatly. Unfortunately this confuses your perceptions of responsibility. You can only see what you want and have little consideration for the needs of others. Part of your anger is when you allow an opportunity pass by only realizing it was there once it's gone. Other times you over react and release pent up anger and emotions on undeserving others. There are several strains caused by this and one of the most significant is your inability to personally relate to your father and authority. Whatever the situation, chances are it was less than functional and possibly violent. Part of your psychological problems is that you feel nothing was ever good enough. If you were neglected you would act up of distance yourself from him. Any traumatic experiences will take a severe toll on your life well into you adult years. This alignment almost always shows a harsh relationship with your father, possibly even abusive.

Mars square Uranus

This is one of the most volatile aspects two planets can form. The square between Mars and Uranus gives you an irrepressible desire to be completely free. Without hesitation or restraint, you project your forceful nature into your environment and onto your peers. No one can tell you what to do, how to do it, or pretty much anything else either. You never learn until you make the mistake for yourself, and it's difficult to listen to those wiser than you. As you mature into your older years you realize the folly of those bullheaded ways. Anxiousness, nervousness, and paranoia can run through your head and cause severe problems in your day to day affairs. The aggressive nature of Mars and the eccentric nature of Uranus are in direct conflict with each other. Both planets rebel instantaneously when not allowed to do what they choose. I believe this is one of the top five most difficult aspects to handle. You're naturally rash and inconsistent in your decision making. Acting hastily causes not only emotional strife, but physical accidents as well. Because you're moving so fast and not always thinking about what you're working on can cause bruises, cuts, and possibly minor burns. The only thing holding you back is your complete disregard of safety and rules imposed by others. Learn to cooperate and you will go far. Remember, the more you resist the more you get tazed or pepper sprayed.

Mars square Neptune

When Mars and Neptune are positioned like this it's extremely difficult and most times impossible to assert yourself without causing severe emotional turmoil. You fluctuate between intense aggression and complete passiveness. You can never figure out when it's the right time to go after something or just let it pass by. Once you see the results of your actions you feel depressed and melancholy for not making the proper decision. Your unconscious tendencies cause you to create anxieties and annoyances within all your romantic relationships. You become attracted so someone who is already taken, or highly unstable thinking that you, and only you, can change them for the better. Your early childhood conditioning caused you to repress your will and desires so much so that you suffer many years into your adult hood. The house each planets occupy will show where you are the most timid, Neptune placement, an overly aggressive, Mars placement. Quite often you just can't figure out what you want let alone how to get it. This also stimulates psychic abilities and vivid dreams. If you choose a path into the higher realms of the spiritual world then you will experience great and unusual things that won't happen to other people. Alignments between Mars and Neptune always implicate the inability to see how your actions will affect you down the road.

Mars square Pluto

Squares with Mars usually give you an aggressive and forceful personality. When Pluto is involved you become possessed on pursuing your goals, and will stop at nothing to get what you want. Whether they are positive or negative is up to you. During the course of your war path you overlook the little problems that might arise and become extremely hostile when they do. The usually negative energies charge you into projects demanding more than you can give. You try and attain the impossible because you need constant reassurance of your abilities and self-worth. Perhaps you were teased or ignored as a child and now as an adult you feel the need to show former bullies how far you have gone. Perhaps you were the bully, picking on those who were weaker in order to feel superior. Either way, this formation produces personal insecurities which never truly go away. Even as an adult you will be constantly challenged to test your competence. Pluto is known as the destroyer, the one who completely demolishes and constructs something new. This can be physically, mentally, or spiritually. You may feel like you have hardships that others don't, and you probably do. Once you can become comfortable with your own personal inadequacies then nothing is impossible for you. This can also indicate a significant injury or illness that requires significant amounts of rest and rehabilitation.

Jupiter square ascendant

This is one of only the few squares which doesn't produce negative energy. Jupiter is flamboyant, optimistic, and philosophic in everything it does. The biggest hang up is your inability to integrate these qualities into your personality. You have big ideas for success which are many times too extravagant to complete. You act passionately towards them and become sour when they don't pan out. You're full of fire and spirit at first, but you quickly burn out if others don't catch on right away. Not wanting to act in moderation you can take anything and everything too far. Sometimes this indicates your parents are able to help you along, giving you more opportunities than most. Despite any opportunities you were denied, you still rise to greatness because of your undying spirit and courage. Many of your failures will come from your arrogant attitude. You can over estimate your capabilities and resources, not realizing it until it is too far down the road. Financial losses due to gambling losses and poor business speculations can be possible. Make sure read all the fine print when entering into a contract. Weight issues are always involved with Jupiter. If you're fat and out of shape stop drinking so much sugar and get out walking three times a week.

Jupiter square Saturn

Because aspects between Jupiter and Saturn are the slowest amongst the personal planets, the energies produced here aren't always felt for everyone born under this alignment. Saturn's purpose is to provide stability and a foundation to build on. Jupiter is the eternal optimist whose flamboyance is unrivaled. Squares are traditionally the most difficult aspect to handle but Jupiter's optimism can balance out nearly anything. Often this indicates your success is only through responsibility and hard work. On rare occasion you're in the right place at the right time, and if you're pertinent you can seize the opportunity. The biggest problem is your over inflated ego thinking it can accomplish more work than possible. You get super size fries only to throw half of them away. Although it may be tough, once you realize your own potential there's nothing you can't do. Spiritually this produces tensions as well. It's difficult to find your place amongst the religions and quite often this indicates you completely separate from the way you were raised. You question everything your parents taught you and the evidence must be abundant in order to change your mind. The biggest problem is when you stick to your views and refuse to admit the opinions of others are valid. Sign and house placement will show which planets is dominate. Saturn's influence will make you responsible and determined to succeed, while Jupiter will make you more bombastic and outgoing.

Jupiter square Uranus

When Jupiter is squaring Uranus this shows you experience major conflicts which inhibit you from attaining your goals. You constantly bite off more than you can chew and the result is a lack luster performance. Exercising self-control and establishing priorities should be on the top of your list. Once you do so you'll find you can solve problems others simply can't. You have a brilliantly talented mind which can create the most innovative of inventions. This can lead you into a prosperous career in technological research and development. Jupiter is already an overinflated wind bag, and Uranus can be the stingy miser who won't listen to anybody. Jupiter rarely produces negative energy, but the square is the most troublesome aspect a planet can have. The absolute worst issue is you're overly optimistic and can't see where problems might occur. No one begins at the top of the ladder and you will need to learn which rung you actually stand on. Jupiter represents ultimate expansion and when the rebelliousness of Uranus is intensified then you'll go to great lengths to maintain your freedoms, even if it means rioting in the streets.

Jupiter square Neptune

This square is a mildly generational aspect which, pending retrogrades influences everyone born over two month span, once every eight years or so. This particular aspect generally indicates spiritual confusion and difficulties establishing your personal philosophies. It often takes several years of listening, thinking, and altering your beliefs from time to time. Squares are the most difficult aspects to handle, but Jupiter can deal with anything thrown his way. Just don't get too down when your first attempt fails. Creatively this creates problems finding an outlet for your abilities. Usually it comes from a lack of resources. Don't consider a career as an artist, musician, or actor. These activities can be a good hobby, but don't bank on retiring rich if you try. No matter how much effort you put forth the dreams in your head never seem to manifest themselves into the real world. Small scale projects like church productions and quilting with old people are the best options. Especially if you can find a niche helping those in need. Consider a trip to a third world country. Seeing and experiencing up close is the best way for you to expand your horizons and further your beliefs. Because this influences so many people in so many ways it's impossible describe everything. It definitely isn't a good starting point but again, Jupiter doesn't produce anything bad, partly because he doesn't admit it. Neptune dilutes your thinking and makes you arrogantly optimistic. Every square is one of the problems in our life. The houses these two planets occupy will be where you experience the most unrealistic opinions and expectations. Because your imagination and fantasies are so powerful you enjoy the escape into other realities drugs allow you to get. Whether it's a strict religious doctrine, or your own personal path, these you're extremely philosophical and spiritual. Afflictions from Venus or the Moon will make you compassionate to a fault so don't be a sucker for a sob story. If you aren't careful you get involved with people who only want to take advantage of you and your resources.

Jupiter square Pluto

This is an infrequent square between the slowest moving planet, Pluto, and the moderately paced planet Jupiter. Because of this, their alignment doesn't occur very often and its powers are magnificent. As with all aspects this can have a varied effect on each individual. You're the most devious of genius and possess immense intellectual abilities. The reason behind this brain power is your driving ambition to know everything about everything. Chances are you become entirely obsessed into whatever your desire is. If your direction is focused into positive endeavors you will become an expert in your chosen field. Areas of medicine, psychology, or any profession where there are no limits for advancement are advised. If this alignment is in close relation to your ascendant the energies of this will be intensified. You may become a complete rebel to authority and a menace to the standard code of ethics. No matter how severe the beating, you will always get up and eventually bounce back. Even if the traumas are exceptionally drastic, your past experiences will be your driving force in life. You will act up and speak out against any existing rules and regulations you see are unfit and unfair. If you become conceited about your authority the moral of your workplace will suffer. You have a grand vision of what you think the world should be like and dismayed when others don't see things as you do. You develop your own personal religious and spiritual views, which you stand by and defend dearly. Although you have your own opinions you understand that others are entitled to theirs even if they are different. House placement will direct obsessions.

Saturn square ascendant

Squares are always difficult aspects to handle, and squares with Saturn usually cause you to be overly serious, reclusive, and depressed. When squaring your ascendant, you express yourself negatively without even knowing it. Integrating your individual responsibility into a group is especially difficult. You never know just where you fit in and constantly overstep your boundaries. You're very difficult to get along with because when others don't agree, you simply pack up and leave. It doesn't matter what obstacles are created, you need to be allowed to pursue your own path. The reason you enjoy being alone is because of the apprehensions when asserting yourself and encountering significant opposition. Extreme competition causes you to shy away and sometimes cower into a corner when confronted. Don't under estimate your abilities and sell yourself short. Fighting is not always your thing because you see the consequences either victorious or not. If you choose to fight you will use every trick you know to protect yourself. Everything you do will be slower than others, speed is not a trait produced by this. Others may see you as cold and indifferent, but the reality is you're serious and responsible. You learn through your experiences and know you receive nothing for free having to work for everything you want. Once you settle down the security you gain from marriage reinforces the confidence you slowly need to develop.

Saturn square Uranus

Fairly rarely does Saturn square up Uranus, and it's a good thing to. If fact this is one of my top five most difficult, and you had better hope there aren't any other squares or oppositions involved. This aspect makes it nearly impossible to change old behaviors and thought patterns. Whatever was engrained into your head as a child follows you into your adult life. Both Saturn and Uranus are slow moving planets, making their alignments considerably more prolonged and significant. It's very difficult for you to see outside your box, and you have a subconscious fear of anything unknown or unfamiliar. It's possible your early conditioning taught you to seek the approval of others as opposed to just being yourself. It's imperative you break away from your adolescent fears and come loose from your shell. You're highly irritable and overly anxious most of the time and you experience serious fluctuations in your mood, attitude, and behavior, causing massive confusions amongst you and your associates. This may also indicate a very unusual relationship with your father. It's possible that he has a different job than others, maybe he passed away or left at an early age, or possibly your relationship is just strained with problems everywhere. Squares add stress and difficulties within our lives and Saturn is the planet that teaches us responsibility, making aspects like these very unfortunate. When not harmonized by more pleasant aspects elsewhere you will have anger management, depression, and psychological issues. Don't become too depressed if you have this in your chart, it can be influenced and the stresses eased by many other things.

Saturn square Neptune

Squares between the slow moving Saturn and the turtle paced Neptune make this alignment very distinct and magnificent. As with all aspects involving generational planets like Neptune, the relationship it forms with your ascendant will dictate how much influence you actually feel. Usually this produces unrealistic fears about possessions, poverty, and personal inefficiencies. You become overly anxious about things and situations which you have no control over and desperately cling onto them. Despite how emotionally distressed you become you will still procrastinate when finding a solution. Then when your first idea is wrong it takes even longer to realize the error. The false fear about your own ability makes you feel inadequate and unable to cope with strenuous situations. What you're actually afraid of is the exposure of your faults and weaknesses. Because you can see your negative qualities you think everyone else can as well. This negative attitude crosses into your professional life causing more and more disappointments. It's possible for you to get sucked into a lackluster job in which you despise just because it's easily gained. If you avoid any challenge that comes along no one, not even yourself, can be aware of your talents and capabilities. You have a knack for organization and leadership when left alone or in small groups. Spiritually this creates tensions when applying your philosophies to life. You have a grand concept of what the universe should look like but it never is and you must accept that. The best outlet for this will be through art, music, or writing. Something where you can turn the ideas buried within your subconscious into an actual structure. Maybe even demonic art carving.

Saturn square Pluto

Aspects between Saturn and Pluto are hard to describe because Pluto wasn't discovered until 1930, and Saturn is a slow moving planet. Due to the infrequency, the relationship with your ascendant is indescribably important. Only a percentage of the millions born during this aspect will feel the power. You love to dominate and were probably a sore loser early in your childhood. If you couldn't be the victor you wouldn't want to play. Because of this you probably developed friendships with younger children because you had the competitive edge and could easily take advantage. You have extreme emotional insecurities, which you rarely let anyone know. You continually construct defensive walls not to keep other people from coming in, but to keep your true self from coming out. With a square between these two planets you find it difficult to live up to your perceived potential, and probably never will. You're only able to assess your true self halfheartedly, never wanting to expose any personal insecurity. All aspects between Saturn and Pluto can cause severe psychological disorders and the square is the worst. The positive characteristics allow you to recognize spirituality better your life and become deeply devoted to religion. You will not accept religion as it is taught to you. Questioning everything you are told is the best way to discover the truth for yourself.

Uranus square ascendant
The best way for any generational planet to cast its influence is through an aspect with your ascendant. Unfortunately, squares are the most problematic of aspects, and Uranus is the craziest of crazy. This particular alignment makes you nervous, neurotic, and extremely over anxious. You're a complete and total rebel who will eventually have to break free from all accepted norms and blaze your own path. Hopefully you have soothing influences from the Moon or Venus. All too often you do something simply because you were told no. It's only after you experience severe traumas from your own mistakes before you learn your lesson. You don't care if others follow your way, all you desire is being allowed to run free. Erratic and spontaneous all the time, your sporadic decisions will get you into trouble as a youth. If you were raised in a strict and confined household your rebellion may lead you down a path of destruction. You have endless amounts of energy to direct, when you direct it positively the results are limitless. Your innovative creativity is off the charts and can inspire you into great and wonderful things. Meditation in a peaceful and relaxing environment is going to be required to prevent mental exhaustion and migraines. At its worst you argue simply to be difficult and cause problems.

Uranus square Neptune
(1867-1874)(1952-1959) (2036-2040)
This is a very infrequent formation which won't take place again until the mid 2030's. Those who have one or both planets aligned with their ascendant possess much more distinguishable energies than those who don't. Because these are both relatively newly discovered, Uranus in 1781 and Neptune in 1846, astrologers still don't know just what to expect from this aspect.

The squaring of two generational planets produces a society which is in constant rebellion, but not quite sure of the purpose or reason. Your generation feels the oppression associated with ignorance and will dedicatedly pursue the expansion of personal and intellectual freedom. Spiritually this is a period of revolutions and rebellions. The straight laced patsies are going to have to accept the wild child running around naked. Whether it be freedom from government, the accepted norms of society, or spiritual persecution, those born during this period will direct and lead the world into a completely new society. Reason being, you feel guilty about your social obligations and don't recognize that you alone can't change the entire world. If you develop extravagant plans without completely assessing all the possibilities you will surely fail or come short of your expectations. This alignment will inspire brilliant artists and wonderful musicians. House placement is always important with generational planets. The houses these two planets occupy will show your most confusion, Neptune, and your most unexpected or unusual events, Uranus.

Uranus square Pluto
(1931-1934) (2009-2014)
        Both Uranus and Pluto are considered generational planets and their influences aren't always prominent in everyone's chart. Because of the slow speeds they travel at close alignments with your ascendant or mid-heaven will magnify their effects. Those born under this aspect will be generational revolutionaries. Like a sweeping wave of the ocean, governments will collapse, new world orders established, and break-trough's in medicine and technology all revolutionize the world. The last time these formed a square was from 1931 to 1934 and WW2 was the impending result. Part of the issue is the lust for power and control causes the wrong people to gain power. This is a period when society must learn through atrocity and clean up the mess once the square is broken and the trine is formed. The ability to bounce back from defeat causes the warring factions to never give up. No matter how badly beaten only death will stop the craziest of crazies. Some of

139

your generation will fail to participate in this social revolution. Many people of this era are those who don't care enough to vote or voice their opinion, then complain about their situation when given the short end of the stick. Others will fight for their freedoms valiantly and desperately. Psychological distress is indescribably intensified. The basic nature of Pluto is obsession and Uranus is purely rebellious. On a personal level this aspect merely intensifies the desires dictated by the other planets.

Neptune square ascendant

Because Neptune is a generational planet it makes alignments with your ascendant much more important. Squares are always difficult aspects to handle, and this one makes you extremely sensitive to the criticism of others. Taking meaningless comments to heart causes you to feel others are attacking you when they're not. Then you snap at people, not realizing how stinging your words really were. No matter what, Neptune always causes confusion to anything it touches. This particular aspect indicates trouble accepting religion and spirituality. Because you can see the multiple validities of all the world's religions you don't feel the need to associate with any. Even if you do take part in a religious sect you do so somewhat grudgingly. This is because you understand spirituality isn't experienced in a church but out amongst the cosmos. Neptune loves unconditionally and this alignment makes you more compassionate towards the injustices you see around you. Neptune sees everything as equal. Man, animal, and Earth, are of no difference to this planet. Part of the problem with the square is you realize how miniscule you are as a human and alone your efforts are meaningless. If you can find an organization where you can work as a collective then you're a wonderful asset. Try working behind the scenes without much recognition for your efforts. Just make sure to take credit where your credit is due.

Neptune square Pluto

If you have this in your charts you have been dead for

140

hundreds of years and are a ghost. It will occur again around 2055, and I will probably have joined you by then.

Pluto square Asc.

Because it's the most distant of the planets, the generational effect of Pluto is only expressed through a close alignment with your ascendant. This aspect shows you feel destined to have a powerful influence on the lives of everyone you contact. You think you can change the lives of others and overly seek opportunities to do so. Basically you're an obsessive control freak. The square is considered the most difficult aspect in astrology, and your ascendant is a very sensitive point, so expect some problems. This aspect causes extreme rifts with authority figures and anyone trying to control you. Whether you admit it or not, you're an ego maniac. You consume resources which aren't yours then becoming hostile when told no. If your parents had complete control over you this will have an extremely negative effect. You can show bad judgments when making decisions because you are convinced that no one should question what you do, even if your error is quite obvious. You need to learn to respect other people's boundaries, even if you feel entitled to intervene. Once you learn how to make good judgments achievements are boundless. You will probably have trouble in personal relationships because your demands are sometimes oppressive. Your lust for power and recognition seeps into all affairs, making compromise nearly impossible.

Trine

Genesis: 16/17
Then God made the two great lights: the greater to rule the day, and the lesser light to rule the night. He made the stars also. God sent them in the firmament of heaven to give light on Earth, and to rule over the day and night, and to divide the light from darkness.

At 120 degrees apart, planets form a trine and walk in

141

harmony with nothing but peaches and rainbows. Well that's the general philosophy, and sometimes there is too much of a good thing. Contemplate an endless ice cream cone. The first few bites are wonderful, but after 100 it sucks. Best friends with the sextile, they are extremely similar, and are meant to ease the tensions from other bad aspects. Any negativity from a trine is because you're too carefree and easy-going. This alignment will tranquilize the harsher squares and oppositions, while complementing the conjunctions in a positive manner. Trine's are the symbolic relief point from the stresses caused by the square. Their purpose is to provide comfort and understanding between whichever planets are involved. In the same manner as the sextile I use a six degree orb on either side, but because of the uncertainty at the 135 degree separation the orb for the trine is different. The no-man's land between the trine and sesquiquadrate is from about 127-132 degrees of separation. Trine's will show where you're the most comfortable and what you will naturally excel at.

Sun trine ascendant

    This aspect allows the energies produced by the other aspects to express themselves throughout your personality. It creates positive energy giving you a happy demeanor towards life. If your Sun is in a fire sign this will be especially true, and your spirit will have to be controlled. Earth signs will be organized, professional, and business like. Air signs will be intellectual and innovative. Water signs will be emotional and compassionate. Most importantly this allows you to use all the influences present in your chart. You have a firm grasp on who you are and where your place in the universe is. There will inevitably be pitfalls and obstacles, but in the end you eventually find your little niche. Even though you seem to have all the energy in the world you rarely take advantage of it, and many of your creative potentials will go down the drain. This is because you feel everything comes so freely and easily that hard work can take a back seat to enjoyment. The biggest problem here is dealing with people who don't share your energy level. Because you think everyone is the same as you, you assume their spirit is as well. This isn't true, and if you don't learn when and where to calm down in you will experience some social dysfunction.

Sun trine Moon

This is one of the most wonderful aspects in all of astrology. There is a harmonious balance between your spirit and emotions. You naturally react to situations in such a way that your will and your habits can continue to develop properly. There's a good balance between the lessons you have learned from past experience and your ability to use this knowledge when making future decisions. Your relationship with your parents was generally favorable to your continual growth. They probably inspired you to become your own individual and not merely a reflection of themselves. This doesn't necessarily mean you have a functional relationship with them. Unfortunately, most of life's lessons are learned through calamity and strife. This alignment helps sooth the negativities we all experience. Your greatest problem, if it can be called that, is your tendency to lack aggression when you need to assert yourself. You may find you waited too long and someone else has gotten there first. This is a nurturing aspect allowing you to respond well to children and they seem to be on their best behavior around you. You seem to meet the right people at the right time, and use it to your best advantage. In positions of authority you feel completely at ease, and exercise your will with an understanding of how others will react to it.

Sun trine Mars

A trine between the Sun and Mars instills you with self-confidence and leadership abilities. It also indicates you have more ethical intentions when you take on a project. You have the drive and desire to finish what you set out to accomplish and very rarely fail. Sometimes your determination and courageousness causes you over look whatever risks are in the way and damn the torpedoes, full speed ahead. Your over confidence leads to failure because you're so eager to see the project complete. It's easy to establish

143

your goals and figure out the best possible way to accomplish them. No single aspect indicates a wonderful life, but this is a considerably good start simply because Mars isn't mad. Strength and competitive spirit are also enhanced by this aspect. Part of your success is you can physically wear out your competitor. This isn't an artsy fartsy type aspect. It won't give you any imagination or creativity, but it does provide the energy needed to finish your project. The Moon, Venus, and Neptune can show you where to direct your artistic inspiration. Children are no problem for you because you accept them at their own development level. Unless they get mouthy, then you have no problem giving them a smack.

Sun trine Jupiter

This is a top ten positive aspect. In particular this allows you to learn the lessons of life through past experiences and inspires you to pass them onto future generations. It's easy to see when you're wrong and where changes can be made for improvement, although sometimes it's only after a vicious battle in which you were not the victor. You understand you can't always get what you want, but when you work hard enough you usually do. You're friendly and agreeable meaning you can pretty much pick which profession you decide to excel in, even if it's criminal. Because you know the limitations of your capabilities it's your ability to get along with others propelling you into success. You're psychically connected to a world of vast spirituality and human consciousness, but any religious beliefs are only as inspirational as your willingness to develop them. Once you find your niche spirituality will play a key role in your life. If you can harness your creative ability many times you start a new ingenious enterprise, sell it, and retire early into a life of comfort. This can also indicate that you make a living in real estate later in life, renting out your many properties. Professionally you should consider medicine, teaching, or theater. If Mars is closely involved then you should pursue a career in athletics.

Sun trine Saturn

144

This is a great aspect to begin your chart with. Saturn purpose is to give your life form and structure and while forming a trine with the Sun this provides many great things. First off, it usually indicates you have a better than average relationship with your father. Because of his teachings you have probably followed in his ways, possibly even professionally. This generally makes you responsible, hardworking, but if you're going to go sell drugs then you're going to go sell drugs. You realize your success in life is directly related to how much work and effort you put into it. The more stash you can sell, the more money you can make. Generally it's the positive traits which shine through because it's easy to accept your social responsibilities and follow through with your obligations. Business and management will suit you, as well as any job in which you can follow a set schedule. It may require working long hours into the night, but you want to know when and where you will be working. The number one key to your success is the ability to use your resources efficiently, getting the most out of everything, and everyone as well. The biggest problem is your inability to see outside your box. Breaking away from your normal routine and habits will be nearly impossible once you get dead set on something. House placement will show where you should try and find your career.

Sun trine Uranus

Aspects from Uranus are usually difficult to handle. Fortunately for you this is one of the easier to accept. Uranus makes you eccentric and crazy most of the time. The trine allows you to accept your unusual personality and use your assets positively. You're inventive and innovative creations often break the mold of the standard norm. Trines are good aspects that project the planetary energy positively. You're very responsible and know how to use your leadership skills in the most efficient and effective way possible. People respect you for the hard work and dedication you put forth. As with every aspect sign, house placement, and exactness of alignment will need to be considered. As the first of the generational planets, Uranus provides us with a revolutionary

145

desire to change the world. It may be the globe as a whole or just your own local community. Neurotic at times, this aspect can often indicate obsession, jealousy, and many times just plain berserkness. Interested in unusual people and things allows you to have a wide variety of friends and social contacts. You'll find your life is filled with several sudden and unexpected changes. Things happen to you that just don't seem to happen to other people. Depending on house placement this can indicate anything from an unusual job to an unusual death. Later in life near your second Saturn return you will most likely experience a mid-crisis. No matter how successful you are, you will go through a significant psychological overhaul that will cause you to change your life dramatically.

Sun trine Neptune

As the battery charging our ego, aspects forming with the Sun are usually quite intense. Trines between the Sun and Neptune will make you dreamy, imaginative, and rather carefree in conducting your business. This attribute can give you a hippie like personality that is quite lost in the illusions of life. Neptune is mystical and magical allowing fantasies to run wild and seem incredibly real. Considerably better than some of the other possible alignments, the trine promotes a harmonious balance between your inner self and your spiritual beliefs. Because humans know very little about their own subconscious it's difficult to predict how alignments like this will turn out. Chances are your creative abilities are better than most, and if directed properly will prove quite useful. This is one of the better modifying aspects, meaning it's easily influenced by other alignments but still adds its special flare. Those with this in their charts will see the atrocities that take place across the globe and desperately care to change it. They will take a responsibility for cleaning up the mess caused by the previous generations. If there is a driving fire from other parts of your chart you may establish one of these environmental endeavors. Generally you will like to stay behind the scenes, letting others have the spotlight, but sign and house placement can definitely change that.

Sun trine Pluto

Trines are considered one of the best aspects in astrology, and Pluto is always like a catalyst with whichever planet it's aligning with. When the spiritual battery of the Sun is involved you possess ambition and many times obsessiveness. House placement will be where you direct most of your intense desires. Although you're extremely determined to succeed you don't care very much about receiving attention for it. Responsible and hardworking, you would rather be a high ranking assistant than a low ranking manager. Your creative and imaginative abilities are immense, and you have a direct connection with the vast expansiveness of the universe. Religion will interest you, but you still realize there's a greater cosmos out there and that humans only understand a little about actual reality. Your psychic powers allow you to unconsciously read into others well. This can make you an excellent psychologist or counselor. Since Pluto was only discovered in 1930 astrologists are still studying the effects of this here on Earth. Continually referenced to Shiva the ancient destroyer, recovery, rebuilding, and rejuvenation are all associated with this aspect. Despite whatever traumas produced in your childhood years you are still able to pick yourself up and get on with your life. This will also stimulate you interest into the darker realms of magic and religion. Be careful when dabbling into the seedy underworld, it's possible to unlock doors you wish you hadn't.

Moon trine ascendant

The relationship each person has between their Moon and ascendant is very important. I consider the Moon in trine with your ascendant a balancing aspect which alleviates the tensions from the problematic ones. This indicates the emotional state of the Moon is positively integrated into your personality generally making you happy and optimistic. Unless the Moon is all messed up by bad aspects from the other planets. Then, it's the problematic emotions that are positively integrated. Basically this allows you to feel the condition of your Moon. Tight formations will allow you to experience feelings as they were meant to be. The absolute best of this is your ability to identify your emotions correctly. When you're mad you know what the source is, and when you're in love you have nothing but rainbows. Nothing is ever determined by one aspect, but this is a great starting point. This gives you a calm and friendly personality attracting many friends. Your emotional state doesn't usually fluctuate or react inappropriately, but by no means does this indicate you're always in control. This just usually shows you can remain calm and mellow under stress. Rarely will you make the same mistake twice, and it's easy for you to learn from your failures and short falls. The Moon affects the relationship we have with our mother. Trines usually produce positive energy adding better ability to accept your mother's inadequacies. You're poised and under control and most of the time pressure situations don't get to you. Performance under the spotlight and in the clutch can come naturally. It may take practice and hard work, but eventually you will get there. Because you realize that you have to make sacrifices in your life in to advance your career, personal affairs may take a back seat to professional matters. Once you find an equal balance with the two you can settle down and remain happy.

Moon trine Mercury

A trine between the Moon and Mercury integrates your intellect with your emotions in a positive manner. You attract many friends because it's easy for them to warm up and sense your sincere feelings. This is a formation which can balance out and harmonize other harsher aspects. Most of the time, this indicates you're able to identify your emotional state and make the proper adjustments. Remember though, nothing is completely set in stone, and this may make you a blundering baby. You will need to talk about any emotional grievances to a trusted loved one, probably a female relative. Any repressed feelings easily turn into harsh resentments. You will have very vivid dreams which will be

148

an inspiration throughout your life. If this is in a water sign you will be too psychic for your own good. You may not be able to handle all the unconsciously received energies from others. Intuition can be developed and you are the very meaning of the term psychic. Magic and the occult will interest you greatly and should be studied. You could be quite the spiritualist. If you choose to express yourself with art, music, or writing, this is the alignment to use when timing your progressed transits. This aspect can also make you a wonderful singer as long as the music is turned up and no one can hear you.

Moon trine Venus

Fortunately for you the Moon trining Venus is one of best alignments you can have. Not only does it make you socially charming and beautiful, it also soothes harsher planetary aspects. The Moon and Venus greatly enjoy each other's company, and the trine allows their gentle to flow positively. Friends are naturally attracted to you, and quite often your social circle will grow bigger than appreciated. Your funeral will probably be over crowded with people showing up from everywhere to pay their tributes. It will be necessary to weed out your social garden and cut ties with acquaintances from time to time. This will happen when Saturn progresses over one of these. Many times your happy demeanor is highly contagious, can cheer up a room just by walking in. Friends will surround you for your entire life because of this. Keeping your private life private isn't always important to you, and you feel by opening up to others they will open up to you. This is definitely not true and you will need to show restraint when divulging personal information. Many people will come to you with their troubles because you are so kind and caring and talk with an open heart. It's quite possible that you choose a career in decoration, architecture, or creative design. Style is very important to you.

Moon trine Mars

Mars is the instigator of energy, motivation, and aggression. When it's the Moon forming an aspect this adds emotion to all

149

your actions. Behind everything you do there is a significant driving force based deeply in your everyday feelings. Your reactions are habitual and many times over responsive. Usually this indicates you're easily aroused and thrown into frenzy when things get extremely out of hand. The Moon is a feminine planet and Mars is a masculine one. Naturally this produces a counter-productive force which is quite confusing at times. Even though there are difficulties for the Moon relating to Mars, the trine is a pleasant aspect which can stabilize the Moons significant fluctuations. Remember nothing is left uninfluenced, and there will always be modifying energies elsewhere. Generally this is a pleasant aspect arousing and intensifying your emotions. Compromise is easier for you, and you realize that in order to get what you want adjustments will have to be made. Part of the problem you experience is the passiveness of the Moon causes Mars to over compensate with aggression. You may act tough and macho, but this is only a cover for the soft emotion produced by the Moon. This can also lead to turmoil in the business and professional world. You don't care to step on any toes rising to towards success, sometimes allowing those who stoop to less ethical ways to eventually prevail. More often than not you realize an opportunity was missed because you were too timid to act.

Moon trine Jupiter

The Moon in trine with a Jupiter produces a glowing personality and an ease relating to people. This is one of the most harmonious alignments possible, soothing the negative energies produced elsewhere. Jupiter is a highly philosophical, expansive planet, and will greatly magnify everything it touches. When his influence is targeted at the exceptionally personal planet of the Moon your emotions, subconscious, and metaphysical abilities are his intended targets. The feelings you experience are more substantial than others, and you sometimes get carried away with them. One problem caused by this is the tendency to over inflate your emotional condition. Moon alignments are easily influenced, but it will take several negative alignments to overpower this one.

150

They have to be considerably greater and closer aligned, but it is still possible for this to intensify the bad. Because Jupiter greatly opens your subconscious abilities you can get lost in your own head becoming your own worst enemy, especially if one of these planets is in the twelfth house. Your usually optimistic outlook on life can cause you to deny the facts if turmoil is caused by the truth. Even when circumstances are dismal you can look on the bright side and see light at the end of the tunnel. Your infectious enthusiasm can generate a feeling of wellbeing among the people you are with. You're very fond of helping out with charitable events, however you would rather just help out than plan and create the function. The energy produced between these two planets will not only enhance all the warm loving qualities of the Moon, but it will also add to the chaos when thing go awry. Your romantic interest is a person of high moral character who is sincere, honest, and spiritually motivated. You love being in love and your relationship will continue to grow with each passing year.

Moon trine Saturn

A trine between the Moon and Saturn indicates you're reserved, cautious and usually hesitant when warming up to strangers. It's difficult to expose your true feelings because it displays weakness and instability. Saturn is a very strict planet who teaches us life lessons through calamity and strife. Fortunately a trine can add stability towards the constantly fluctuating Moon. In your early training you grew to possess a good form of common sense. You're emotionally secure and able to look at most situations logically and responsibly, realizing you must invest personally in order to reap any benefits. There is a sense of refinement in your appreciation of art and music. Unusual, abstract art will not interest you unless the lines are precise and color scheme matches. Instead you enjoy things that stay within the traditional norm. Architecture and design are two professions in which you would excel greatly. When in competition you play by the rules and expect others to do so. This trine will also add a great deal of emotional attachment to your father. Anytime you think

151

you have failed in his eyes will affect you tremendously. You will be able to handle responsibility early and your parents will be able to leave you in charge of any siblings without fear. At the absolute best this allows you to accept all responsibilities. The reason you are so reserved, cautious, and hesitant, is because you know how to stick to tried and true methods.

Moon trine Uranus

This aspect makes you emotionally excitable and highly original. Although trines are generally revered as positive and harmonious, this one can indicate that the craziness of Uranus is flowing freely throughout your emotions. Your eccentric personality attracts many friends from many different areas of life. With your eager mind and insatiable curiosity you can hold your own in an argument because you know the facts. Any facts you don't know you simply make up and just believed as true, which sometimes can cause serious problems. Maintain your honesty even when it comes to little white lies. Even though the emotional state you're in can fluctuate so dramatically at times, this trine is significantly more harmonious than most others. Neither one of these entities can be considered as stable, so no matter what their relationship, chaos is always possible. You possess large amounts of energy and when you decide to settle down, and your partner must possess the same. It can take you some time and effort before you finally find someone you are compatible with. This relationship can make you a completely rebellious revolutionary. Because Uranus will always break free of restrictions, the attachments caused by the Moon constantly conflicts these interests. Aspects between personal planets and generational planets aren't always prominent and you may not even experience this energy at all. That case is highly unlikely since the Moon is one of the major factors determining the entity you see yourself as. You will need to get away and clear your mind frequently, if not it's your own psychological destruction you will have to endure.

152

Moon trine Neptune

Both the Moon and Neptune possess a significant influence on our emotions, subconscious, and spirituality. This is a balancing alignment which helps ease the tensions produced by harsher influences elsewhere. On problem is, this relationship can be easily modified by outside forces. Serious afflictions from Mars, Saturn, or Uranus will make this relationship go considerably sour. Neither the Moon nor Neptune can stand up for themselves very firmly. Positive aspects from those three planets will help you direct your imagination towards productive outlets. The ultimate compassion of each planet can be so strong you spend more money on others than yourself. You're generally interested in the welfare of loved ones and overlook your needs for theirs. Be careful not to enable any drug addicts. This is a very psychic alignment and whether you accept it or not your intuition is profound. Part of your creative skill set is the ability to tap deep into your inner subconscious and see the other realms out there. As long as you can distinguish fact from fantasy then you're fine. Just make sure not to get caught up in your illusions. Artists, musicians, and actors are always inspired by a relationship like this. Their house placement will show where your abilities can be the best directed, especially if Saturn is in harmony as well.

Moon trine Pluto

More often than not the trine between your Moon and Pluto balances out several of the more problematic aspects other planet cause. This is because they allow you to rebound from serious emotional traumas better than most. When the horrific yet inevitable circumstances arise you begin the healing process faster than most. It usually comes after an extreme emotional outburst. You're a deep feeling individual who habitually resorts to emotional instincts when unexpectedly aroused. The sometimes instinctual reaction to sulk and cry into your pillow only increases the sorrow. After intense feelings of depression and loneliness you eventually dry your eyes and suck it up. Once you're done grieving, going back into a normal routine is simple and easy. If

Mercury is involved you would make a great child psychologist. Your warm and caring nature allows them to open up to you freely and honestly. Nursing and hospice care would also be career options to consider. Whichever houses these planets are occupying will determine where you go to vent your pent up frustrations. This will also make you psychic and possibly interested in the occult. Both of these planets greatly affect our subconscious. Your imagination is so vivid it is sometimes impossible to decipher fantasy from reality. Finding hobbies, possibly careers in art or music will be positive outlets for your creative abilities.

Mercury trine ascendant

This aspect provides you with intelligence, energy, and an extremely talkative nature. Chances are you're a constant chatter box and it's very difficult to sit still for very long. Trines usually indicate positive energy flowing and this energy is mental. If Mercury is heavily afflicted then this aspect can easily turn sour. It's simple to communicate with others because words come easy. When planets directly align with your ascendant you the person takes on distinct characteristics of such planet. Mercury is extremely childish, and brilliantly smart. The jack of all trades yet master of none. The signs these two are in will sway this relationship into drastic possibilities. Positive influences make you extremely talented at math, music, or science. Bad influences make you have mental illnesses. Mercury is constantly curious, and rarely focuses onto one thing for very long. On other side of possibilities, when influenced negatively this can make you completely irresponsible and cause complete refusal to mature into the adult world. More often than not this merely indicates you have a good head on your shoulders.

Mercury trine Mars

Mercury aligning with Mars makes you smart, energetic, and usually well spoken. Trines allow the energy between the two planets to flow positively, and in general will require substantial negative afflictions to turn this aspect sour. Remember this merely allows the energies of Mars to flow freely through your Mercury influences. Words are much more powerful than most people realize and if you get carried away with slander and back biting issues obviously arise. Aggression, action, and competitiveness, are all attributes of Mars. Integrate that with Mercury's intellect and you become extremely quick witted and clever. Focus and direction will be key when determining just where you're able to direct your talents. Sports, gambling, or anything which can distinctly prove you are the victor will be enjoyable. Although this aspect doesn't usually direct a career path, your brilliant conversation skills would make an excellent lawyer, politician, or news reporter. Even if you know nothing on a subject you're capable of making what little knowledge you have look like you're educated. Be careful not to get your foot caught into your mouth, as this may happen on several occasions. Your intelligence, curiosity, and athleticism are all energized and accentuated by this aspect.

Mercury trine Jupiter

This aspect makes you very intelligent, with a high level of philosophical comprehension. Jupiter gives you an optimistic outlook on using your ideas to their fullest potential. The knowledge you attain throughout your years makes you an encyclopedia of knowledge, but where and how you direct that knowledge is up to you. Because of this you can become pompous and arrogant about how smart you are. In school you probably didn't pay much attention because you naturally understood what was being taught. Just remember there are others out there better than you at many things. Not getting caught in your own ego will be important. Education is your specialized vocation and you enjoy passing wisdom along. The high standards you set for yourself and your associates allow you to use your acquaintances advantageously. Because you can be trusted with responsibility and authority your superiors will eventually see your special abilities and promote you through the ranks. This will undoubtedly cause rifts with co-workers who feel they are more qualified. At worst, this aspect intensifies the childlike qualities of Mercury. It may take you a while to truly grow up, and chances are you never will.

Mercury trine Saturn

Your success is limitless because you understand how to use your resources in an organized and efficient manner. Gathering all available knowledge and information, you don't form a solid opinion until you can be reasonably educated. Once you do become educated your beliefs are impossible to sway. Solving problems is easy because you see the multiple options available. You have a conservative mentality and can get to the finishing point in the most direct process. Leadership is natural, and you go about your own business expecting your associates to follow. Whether they choose to is not your responsibility, as you don't need to baby sit professionals. You still just go about your own things like nothing happened despite their decision. Education is on the list of high priorities and you understand this is an ever advancing world and you will need to keep up. You will excel in careers which require exact precisions and measurements. Being spot on is important to you. Aligning your responsibilities with your cognitive thinking will come more naturally than most. This isn't a destructive aspect and generally produces positive characteristics. When influenced properly else where you may mature and develop responsibility earlier than your peers. If your friends are older than you it's because you prefer their maturity over others your own age.

Mercury trine Uranus

When these planets are positioned as such, you desire to be a free thinker who's allowed to do they please. You're very talkative and have an extremely unique mind set. Most of the time, you're quick to make decisions and often act out hastily. Mercury is the fastest of the personal planets and Uranus the speediest of the generational ones. These formations are what make us the different individuals we are. Curiosity, nervousness, and intelligence are all ruled by the planet Mercury. Uranus takes all of these and progresses them into the future, evolving them into something new. When influenced by house placement and other planets this aspect can make you completely rebellious, no matter what self-destruction is caused. Exact alignments with Uranus are always difficult to handle and hopefully this one is outside. Anything closer will intensify your anxiety and restlessness exponentially. Your curiousness into several subjects will need to be kept in check. Mercury is known for quickly dropping one topic for something new. Squirrels, butterflies, and rainbows can be constant distractions. Subjects of nature, science, and religion inspire deep thoughts and insights igniting your knowledge seeking mind. An unfortunate possibility with this aspect is a severe speech impediment or mental illness.

Mercury trine Neptune

Mercury alignments with Neptune inspire spirituality, creativity, and compassion. The trine will allow the energies between the two to flow more harmoniously than most. It may take a while, and you sometimes never do, but if you can harness your imagination the options are limitless. Neptune is one of the softest influences on Mercury which never produces hostility. You may not be the granola eating pacifist, but violence usually deters your attention. Many times this produces fanciful ideas that are just too hair brained too succeed. If you can't determine which are good and which are bad then expect many lackluster performances. Deep down you're brilliantly psychic and possess connections with multiple realms of existence. You may experience prophetic dreams and periods of waking intuition. Because your skills are subconsciously developed you don't understand them and won't know they're there until they pop up. As a child you probably spent more time daydreaming about recess than listening to the teacher. Your imagination is so vivid it often pervades into your reality without you even noticing it. You're constantly in and out of your own dreamland and if you're not careful then the results are often very disappointing. This inability to determine fact from

157

fiction makes you susceptible to fraud and deceit. It also causes you to fall behind in class because the teacher made several valid points while you were out chasing imaginary squirrels.

Mercury trine Pluto

Mercury's alignments with Pluto are usually very easy to handle. This is because Pluto acts as an intensifying catalyst with whatever it touches and Mercury influences your brain. Relationships between Mercury and Pluto make you very inquisitive and constantly seeking to gain deep insight into everything. Once your brain focuses in on something it's your only interest. This can spark your curiosity into the fields of psychology, medicine, or religion. Similar to its distant relative Neptune, Pluto has a very powerful connection with the mystical, magical, and unknown realms of the universe. With the help of Mercury and other outside forces this can make you exceptionally psychic and intuitive. Considerably better than squares or oppositions, the trine allows you to accept these talents more openly. Chances are you experience future telling dreams and conscious intuitions as well. All and all this is a good alignment which will help you get over the harsher ones. Although we only know a little about Pluto, we do know it's responsible for complete destruction and rebuilding. Sometimes when afflicted by Venus you become intensely attached and will suffer extreme abuses in order to maintain your grasp.

Venus trine ascendant

This is a wonderful aspect making you charming, generous, and socially graceful. Usually friendly and compassionate, others take liking to you quickly and you enjoy their affection. You have a flair for the dramatic, and enjoy talking about your affairs as well as those of others. Although generous in nature you don't frequently spend money on gifts, but when you do it's lavish and extravagant. Delivering the token in person is also important to you. The direct personal contact allows you to enjoy giving as much as they are receiving. You possess a refined and distinct style of art, music, and beauty, expressing this by displaying various artifacts throughout your home. The clothes you wear also reflect your personal style. Chances are you have more clothes gathering dust in the closed than you know what to do with. Relationships are vitally important and Venus can be obsessed with finding the perfect partner. She is a very needy planet that requires constant affection from loved ones. If someone isn't showing you the attention you feel you need your attention is easily swooned elsewhere. You may bounce around from one seemingly dysfunctional relationship to another until you find someone you can settle down with.

Venus trine Mars

Because Venus and Mars are such personal influences the relationship they form with each other is critical. Trines are amongst the best aspects planets can form and these two in harmony is good simply because they're not fighting. Usually this indicates you know how to integrate your ego into your relationships and get along with most everyone. You know how to function within the niche you choose to live in and express yourself freely. It gives you a good understanding of who you are and where you want to go in life. Their relationship with Saturn is important because it will show where you're responsibility is and how easy attaining it will be. Public speaking is easy because large groups don't scare you. You're extremely social and love the attention a spotlight provide. Most of the time you're level headed and calm, but just like everyone you have a breaking point. Unless extremely afflicted by other planets the aggressions of Mars are calmly soothed by the feminine touch of Venus. More often than not, your disposition is pleasant have and you look for the better qualities people have to offer encounter. Venus is always falling in love and Mars stimulates these tendencies. Your partner won't like you socially flirtatious nature and it will definitely cause problems. This is generally a good aspect allowing you to understand the difference between right and wrong.

159

Venus trine Jupiter

Hooray for you, these two planets are so wonderful they're known as the greater and lesser benefic. When separated by trine their energies are allowed to produce optimism and exuberance. In turn, this sooths the anger and hostilities created by harsher aspects in your chart. The biggest problem is the houses they occupy show where you're lazy, Venus' position, and lucky, Jupiter's position. You possess a calm, relaxed attitude allowing you to view things with an open mind. Because you naturally think everything will work out in the end, very rarely do you feel down and blue for long. With your charm and open heartedness, you can bring people out from sadness and depression without trying. Success in life seems to come easily because of your ability to meet people half way. You instinctually know when to make concessions in order to cooperate and maintain harmony. You're usually well behaved, and seek out the company of well-mannered and respectable associates. Because of this you usually establish a good reputation and public standing. Politics and social work may be fields where you find an interest and success.

Venus trine Saturn

Saturn is the stabilizing planet structuring their foundation in life. When in trine with Venus she adds a feminine touch with her grace and style. The most prominent need is your desire to have a well formed and structured relationship with everyone. All your personal contacts need to fit into their specifically determined place, and when they don't you get into a tizzy. First off, you're hesitant to warm up to random strangers and cautiously introduce yourself after they have approached you. Second, you're optimistic and reasonable, and you know who to turn to when you need advice or help. Your childhood years prepared you to accept the self-discipline and responsibly needed for success. With the Moon's influence sometimes this indicates an overly strict mother or an overly passive father. You succeed because you know how fulfill the needs of others while maintaining your own as well.

Whatever path you set for yourself straying from your norm will be difficult. It's best you to just stick to the rules. The clubs and social circles you belong to will reflect your refined personality. You will also hold office and be a prominent member of these clubs. In romantic relationships you are devoted and loyal, expecting your partner to be the same. Staying between the framework of a normal relationship will be best for you.

Venus trine Uranus

Alignments with Uranus are always difficult to handle, but when aspecting Uranus, it's best to have a trine or sextile. This relatively harmonious planetary relationship allows you to be unusually cheerful despite all the trials that life may throw you. You love forming relationships with interesting characters and adore those who are exceptionally unique. The clothes you wear, friends you have, and interests you acquire are all direct reflections of your individual personality and your desire for the unusual. This doesn't mean you are a face painting zombie freak, but style and manner are both important to you. You may also be a zombie freak. Venus represents all our relationships, whether it's business, romantic, or casual, and how we deal with the world is directed by her. Uranus is rebellious and adventurous, which in turn can make you overly controlling about everything. No matter what the relationship your freedom is exceptionally important to you. If you feel unnecessarily restricted your behavior becomes inappropriate and rash. Fortunately trines are usually positive and can make you optimistic about the future even when you're down. There may even be a definite interest in the occult and darker side of world religion. If positioned in the third or ninth houses this can indicate travel to unusual places. You are well adept of self-control, because of this positive attribute you will probably marry well. You expect a lot out of your partner and are willing to do everything expected of you. In your profession you are well suited for authority and management.

Venus trine Neptune

Venus and Neptune are both very artistic inspire creativity. The major problem with this aspect is neither planet possesses much aggression. Both are easily swayed by outside forces, making you dreamy, fanciful, and ignoring anything you see as bad. If you're not careful this can make you completely deluded to the abuses you endure through life. When your dreams and reality can't be separated mistakes are made and dysfunction occurs. In no way should this be interpreted as a bad aspect, just be aware that it can go sour with afflictions elsewhere. Your great appreciation of art, music, and theater shouldn't be ignored. If you can direct your imagination properly this is an excellent modifying alignment to go along with a driver. Because you can see the beauty and innovation behind everything you're able to take the better aspects of multiple things and conglomerate them into one. Even if it's as simple as cooking or basic home projects, you enjoy the unique and interesting things in life. You have an endearing quality that allows you to accept the failures of others as long as they are honestly trying. Neptune also induces interests into the occult and mystical. If you choose a path of spirituality, time your meditations and contacts with higher realms to this trine and find magnificent results. Talented astrologers can tell you when the full and new Moons will ignite the inner spirits who contact your soul. Psychic visions, telepathic messages, and vivid dreams will also be induced by progressive planetary transits.

Venus trine Pluto

With Venus and Pluto forming this relationship you seek out the fullest emotional and creative experiences that love can bring. You believe there are spiritual benefits from your personal contacts and social affairs. This can make you very involved in church or community activities. Despite your intense desire for the higher consciousness within the universe, you may suppress your creative potential until you find that someone you can truly open up to. Your romantic partner will bring out the best in you. Once you fall in love you do so deeply and passionately, feeling the happiest in committed relationships. You derive person and emotional security

162

when you can not only develop a plutonic friendship but a spiritual connection as well. It's entirely possible you gain a high position within a religious sect. You enjoy teaching others how morals and values can enrich their lives. This influence can also make you exceptionally artistic. You should pursue and interests in music, theater, or the arts. At its best your spiritual connection to the outer world manifests itself in this world in the form of music or art. The obsession to express your creative side shouldn't be restricted.

Mars trine ascendant

When Mars is positively aspecting your ascendant it makes you assertive and athletic. The trine allows you to direct your efforts and energies towards prosperous outlets. Others are inspired by your enthusiasm, and rally around you to support your endeavors. When you're forced to think on your own you can do so with ease. Despite all the negativities aspects Mars can produce, this is one of the easiest to handle. Remember Mars always needs somewhere to go and something to do. He's also a sore loser and will just pack up his stuff and leave when he knows he can't win. Sometimes you succeed simply because you surround yourself with competition you can dominate. Being completely independent is extremely important to you, and you should generally be left on your own. Sometimes the trine can indicate negative energies are flowing freely. If Mars is heavily afflicted by Saturn or Uranus you can be very angry and violent. Your volatile temper might get you into trouble sometimes. Going crazy with your check every payday will lead to financial troubles. Although you may not be athletically inclined you will still enjoy the competitive nature of sports.

Mars trine Jupiter

This aspect between Mars and Jupiter indicates you can direct your energies in a well-organized manner. Not only does this blend your physical energy in a positive way it also allows you to focus mental energy on productive things. You create legitimate, attainable goals and have the determination to see them through. However, when the challenge seems unimportant or useless you couldn't care less. When you don't care about something, you really don't care at all. Physical strength is one of your assets and you can work long hours of hard labor. Competitive and athletic, sports or activities where you can prove your abilities will be important outlets to release your pent up aggression. This aspect also makes the impulses in your brain stronger and faster than others. The electric nerves move too fast most times and this causes you to make quick, rash, and most times inaccurate decisions. You get by because your intuitive nature allows you to eventually make the right move at the right time, and luck will seem to play a factor at just the right time. You have an easy come easy go attitude sometimes and that will cause you to spend more money than you should. Gambling, drugs and addictions can also be enhanced by this aspect. This is a driver aspect that can be wonderfully used when modified by Moon or Venus contacts. House placement will be a great direction as to where this energy should be focused.

Mars trine Saturn

Mars and Saturn are known as the Two Malefics and aren't given that name without reason. Even trines will produce an intense energy which can really only be described by experience. Generally speaking this indicates your ability to use your resources responsibly. This is definitely a driver aspect producing action, aggression, and determination. The house placement of these two will show where you direct your attention most productively. These are two of the slower moving personal planets, and their alignments shouldn't be taken lightly. Positive aspects from Mercury can make you brilliantly smart. If this occurs in the air signs of Gemini, Libra, and Aquarius, you can expect this aptitude as well. The trine is one of the most opportune alignments these two can have, and hopefully you use this energy well. You naturally understand harsh feelings can lead to further problems when not attended to. You're hard working and determined to do

164

whatever you want. Even if you get involved in the criminal way of life, you may have a long and luxurious career dealing whatever drugs you choose. The nature of Mars constantly desires more and Saturn will restrict this into only a few interests. This is a great building block because it shows a good balance between what needs to get done and how to finish the project.

Mars trine Uranus

Other than Saturn, Uranus is the most problematic planet for Mars. Difficulties are created because the rebelliousness aroused stirs up an independent spirit who must strike out on something alone. Fortunately, if these two have to be in aspect, the trine is one of the best. This allows you do accept your unique personality in ways that are somewhat productive to society. Because you tend to find an abstract niche to click in with, only a few will accept you and there will definitely be some haters along your way. Despite the fact the trine is associated with positive energy sometimes this only indicates the stubborn characteristics of each planet are there. Both planets refuse to listen to reason, and there's no sense trying to teach you until you want to learn. Only bumps and bruises will get your attention, and even then you make the same mistake thinking you were right the first time. Your innovative brilliance shows you're intelligent, but only after you have beaten yourself up in the process. These two planets are trouble makers, one throws gas on the fire the other had started. Sometimes you can be the highly technical surgeon, others the ingenious hill billy. You may be a redneck, but your whiskey still and chicken coop are top notch, and the envy of your toothless friends.

Mars trine Neptune

Aspects with Mars aren't always easy to handle, but the soothing effects of Neptune can calm down outside forces. Usually, when Mars and Neptune form a trine it indicates you successfully integrate your aggressive nature with your social responsibilities. Unless there are serious afflictions elsewhere you should possess a firm grasp where your ideas can take you. You're extremely complex imagination will give you vivid, sometimes psychic, dreams. If you can turn these visions into an actual reality then you may find great success in theater arts, music, or painting. Neptune is the ultimate humanitarian and the assertions from Mars may spark your interest towards relief efforts, or environmental clean-up. There's a driving ambition for you to serve and help others, especially those who are completely unable to defend themselves. This can also lead to issues in the work place because you feel you're accomplishing larger amounts than your co-workers when you're actually not. At its worst this makes you completely delusional as to how your actions will affect reality. When heavily afflicted, this can make you a career criminal who can't stay out of jail. Call the prison and reserve yourself a cell.

Mars trine Pluto

Mars and Pluto aligned like this indicates you have a strong drive to accomplish your goals productively. When you direct your ambitions towards the house placement of the planets you successfully complete what you start. You're a natural problem solver because your psychic abilities allow you to understand things you know nothing about. Many times this creates problems in the classroom because you seem to already know what the teacher is showing you. Chances are you're a C average homework student, but a straight A test taker. You can excel at activities which require long periods of stamina and endurance provided there is support from the other planets. Sometimes this can indicate you become passionate about the seedy underworld of life and criminal activities are products of both planets. Generally, this is a great starting point and you're naturally drawn towards what you will succeed in. Pluto is the least known of the planets, but the intense passions have definitely been noticed. If the aspect is closer than five degrees it becomes exponentially more volatile. Careers in medicine and psychology can prove very satisfying. Your athleticism increases as this aspect grows closer, and if it's within two degrees you might be a professional athlete. The passionate lust may also indicate you have multiple children with multiple

166

partners.

Jupiter trine ascendant

Very rarely does Jupiter produce negative energy, and even
rarer does it happen when a trine is involved. In fact, this can be so
overpoweringly wonderful you poop nothing but sunshine and
rainbows. This is one of the aspects relieving the stresses caused
by other bad aspects. Basically, you have a wonderful outlook on
life because you know everything ends up for the best. Always
expecting to succeed, when you fail it disappoints you greatly.
Sometimes it inspires you to try harder. You're only depressed for
a little while and bounce back quickly getting back into your
normal groove. You understand personal effort will result in
personal success. This attitude inspires you think highly about
achieving greatness. Because you have such a pleasant demeanor
your supervisors appreciate you more than you think. Every aspect
has its down side. This one can make you lazy, over indulgent, and
arrogant. Many people born with this have an advantageous
childhood. Sometimes they do well with it, sometimes not. If
properly aspected by other planets this can make you brilliantly
smart. Self-control along with hard work and determination will
guarantee success in any field you choose. This can also indicate a
luxurious life, full of amenities.

Jupiter trine Saturn

With a trine between Jupiter and Saturn you easily recognize
the lessons learned you're your experiences throughout life.
You're usually responsible and have respect for the laws and
regulations set before you. The goals you place on yourself are
usually well within the limits of your capabilities and success is
never a surprise. Whatever profession you choose you'll be able to
work well by yourself or within a group. There is a clear concise
way in which you conduct your business. You're straight forward
and could care less about trivial details. Concerned with your
contribution to society, you strive to make your environment a
better place for everything, not just everyone. This is one of the

167

best structure aspects for the Sun, Moon, and other planets to build upon. If Neptune is involved in any way there will be an interest with environmental preservation activities. Jupiter is known as the greater benefic and Saturn is the greater malefic, with these two planets working in accord you will have a good understanding of not only what you care to do with your life, but how to get there as well. This biggest confliction between the two is Jupiter's flamboyance, while Saturn wishes to remain back stage with little or no recognition.

Jupiter trine Uranus

A trine between Jupiter and Uranus indicates you have the ability to use your vast intelligence productively. This is a slower forming alignment that isn't felt by everyone born under it. In particular this can make you brilliantly smart and some of the greatest scientists ever will be produced by this. Jupiter is a spiritually expansive planet who will raise your consciousness into a new level. You're unconsciously alert for any mental challenge, and never shy away from a chance to learn something new or interesting. Your unusual philosophical views will question which ever religious dogma you were taught, if any. The belief system you develop is going be completely different than those of your parents. In business and adventure you take risks that most wouldn't touch with a ten foot pole. You can be the eternal optimist and your spirit will never break, or believe it can fail. Although trines are generally good aspects, Uranus is rebellious and known for acting crazy. Unfortunately, it's possible that you experience a massive catastrophe. This will be to help you grow into a stronger and better person. This can also indicate an unusual monetary winning or inheritance. Especially if placed in the fifth or eighth houses.

Jupiter trine Neptune

Trines between these two spiritual and intellectual giants are among the best in astrology. The only bad part is not everyone gets to feel their energy, and even fewer put it to good use. Reason

168

being, Jupiter is lazy and so is Neptune. Despite the fact you have all sorts of creative inspiration, unless you possess fire elsewhere, most ideas never leave the boarding station. All the trine does is allow these two to function in a proper manner. As one of the generational planets, Neptune always needs a close contact to your ascendant to in order to emphasize its influence, and the house placement is just as important. In two basic terms Jupiter equals ultimate expansion and Neptune is unconditional love. You have a deep understanding of the spiritual world and are extremely psychic. Although you maintain your beliefs firmly you're not opposed to listening to others. Everything produces knowledge if you know where to look. You're open minded and fair, believing everyone has a right to their own opinion. This will lead to in depth discussions about higher realms of the universe. You recognize life on Earth is only temporary and humans are merely a speck amongst the cosmos. Activism within environmental groups focused on cleaning up and repairing the damages caused by past generations will be started by those inspired by this. Interests in surgery and more advanced forms of science and technology will suit you well. You will change the world if you can get your focus and determination pointed in the proper direction. The biggest nuisance will be you inability to see your over inflated ego. Some individuals with this will be pompous and very arrogant.

Jupiter trine Pluto

Because Jupiter is a slow moving personal planet, and Pluto is the slowest of all, their aspects are semi generational and require an alignment with your ascendant in order to reach their fullest potential. The trine allows positive energies from both planets to flow in harmony. This is one of the best relationships they can have, and wonderful things will be produced. Jupiter is the planet of higher philosophy, religion, and conscious progression who takes the obsessions of Pluto and puts them to good use. The intellectual expansion here produces a fascination into higher realms of universe and deeper into human life. Knowing only a little about something isn't good enough for you. You require

169

obtaining as much information as you can about someone or something. Optimism, flamboyancy, and the ability to bounce back from extreme adversity are all qualities this aspect produces as well. The worst scenario causes you to over exaggerate your opinions and abilities. Because you think so highly of yourself when trying something new you instantly think you're the champ. Unfortunately this can indicate a massive atrocity occurs in your early years. If this is the case it's only to teach you lessons not everyone has to learn. Because of the abuses you endured in your early years will teach you how to cope with grief, anger, and many other negative emotions your torments created. Once you put the past behind you helping others find their path will give you great personal satisfaction. Counseling or social service work should be considered as professions.

Saturn trine ascendant

Your ascendant is the most powerful point in your natal chart, and when Saturn is aligning with it you're instilled with determination and responsibility. Trines and sextiles are the two most positive aspects planets can form and the stability from Saturn is greatly appreciated. This formation allows the functional qualities of Saturn to project them throughout your character. If it takes you a while to catch on to things don't be discouraged, this is merely the reserved and cautiousness from Saturn. Although this is a usually pleasant aspect one downside to this is the depression and feelings of inadequacies this will sometimes cause. As a child you may have felt like an outcast because you lacked interest in the childish games of your classmates. If you isolated yourself in your early years it will be difficult to break away from these tendencies. Consider having older friends. Because you were able to accept responsibility at an earlier age this gave you the opportunity to develop your skills and gain knowledge sooner than your peers. This gives you a distinct advantage in competition because you're starting ahead of the pack. Even if your parents weren't able to give you all the advantages your friends had you still use what little you have effectively. Whether it be information, money, or physical possessions you will usually find a way to get the most out of everything.

Saturn trine Uranus

Although their alignments are very powerful, they need to form a relationship with your ascendant in order for the energies to be released. With Saturn in trine to Uranus you learn your life lessons easily and naturally acquire the discipline needed to succeed. You're always thinking about your future and how your present actions are influencing it. Even though you enjoy your material possessions you have an ability to detach yourself from them and simply see them as things. What you are stubborn about will be the methods you take. Saturn never strays from the proven path and Uranus strips naked before running wildly through the bushes. Naturally they have constant conflictions when trying to cooperate. You would rather make changes to the current plan then come up with a completely new one. You clearly see how your innovative and progressive ideas will benefit society and have difficulties when others don't share your vision. Quite often this indicates you have an unusual job or injury. Leading by example others will readily accept your authority because you can assert it without being arrogant and condescending. You hold yourself in high esteem and want others to remember you for your contributions to society and concern for others. Best of all it can show you appreciate the eccentricity of your father. His uniqueness brightens your day because it distinguishes him from others.

Saturn trine Neptune

Alignments between Saturn and Neptune are infrequent and can be very tricky when determining the influence each individual feels. Because the trine is a very positive aspect the qualities of both planets are usually in check and functioning properly. When influenced negatively this aspect makes you completely confused and diluted about most areas of your life. Neptune trines make you fanciful and dreamy. If these energies are allowed to run loose you may live off in dream land and refuse to accept reality. Saturn's

171

prominence will make it impossible to focus on more things than one. Because you enjoy escaping the realities you're bound to, drugs and alcohol may play a distinct role for you. If positively influenced you may find success in a career involving music, art, or theater. The psychic and intuitive abilities this aspect generates can make you very sensitive and receptive to your environment. You pick up on the subtle, subconscious signals that we all project. Sign and house placement will determine how fast and strong these signals are received. There is a direct link between your spiritual energy and the magical realm of Neptune. Just as Neptune is a generational planet, aspects formed are also generational. Those with this in their charts will take a responsibility for cleaning up the mess caused by the previous square. Environmental and humanitarian groups will be established in record number. If there is a driving fire from other parts of your chart you may establish on of these environmental endeavors. Generally you will like to stay behind the scenes, letting others have the spotlight.

Saturn trine Pluto

Trines between Saturn and Pluto occur for a moderate duration of time, at odd intervals apart. Like all alignments between Saturn and a generational planet, the relationship with your ascendant will be vital in projecting their power. The trine between these two can be one of the most productive of all. When positively influenced, this aspect will give you the ability to concentrate for long durations of time. Your professional goals are extremely ambitious and Pluto's obsession will seep its way into your career. As with all aspects with Pluto the other negative effects are possessiveness and jealousy. House placement is where you will show the most ambition to succeed. This will cause severely psychotic behavioral patterns for a few individuals. Not everyone born under this becomes an outstand citizen. Some will direct their energy into negative endeavors and turn into criminals. You can be manipulative and not always take the most honest route to the top. Obsessions with power and control are almost always produced by Pluto. For the most part, this aspect allows

172

you to accept large amounts of responsibility needed for large projects. Remember that Saturn is the structuring force giving us blocks to build with, and Pluto is the most intense of the planets. Their combination always makes you intent on productivity. Meaning you always need to see results from anything you do.

Uranus trine ascendant

When planets are influencing your ascendant you prominently display the traits of that planet throughout your personality. When that planet is Uranus, it makes you eccentric, original, and completely unique. It's pertinent you're allowed to blaze you own path, because when restricted you rebel hastily and most times immaturely. You enjoy expressing your creativity and have a flair for the innovative. Things that are normal and bland have none of your interest, and you crave the excitement only originality can produce. The potentials for your creativity and imagination are limitless. The only thing possibly restricting you is the funds necessary to exploit your imagination as well as finding proper direction. Because you generally refuse to listen to others you may find it difficult to cooperate within the small groups which are essential for growth and success. This can also produce nervous, highly anxious, sometimes obsessive behavior. As a child you were probably quite a trouble maker, or at least very restless. You're insatiously curious, and everything will interest you. From the little bug crawling on the floor to the blue water in the bathroom toilet, everything can be used as a toy, and usually is, right before it goes into your mouth. You don't seem to care about what others are doing as long as it doesn't affect your freedom. Rules and schedules will get tiresome and boring after a while, try not to get caught up in a routine.

Uranus trine Neptune
(1939-1947) (2048-2055)

Aspects between Uranus and Neptune are among the slowest moving and longest lasting in astrology. They occur so infrequently and affect so many millions their influences aren't felt

173

by everyone. This will next happen when Uranus is in Virgo and Neptune is in Taurus during the mid 2000's. Alone it represents your attraction to independent creativity. Aspecting other planets will allow you to express your ideas in a functional manner. You're able to imagine things on your own and often the fantasyland create invades into reality. You The trine indicates you have an independent imagination and you know how to use it more effectively than others. You accept you're creatively unique and when put to good use your talents separate you from the crowd.

Uranus trine Pluto
(2023-2027)

Last forming in the early 1920's then again a century later in 2023, this is a slow aspect which affects each individual extremely differently. Not everyone feels the energies released, and one or both planets need a prominent alignment with your ascendant to fully experience it. Pluto is the champion of ultimate obsession and Uranus is the inspired genius. The trine usually indicates a time of prosperity where humanity corrects many of its mistakes perpetuated during the previous square. Since Pluto's discovery in 1930, we have yet to know an actual trine is forming by these distant planets. Occurring during the middle 2020's we can only guess what influence this will bring. I assume by then space aliens will make themselves known and ghosts will be shortly behind. This is a long lasting aspect which forms of and on for around three years. Because of the slow moving nature of these two this alignment will next occur when Uranus is along the cusp of Taurus and Gemini, and Pluto is between Capricorn and Aquarius. Trines generally release positive energy and most of those born under this sign will be much more emotionally stable than those born with the square between the two. Uranus is definitely too unpredictable to forecast accurately and Pluto hasn't even been known about for even a century yet. During their transit of the Earth signs each plant tuned the psyche of humanity towards the holistic and natural aspects of the universe. Now as they progress into the more scientific air signs we will discover how to integrate technology

174

into the metaphysical sciences. Hopefully this means spirituality and science can bond together with astrology and astronomy holding hands like before the telescope.

Neptune trine ascendant

A trine between Neptune to your ascendant possesses you with an extreme sensitivity which causes you to be unsatisfied and unrealistic towards life. Because you become so deeply attached to things you're disappointed when others don't feel the same. Your emotions are intense, and influences from the Moon or Venus can make them fluctuate dramatically. Neptune is notorious for confusing you and diluting your judgment. The fantasies you get lost in seem so realistic you can't always decipher fact from fiction. Whether you admit it or not you're a constant dreamer and enjoy spending time in realities elsewhere. If you're not careful, this can lead you into severe drug or alcohol abuse. You're a complete romanticist at heart and are always seeking the ideal relationship. Sometimes you feel you must be the one to make the most concessions in order to get along. This can perpetuate into several abusive relationships whether it be professional, romantic, or otherwise. You have a vivid imagination and are extremely creative. If you can use your negative emotions properly you may an outlet in the theater arts, creative design, or music. When you can bring your abilities into the spotlight, the warmth and acceptance from the masses will bring personal satisfaction. All generational planets need an aspect with the ascendant, and although the conjunction is the most powerful, the trine is one of the most wonderful.

Neptune trine Pluto

If you have Neptune forming a trine with Pluto you are dead and will need to contact someone on Earth through telepathic means.

Pluto trine ascendant

Contact with your ascendant is what allows Pluto to

175

accentuate its influences within your personality. Fortunately for you the trine is one of the best aspects you can have, and Pluto's destructive forces are usually calmed down by this mellow relationship. The obsessive properties of Pluto are generally directed into positive outlets and you bounce back from adversity easier than most. When a trine is formed it gives you an infinite source of energy to draw on when using your creative abilities. There is nothing you can't accomplish once you set your mind to it, and nothing will keep you down for long. This doesn't mean everything will be handed to you effortlessly, but whatever the pitfall you will get up and try your best again. No matter what negative or traumatic experiences you may have in your past you can see through them and focus on the positive personal growth you receive from it. You're eager to establish a secure future for yourself and family. This may indicate that you marry and start a family later in life once you have a firm foundation in place. As you instinctually recognize you failings and shortcomings, you effectively identify and reform anything that is no longer useful or productive. Unfortunately this may also indicate a catastrophic tragedy which you must pull yourself through. Probably associated with death you may lose a loved one unexpectedly and entirely too soon.

Quincunx/Inconjunction

Matthew 24:29
Immediately after the tribulation of those days the Sun will be darkened and the Moon will not give its light. The stars will fall from heaven, and the powers of the heavens will be shaken.

150 degrees apart, planets form the quincunx or also confusingly called the inconjunction. I have found this alignment very similar to the 135 degree separation called the sesquiquadrate and have deemed the two Bigfoot (quincunx), and Sasquatch (sesquiquadrate). These aspects produce confusion about whether

to be good or bad. Both are easily influenced and will swing whichever way the other planets dictate. Bigfoot is the midpoint between the trine and opposition, while Sasquatch is the midpoint between the trine and quincunx. Of all the major aspects this is the weakest and easiest for other planets to mold. This leads me to use a smaller orb of three degrees, expanding to five if one of the planets is in a ruling or exalting sign or house. Many times they indicate the outside forces causing problems in your life.

Sun quincunx Ascendant

The biggest problem caused by this aspect is your inability to integrate your spirit into your personality. Negativities are felt because the quincunx represents the stressful energies between the free flowing trine, and the problematic attraction of the opposite. You never do anything unless you can go all in and give one hundred percent effort, but finding that niche just doesn't seem to happen. Desperately seeking approval, you're determined to be known for your accomplishments throughout the community. If you're forced to work behind the scenes you eventually develop a secret desire for the spotlight. As you realize what you do well and what you do not, you eventually lose interest in anything which doesn't come naturally. Dedication is never an issue once you do find where you belong. When the Sun aspects your ascendant it shows how easily the rest of the energy throughout the chart meshes with your personality. Unfortunately the quincunx is a dysfunctional flow between the two. You express yourself in ways that don't conform to the norms of accepted society. Most of the time one of two things will happen. You're either normal, and don't know where you want to fit into the responsible side of society. Or, you accept your unique personality, and find your niche amongst fellow misfits and oddballs.

Sun quincunx Moon

A quincunx between the Sun and the Moon creates emotional insecurities and uneasiness relating to others. The

177

resulting stress causes you to lash out inappropriately, taking out the pent up frustrations on undeserving loved ones. You desire to hold on to past friendships and relationships so desperately you still make concessions even after someone has departed. You feel obligated to bend over backwards yet never force others to do the same. Many times you don't realize your own self-worth and settle for a life of servitude. Even though you're usually smarter than those you serve. You're extremely compassionate and often fail to recognize the importance of your own personal needs. Positively, your ability to listen and learn from other people allows you to apply their insights productively. If you can figure out how to not take slight comments too personally you won't get into useless arguments. This isn't the worst relationship between these two, but it definitely isn't the best. Part of the problem is it's so easily influenced by the other planets. Positive aspects will show where your compassion can be put to good use, while bad aspects indicate you're a pushover who endures excessive abuses.

Sun quincunx Mars

This planetary positioning is similar to the square, and shows severe discord within everything you do. Nothing ever flows as smoothly as planned, and the effects are exceptionally aggravating. Although you're eager to show your abilities, you continually do so to the wrong people and at the wrong times. Your spirit doesn't know where to direct your energy so it either dissipates, or is used inefficiently. The ineffective changes you try to make only fuels your psychological fires. When you do the same things over and over again you actually expect different results and are dismayed when the same thing happens. Disappointed from your perceived failure, you become irritable and angry, lashing out inappropriately. Inherently distressed with constant problems, you consistently bring on the turmoil yourself. Because of this you will endure extreme abuses from others in order to prove your loyalty and worth. You want others to remember you for your accomplishments and what you have done for them, yet you can't seem to get out of your selfish desires. Try putting your ego aside

178

and become a great number two guy.

Sun quincunx Jupiter

This alignment almost always infuses confusion and uncertainty into your abilities, and your confidence is hindered because of it. In turn, you over compensate this lack of security with aggression and boldness. No matter how powerful you appear on the outside deep down you're constantly reevaluating yourself, your possessions, and your philosophies. Because of this inferiority you're determined to prove your adequacies to others, welcoming competition. Jupiter has a tendency to over inflate itself and your ego may follow suit. Many times your mind will think you're more capable than you actually are. When your big ideas don't come through it's usually because you've over-estimated the time requirements and resources needed. It's through the praise and approval of your associates in which you find personal security. You can be sensitive to criticism and over react when someone subtly hints at it. Education is important and even though you may not have enough finances available, you still find a way to educate yourself. In the professional world you advance your career partly because you take on the responsibilities of others. Make sure you get credit for your hard work and effort, don't allow others to take your spotlight. In your occupation you fall into a role of are a refined specialist. Focusing and maximizing efficiency in one particular area. Sometimes this can indicate difficulties getting the training you need to meet your own expectations.

Sun quincunx Saturn

This aspect usually indicates you're mostly careless about your health and personal well-being. Working under someone else's command isn't very easy for you. However there are always exceptions when modified by other planets. It can also turn you into a stickler for the rules, maintaining the strictest of diets and most stringent health regiments. Expect the second option if Virgo or the sixth house is involved. On a every level you have the inability to say no when someone asks for help, and deeply resent

179

it when your services are repeatedly asked for. It's most likely during your childhood you took on more of the daily tasks than your siblings then cried about how much more you do. People who are over aggressive and boisterous don't appeal to you. It's the subtle fear about others authority causing you to shy away from those who are brash. When you find a job chances are you accept work where there is little room for advancement. Getting stuck in the ruts of work will be a running theme throughout your life. This isn't because you're incapable, you're just not as aggressive as your competitors and they get the upper hand. As you strive for personal recognition and significance you experience serious setbacks unless you can detach yourself from others support and learn to be self-sufficient. Don't look past completion of whatever you choose to do. Future tripping will only distract you and hamper your personal progress. Also remember not to compare your success with that of others, and accept the loss when you try your best.

Sun quincunx Uranus

This aspect between the Sun and Uranus indicates you frequently deprive yourself by caving into other people's demands. You're kind of pushover and collapse when overly strained. Hopefully you have stabilizing aspects from Jupiter or Saturn to give you a sense of self-worth. You have to be careful not getting trapped by others telling you you're the only one who can help. When the Sun alignment with Uranus they also produce rebelliousness, eccentricity, and anxiousness. The influence from other planets as well as house placement will be important when determining just where you excessive energies are directed. Remember everyone is crazy in their own individual way. In the professional world you will have to avoid your co-workers placing their assignments on you. You may get so caught up doing the work for others that you fail to complete your own projects. Make sure your associates don't get the credit you have earned and deserve. You enjoy your freedom and must be left to march at the beat of your own drum. When your freedoms are denied you will react intensely. You will find your life is filled with unusual events, and people. Things happen to you that just don't seem to happen to others. This is most definitely a driver aspect that will need calming relationships with other planets. If you're completely nuts and your life is in shambles this alignment can be a reason why.

Sun quincunx Neptune

Many times this aspect makes you consider your responsibilities and problems are more important than others. You allow dysfunctional people into your life thinking they will solve your issues for you, and refuse to accept when they can't. As you casually turn your back to your problems it simply causes you to sink deeper into your quicksand. You're attracted to problematic individuals, and many of your relationships will end in disappointment. Getting what you want is important, but you just don't know what you want. Make sure you don't turn into a dumping ground for the negativity of others. You will experience drama in your work place because of your inability to avoid useless gossip. Until you choose to address this issue you will continually have others invading your personal life. Your interest into the affairs of others has consequences. It's difficult for you to grasp religious or spiritual concepts. You see the greater picture out there, but your ever expanding mind realizes no matter how advanced you think you are, in reality, humans are tiny specks of water, walking on a tiny speck of dirt, way out in some dark universe. This aspect also indicates creativity and psychic ability. If you develop your talents you can be a very talented artist, musician, or writer.

Sun quincunx Pluto

With this aspect you accept responsibility others avoid then resent it bitterly when you produce more than them. Eventually everyone starts expecting you to take on their endeavors then become surprised when you decline. Your over emphasis on superficial matters will only bog you down. It will be necessary to establish boundaries with how far you intrude into the lives of others, as well as how far they are let into yours. This can also lead to an attraction into the religious, occult, and mystical. Pluto is ruler of the underworld causing complete and total chaos to those with him dominant in their charts. Remember that anything and everything will be modified and this shouldn't be taken as a completely harsh aspect. Pluto gives you the ability to bounce back from extreme adversities and rise up from total destruction. Only after being completely removed can something else be built in its place. One problem is you must go through complete hell to get there. It isn't easy hitting ground zero and resurrecting something amazing is entirely possible. If you can us your inferiorities as a driver you can achieve greatness in many areas. This can also make responsibility difficult. You will have to accept your duties at work and around home before any happiness can be achieved.

Moon quincunx ascendant

With the Moon aspecting your ascendant like this you're so determined to be helpful that you let others abuse you over and over again. You can't say no and the process continues to repeat itself over and over again. Emotionally, you're extremely vulnerable and easily deceived. You lack the ability to separate those who do deserve your attention from those who don't. Because you're so eager to serve the needs of others you make for an exceptional employee. You're able to compensate for your lack of education with your natural ability to adapt to your environment. You're very receptive to not only the physical needs of others, but their emotional needs as well. You absorb the energy of the room easily and must be careful to get into the mob mentality. Be careful not to buckle under peer pressure as well. Many times it's extremely difficult for you to correctly identify your emotions. What's even more strenuous is properly displaying them towards the public. Your relationship issues are construed from the mixed signals you send your loved ones. Because you feel one way but act nearly the opposite they in turn react inappropriately as well. This aspect is easily influenced and the alignments with other planets will definitely modify this. The houses the planets are positioned in are where you will be the most secure and attached to.

Moon quincunx Mercury

When the Moon and Mercury are positioned like this it causes emotional and psychological tension. The biggest malfunction is the difficulty separating your emotions from your intellect. This makes rational thinking seemingly impossible. You're mind is constantly cycling through your feelings, allowing them to dictate your actions. The inability to stop causes your emotions to spin so fast and out of control you cannot rationalize how your actions are responding. The messages you send don't always coincide with how you're feeling and the confusions follow suit. As you inject feelings instead of facts your view becomes clouded and unreasonable. You detect criticism where none was intended and respond abrasively and possibly violently. Even as guilt sets in for your inappropriate behavior you still repeat the negative actions that got you there in the first place. This vicious cycle repeats itself over and over, causing severe migraines or nervous breakdowns. Also adding to your strife is the inability to accurately assess and express your emotions to others. Although you may talk about personal issues with others, many times you realize it's the problems of others you're conversing about. Focus on yourself once in a while with quiet prayer and meditation. This should relax your excess psychological stress. This aspect will also add problems relating to your mothers and females as well.

Moon quincunx Venus

This aspect usually indicates you're submissive to others and continually put their needs above yours, especially within your relationships with women. You make large concessions to those you feel obligated to and are in turn get used as a door mat for walking on. Both the Moon and Venus are emotional planets which are easily influenced. The discord produced by this separation causes intense fluctuations and you'll experience

183

extreme ups and downs. Because these two are so dependent on others when they align like this their dependency can be magnified. You desperately seek approval of and take on others responsibility as if it were yours. This is one of the more difficult relationships between the Moon and Venus. The biggest problem you have is integrating your emotions into your relationship. Because you don't truly know how you feel about someone if they're a shitbag you don't realize it until it's too late. If there are no stabilizing aspects elsewhere you're an emotional train wreck, always nearing a crash. The natural reaction to intense situations is usually unbalanced, and establishing your emotional priorities needs to be high on your to do list. Once you figure out your feelings the proper behavior will follow. Helping other is difficult because you overextend your resources leaving nothing for yourself. When you decide to help others make it crystal clear what your role is along their intentions. Don't rush into any binding agreements without reading the fine print below the dotted line. Many times you will loan things to others, never to see them again.

Moon quincunx Mars

This alignment between the Moon and Mars causes a lack of self-control when expressing your feelings. The conceited aggressions of Mars don't get along with the nurturing characteristics of the Moon. They basically tear you apart between what you want for yourself, and what you can spare for others. You need to be consciously aware about respecting personal boundaries and acknowledging the emotions of others. Thinking your opinion will always help the situation, you forcefully put yourself into the affairs of others. This obviously causes associates to become offended by your aggressive nature. Chances are you learned your bad habits from your mother and many times this shows that she frequently crosses your boundaries. She sticks her nose into your business when you want to be left alone and you take it out into the world around you. It's possible you were a trouble maker as a kid and she had to constantly supervise you.

184

Now that you're an adult, she has issues letting you go. Not sure when to run away or fight you may end up like a deer in the headlights seemingly hypnotized until impact. This is one of the more stressful aspects the Moon can form with Mars. Fortunately it's easily modified by the other planets. Their condition will usually dictate whether this alignment turns sour.

Moon quincunx Jupiter

This planetary alignment causes you to become overly sensitive and underestimate your abilities. Jupiter expands your emotions in such a confusing way that you compensate by over reacting and being too enthusiastic. It's difficult for you to control your emotions because you experience such drastic fluctuations. When you don't know how respond you do so in a loud and dramatic fashion thinking that can stimulate your courage. It won't matter if you're babbling a bunch of nonsense as long as you can hear yourself talking. No alignment with Jupiter can be considered bad but, this aspect's biggest problem is it won't help ease any tension the other planets are causing. Both the Moon and Jupiter provide hope when things are down. The quincunx doesn't allow them to work synergistically and it pops that little bubble of happiness. Your personal insecurities cause you to take on the basic needs of others hoping it will distract you from your own problems. When you allow your family to constantly take advantage of you once you finally stand up for yourself they think you're mad at them. After all material and physical resources are consumed you're left with nothing for yourself. As you mature you understand there's a significant amount to learn, but just can't seem to establish a concrete belief system. Every time you think you've solved something, life changes completely. You will continue to spiral round and round in this painful process until you can establish control between your intellect and emotions. You will definitely need to find activities outside your occupation. If not, you will just set in a standard routine of get up, go to work, come home. The best thing about this aspect is the fact the degree of orb is so small. I use three degrees, but expand to seven with ruling

185

signs and houses being involved. The houses occupied will show where you experience the most emotional connection, by the Moon placement. While Jupiter's positioning will indicate where you're the most arrogant and comfortable.

Moon quincunx Saturn
Sometime called the sesquiquadrate, this relationship between the Moon and Saturn causes you to be emotionally uneasy and reserved. You have an unnatural insecurity about your own abilities which causes you to shy away from situations which are emotionally tensious. The cautious nature of Saturn restricts the loving feelings of the Moon creating the turmoil you experience almost daily. It's difficult to show your true feelings and this may cause to have significant delays in your romantic and marital life. You feel extremely guilty when you disappoint your loved ones, and are especially hurt when they do the same. It won't be until you can establish a distinct priority between what you need for yourself and what others actually need from you before you can find a stable balancing point. Relationships will start off slow and greatly hinder your romantic life. Many times you will fall for someone already involved, or you wait too long to make your move. This to, will eventually pass with maturity. This is an easily influenced alignment, and the other planets will definitely modify it. House placement is key because it will show where you're the most emotionally insecure.

Moon quincunx Uranus
When these two planets are aligned like this it means you must be free of all emotional hang ups until feeling completely independent. You're skilled at handling reoccurring crises because as soon one issue is finishing another pops up. As time passes you naturally fall into a place where everything just flows. Many of these problems are a direct result of the early conditioning set upon you as a child. It's possible that your parents coddled you and gave you everything you needed, causing you to not be able to fend for yourself. Also, it's possible they were completely neglectful,

186

causing you to feel unloved and unwanted. Either way, the natural confusion caused by this aspect can make you excessively emotional and unpredictable. Now as an adult you tend to react inappropriately and immaturely, getting caught up in bad decision after bad decision. Your emotional energy level is extremely high and in constant fluctuation. Up one minute and down the next you will experience a whirlwind of emotions throughout your life. In romantic relationships you need space to be on your own. Once you feel like you are bogged down into a boring relationship you will act out erratically and unpredictably. Too many alignments with Uranus will make you unstable and ridiculously rebellious.

Moon quincunx Neptune.

This alignment stimulates your imagination and curiosity into the abstract forms spirituality. Accepting there are higher forces than we can see is easy, but pinpointing your beliefs is difficult. Religions as a whole doesn't always make sense and you can't quite figure out where you fit in. Both planets have a significant impact on your subconscious and innermost mind. Unfortunately this amplifies the confusions always caused by Neptune. You're quite uncertain about life on Earth and the existence of humanity. These energies are very sensitive and easily swayed by the other planets. The very nature of the quincunx is confusing, and Neptune is King Triton of confusion. Your clinging emotions make it difficult to separate yourself from anything and anyone. You become so attached to someone or something you will endure severe amounts of emotional or physical abuse. Neither the Moon nor Neptune are aggressive and require a backbone from elsewhere. They're both emotional sissies and would rather look the other way when the situation gets iffy. No matter what your situations are, you constantly seek out something causing stress somewhere in your life. Even if things are running easy and smoothly, you still focus attention on any negativity and dwell on that instead. In your working environment you over extend so much many of your co-workers may see you as a brown nosing suck up.

Moon quincunx Pluto

What I call the Bigfoot is difficult because it can sway so many ways. Pluto is more of a catalyst than a dictator when analyzing any aspect. It's like the gasoline you throw on the fire to flare it up. As the ruling influence of your subconscious mind, the Moon sitting quincunx to Pluto suggests you have to learn balance between emotional compulsiveness with objectivity. Chances are during your childhood years you were expected to give into all the powers of your parents. When you refused submission, they made you feel unloved and insignificant. Because of this harsh upbringing you still feel you must submit to the powers of others in order to gain approval. Now you tend to over react to their demands. Because you were so repressed of personal freedoms as a youngster, as an adult you feel compelled to restrict others as well. This makes you a poor supervisor and you shouldn't try to lead large groups of people. There is definitely a malfunction in your brain that obsesses you with power and control. Once again this will be intensified the more you were held back. You have an illusion that anyone who uses you cares for you in some way. This is completely not true. The truth is you're a glutton for emotional punishment and will have to get over many traumatic experiences. If severely afflicted by other planets this indicates an extremely abusive past. Be consciously aware when becoming emotionally involved with others who have wooed you with their charm.

Mercury quincunx ascendant

This is a somewhat bad aspect which usually adds stress and tensions into your life with migraines and anxiety problems. Mercury controls intellect and the central nervous system and this isn't a great starting point. It's difficult to grasp concepts quickly and even when you do you don't know where to direct your knowledge. By no means is this considered a chart wrecker and other the physical ailments, there isn't too much negativity. Granted if Mercury is in poor condition relating to the other planets, this doesn't help alleviate the issue. This particular aspect indicates you try understanding everything about those you associate with and focus on useless facts. When you do face a challenging confrontation you tend to give others the benefit of the doubt and usually submit. Verbal arguments are best avoided, because once you get carried away things get really bad, really fast. Although you give people the benefit of the doubt too often you're still aware of their lacking integrity and character. Your evaluations and conclusions about people are generally spot on, and you're fooled only once in a while and for a short time. As you worry over matters in which you have no control, if someone ever tries to talk about your short comings you change the topic quickly. This also gives you an overly aggressive way in which you communicate to others. When offended, you're quick to confront someone verbally, and a tongue lashing from you can be quite brutal. As you grow and mature you have to realize that your instant responses don't always produce the desired effects. Your tongue is a powerful weapon and you will have to use yours wisely.

Mercury quincunx Mars

Aspects between Mercury and Mars always make you talkative and energetic. This time without much direction towards anything. You may be intelligent, curious, and determined but you just don't direct it towards a proper outlet. Left alone this is an agitating relationship between your intellect and your aggression. Chances are you only care to gain enough knowledge to carelessly pass by, never truly grasping a concept. Unfortunately your inability to focus on productive outlets can make you a social gossip queen. Just like thinking, you're always talking about unproductive topics. You're naturally over impulsive, the swift and head on way you attack things isn't always the easiest and most efficient. Oftentimes you will have to waste resources fixing little mistakes you made by moving too fast. This usually makes you verbally aggressive and irritable. You may have a long fuse before you blow up, but once you do it's game over, much like a volcanic eruption. Consistently taking on others responsibilities, you then

189

become resentful when you have no time for yourself. You need to make a list of thought out priorities in which you can stick to. If soothed by other planets this is merely a catalyst to your intelligence.

Mercury quincunx Jupiter

This aspect between Mercury and Jupiter usually indicates you have difficulty expressing your intelligence and creative abilities. You have lots of energy and inspiration but can't seem to find anywhere to direct it. The problem is there are so many outlets sparking your curiosity, just not enough time to do everything. They all look interesting so instead of focusing intently on one, you focus loosely on all of them. Once a decision is made you're unsure if you made the right one and continually question your choice was correct. As you constantly second guess yourself, you habitually ponder the "what if's" in life. Although you're smart you don't always show practical common sense. Childish pranks and immature jokes will amuse you and irritate others around you. This may also cause you to be immature until your later years, if you grow up at all. If you don't confront and successfully handle the unproductive habits developed as a youth then you are doomed to a life of inconsistent work and money. The earlier you accept your responsibilities the better off you will be. You also talk a lot more than you need to and generally choose the wrong words at the wrong time. Tone and emphasis are something you need to learn or you're going to inadvertently piss off several people.

Mercury quincunx Saturn

This aspect usually means you take your responsibilities very seriously and place too much emphasis on these qualities. All too often you feel your self-worth and the worth of others is within the possession and positions someone has. Although you know how to earn a good living the worries of possible financial crisis are always in the back of your head. You go to great lengths proving your worth through work ethic and determination. This can also make you extremely organized and neat, or on the opposite side, you may be a complete hoarder and keep everything you ever own. Your attention to minor detail makes you impatient with others most of the time. When people don't do what you tell them, or they ignore your ideas, you become extremely agitated and aggressive. It will also be difficult for you to accept any failures of your past. When things didn't go as planned you can turn melancholy and become extremely depressed. You will have to establish your priorities before you can separate them from your responsibility to others. Saturn really likes getting into a set routine and staying there. Mercury is a very mutable planet that merely acts as the intelligence towards where ever he is directed. This particular alignment will usually go one of two ways. If you're not dead set in a standard routine then it nearly impossible for you to find one. When influenced poorly this can also make you refuse to accept any of your social responsibilities.

Mercury quincunx Uranus

This aspect causes psychological stress, nervousness, and high anxiety. Alignments between these two planets are usually difficult and require soothing influences from elsewhere. You suffer severe disappointments and punishments when you attempt to help others. You're insatiously curious and an intellectual powerhouse. The biggest problem is your inability to focus on one thing long enough to become an expert. Your hesitant and sporadic spurts of enthusiasm are always followed by intense periods of mental anguish after not completing what you start. If you find a profession where your self-imposed obligations to society are met, this will quell some of the mental anxiety causing your problems. Careers dealing with small, local welfare programs, medical research, or rehabilitation can provide you with the subconscious release needed. Until you can establish a list of priorities you will be at the mercy of others who can find things for you to do. This aspect can also make you high strung, nervous, and paranoid. Not to be considered a bad aspect, this is one of the easier not so happy alignments for these two planets. It mostly shows you have attention deficit disorder and can't focus on anything longer than a fart.

Mercury quincunx Neptune

This aspect makes you feel extremely guilty when you don't respond to the needs of others. You think it's your duty to take on the world and often make promises you know you can't fulfill. When you fall short of living up to expectations you merely shrug your shoulders and say "At least I tried." It's as if you're dead set on constantly persecuting yourself. You worry over problems that don't exist, and obviously deny to the ones that do. The stress and tensions you place on yourself may be fictitious, but the physical exhaustion will be real. The problems fabricated in your mind eventually materialize into the real world and quite often you imagine your problems true. It's difficult to express your creativity and you often get set in job where you're not allowed to use it. It's best for you to work alone, or at least have your own set work area. Make sure your responsibilities are clear and predetermined. Your generosity towards others will be noticed by your coworkers and used against you. Accept the credit you earn and don't allow your opponents to use you as a door mat. Neptune has a way with diluting your perceptions of reality. Because Mercury has so much control over brain power this can cause significant misinterpretation of the truth. Be careful not to get caught up in your lies. Honesty will always be the best path.

Mercury quincunx Pluto

This planetary alignment indicates you accept an overwhelming amount of responsibility throughout your life. The early direction set upon you by your parents conditioned you realize your duties, and attend to them immediately. As a child you may have become bitter and resentful because of the excessive workload forced upon you. This established a subconscious pattern causing you to respond to your tasks with an obsessive desire to finish immediately. When things don't go as quickly and smoothly as planned you become easily aroused and agitated. Because you accept so many responsibilities you eventually over step your boundaries and directly interfere with business which isn't your

192

own. Be careful not to step on the toes of others because when you do cross these borders as it destroys your social circle. If you can learn the limitations of your capabilities there isn't anything you can't accomplish. Unfortunately this aspect can also show your inabilities to get over your past. Part of the driving force behind you is all the traumatic experiences you don't want to deal with. Whether they are grand or minute, the grievances you experienced as a child will eventually surface themselves into the open. Use these driving emotions productively by directing them into art, music, or medicine.

Venus quincunx ascendant

Forming an aspect with your ascendant is the most powerful way for a planet to project its influence. Despite the general displeasure usually caused by a quincunx, for some reason this one is easier to handle. The beauty and social graces of Venus may not be radiant in your personality, but there's definitely a hint. You're biggest problem is your inability to relate to people on an individual level. Venus is the most social of planets and when influencing your ascendant she gives you a passionate desire for group attention. In this alignment you don't know where your help is needed and where concessions must be made. Once you get too involved with the affairs of others you become distracted from tending to your own. Valuable time and resources are spent handling the problems of your associates leaving little for yourself. Within your family you're the one who wants everyone to maintain contact with each other. It will probably be your home where many family functions take place. Like a broken record, you continually make the effort to organize an outing or get together, only to be disappointed when others don't show the same enthusiasm.

Venus quincunx Mars

Venus and Mars have a very particular relationship and the signs, along with house placement are both key when interpreting their effects. This aspect makes you intensely passionate, with

193

extreme desires. Despite all your energy and aggressiveness you still have difficulty satisfying them. The reason for this is you constantly want everything out of everything. You want so much and want it all at once, when things take time your impatience kicks in. No matter what the alignment, you become demanding and needy, constantly calling upon others for some form of assistance. Venus and Mars are nearly complete opposites who don't get along, yet are still insanely attracted. Sometimes, the passiveness of Venus causes the aggressiveness of Mars to over assert itself making you an outlandish braggart who always has to be the best. When you lose there is always an outwardly circumstance preventing your victory. You never admit your competitor was just plain better. Conflictions between these two planets cause you to be impatient and irritable. There will be days when anything and everything makes you mad for some reason. When the influence of Venus is stronger you often go far out of your way to help fill the needs of others. So much so, they eventually come to expect it, causing you to become resentful and bitter. You will need to realize others have an easier time than you. It will seem like you have to work harder and longer to accomplish the same thing they do, and the truth is it does. Quit comparing yourself to others and figure out how to do your own thing.

Venus quincunx Jupiter

This aspect causes you to over inflate the expectations and demands of others in all your relationships. Because you don't realize what your personal needs really are, you don't know what to ask of others. Hoping it will fill the unconscious void, you pour out your assistance, only to get taken advantage of. If you aren't selective about when you concede everyone will trample on you. Venus always needs to feel loved and isn't happy unless in a committed, significant relationship. This causes you to casually bounce from one romantic flair up to the next. Chances are you get married just to play wedding and end up in a messy divorce. Delusional Venus actually thinks there is a perfect partner out there. Professionally, this planetary combination doesn't indicate a particular profession. Your social charm will allow you to succeed in many different fields. Because of your submissive nature, managers and superiors recognize the profits they can gain from your efforts. Your co-workers will realize this as well and use you as their work horse also. In any career you choose you will never get recognition for all your efforts, make sure that you get credit for all your work.

Venus quincunx Saturn

This is a less fortunate aspect making your responsibilities seem excessive and burdensome. You resent it when others always ask for help and don't accept no as an answer. There are other things you have planned for your time and it doesn't always include the people who wish it. Many times you over react when someone asks for a small favor. Although you may not say anything, deep down inside it bothers you greatly. Bad alignments from other planets only intensify the anger, and only a few pleasant ones can truly east the complications. On the occasion you do help someone you expect significant praise and gratitude. If someone doesn't say thank you it greatly offends you, especially if you went far out of your way to help. Your biggest issue is you don't recognize your responsibilities in your relationships. You either make concessions when standing your ground is more important, or refuse to give in when you need to compromise. This aspect causes serious relationship strain which can't be avoided. Once you recognize this flaw it's easy to deal with. Just make a conscious effort to change and the behavior pattern will eventually evolve along as well. Deep inside what you really desire is admiration and approval from the public. Whether it's your education level or success as a professional. It's this driving force pushing you towards positions of leadership and authoritative roles.

Venus quincunx Uranus

Aspects between these two are unique in the fact they don't last for very long, yet still require a close alignment to your ascendant to be fully experienced. If you have this aspect in your chart you often neglect the needs of yourself to attend to those of others. Anytime you finally do something for yourself it isn't without sacrifices. As you continually do things for others without being asked they eventually become expectant of your generosity. Sooner or later, you take on more responsibility than you can handle and have a break down. If you're not careful of your own psychological state you may suffer from hyper anxiety and nervous disorders, even schizophrenia. You can ease your tensions by not immediately responding with help. You may have to watch a loved one suffer rather than take your time and effort to solve someone else's problems. Allowing your loved ones to make mistakes is vital to their personal growth as well as yours. Don't offer complete support until you have been asked to do so. In romantic relationships you need someone that is a little eccentric and sporadic. It may take many love affairs to find your eventual partner, but when you do the bond will be lively and energetic. Whether romantic or plutonic make sure you are not used as a door mat. You don't need to buy the affections of others with your service.

Venus quincunx Neptune

Aspects between Venus and Neptune are especially wonderful because both planets are associated with beauty and art. Neptune adds a creative inspiration from different realms and Venus is the definition of gorgeous. Unfortunately, Neptune exponentially multiplies confusion and Venus integrates this into your relationships. The quincunx is very sensitive aspect which is easily influenced by other planets. Venus and Neptune are just as influenced and it's possible this is the weakest aspect in your chart. Basically this aspects show an unusual display of affection between you and your associates. You treat your loved ones in a different manner than most and your loose associates enjoy your off beat style. Usually this aspect is expressed by the clothes you wear and the possessions you collect. The spiritual side of Neptune draws you to individuals who share the same religious beliefs as you. Although you may accept the individuality of others, your social circle will be with those in your same spiritual sect. You can be extra sensitive to the feelings of others and their criticism as well. Sympathy can be your greatest asset and biggest liability. When you exclusively pay attention to the needs of others you eventually realize there's nothing left for yourself. Violence abhors you, and if you're an aggressive fighter, it's from elsewhere in your chart.

Venus quincunx Pluto

Aspects like these produce tensions in all your emotional relationships, whether it's romantic, plutonic, or professional. The reason for this is you give yourself excessively towards everyone, even more so to the ones you love. It will be necessary to learn moderation within your relationships. Pluto is a planet of complete obsession and can cause you to become a total control freak. Be cautious when forming close relations with those telling sob stories, Venus is easily swayed and also overly compassionate. Your generous nature wants to help everyone, but your resources are only so limited. When others realize this they may try to take advantage of you. It's your desire for intense personal contacts that can turn your behavior into obsessive. If Mars is involved you will want to be the dominant force in all your relationships. When someone resists your control you lash out emotionally and sometimes violently. Hopefully there are other aspects in your chart calming down the strenuous energies produced by this. If you can manage to stay out of the affairs of others then you will find that others will stay out of yours. The jealousy of Pluto also reveals itself when positioned like this. Part of the reason for your relationship failures will be your inability to submit to your partner's demands.

Mars quincunx ascendant

This relationship between Mars and your ascendant indicates you always take on more than you can actually do. You have an aggressive and restless attitude which is sometimes too bold for its own good. Because you feel others will see you as a failure you strive to accomplish as much as you can all the time. Any clubs you're in you want to hold a prominent office. As you mature you'll get restless at any occupation in which you're not your own boss. You're actually very driven by fear or anxiety by covering it with a macho bravado. This aspect really isn't a good starting point for Mars. There's a natural chip on your shoulder making you think everything and everyone is in competition with you. If you're constantly on the defensive people naturally assume they've done something. Then you get offended if they respond negatively and the fight ensues. The negative energy is easily relived by the other planets, but be very aware if Mars isn't calmed down. This alignment can definitely trigger hostility and violence when negatively aspected. Its basic nature confuses the way you direct your ambition. Since you don't know exactly what you want you don't know how to get it. Life will be more enjoyable when you find a profession where you have a distinct set of responsibilities which are set by someone else. Many of your individual projects will fail because you don't see the actions needed to succeed and won't ask for help. Learning to cooperate is always the best path.

Mars quincunx Jupiter

An aspect like this usually places unneeded stress and tensions where they don't need to go. This particular alignment indicates many problems trying to establish the priorities in your life. Any alignment between Mars and Jupiter stimulates aggression and this aspect is more strenuous than gracious. You feel you're allowed to overstep boundaries which others are not. This casual way of interjecting yourself into the affairs of others causes most of the breakdowns in your personal relationships. It's the assumption others cannot fend for themselves which makes you feel the need to respond. Most of the time you're simply the harping critic who can't shut up until things are done their way. Take time to honestly analyze how your actions and words are affecting the situation. Although you don't want to, the responsibilities on your part are always factors as well. In romantic relationships you're best suited when your partner meets your needs more than theirs. If you aren't the dominant force in the partnership it won't last very long. The sign and house placement will be important. Whichever house these two occupy will be the ones you aggressively pursue. This can also make you extremely athletic or competitive. It will be vital for you find an outlet for your physical energies. Choose an endeavor in which you can prove yourself a victor.

Mars quincunx Saturn

Aspects between Mars and Saturn are always problematic. This particular aspect causes you to have difficulty determining which responsibility to direct your effort and resources towards. Not only do you have problems figuring out your responsibilities, but when you do apply your focus you physically destroy yourself in the process. Perhaps you're desperately trying to prove your self-worth to others, thinking they will only like you for how hard you work. Once you learn to focus your abilities into a constructive project you will go far. Although working with others is difficult for you, functioning as a team can work if you're given individual responsibilities. Sometimes simply the supervisor title can sooth your ego. In your elder years as you eliminate exercise and physical activity from your daily routine arthritis along with other joint and muscle ailments will set in. Negative aspects like this are considered driving forces in a natal chart. If you don't allow the pressures to overcome you the energy provided by this can propel you into a long distinguished career, usually in the field of your choice. If you don't overcome to these unfortunate pressures chances are you get sucked into a dead end job with not much room for advancement.

Mars quincunx Uranus

It's plain and simple Mars and Uranus just don't get along. Rebellious Uranus always has to be different and completely unrestrained. Unfortunately, so does Mars. House placement is key because this is where you're going to experience the most

199

unexpected and often times violently catastrophic incidents. As with everything else, the tighter the aspect, the more potent the eruption. Basically, you think you can do anything you want. Neither planet handles the normal conditions of society, nor do you usually respond predictably. Your naturally aggressive habits are highly charged by your desire to break free from everything. This can make you a rebel without a cause, bouncing to and fro.

Not only do you need to exercise your body but you need to work your mind as well. Puzzles and games of strategy can be extremely interesting. Known as an inconjunction by some standard terms, this alignment makes you to outcast from your peers. You develop a different personality despite whatever is placed in front of you. Unfortunately, if Pluto and Saturn are poorly involved and closely aligned this can make you psychotic. Negative aspects between these two are among the top ten most difficult to handle. You have an insatiable drive to compete, and must be the victor above all costs, even if this means acting less than ethical. Freedom is something you cherish and when it's threatened you're not hesitant to react, and do so instantly with significant force. Life is a constant surprise for you and you can expect random accidents do to your hasty movements. Being reckless and careless causes you to severely injure yourself at some point in your life. You may have frequent trips to the hospital for minor stitches and bumps. Consider a professional career in extreme sports.

Mars quincunx Neptune
You're determined to assert yourself in a positive and constructive way, yet all your results seem disheartening. There's an over anxiousness about you, and in your hurried impatience you overlook the important pitfalls hampering your ambitions. This increases your high anxiety and psychological strain. Despite hindrances you refuse to change negative attitudes and put more energy into useless endeavors, thus perpetuating a vicious cycle of aggravation. Find an occupation in which you set your own production rate or schedule. Your work should not be so physically

demanding that it exhausts you. Avoid labor involving heavy machinery or potentially dangerous substances. You have lofty goals for humanity and strive to help others realize the spirituality you possess. Relationship wise you're drawn to people who make excessive demands of you. You're highly psychic and see intentions of others before they are stated. Vivid and prophetic dreams are associated with this aspect. Especially one of the planets is located in the twelfth house. Schizophrenia, Alzheimer's, and bi-polarity are associated as well and should be monitored accordingly. Anti-depressants and other psyche controlling drugs should be used carefully and in moderation. Upsetting the natural balance of your subconscious can prove to be more destructive and counter-productive than helpful. Prayer and meditation will always be best to help with the psychological strain.

Mars quincunx Pluto

The quincunx between Mars and any planet is difficult to handle. This one causes you to over react towards the simple daily pressures of life. When you take on more responsibilities than you can handle others see you as a work horse they can use at their disposal. You're driven to accomplish as much as you can with your little amount of time. With so much to do and so little time the nervousness creates tensions and migraines plaguing you throughout life. When you don't live up to the high expectations others have placed on you, emotions of guilt, inadequacy, and depression can set in. Disappointment hits you especially hard. Getting over any childhood traumas will be exceptionally problematic. You may cover up your repressed emotions with addictions to drugs, sex, gambling, or even work. Whichever your demon, once you immerse yourself into one of these there will be irreparable damage. These mistakes only perpetuate the cycle of destruction. Rehabilitation or professional counseling might be needed to correct these behaviors. The best thing about this alignment is the small orb it requires to be dominant. If this is more than three degrees separated don't worry too much.

Jupiter quincunx Asc.

Despite being extremely powerful this alignment is easily influenced by sign, house placement, and relationships with other planets. When helping others you're always generous to offer services. You truly want to help to everyone, but are unable to limit the number of people you support. Compromising even when you shouldn't, you're an enormously talented person and shouldn't sell yourself short. Because you place the attributes of others above your own many times you're left with the scraps under the table. If you're not careful you'll willingly accept the junk end of the stick, just to settle peacefully. People will take advantage of your submissive nature and try to push you around. Don't allow others to take the credit and accolades for your hard work. You have good intentions when you start endeavors of your own, and this aspect provides you with the fire to complete most of the projects you start. This can also signify some luck gotten within those chosen projects. If Jupiter is in your sixth house from this aspect you will be directed towards the projects of others, while if it is in the seventh house your energy will be projected towards yourself and your own issues. This shouldn't be taken as a bad aspect, no alignment with Jupiter is bad. The worst case scenario makes you over inflated about your opinions and ego. Basically it enlarges whatever it's touching.

Jupiter quincunx Saturn

Being the two slowest of the personal planets, when Jupiter and Saturn align it's usually in dynamic ways. Some individuals will use this energy in positive ways and others won't. The biggest problem with this particular alignment is the inconsistency of the Bigfoot in general. They can make you brilliantly smart and resourceful. It's just difficult for you to see your strengths and weaknesses. All alone this is usually an unpleasant aspect which indicates you place excessive burdens on the responsibilities in your life. You take on many projects or activities, only to complain about how much of your time and resources they consume. It's difficult for you to justify your selfish feelings and actions causing severe mental anguish. Feeling you have to sacrifice greatly in order to make the needed concessions, you secretly hold onto grudges you bury inside. It's only after you've reached a boiling point do you finally release your frustrations. What you really need is the advice of a trusted and objective third party. Saturn loves responsibility and Jupiter expands everything it touches. Because there's so much on your plate directing your time and resources efficiently or effectively is nearly impossible. You can't be in two places at once doing three things while you're there. Focusing on a significant few endeavors will prove more fruitful and less stressful. Jupiter and Saturn are the slowest of the personal planets and their alignments need an influence from your ascendant to provide significant energies. House placement will also guide the stresses into certain areas of your life. You're career and public perception will be very important. Consider politics or teaching at high academies.

Jupiter quincunx Uranus

When Jupiter is aspecting Uranus like this it usually indicates your life if full of unexpected triumphs and challenges. House placement will determine where you're most likely to experiences these incidents. Many times your higher aspirations will fall apart simply because you have set your expectations too high. You strive to identify yourself as a unique individual, but can't seem to find your niche. In doing so you may alienate your close and distant associates with your radical points of view. This does not mean in any way you're closed minded to the opinions of others. The actual fact is you understand everyone has their own interpretations and opinions. Although you're rigid in your own views, when someone points something out you hadn't thought of you openly embrace any changes you feel will be positive. Erraticness, eccentricity, and innovativeness, are all qualities produced when Jupiter is facing Uranus like this. When harnessed your excess mental energy will challenge you with new and innovative ideas. Once you find a way to profit from this, your success is limitless. This particular separation is easily swayed by

203

other planets. These two will basically enlarge whatever energies are touching it.

Jupiter quincunx Neptune

Sometimes I call it the Bigfoot but it's actually called the quincunx. The relationship between these two spiritual giants is an interesting one. It gives you greater insight towards improving humanity as a whole. Jupiter is the planet of higher learning and philosophy, while Neptune is the planet of the cosmic mysticism and oneness with all. Sometimes you take on greater responsibility in the problems of others than you need to. You may also cross boundary lines when keeping your nose to yourself. You will lose friends because of your inability to give them their space. You're not a therapist to everyone and must recognize it. When you're unable to find situations requiring you to help others, you create imaginary issues in your head. As you try to be a friend to everyone others will make excessive demands of you. You grudgingly accept already knowing you've gotten into more than you want. You feel you have to say yes because if you say no that person will be offended because of all the other contributions you have made in the past. When negatively aspected or placed natally you may acquire a disease or illness that is difficult to diagnose or cure. More often than not this merely heightens you sense of beauty and imagination. At its worst you become so fascinated with your dreams you fail to recognize responsibility.

Jupiter quincunx Pluto

With Jupiter and Pluto aligning like this you're the ultimate opportunist, successfully taking advantage of every situation, and every person. This doesn't mean you're unethically ruthless, but you stoop to seedier actions behind your even shadier thoughts. Unless controlled by morals and ethics you can be the most devious of devious, not caring who must be trampled in your path. Because you feel the pressure of responsibility you may reject them completely. On the other side you may completely ignore the responsibilities of yourself and solely focus on those of others.

You're an incredibly intelligent individual who just doesn't know where to direct your mind. As this aspect grows closer in exactness you become more and more possessive and obsessive. The aggressive nature you display is only a cover up for a deeper insecurity. If you can fully inform yourself about your surroundings and situation this will ease your unnatural intimidation from others. Formations between Jupiter and Pluto are mildly infrequent. Pluto is the slowest of all, and Jupiter is the middle of the pack. Thus making their alignments fairly more potent than most. If this energy is present in your character, you will spiritually feel it, and psychically know it.

Saturn quincunx ascendant

This aspect from Saturn is never good, and as with every other aspect more than one thing can come from this. Many times you take yourself and your responsibilities way too seriously. You're dedicated to social duties, and can never just kick loose or let go. Even when relaxing, business, bills, or personal pressures will be overly present. Or, the complete opposite is possible. In that cause you flee from responsibility like it were the black plague. Most times there is no happy meeting place between the two. Either way, you need to be cautious or precise in everything you do. It will take a while to warm up to others, and even then you may seem cold hearted and insincere. Unfortunately, sometimes they will be correct, you are cold hearted and insincere. You may think you can help the situation, but several times you will just be interested in hearing the dirty laundry of others. If you pay attention the affairs of others the distraction provided allows you to defer your own. Some astrologer's may disagree, but I feel this is one of the most frequent aspects in those who suffer from a midlife crisis. Whatever your current situation, on your second Saturn return you will turn 180 degrees and begin acting the opposite. Those who immersed themselves in business and career will face depressions regarding too much responsibility. Individuals who rejected their duties will frantically scramble to put the pieces together. At its worst you're a shrewd, hard headed businessman. At its best your accept everything thrown at you with a grain of salt, and handle the work appropriately.

Saturn quincunx Uranus

Because Saturn is the slowest of the personal planets, and Uranus is the fastest of the generational ones, their alignments are infrequent and occur at very uneven intervals. Generally, this indicates you have difficulties establishing the priorities of the obligations you take on. Your "to do" list is hard to come up with and once you do you realize you left things off. The houses these to occupy will be the two areas of life you experience the most troubles. Things seem to never fall into place, and you can't seem to get all the right pieces into the right places in order to create a functioning machine. Whether it's education, experience, or funding, there are never enough resources for your ideas. Although you never admit it you're easily intimidated by those more aggressive. If the aspect is tightly aligned, within three degrees, or closely related to your ascendant, the powers are magnified exponentially. This is what I call a structure alignment meaning it's meant for other planets to build upon. When properly influenced you become dedicated to your craft and fixated on being the best. It's your dedication to calculated precision giving you the advantage over your competitors.

Saturn quincunx Neptune

This aspect between Saturn and Neptune causes to feel your talents and resources must be justified. Everything you do must fit into place with another and you fall into routine easily. Saturn and Neptune are both slower moving planets and their alignments are monumental. Although grand and spectacular, in order to experience the full effects of this relationship you need a connecting aspect with your ascendant. Otherwise house placement becomes more important. It will show where you will experience the most confusion about your responsibilities. You constantly seek ways to improve your talents and knowledge usefully but can't find the proper education or training. The spiritual attributes of Neptune may compel you into a career amongst the spiritual and religious. Not necessarily an ordained minister into a set doctrine, you may seek out to find spirituality all by yourself. You wish to bring organization to any chaotic situation and many times will bite off more than you can chew. Throughout your life you will be plagued by too much to do and too little time to do it in. The illusions of Neptune cause you to think you will be defined by what you accomplish in this lifetime. This is because you consistently volunteer your time and resources to anything you are asked. When negatively aspected by other planets this can cause you to be a hypochondriac. Along with this you may also suffer from obsessive compulsive disorder or hoarding.

Saturn quincunx Pluto

Alignments between Saturn and Pluto are few and far between. As the slowest of the personal planets, Saturn is restrictive and incredibly overly cautious. Pluto, the slowest of all planets, is passionately obsessive with intense powers of destruction. This is definitely a generational relationship, and the influence they have with your ascendant is key when determining their significance. Usually this causes you to take all your obligations and responsibilities way too seriously. Your status amongst your peers is important and you feel you can impress them by what you accomplish. This occurred 1999, once more in 2005, but not again until 2033. This is a slow and irregular alignment which isn't prominent in very many charts. Deep inside you're intimidated by being singled out, and don't care about attention and ballyhoo. Although you deeply desire to participate in improving the social injustices around the world, many times you just don't find the time to do so. If you're not directly affected by an issue you may turn a blind eye, or casually brush it away. You can be quite worrisome and suffer from high anxiety and nervous disorders. If you can't establish an order of priorities within your life you will eventually suffer a midlife crisis or nervous breakdown. This is a horrible starting point for aspects from other planets. Bad aspects from Mars or Uranus will produce such atrocities words can't describe them.

Uranus quincunx ascendant

Uranus is a planet of eccentricity and innovation. When aspecting your ascendant in such a manner this makes you inventive and clever, always looking to gain knowledge and solve problems. Your mind is constantly on over drive, sometimes uncontrollably. This is an aspect when influenced by other planets can produce severe paranoia, anxiety, and nervous disorders. The high energy level you possess makes it difficult to wind down. Rather than turn to drugs or alcohol to subdue any insomnia you should try reading in a quiet place with no electronics around. Your outlandish ideas will not always go over easy with others. Going against the grain is normal for you, and the straight laced yuppies don't like you different lifestyle. Uranus always seeks out new ways to research, develop, and then improve. The biggest problem you experience is the inability to find that one subject sparking you interest. Everything is so fascinating that one topic is never enough. Uranus is the ultimate revolutionary Once you learn and your one individuality integrating into your niche of society will feel much more comfortable.

Uranus quincunx Neptune

Occurring during the late 19th century, then again in during the middle of the 1920's, this seldom seen aspect won't come around again until the middle 2060's. Despite its scarcity, this is an unstable aspect whose influence will be felt for generations to come. This alignment will make the masses of people passionately disturbed by the injustices of society. As seen by the crash of the stock market in the late 1920's followed by the great depression, and subsequently world war two, the social magnitude of this influence should not be over looked. Not only does this revolutionize society, technology and medicine are influenced as well. The advancement of the television, radio, in the 1920's and the development of x-ray during the previous quincunx during the

1890's, we can only speculate and imagine where we will be when this hits us again. Since this is such a long lasting generational aspect the exactness of aspect to your ascendant will determine how influential this one is.

Uranus quincunx Pluto

This is a rare and influential aspect that affects large masses of people. Occurring in the early 1910's this seldom seen alignment won't form again until around 2035. Because Pluto wasn't discovered until 1930 we can only speculate the actual results from this formation.

Neptune quincunx ascendant

This separation between Neptune and your ascendant suggests you're constantly trying to gain the approval and cooperation of others. Most times it doesn't go as planned and you screw things up even more with your delusional ideas and conclusions. Quite often your instinctual reaction won't be based in facts and reality. Instead you see things how you want and not how they are. Neptune is a mystical and magical planet which often confuses people. Despite all the wonderfully creative ideas floating through your brain, it's difficult to establish any distinct form in the physical world. Whether it's art, poetry, or music, there is an endless amount of inspiration for you to tap into. Because it's so difficult for you to capitalize on your own abilities it may be a good idea to find someone or somewhere you're not the ultimate authority. One problem with this is you can be gullible and easily taken advantage of. Carefully look into any fine print before you make any monumental decisions. Neptune is one of the generational planets and alignments with your ascendant are the best way to feel the energy. The condition of Neptune is more important than can be described. It will show the intensity of the confusion.

Neptune quincunx Pluto.

Good luck if this is in your chart. No one reading this will ever have this aspect. Aliens will invade and destroy Earth before then.

Pluto quincunx ascendant
When Pluto is aspecting your ascendant like this you often take everything in your life too passionately, and it's difficult to come up with outlets on your own. People seem to have an ability to conform you to their desires and use your resources as their own. Sometimes you're overly concerned about the environment around you, and the services you volunteer take up excessive amounts of your life. After over committing your time and resources you're left with almost nothing for yourself. Part of your major problems will be the inability to see outside the box. Once you set your sights on something there are theoretical blinders preventing you from seeing things from a peripheral view. Because of the insecurities this produces you should think twice before going into business for yourself. The security provided from careers in teaching, social work, or medical services will provide you with a more satisfying job. You think very highly of your opinion and can become obsessed when enforcing it. When others disagree, you argue convincingly and become upset easily when the facts prove you wrong. After sulking for a while you realize it's time to get over it and move on. The competitive spirit within you is intense yet secretive. You deeply desire the opportunity to show off your talents and achievements, but when tensions are high the pressure increases so does your volatility.

Opposition

Ezra 3:5
Afterwards they offered the regular burnt offering, and those for the new Moons and for all the appointed feasts of the Lord that were consecrated, and those of everyone who willingly offered to the Lord.

Of all the aspects the opposition is easiest to guess simply by name alone. When two planets are directly across from each other they form the second most difficult aspect to handle, and arguably the second most powerful over all. Some astrologers will say the square is second in strength, but I disagree. Squares may produce more intense negative energy, but there are positive parts of the opposition that aren't associated the square. A square is just pissed off completely. Along with the square, the opposition is a conflicting relationship between two planets that just won't cooperate. Planet A lacks the qualities planet B possesses and vice versa. Like magnets, they wildly attract because one wants what the other has, yet both energies are so different they hate each other. In essence one completes the other. The purpose of the opposition is to arouse enough emotion you off you get up and do something. Any agitation created by the planets involved is so strong you can't resist action.

Sun opposite ascendant

The Sun opposing your rising sign shows you're easily impressed by others and desire they be as impressed with you. Aspects like these are usually driving forces behind many business minded individuals. You attract powerful and influential people because you enjoy their company thinking if you associate with them you are as successful as them. Part of this is because you have an insecurity about yourself and think if you're surrounded by successful people you in turn are successful as well. In a sense you're confused about how to attain your goals while helping others achieve theirs as well. It's the constant struggle to identify what you can do for others which depletes your resources. Although you're misunderstood most of the time, with positive aspects elsewhere there's nothing to fear. Worst case scenario is you never truly integrate you spirit into your personality. It's basically impossible to identify who you truly are. In personal relationships you try too hard to do everything that is expected of you. There's an underlying need to become independent of the security your parents provided, and transfer your need to belong to someone you can relate to personally. Before asserting your own opinion you always look from the other's point of view. This can be a definite asset in politics and business.

Sun opposite Moon

When the Moon is in the opposite sign of the Sun it means there was a full Moon on the day you were born. An opposition is one of the most personal relationships between these two and your personality will show it. Being born under a full Moon provides you with a sense of spirit which isn't in most people. You're basically larger than life. Like the bright night sky produced by a full Moon, you enjoy being seen and appreciated by the masses. Despite this attraction for attention you still act with a hesitant stint of enthusiasm. This is the emotional fluctuation caused by the lunar side of the energy. You switch from the ego centered behavior of the Sun and emotional habits of the Moon. Your greatest asset is your ability to love everyone to the fullest. Emotions are experienced as they were meant to feel, but the handicap is your unwillingness to let go of the past. You can never do anything without emotion. Don't wait for others to walk the path for you, blaze the trail yourself. Strains in relationships will continue to exist until you can determine where you stand and identify it honestly. You can get caught up in self-pity when matters don't progress the way you want them. Remember it is the success after the turmoil determining your character, not the unpleasant experiences.

Sun opposite Mars

The opposition between the Sun and Mars causes you to be a determined and competitive fighter who stops at nothing to succeed. This aspect makes you energetic, athletic, and sometimes excessively violent. You never back down from the opposition and will continue fighting long after defeat. Just as you never retreat from a competition you naturally seek them out. Because you respond so aggressively towards every challenge others may see you as arrogant and conceited. You're constantly causing dissention within the ranks, and it's very difficult to take orders from others. As you continue to pursue adversary after adversary you eventually realize all your fighting was nothing more than a blatant display of your dominance. Your passions are intense and you often dive in head first without looking before you leap. The hyper aggression you experience can be subdued by large amounts of athletic activities. Sports requiring extreme amounts of strength, endurance, and concentration are right up your ally. The physical reward and admiration from your peers achieved through this will provide you with a sense of inner security. This is a driver aspect which can be extremely detrimental when poorly afflicted. If there aren't any harmonizing aspects calming this one down you will walk through life angry, with an unnatural chip on your shoulder.

Sun opposite Jupiter

Although oppositions are usually less than fortunate, no alignment with Jupiter can be considered bad. Alone it blesses you with a natural intelligence, absorbing information and applying it more readily than others. Learning from your mistakes the first time will allow you to mature faster than most. Knowing how to make a good first impression is your strong point. Putting your best foot forward will get you very far in business or politics. Because you're always so optimistic and hopeful about life you assume others feel the same. When they don't have the same amount of energy you project yours even more. This causes tensions when others just want to be left alone, you must remember others will need more space than you do. As with every aspect there is a negative side to this. You never do anything half-hearted. If uncontrolled, addictions or obsessions will ruin your life and all your personal relationships. Letting go will be difficult. Stay away from drugs and gambling as these can lead to your downfall. Unfortunately this also produces an over inflated ego and perception of yourself. Your overly confident attitude will eventually cause people to think of you as conceited and rude. Be careful not to express your opinions too forcefully or over zealously.

Sun opposite Saturn

An opposition between the Sun and Saturn puts your life into constant crisis and turmoil. Your biggest problem is you don't place much emphasis on responsibility or accountability. When nothing is wrong you make up non-existing problems simply to give you something to complain about. Your personal insecurities are always in the back of your mind and you can never seem to shake them and get on with business. Quite often this is produced by a difficult relationship between you and your father. Whether your parents divorced and you felt neglected by his departure or you his attention was never enough, either way the traumas produced during your childhood will usually follow you into adult life. In youth responsibility is generally not a priority and if you don't learn work ethic you're doomed to a repetitive cycle of failed job after failed job. As you grow comfortable with yourself, your romantic partner will be a great source of advice and strength. In females many times you will fall for someone older and in men your partner will be more responsible than most. Whether you're male or female your chosen partner will be a great source of advice and strength for you. Once in a relationship you are deeply committed and fall completely in love. Once you accept your responsibilities in life you're determined and driven to finish whatever you start come hell or high water. There will be difficulties in everything you do and you need to just deal with it. This can also indicate an extreme opposition to control and authority. You won't respond well when you feel restricted by the powers of others and my act out irrationally when confronted.

Sun opposite Uranus

This is quite an exciting aspect which is highly volatile, and doesn't always respond in a rational manner. You have lots of energy, intelligence, and rebelliousness. Sometimes this aspect makes you high strung and irritable, getting frustrated where frustrations aren't needed. As a child you probably chose to hang out with others younger than you because of the advantages age sometimes brings. The fear of overwhelming competition is one of the driving forces in your life, and you seek out competitors you feel are inferior and can be dominated easily. Because of this, it's possible you venture out and begin your own business alone. You possess enough creative and innovative ideas if you apply effort and hard work success is inevitable. Uranus is highly revolutionary, unconventional, and ingenious. You're constantly on the go, bouncing to and from one project onto the next and must be cautious not to leave any loose ends. This can provide you with an excess amount of nervousness which can produce good things, depending on where you choose to focus this energy. You inspire to de different than others and love anyone as crazy as you are. The qualities of Uranus are very prominent and push you to do things that no one has ever done before. If you go into business for yourself it will be in a field that is incredibly unique and unusual. Once you do harness your differences and erraticness there is no limit to where you will go. This alignment will also produce cases of insomnia, high anxiety, and possible neurological issues.

Sun opposite Neptune

Opposite planets attract like magnets, one has what the other wants. An opposition between the Sun and Neptune usually indicates that you constantly face challenges which are problematic and hard to understand or diagnose. In your childhood years you had a misunderstanding about authority, you felt you were singled out for discipline and everyone was against you. It's easy for you to create illusionary problems where none have existed. You're overly doubtful about your own capabilities and place others ahead of you thinking they are more educated and qualified. Sometimes this is true but most times this is not. If you're reluctant to educate yourself or receive specialized training this will become true. Neptune always produces confusion and illusion, when the Sun is placed here those attributes are intensified. Eventually, you will seek out relationships which have little or no commitment. That way if they fail there aren't feelings of guilt on your part. You can be a dreamer and an extremely psychic. This can also cause an over active imagination. Any fantasies you create are so seemingly real you can't tell them apart from real life. As you chase these deluded ambitions they distract you from what is really important. This is also a spiritually problematic alignment as well. Although you sense there is a greater being out there you can't seem to pinpoint your beliefs. Spiritually this aspect may cause you to sway from one religion to another, picking up points of each along the way.

Sun opposite Pluto

Yet to experience one hundred oppositions we don't really know much about this alignment. The reason for this is Pluto wasn't discovered until 1930. Generally, this aspect puts you on the defensive when you experience the slightest resistance. You instinctually assume your competitor is better, stronger, and more qualified than you are. This produces extreme insecurities and inferiorities. If you can't win you just won't play. Many times you will attack first, thinking it would be a good defensive move, when you're wrong you get deeply depressed about the situation. A natural extremist, obsession can set in when you fail to look at everything around you. It will be difficult to let go of your past, and you undoubtedly experienced traumatic events which still plague you today. The more horrendous the act the more the vengeance will cling onto it. Eventually through prayer and meditation you will over-come these calamities and reach a personal level of nirvana. Remember a plant needs a strong root system in order to grow tall. Sometimes the catastrophic events you endure are meant to strengthen your characters roots. Any alignment involving one of the generational planets possess one consistent similarity, the closer the aspect to the alignment the more volcanic the explosion.

Moon opposite ascendant

When the Moon is opposite your ascendant you're in constant need of love and attention. Deep inside you're desperately attached to the affection you receive from others. You involve yourself in the personal affairs of everyone you know and sometimes casual acquaintances. Many times you uninvitingly interject yourself into the business of your friends, and quite often over step boundaries. This is because you believe immersing yourself into the lives of others will bring them closer. When this isn't the case and your advances are rejected you become completely offend and confused why they don't want you close. You partly impose yourself on others hoping they will turn to you for emotional support and advice. Although your kind nature attracts a vast array of friends, some aren't interested in friendship. Not all people have your best interest in mind and you're especially susceptible to their deceit. You function well in social environments and will be best suited for professions relating to the public. Feeling alone is intolerable and sometimes your cantankerous nature makes it seem so no matter what the situation. Despite your social contacts, it's easier to deal with the problems of others than your own. When you submerse yourself into their entanglements it provides a sufficient distraction from problems of your own. This can also indicate severe tensions between you and your mother. If severely afflicted by planets like Mars, Saturn, or Uranus this can be a debilitating emotional powder keg. It's possible that you over react to every situation and rarely control your emotions. This is because you're so confused about what you are truly feeling and can't identify the problems. When the problem can't be realized, neither can the solution. In turn your habitual over emotional reactions are usually incorrect ant proper adjustments aren't made.

Moon opposite Mercury

Oppositions are definitely not the most harmonious of alignments. Because both the Moon and Mercury are so easily influenced they can never seem to make up their minds, and both fluctuate dramatically. Mercury is constantly curious and seeking something new, but the Moon always needs support and reassurance from things which are familiar. Since you can't identify how you are feeling it's nearly impossible for you to

217

convey that to others. One of the major malfunctions is the inability to separate your emotions from rational thinking. Mercury controls your intellect and cognitive thought, while the Moon rules your subconscious and habitual reactions. The opposition makes each essence completely counterproductive. One planet has and understands what the other wants. Logical thought process tells you to do one thing while your emotional instincts direct you otherwise. Despite the lack of stability its influence can be very detrimental and shouldn't be taken lightly. Not much good can be produced when your brain and your emotions don't function properly. This can also indicate extreme communication breakdowns between you and females, especially your mother. The two houses they occupy will be where you experience the most emotional confusion.

Moon opposite Venus

The Moon opposite Venus makes you stingy and rude, although most times you don't even know it. It's not one of the more pleasant alignments and hopefully you have harmonizing influences elsewhere. You're easily offended and become extremely vocal once you are. Displaying your displeasure isn't difficult and chances are you're very hyper critical as well as invasive. When your needs aren't met you turn into a diva, requesting others do things you can easily accomplish alone. I call it damsel in distress syndrome. Although there will be a lot of negative energy, there are also positives to everything. When in love you're completely committed, and require your companion to be the same. Tensions will arise within all your relationships whether in romance, friendship, or family when you fail to bend as much as you instruct others to. Because you're so demanding you always seem too busy with your own issues to help others. With no intention on your part, the subconscious signals you send alerts others you don't really want to help. Sometimes you do, but do so grudgingly. The basic nature of this alignment is the emotions of the Moon don't know how to function within your relationship. You don't know how you truly feel and can't make an accurate judgment. Once you figure out how you feel your life will balance itself out.

Moon opposite Mars

With an opposition between the Moon and Mars you believe every relationship is always in a state of crisis. Quite often you make up preposterous and completely inaccurate issues to dwell on. You have severe difficulties compromising, which in turn leads to more strain in your relationships. During childhood you would scream and cry over the most insignificant matters, and possibly still do as an adult. Your highly charged emotions cause you to react harshly to criticism, no matter how constructive and needed it might be. You're outgoing and assertive when you meet people, but in the process you usually choose to befriend people who are temperamentally unstable. Many of your romantic relationships will fail because you're attracted to the material things and base your relationship within those few possessions. You're pushy and overbearing, if anyone refuses to submit to your demands you react instantly and sometimes violently. Your complete resentment of criticism will cause disturbances in your work place. Expect frequent arguments with your co-workers, superiors, and law enforcement as well. You will have to learn to control your actions when you are hostile. This is definitely not a good starting point for your Moon. In the most basic of terms total emotional instability is what this causes.

Moon opposite Jupiter

Oppositions between the Moon and Jupiter cause you to be extremely emotional and confused where to direct your passions. You're compassionate and caring to a dangerous level. Many times associating with the wrong person winding up in a mess of trouble. If you always extend a hand to those with fewer advantages it only causes needless expenditures of valuable resources. Whether it be overextending your time or spending too much money frivolously, this constant circle will continue until you can address your problems. You continually give others the benefit of the doubt despite the lack of proof behind their statements. Don't become too emotionally enveloped until that person has shown you the same feelings. Your romantic life will suffer because you feel your partner is continually using you. This is because you put the needs of others before yours and they grow use to your services. Eventually everyone just expects you to do certain things and when you speak up or become resentful they simply stand there wondering why. The most basic philosophy of this aspect is the expansion of emotions. Higher consciousness will be revealed through extremely emotional circumstances. Sometimes good. Sometimes bad.

Moon opposite Saturn

The Moon opposite Saturn instills you with an elevated sense of responsibility and emotional restriction. You either feel completely enslaved to your personal duties, or reject everything required of you. Many times issues with pessimism and depression are associated with this aspect. Quite often you will take life too seriously, with no experience ever being casual or superficial. During youth responsibility was taught as part of growing up and you miss your childhood. Many times this causes emotional tensions with one or both of your parents, probably your father. No amount of attention was ever enough, and if he truly did neglect you the emotional trauma is especially scarring. The biggest problem between you and them was the lack of emotional connection. Maybe he was stricter and more demanding than most parents. Possibly he wasn't part of your life and the absence hurts tremendously. This isn't to say you don't love you parents, but there are serious difficulties when bonding. Because of this you tend to grow responsible early and seem to get along with older people more than those your own age. This is not usually a pleasant aspect creating a wall between your ability to express your emotions and your personality. If your upbringing was positive then it will be difficult to leave your home and family. If it was negative it will be impossible to let go of the scars from the past. Until you do so happiness and success will be difficult, if not impossible.

Moon opposite Uranus

Oppositions between these two usually cause extreme mental and emotional disorders. It's nearly impossible to integrate your emotions and your intellect into your behavioral process. You either act instantly and emotionally, or not at all, spinning in circles on how to handle the situation. Eventually the circles lead to nowhere and the emotional reaction comes out. Basically you're a complete basket case. You need positive energy from other planets in order to mellow your ass out. Get away by yourself for meditation and personal reflection. Part of the problem is you're extremely psychic, and have difficulties separating your unconscious habits from the way you react. When you don't identify the problem you only repeat the mistake. Your romantic alliances are usually strange and different. You may get involved with a foreigner or someone from a completely different back ground. If Mars is poorly aspecting this you may get into abusive relationship after abusive relationship. Perhaps these complications are just a way to avoid responsibility. If your life seems too tragic others will start doing stuff for you. This in turn will lead to you making mountains out of mole hills, hoping someone will come to your rescue. The Moon is the most unstable of the planets and Uranus is the most erratic. You're generally an odd ball marching to the beat of a different drum.

Moon opposite Neptune

This is absolutely not a psychologically stable alignment. Oppositions between the Moon and Neptune cause your fantasy world and imagination to run amuck. You're constantly day dreaming into your own created world, refusing to accept reality. These two can definitely turn you into a psychological space case when aspected by other planets. This is because you're highly tuned into the psychic realm of the universe. Buried deep within your subconscious are locked up secrets to the cosmos. Through prayer, meditation, drugs, or alcohol, you experience life in different ways than others. If you were neglected as a child you probably created imaginary friends to spend your time with. These so called "imaginary" friends were actually spirits or ghosts, communicating from a different frequency. Your many interests pull you into many different directions, causing stress and tensions when commitments aren't fulfilled adequately. All too often your talents go to waste. The limited resources you grew up with forced you into a situation where you don't get your primary choice. When you can't earn a decent living with your creativity skills you must submit into a profession you dislike. Don't expect to ever be truly happy with your job. Poor aspects from Mars or Saturn can turn this real bad, real fast.

Moon opposite Pluto

Oppositions between the Moon and Pluto indicate you show your emotions openly and are very hurt when they aren't returned. Possibly a memory of punishment and injustice involving your parents left you with trauma which seems unable to pass. The emotions controlled by the Moon are spun into complete frenzy by the destructive forces of Pluto. Both of these entities are extremely possessive and the obsessions of Pluto are embedded deep into your inner subconscious. This can make you unreasonably jealous not only of your possessions, but your loved ones as well. You cling to things like the world will end with their departure, leaving you standing there crying. Difficulties arise because the constant fluctuations of the Moon and Pluto's inability to react quickly. Although the influences from Pluto are as subtle as he is distant, once the powder keg explodes the effects are easily noticed. This usually indicates a complete emotional breakdown where you need to draw great amount of personal fortitude to accept. This will probably occur when Pluto is has progressed to form a square. Expect the turmoil to start boiling around your thirtieth birthday. Because of your strong emotional needs you will get too involved too soon and get instantly attached. Examine every situation carefully before making any definite or long term commitment.

Mercury opposite Ascendant

Mercury oppositions usually produce one of two entirely different effects. Either you're extremely talkative and won't shut up. Or, you're exceptionally quiet, and tend to yourself a lot. Much of this will be determined by others planets modifying this little one. Mercury controls your intelligence, communication skills, and the body's central nervous system. Oppositions will cause difficulties in one of those three things. You're slow to express your true feelings. Wanting to fit in with the crowd you usually wait until others have stated their opinion, only then will you casually agree with them. This isn't because don't have opinions of your own your just don't care to get into heated debates with others. If you never disagree with anyone others will eventually see through it and expose the hypocrisies. Deep down you desire to be the most agreeable person ever, gaining self-worth and personal security by the acceptance of others. You can be slow to catch on and will say the wrong thing at the wrong time. If the occasion requires you bend the truth about your back ground in order to make a good impression you're all for it. If you're extremely talkative and have the gift of gab, you love to use it, sometimes about things you shouldn't. Try stay out of the personal affairs of others to avoid unnecessary drama. Very talented at relating to others, you will find success at any profession where you have direct contact with the public. This can also indicate a speech impediment or mental disorder.

Mercury opposite Mars

This aspect gives you an insatiable curiosity and boundless intellectual ability. You have an extremely active mind that never quits spinning. You're not always thinking about something productive or useful, and if you allow your mind to wander nothing will ever get done. You constantly seek out opportunities to show off your vast amounts of knowledge but can't seem to find the right outlet. Sometimes you actively seek a verbal competition and get into many altercations because of petty arguments. Because of this naturally aggressive attitude towards others, they eventually

223

become offended and see you as conceited and mouthy. You have to make significant efforts to compromise and get along with others. It will be this attack before you're attacked attitude which causes most your problems. You never look before you leap, and should take time to smell the roses you will need to slow down and assess every situation carefully. Your speed and carelessness way of doing things will cause many minor and sometimes major accidents. Be prepared to spend some time in the emergency room throughout your life.

Mercury opposite Jupiter

An opposition between Mercury and Jupiter gives you a fertile imagination with high expectations for yourself. You're full of inspiration but many times lack the focus and determination to finish anything you start. Mercury is known for picking something up, gaining enough info to satisfy his current curiosity, and putting it down for something newer and flashier. Jupiter just makes this worse. It will be necessary for you to learn focus and attention. Your sometimes childish attitude thinks you can accomplish great things with little or no effort. If you fall into a profession where there is little room for advancement you will become melancholy and depressed. You need to always expand your knowledge and continue learning new things. This aspect can also act as a catalyst used to energize aspects from other planets. The expansive and philosophical qualities of Jupiter will give you a spiritual outlook in life. You may not be part of an organized religion, but you realize that there are force out there greater than human nature. If you choose a path of spirituality and enlightenment your cosmic abilities are profound.

Mercury opposite Saturn

The opposition between Mercury and Saturn causes you to isolate yourself and then become depressed about being alone. Not necessarily the most harmonious of aspects, this can make you stingy and opinionated. Your rigid views constantly put you on the defensive. Getting so set in your ways you take any opposition as a direct personal attack. Until you can give up your disagreeable nature your mind will be in constant turmoil. Because you have considerable intellectual abilities you tend to think you are always right and the ideas of others don't really matter. Unless aspected otherwise you will be slow to warm up and reluctant to share. The isolationist within you causes you to have few associates, and then alienate the ones you do have with your hyper critical tendencies. If you get involved in the affairs of others you will drive several wedges between you and your friends. Be especially careful if you do decide to become a recluse. The psychological damage caused by isolation isn't pleasant and can lead do deep, dark cycles of depression. At its worst this indicates the inability to communicate with your father. This aspect can be easily modified. It usually indicates the difficulties figuring out what you want to do in life and you'll probably settle for mediocrity in your career.

Mercury opposite Uranus

You possess an extreme amount of intellectual ability, but basically, you're a misunderstood genius with a knack for incurring wrath from others. This is one of the most interesting alignments Mercury can make. Both Mercury and Uranus are brilliantly innovative, and when they oppose like this, the intelligence is there, but requires a direction to focus on. Other alignments will turn you into a prodigy of music, science, or art. Any aspect with Mercury is mainly influencing your brain, nervous system, and sometimes physical agility. If Venus is involved then you either have a beautiful singing voice or strong public speaking abilities. When this aspect is exact, or in a fire/air polarity then speech impediments, nervousness, or mental disability will most likely exist. Many times you feel your opinions are the only valid ones, and assume everyone will just agree with you. When they don't you become angrily agitated. You may also develop a "know it all" attitude towards those below you in your profession. If you develop and interest into science or technology don't shy away from it. Although Mercury aspects don't indicate direct careers, finding employment in the fields of medicine or research and development can prove interesting and lucrative.

Mercury opposite Neptune

An opposition between Mercury and Neptune bolsters your imagination and creativity, just not in a productive way. You have unique and original ideas but you struggle to identify a distinct style. Whether it's art, writing, or music, there's a desire to create and get lost in your own personal dream world. Be careful not to get too lost in your fantasies, there will be difficulties deciphering between the truth and fiction. When left unchecked this aspect can throw you into a whirlwind of delusion and confusion, the two things Neptune does best. Because Neptune is a generational planet there will need to be a relationship formed with your ascendant for this energy to be fully functioning. Unless you have other aspects altering your chart you will find competition useless and unnecessary. Because Mercury has a direct effect on your cognitive thinking abilities, when influenced by the compassionate and humanitarian properties of Neptune you may become dedicated to changing the world. When you don't plan your actions carefully you find significant flaws in your ideas. Quite often your imagination is grander than in actual reality and your dreams are simply too big. Finding a way to use your creative talents will not be difficult what will be tough is staying focused long enough to see things through. With psychic abilities and a heightened intuition you can see and predict things before they happen. You are very keen on the emotions and feelings of others and are a sucker for a sob story. Any person with a sad tale will not be turned aside.

Mercury opposite Pluto

Alignments between Mercury and Pluto make you psychic to the truest sense of the word. You have great intuition and can read into the unbroadcasted motives of others. Your intellect is keen and you see the broader picture to the universe. You easily grasp onto metaphysical subjects and can accept the abstract as true. The fact of the matter is you are a witch, wizard, magician, sage, or whatever you would like to call it. Even if you reject your abilities the glimpses of conscious intuition as well as psychic dreams will be prevalent throughout your life. You're a ghost magnet and will probably experience several paranormal activities. This also makes you very sensitive when others question your intelligence or credibility. You're quick to defend yourself, and lash out verbally when opposed, if Mars is involved as well you may get physically violent as well. Pluto is the emperor of obsession and jealousy. When he and Mercury align in any way it indicates a mind which locks into one single thing. At its worst this aspect makes it impossible to think about anything other than is what's in front of you. This particular formation can also cause you to become dangerously focused on only one or two things. Whether it's people, possessions, or philosophies Pluto isn't known for letting go easily. Those who completely reject do so with the utmost passion. It can also indicate an interest into medicine and psychology.

Venus opposite ascendant

The beauty and refinement of Venus draws you towards the sophisticated lifestyle. Enjoying the finer things in life, you're clean, well dressed, and overly concerned with the way you appear to others. All too often you see people for more than they actually may be. You consistently give people the benefit of the doubt no matter how undeserving they really are. It's this over appraisal of their talents which causes you to give them too much credit when you know you shouldn't. You think everyone you associate with is of the highest of characters and are shocked if they don't live up to your expectations. Although you appear confident on the outside, deep within there is an issues with your own personal character flaws. As you mature and can identify these insecurities they become more easily dealt with. It can be difficult for you to do things on your own. If you can find someone that you can rely on for help you make a wonderful partner. You turn your nose up at the seedier underworld of life, and have no interest in associating with those who don't care enough to groom themselves. At the

227

absolute worst this makes you completely dependent on someone else. When heavily afflicted you see all your flaws and think you're incompetent.

Venus opposite Mars

Other than the square, the opposition is the most problematic alignment for Venus and Mars. Oppositions between these two make you passionate and highly volatile. Many times you're a diva like queen, over dramatizing the little nuances in your life. You're usually absorbed in yourself and what you want. In love, you're a glutton for punishment and endure severe abuses. You're not very compromising and become highly irritable when you don't get what you want, when you want it. As a child you probably threw hissy fits and tantrums when you were told no. If not you have magnificent calming influences elsewhere. You unconsciously project an animal like magnetism that naturally offends some people, especially those of the same gender. The truth is that you are very sensitive to criticism and the opinions of others. When people judge or treat you harshly you become enraged and sometimes physically violent. Until you can learn to compromise and get along with others you will constantly experience the social and professional estrangements. Pay attention the emotions and feelings of others. Your self-centered nature may be taken as cold heartedness and turn potential friends away. House placement is key because it will show where your relationships will experience the most problems.

Venus opposite Jupiter

No aspect between Venus and Jupiter can be considered bad, but of the possibilities the opposition is one of the worst. Although there are negativities to the opposition, they're mostly because you've spent too much time and money on fun. Drinking and living the high life causes your resources to dwindle, and is the main source of your financial woes. Psychologically this opposition causes you to constantly second guess your final decisions, and frequently contemplating what could have been.

Part of the problem is that Jupiter's expectations are always higher than accomplishable and Venus places this philosophy into your relationships. This aspect most definitely doesn't give you a back bone, and quite often it indicates you become completely dependent on your partner. You make concessions to others thinking their admiration will be gained from it. When influenced positively this makes your artistic ability extremely profound. Nothing appreciates the finer arts more than Venus and Jupiter is a close number two. That is why you spend all your money on possessions.

Venus opposite Saturn

When Venus is opposing Saturn you underestimate your self-worth and need constant competition in order for reassurance. You have to examine all your good qualities and continually remind yourself you're as talented as others. As a child you were probably convinced you weren't as intelligent or capable as your classmates. Because of this inferiority complex you make concessions to others thinking it will win their approval. Over dramatizing your everyday responsibilities will get on the nerves of your loved ones. It's true you do a lot, but many times you think you deserve more credit and attention than you actually get. This starts an emotional chain reaction leading into a vicious circle of arguments and fights. Know your role and shut your mouth. Romantically, it's best to wait until later in life before you marry. Take your time and pick your mate wisely, the financial stability of your spouse will be important. This will make you only when you are in a secure and comfortable relationship. If you rush into a marriage you will end up with nothing but a sorrowful broken heart. At the worst this indicates a terribly estranged relationship with your father. Even if he was involved in your life he was probably neglectful, and possibly abusive. Sometimes when afflicted by other planets this can indicate an affair with an person with a significant age difference.

229

Venus opposite Uranus

This opposition causes you to be emotionally volatile and unstable. Uranus is highly unpredictable and Venus places this essence into your relationships. You're attracted to individuals who are exceptionally unique and have their own sense of style. The more someone expresses their individuality the more you're interested. Part of the problem is you must be completely free and allowed to do as you please. Committed relationships only bog you down so you flee somewhere less restrictive once the restraints are felt. If you marry in your early years chances are it will end in divorce. This is because you eventually realize how much your flirtatious freedom actually meant. Venus is completely dependent on being in a structured relationship and Uranus wants nothing of the sorts. It's possible you marry four or five times before you realize only casual relationships are the only thing for you. Uranus inspires brilliance. The influence of Venus can then direct this intelligence into art, music, or theater. Your creative talents dwell in the realm of the abstract. Stay true to your imagination and your creation may change the world. Other than a square this is the most problematic aspect for any planets to have.

Venus opposite Neptune

An opposition between Venus and Neptune causes you to have a vivid and sometimes distorted imagination. All alone this makes you dreamy and fanciful with nowhere to direct it. This aspect requires a driving force where your creative abilities can be utilized. When properly aspected this can make you a wonderful artist or actor. This is because you can get lost in delusional fantasies easily. The dream world is difficult for you to separate from reality and if you don't ground your thoughts chaos ensues. You're gullible to a fault and can get taken advantage of easily. Neither of these planets handles their problems directly. Both are prone to becoming dependant on others. These planets both represent unconditional love. Venus requires something in return, but Neptune asks for nothing. You're very spiritual, but you learn more from listening to others than you do by reading and thinking

230

for yourself. Once you hear something that makes sense you apply the philosophies to your life as you choose. Once you can establish a distinct difference between reality and fantasy then you can tap into your vast amounts of creative abilities. You believe others are more capable than they really are, and expect them to accomplish things they simply can't. The self-doubting ways of Neptune are interjected into your relationships by Venus and you have to come to grips with your own insecurities. Challenging yourself to things you believe you aren't capable of will be extremely difficult. Because of your sensitivity you will need to develop a personal relationship with your coworkers. It won't be until you turn your guard level down and allow others in before you will feel any sort of personal comfort.

Venus opposite Pluto

Oppositions from Venus are difficult to handle because they produce tensions within certain aspects of all your relationships. First off, their house placement will show what you cling onto the tightest. When the opposition is with Pluto it makes it nearly impossible for you to get over the past when broken by failed relationships. Chances are you fall painstaking in love only to be shattered when let downs occur. Then you become passionately vengeful and start slashing tires. Part of your romantic mishaps will be caused by your desire for complete control and dominance over your partner. This alignment can make you forcefully controlling and manipulative. When negatively influenced from elsewhere you sink to the most devious of ways to attain your supremacy. You have intense emotions that cloud your judgment and ability to make rational decisions. Because of your fear of emotional responsibility and attachment you may avoid personal contact with others. One unfortunate possibility is the intense desire to seclude yourself from everyone and everything. Money will be the cause of many problems in any permanent relationships. Both Venus and Pluto are driven by passion for possessions, although for entirely different reasons. The actual problem is the excessive demands you make of your partners, and

231

their possessive attitude towards you. This also gives you a darker possibly more sinister perspective on art. Old ancient texts, paintings, and other arts will decorate your walls. Skulls, bones, and things associated with death of regeneration will interest you. Be cautious to open up freely to others, you should avoid close friendships until you are sure that person is worthy of your confidence.

Mars opposite ascendant

This is a bad aspect, just plain bad. Because of this you attract people who want to threaten or harm you. You seem to enjoy the strife, and have a chip on your shoulder challenging others to knock it off. The fact of the matter is you have little self-confidence, and the over aggressive bravado is just a cover up of your true feelings. Experiencing the tender and sentimental emotions in life scares you, and you build up walls of defense to keep them at bay. When others try to break those walls down you feel they're invading into your personal life and become agitated. It's the fear attracting you towards others who are frightened by emotions as well. Because of the distractions they provide, you're not happy unless there are severe tensions in your life. If there are no problems, you create an imaginary one, just to have something to complain about. Unless directed into positive outlets you can be violent and rude. Competitions where you can prove your abilities to others will be a good outlet for this energy. The aggressive energies of Mars flow out easily when it is positioned like this. As you mature and harness this excessive energy, the determination produced can drive you into a happier life. Chances are you grew up angry. If you were teased or picked on as a child, these scars will follow you into your adult years. It is easy for you to hold onto grudges and ill feelings. Professional help may be needed in order to deal with these psychological traumas.

Mars opposite Jupiter

When Mars is opposite Jupiter you become highly volatile and competitive. Your aggressive nature constantly seeks out challenges which can prove your abilities. However, this overly dominant personality will often take on more than it can handle. Because you feel your opinions are superior it's very difficult to compromise and get along with others. Completely resentful of those who wish to force their authority upon you, you react instantly and sometimes violently when someone does. This reaction will also cause you to alienate your friends and colleagues. When severely afflicted by other planets, especially Uranus, this can be a chart wrecker, making you angry and resentful at the world. You will need deep meditation and personal reflection in order to combat your overly pessimistic demeanor, and an athletic outlet is also needed. If you can't stop being angry and let go of grudges the only person suffering will be you. Once you learn to be comfortable in your own skin the sky is the limit for your success. As you mature and learn to forgive yourself and others for the harms they perpetuated then your life will settle down and fall into place. The biggest malfunction is your overinflated ego that believes failure is impossible. This attitude makes you take on more responsibility than you can accomplish and become bitterly resentful when others point out your failures.

Mars opposite Saturn

When Mars is in opposition with Saturn you have a direct confliction between what you want and your responsibilities in getting it. You fluctuate between periods of heightened energy into periods where nothing gets accomplished. It will be nearly impossible to succeed until you can direct your passions productively. Once you accept your responsibilities to yourself and others the tensions caused are certainly relieved. This can be a long and painful process, especially if there are severe afflictions elsewhere. Saturn and Mars have earned their malefic name for a reason, and it isn't a good one. Possibly the most unfortunate part of this is the strain it places on your relationship with your father. It's possible he was neglectful, or even physically abusive. Either way the trauma you endure causes you to become subconsciously angry and irritable. Because of his lack of support and positive

233

reinforcement you develop the feeling that your competitors are more qualified than you are. This is only sometimes true, and you must realize your own skill set. Once you learn your own capabilities you become comfortable in your own skin and function properly. It won't be before you learn the awesome powers of forgiveness until you will experience inner peace. If the Moon is negatively involved this can indicate severe tensions with your mother as well. Your overly inflated view of your abilities is only a cover to hide the deeper insecurities which haunt you. You are either all in or all out, and there will be extreme difficulties finding a happy medium somewhere in between. Meditation and reflection will help you focus and ground your negative energies.

Mars opposite Uranus

This aspect is bad. Really, really, bad. Alignments between Mars and Uranus are always difficult to handle and other than the square an opposition is the worst. You have extreme amounts of energy and explode violently when not properly directed. This alignment makes you an intense competitor, and losing is never an option. You thrive on competition and have a natural ability to gain dominance over someone. The simple fact, you're arrogant. You possess an ego which always needs to constantly express itself and always be kept in check. This isn't to say you can't be calmed down by other planetary influences, but there's a lot of gun powder in the keg. You believe you're destined to succeed and nothing can stop you. This planetary relationship can cause you to have several cases of uncontrollable aggression. Depending on which sign and house placement this aspect takes place in will determine just where you direct your aggression. As with everything there are good qualities produced by this. Sign and house, as well as positive aspects from the other planets can produce brilliant and innovative inspirations. Where you direct your intelligence is up to you. These oppositions occur about once every three years and are definitely an unusual aspect to have in your chart. If Mercury or Venus is in aspect as well you may have a wonderful singing voice.

Mars opposite Neptune

Dreams, intuition, and psychic abilities are in the realm ruled by Neptune. When Mars is opposing them their energies become active, but not always productive. Your dreams are vivid and prophetically psychic at times. Quite often you wake up having difficulty separating the dream world from the real world. If you choose to use and focus this energy into something productive you can be a brilliant artist or musician. The mystical and the magical will interest you, and these fancies shouldn't be ignored. You enjoy anything that sparks the imagination along with any creative possibilities. Your subconscious is deeper than others and your connection to the spirit world is there for the taking. Although you may be fascinated with the occult take special caution. There may be doors better left shut, your intense curiosity may expose you to things not to be trifled with. Make sure not to get too carried away if you do get into the world of magic, your views of reality aren't always accurate. House placement is important because of the confusions it causes. Their placement will show where you need to be the most careful when taking action.

Mars opposite Pluto

The opposition between Mars and Pluto indicates the inability to control your energy and aggression. Your defiant attitude causes others to respond negatively without you knowing why. Because you're constantly on the defensive, the style and manner you talk places others there as well. You have a magnetic way in which you can control people, and constantly use your charm to woo the affections of others. You can be obsessed with power and control, going to extreme measures to acquire both. It will be important for you to determine if your motives are out of your desire for authority and if they're logically sound. Most of all you will need to assess the possible positive and negative outcomes of all your actions. This aspect can also indicate a major injury or illness you're forced to overcome. You possess amazing resiliency, and can recover from traumatizing events quickly, but those events have to occur before you can rebound. It's pretty much guaranteed that you will experience harsher situations than most. Domestic turmoil and personal affairs can cause extreme jealousy and possessiveness. You may also have severe anger management problems which will need to be dealt with by a professional counselor. This is a very explosive alignment and hopefully you have soothing influences from the other planets, mainly Venus or the Moon. If not you will be uncontrollably angry.

Jupiter opposite ascendant

When Jupiter is opposing your ascendant, this is a good indicator of a bombastic, flamboyant, and inspirational personality. Unlike most oppositions this one can produce large amounts of positive energy which you project outwardly to others. The generalized adjectives of optimistic, generous, and compassionate are all overly used when describing Jupiter. Granted there are several wonderful possibilities with this aspect, there are a few ways this can go amuck. This can give you an over inflated opinion of yourself, your abilities, or your possessions. Your gregarious nature can cause others to see you as arrogant and conceited. Because you over emphasize your ideas and resources others follow along blindly, only to be let down by your failure. If you're not careful you're going to constantly bite off more than you can chew, resulting in lack luster production. Don't take this as a bad alignment, just remain cautious when trying to analyze yourself or your supporting crew. Part of the reason you do succeed is the fact you always see the light at the end of the tunnel. Jupiter is the gentile giant who's massive both physically and spiritually. This aspect can make you larger than life and a legend even if in your own mind.

Jupiter opposite Saturn

An opposition between Jupiter and Saturn causes serious fluctuations between over confidence in your abilities to an unidentifiable insecurity. You aren't completely sure about what you're capable of and how to go about getting that accomplished. Constant reassurance from your peers is needed to fill this unnatural void. Chances are your parents conditioned you to think you weren't as useful as you truly were. It's possible they did everything for you and you failed to learn to fend for yourself. They may have also criticized you exceptionally harsh. No matter how good you were they always pointed out faults and where improvement was needed. More often than not this comes from your father or male figure head. In the professional world you have a yin yang like quality about you. You consistently seek out the challenges set forth by others if their approval isn't instantaneous you alienate them and reject their opinion. Make sure not to surround yourself with nothing but "yes men" as this will only over inflate your already large ego. As you climb into prominence within your chosen professional ranks be careful not to become too over confident. If you think you can never fail you eventually will and be devastated. Realize that everyone has valid points from time to time and you can possibly learn from all your acquaintances.

Jupiter opposite Uranus

Oppositions are usually very difficult to handle, but if you're lucky Jupiter can use the energy of Uranus to the fullest. You're a highly eccentric, highly individualized person who has vast amounts of useful knowledge. Since your childhood years you realized you were very different than your peers. You're quick to act, and easily adaptable to any situation. You can pull yourself through difficult times faster than most. This is because of your wonderful outlook and optimism on life. There is always light at the end of your tunnel and although you still have to face problems most people don't, you always pull through. Religion and spirituality should play a large role in your life. If you don't meditate you should meditate because locked in your head are hidden secrets to the universe. Your unique personality will attract friends from many walks of life. Caring more about behavior than appearance, you tend to wait on judging others until a solid opinion can be formed. Eccentric and innovative as you mature into your older years you will only get crazier. Late in life mental disorder such as Alzheimer's, dementia, and bi-polarity can be an issue. Your larger than life ego is the biggest downfall and you're going to need to watch your arrogance. Most of your failures will occur because you have failed to recognize the resources, skill, and effort needed to finish. Aspects from Saturn will stabilize this and allow you to direct your attention into productive projects.

Jupiter opposite Neptune

This aspect often indicates you make plans and promises you're incapable of keeping, or won't fulfill. It isn't because you don't try hard or care, you just think too big for your britches. When you make these plans and promises you do so honorably and with the best of intentions, but for some reason you just fail to come through. It's possible you feel the expectations of others are too high and you can never live up to them. Most often it's because you have over inflated opinions about your abilities and resources. The resulting effects cause you to feel alone and alienated when you fail to complete something. Many times you're in disagreement with others who insist they are smarter and more competent than you. Your desire to prove everyone wrong traps you in a spiraling web of anxiety and depression. When accepting duties make sure not to accept too many responsibilities in which you will receive no compensation. Quite often you bite off more than you can chew and have difficulties handling the after effects. Be cautious when partaking in drugs or alcohol, this aspect can and usually will produce obsessive addictions. Unfortunately this means you must experience spiritual expansion through difficult circumstances. Difficulties accepting and applying spirituality is another disadvantage of this relationship. Either you establish a strict set of dogmatic laws for yourself, or you completely resist religion. Part of your problem is you see the vastness of the universe and don't accept the follies of organized religion. Other times you do understand higher philosophies, it's just nearly impossible for you to figure out how to apply them to your life.

Jupiter opposite Pluto

Although this can intensify bad aspects it usually doesn't. By no means does this indicate your life is full of peaches and rainbows, but for most people this is going to be used as a comforting alignment. Unfortunately the extreme energies can only be released by catastrophic events. Many times this indicates a sudden horrific experience you have to dig deep within yourself to resolve. The house placement of Pluto is where that event will occur, and the placement of Jupiter is where you need to go to resolve it. Quite often this will be related to death, loss of property, or a significant hospital visit. Death is inevitable and those situations are always difficult. When it does occur it's always meant to open our eyes to the universe and accept our own mortality. Psychologically this alignment causes you to be intently focused on only a few issues. All your attention and efforts can be directed toward only a handful of endeavors. This is one reason you're so successful. Because you give your all into your chosen projects they usually turn our well. Obsession is always mentioned when dealing with Pluto, and the expansive properties of Jupiter can create quite a demon in your head. This is a driver aspect that is going to be modified by other planets and house positioning. The relationship with your ascendant is important as well. Generational planets like Pluto always need an aspect to the ascendant to release the most potency. You love discussions debating religious, social, or political philosophies. When others don't agree with you, you simply state your point more forcefully. Sometimes you feel if you're louder and more flamboyant that will make you accurate. At its worst this over inflates Jupiter's already big ego, and you're an arrogant bastard. At its best you're the ultimate humanitarian who gives up everything to help those less fortunate.

Saturn opposite ascendant

When Saturn is opposing your ascendant this indicates you're usually on the defensive and quick to raise your guard. You're generally over cautious and extremely slow to warm up, it's difficult for you to deal with large groups of people who you don't know. You prefer others take initiative and make the first move. You do this because you feel if they are the ones approaching you, they have already accepted you, and your defenses can be lowered. Your major malfunction is you instinctually assume no one will like you and can see all your faults. This in turn causes you to form the unnatural phobia towards strangers. Just because you're naturally reclusive doesn't mean you're not intelligent and don't work hard. Saturn is the most responsible of the planets. The opposition to your ascendant usually creates tensions when accepting responsibility. What's occurring is you're unconsciously over compensating for your inadequacy. If you don't try you can't fail. Romantically it causes trouble because despite your closeness, you still have trouble opening up to your partner. Chances are you had a less than functional relationship with your father and it has followed you along. Although you're completely capable of thinking for yourself the sheltered way in which you were raised causes you to think differently. If your childhood was abusive or neglectful this aspect will make it nearly impossible to handle the trauma. You will need to search deep within yourself and forgive the individuals that have harmed you.

Saturn opposite Uranus

Saturn in opposition to Uranus shows you're an independent and competitive individual who probably doesn't get along with others too easily. It especially indicates an interest finding an unusual profession. It can also show you have different education than most. Probably from the school of hard knocks. You think you're in constant competition for no specific reason. When you're wrong you go to great lengths to prove your correctness. Even after you're proven wrong multiple times you still have doubts and get incredibly irritable. Although you're intelligent your logic isn't always sound and based upon factual evidence. You're definitely a unique and innovative individual. At its best this indicates success at a very strange and unusual job. Or your father had one as well. Your mind is filled with numerous zany ideas, and it's important to acknowledge others can help stabilize your crazy endeavors. This is one of the most difficult alignments to have. Saturn is restrictive and hates everything new. Uranus hates everything old and wants to create something new. Obviously this generates a conflict. House placement is vitally important because it will indicate where you have the most unexpected issues with the work involved. You associate yourself with people who have as much drive and energy as you do. If you can refrain from assuming you should be starting on top there are no fields in which you can't succeed. If you do attain a position of authority make sure it doesn't go to your head, remember what it was like when you were the low man on the totem pole and act accordingly.

Saturn opposite Neptune

All alignments between these two are very tricky to describe accurately. Both are slower moving and their alignments, especially the opposition, occur very seldom. The houses they occupy and their relationship to your ascendant are critically important. Saturn opposing Neptune generally indicates you don't like competition and naturally distrust most people. Your refusal to accept competitions are due to your intense fear of failure. This planetary combination can make you a hypochondriac, highly paranoid, or even obsessively compulsive. It's possible you're a hoarder as well. Sometime individuals will be very confused about their responsibilities to society. Although you see the atrocities and injustices around the world you still may not be driven enough to start something of your own. It would be best for you to join a group which has already gotten things off the ground. You can be a wonderful assistant, using your organizational and imaginative skills to progress your program. If you were raised in an abusive or neglectful environment this will turn you into a recluse, shying away from everyone unfamiliar. Prominent aspects from Neptune can make you gullible and easily fooled. Because it's so difficult for you do determine truth from fiction others will recognize this and use it to their advantage. This issues caused in your romantic relationships are instigated by your inability to recognize your duties. You can also be fooled by the simplest gesture, thinking it

241

means more than it does. Chances are that you will experience romantic letdowns throughout your lifetime.

Saturn opposite Pluto

The biggest problem with an alignment between Saturn and Pluto is the infrequency it occurs. Because of this, not everyone experiences their relationship in the same way, and house placement is vitally important. It will show where you obsess about the most responsibility and the area of life to take most seriously. Oppositions with Pluto also indicate others frequently walk over you in their quest for power. You consistently put yourself into dangerous situations which are questionable at best. If you immerse yourself into the seedy underworld of society you will find it difficult to get yourself out. The friends you associate with must be analyzed thoroughly to determine their true intentions. If you can't realize not everyone has your best interest in mind then the continual spiral of turmoil will continue. Make sure there is evidence of productivity before you accept promises of financial gain. This aspect is not a good one by any means. This can also indicate that you will experience severe abuses from your father or male parental figure. If you were abused as a child the emotional traumas produced may be nearly impossible to recover from. Emotionally clingy, any horrific experiences as a child will scar you significantly. It won't be until you can forgive your abusers before any emotional healing can take place. Not only can this make you a doormat for others to walk on this can also make you intensely jealous and possessive.

Uranus opposite ascendant

This can be one of the more interesting influences someone can have. When in opposition to your ascendant, Uranus makes you eccentric and well, just kind of loopy. You're most definitely your own unique character and don't care who knows it. You demand all the freedom to pursue whatever you choose, the only problem is choosing that endeavor. Relationships only stand in the way of your spirit and are sometimes seen as a burden. You attract people who demand independence as much as you do. As you develop your relationship with them you become annoyed by what you're expected to give up in turn. Once you feel too restrained the relationship must end. Your enthusiasm is shared by those who defy authority and assert their rebelliousness. In the professional world, not surprisingly, you must work alone and at your own pace. Your ingenuity and innovative skills are off the chart and you think outside the box at all times. You're fascinated by things that can move, blink, or buzz. Technological research and development or medical advancement can prove to be productive outlets for your intelligence. Determined to do whatever you want, whenever you choose to, you let nothing deter you from your path. If there is no path to where you want to go, you will just tromp through whatever is there creating your own. Others who choose to follow are met with open arms. If Mars is involved the psychological stresses will turn you athletic, combative, and violent. At its best this makes you the most brilliant of geniuses.

Uranus opposite Neptune
        Occurring in the early 1900's this rare and powerful aspect affects the generations of the world, not just individuals. Not aligning like this again until 2080 the relationship of these to planets will propel humanity into spiritual divineness, and oneness with our universe. This aspect indicates that people become unaware of the freedoms they possess. Generational aspects take time to form, last a long time, then take more time to separate. Aspects formed by other planets, especially the ascendant will add their own personal potency to this equation. Due to the infrequency of this aspect there aren't many, if any, alive with it in their charts. Those who do are nearly dead.

Uranus opposite Pluto
        This aspect is extremely rare. Occurring in the early 1900's this aspect won't form again until 2048. No one alive will have this aspect.

Neptune opposite Asc.

The relationship Neptune has with your ascendant is more important than any other planet or point. Similar to the conjunction, you possess a vivid imagination and have immense artistic abilities. Problem being, you don't know how to integrate these energies into your personality. Lots of your abstract visions are only understandable to you. Remember that Neptune is least dominant planet and only adds an essence of spirituality and cultivated creativity towards wherever other planets direct it. Along with the Quite often you're too sympathetic making you an easy target for those wanting your resources. Be cautious of everyone you meet and make sure their intentions are positive. This planet is mystical and magical compelling you into a world of spirituality. Whether it be in a strict religious doctrine or your own personal path, the spirit guides within the universe are spiraling throughout your head. Although you possess natural creative skills this doesn't mean you know how to use them. The timid nature of Neptune doesn't allow you to aggressively pursue all your ideas and passions. If you aren't careful you will become dependent on others and refuse to fend for yourself.

Pluto opposite Ascendant

This aspect indicates the skills you possess in attracting strong and influential people. You have a deep desire for close personal relationships. So much so, you may become completely obsessed with someone. The energies of Pluto are intense and passionate, causing you significant turmoil and distress. When negatively influenced by other planets this aspect can cause you to react instantly and destructively, without ever contemplating the consequences. Infatuated by power, you aggressively pursue positions of authority and dominance. When your superiority is questioned you become extremely bitter and sometimes enraged. Because you generally get what you want areas of politics and financial activities can be proper professions. Unfortunately this aspect can also indicate you must face many more relationship difficulties than most. As one of the three generational planets aspects formed the ascendant make the influence of Pluto greater. As the most distant planet, Pluto is compared to Shiva the destroyer. It isn't a personal planet and generally acts as an amplifier for the energies produced elsewhere. This opposition always indicates a sixth or seventh house placement, which shows the destruction coming by way of other people. Sometimes you find other secretly working against you in the workplace.

Sun signs

Sun in Aries
    Aries is the cardinal fire sign, ruled by the planet Mars. Leo maybe the king of the zodiac, but Aries is the crown prince. He's the brave Lancelot of King Arthur's court . It's the sign of inspirational beginnings, igniting brilliance and intelligence. You're full of great ideas, many of which never take off. In general Aries is the arrogant attention seeker always showing off. When you don't receive the attention you feel is due you simply act up more. The spotlight is a natural place for you. Aries is usually over inflated and full of its own ego. He's also as the person climbing into the tree saving a stranded kitten. You're a go getter, the first to volunteer, the first to start fussing, and then the first to break off on your own. Determined and pioneering, you seek to venture off where most are terrified to travel. Blazing your own path is a trend amongst most Aries. This makes you stubborn, hot headed, and difficult to deal with. If your parents were inattentive and ignored you then this can produce severe emotional trauma. When directed negatively towards the other planets in your chart the intense energy produced can and probably will cause severe psychological issues. Represented by the fire ram you're rambunctious and daring. You probably like causing mischief and trouble, requiring constant supervision as an infant. A wonderful idea person, you get agitated when your suggestions are casually brushed aside. The ego inside you is bigger than you care to admit and will be the cause of many problems in your life. You have no difficulty

245

apologizing when you realize you're wrong, the issue is admitting your mistake. Going from calm to raging mad isn't difficult, and even if your fuse is longer than most once you snap, you're a goner. Aries always likes being in charge and if you can't lead the pack or dominate easily you're likely to storm like a tornado of fire spitting obscenities all the way.

Sun in Taurus

Taurus is the determined, stubborn, and bull headed Earth sign. Slow and steady is the pace for those born during the second sign of the zodiac. The ruling planet Venus and the exalting luminary of the Moon will be very influential in your chart. Generally speaking Taurean's are very fixed in their ways. Once Taurus sets in to something it's nearly impossible to get them to stop, or get them going again. Whether negative or positive, someone born under this sign rarely strays from their normal path. Breaking habits are extremely difficult. Any addictions to drugs or alcohol will lead you down a dark destructive path. Intellect and brain power take a back seat to strength and hard work. Hopefully you will have other planets with good house placement and aspects to give you some mental aptitude.

If Mercury is the sign of Gemini or Aries, then you're in luck. In that case, this positioning will give you both brains and brawn. Intelligence aside, you're a loving caring person deeply devoted to your friends and family. If you're lucky enough to have some intellectual endowment, business and management will suit you well. You can be organized, motivated, and trust worthy enough for your superiors to give you more responsibility and authority than most. As the fixed Earth sign, Taurus is naturally drawn to Earthly things. You take great pride in your home, your family, and the possessions you acquire throughout your life. If you aren't careful you may become materialistic and superficial. You can rise to great power, authority, and social status. So much so it will drive you crazy. As you reach your second Saturn return you will begin to feel the pressure of everything you have gained throughout your life, and your Responsibility will bog you down

246

when you need to get away. This will be when you will realize how many important family moments you may have missed because of work.

Sun in Gemini

Quick, agile, and clever are always the first three adjectives describing Gemini. These comedians are the pee drinking jackasses like Ryan Dunn and Steve-O. They're brilliant lyrical geniuses like Kanye West, and actors like Johnny Depp. Mercury is the ruler and the Sun's relationship with that tiny planet is vital. Individuals with this Sun sign have nervous disorders, paranoia, and sometimes speech impediments. The biggest problem for Gemini is the complete inability to focus on one thing for more than thirty seconds. You're distracted easily, and anything moving or flashing sparks your curiosity. You get into one thing, only to start thinking about what will be done next. Most Gemini's have a dual personality and no one can cover up their sorrowful emotions better than this sign. Their adaptability and ability to catch on quickly provides an instant advantage. Music, foreign languages, science, and technology can be interesting to the point of a career. As a child they get into everything, trying to figure out how the little wheels spin. Gemini is always a trouble maker and the master at mischief. Gemini is the ultimate smart mouthed sidekick who never shuts up.

Communications are the specialty for Gemini and you should consider a career in that area. Having social interaction with others is very important and your profession must allow you to be around the public. Just make sure not to get caught up in useless gossip. Stay away from any hardcore drugs. If you choose to partake in any speed drugs then you're in trouble, the last thing Gemini needs is more energy. Addictions will get to you hard and fast, destroying your life quickly. If your Sun is in tight aspect with Mars you will be extremely athletic, possibly even a professional. Many times you will run yourself ragged, simply because you burn up so much energy so quickly you hit a wall are completely spent. When it's time to go to bed then it's time to go to bed. Everything you do is sporadic and you must learn to use your energy in short bursts, not long durations. Aspects from other planets in will provide you with focus and direction. Most of all remember to slow down and pay attention to what is in your hands, not what you think you're about to do next.

Sun in Cancer

Cancer is the kindest, warmest, most tender hearted sign in the zodiac. They're absolutely infatuated with their family but unfortunately, cardinal water sign is represented by the crab for a reason. Although nothing is more important than providing for your immediate loved ones your tendency to allow dependence is your greatest flaw. If you're not careful you expend too many of your resources on the trivial matters of your family. Your siblings may become drug addicts because you constantly support their habit. Because you hate to see them suffer you continually repeat the same behavior. You're ruled by the Moon, and the maternal characters are never stronger than in this sign. Jupiter is the planet second in strength and if there's an alignment between the two the potency will be massive. Like the crab which represents it, you have hard exterior shell that's difficult to crack. Gaining your love is a slow process proven only by several emotionally bonding circumstances, which occur over an elongated period of time. The claws of Cancer always refuse to let go and once someone gains your love you're never going to forget the emotions they invoked. When you become distressed, your natural instinct is to scurry away into a safe hiding spot and sulk. Once gloominess and depression set in, a cycle of calamity is created. Cancerians are the reason psychologists, psychiatrists, and counselors are still in business. You're more fragile and easily broken than you care to admit, and hopefully get a backbone from elsewhere. Beneath the outer crab shell is a delicate soft interior which is quickly bruised. Anyone who becomes part of your life will never be totally forgotten, and if you're harmed, rarely forgiven.

Sun in Leo

Leo is the grandest, most extravagant sign of the zodiac. Ruled by the Sun, this fixed fire sign is known for flamboyance, boisterousness, and attitude. Everyone born under Leo has to be the king of the kingdom and rule their domain. Whether it's a large company or your small family, no Leo is without their reign. To you the world is nothing more than a grand theater production in which you're the sparkling star. You love attention and will always return the favor with wonderful praise. You have a flair for the dramatic, and creating mountains out of molehills will be one of your specialties. Chances are you're loud, arrogant, and relatively self-centered. Other than Libra no one enjoys expensive and lavish things. Nothing is too extravagant. Even if your bank account is overdrawn you'll still find a way to eat at the most expensive restaurants and purchase the latest forms of fashion or gadgetry. Your public image is important, and it's easy to get caught up in public affairs. People will always be invading your personal space, and you'll be crossing boundaries as well.

This is the most regal sign, and when others don't give you an instant amount of respect you offend easily. Leo's love things being brought to them. Pretty much everything must be placed in front of you to attract any attention. Leo's are occasionally shy, but only at first. Get to know one and they won't shut up. All fire signs are known for having little time for hard work and you will have to realize not everything manifests instantly. Because there is so much natural talent within you, if something doesn't come effortlessly there is something more convenient to do. There is some area where you are going to be simply better, faster, or smarter and most people. Sometimes you're simply just better looking, and yes that can mean no brains. Leo isn't as smart as Aries or Sagittarius they just compensate with dominance. You enjoy the spotlight and attention of a grand entry and because it makes everyone look for you you're rarely on time. You want everyone's eyes on you and keeping them waiting does just that. You're generous and openhearted to everyone close. But like the lion Leo emulates, once you're crossed the claws come out, and you slash at the throat. Pride and egotism will often be your

249

downfall. Once you realize that the playing field is generally even and no one owes you anything success will be found in whatever you choose.

Sun in Virgo

Three words always used to describe Virgo are neat, organized, and analytical. Represented by the fair maiden and ruled by Mercury you're neither physically dominant nor aggressive with this trait. This is possibly the most timid sign of the zodiac and you will need to develop a backbone in order to survive. You always need to feel your services are required or helpful. Not only that, but your opinions must always be heard. Because of your constant desire to be loved and accepted you may tolerate an abusive relationship long past its departure. It's easy for you to get set in your ways, and never want to break away from your standard routine. This is because it indicates your thinking was wrong, and you never want your thinking to be wrong.

Admitting you made a mistake is very difficult because, once again, it means your thinking was wrong. You think it's impossible to be incorrect, and this constantly causes problems in your life. If you can learn to keep you opinions to yourself it's easy for you to get along with others. Realizing that other points are valid, and thinking in different ways can produce interesting results which will be extremely beneficial. When influenced by other planets this can make you a hoarder, hypochondriac, or have obsessive compulsive disorder. Professionally, this doesn't indicate a distinct career, but things requiring precision, organization, and patience should be considered. Your greatest asset is your ability to get along with those less fortunate. Because you love feeling needed you may attach yourself to someone dysfunctional and suffer from the abuse. This definitely isn't the strongest of placements for the Sun, but only because it doesn't inspire much fire alone.

Sun in Libra

Libra maybe the sign of peace and harmony, but this doesn't

mean you're peaceful and harmonious. When Libra's think they've lost control they scream louder and louder thinking their words will balance the situation. As the cardinal air sign, this makes you a neurotic basket case, who has think they're in control at all times. You possess great drive in attaining leadership because this means your opinion is final. This biggest problem here is your unwillingness to compromise more than fifty-fifty. When you're the beneficiary of imbalanced judgments or consequences there are no problems. But if you're the recipient of unfair results no sign is more offended and vocal. I also consider Libra the most oblivious sign of the zodiac. There is no one out there who can turn a blind eye to their inappropriate behavior, then criticize others for the same thing. Venus is the ruling planet and her influences along with house placement are vital. Libra is entirely dependent on others and this is my damsel in distress, who can't do anything for herself.

Venus is the ruling planet of this sign, and like the beautiful maiden you're helplessly falling on love time and time again. Once you settle down you're capable of commitment only when it's on your terms. Because this is an air sign, it greatly influences your cognitive thinking. Too much air can make you flakey and ditzy. Once the scales start tipping your mental imbalance causes you to make rash and sometimes inappropriate decisions. When your Sun is placed in Libra this intensifies your desires for close personal contacts. You want to be friends with everyone, and casually change your views to fit in with a conversation or crowd. Venus doesn't like fighting and confrontations. You will avoid physically involving yourself at all costs. Because of your usually delusional views on love you to will enter many dysfunctional relationships before you finally find your soul mate. Libras love the social scene, and adore the attention provided by the spotlight. Whether it be in the Hollywood limelight, or just the small town community politics, public admiration is very important to you.

Sun in Scorpio
Scorpio is the most secretive, seductive, and sexual sign of

the Zodiac. Currently ruled by Pluto and formerly ruled by Mars, the emotional intensity of Scorpio is matched by none other. Neither is the deviousness. As the fixed water sign you have an extreme personality, and your emotions often control your actions. Scorpio's react instinctually, and though their secretly slow showing emotions rarely do they reveal their true character. Your undying emotional attachments rival only fellow water signs Cancer and Pisces. Anyone who gets close to you is never truly gone, neither are the interesting individuals you casually meet throughout life. Never wanting someone else, especially an opponent, to gain an advantage, you mask your actual intentions or identity to others. As you cautiously allow your inner self to reveal itself, the true inside is nothing like the outside. Even when you think you know, you have no idea. Scorpio is the demon's spy, lurking in the darkness of the shadows, waiting to pounce. Like the pied piper you lead others into the world of your creation, only after they pass your tests. The mysterious and occult will fascinate you. Deep down inside, you're probably a witch.

You will fall for the wrong person several times before you can find your Earthly companion, and even then you may still wander. Because of the reclusive nature of Scorpio it's the most unknown sign of the zodiac. Only those who are possessed by it can describe it. As the most devious sign, it can release all the disturbing aspects in life and lead you into a destructive cycle of misfortune. You never forget a kind act, a vicious insult, and you hold a grudge farther than the grave. Letting go of your emotional upsets won't happen until you learn to forgive those who have harmed and disappointed you. If you reach deep into your subconscious you will discover realms as vast as the universe and beyond. The psychic and spiritual energies produced by your cosmic battery can and usually will produce tensions accepting who you truly are. Deep, inner self searching will be the only way to truly release your soul.

Sun in Sagittarius
Optimistic, enthusiastic, and energetic are always words used

252

to describe Sagittarius. Whether it's your Sun or your Moon there is plenty of flair and personality in here, especially in the later stages of the sign. As the mutable fire sign you get along well with everyone and make many friends along the way. Although friendly and talkative you only care to have a select few you truly open up to. Many times you're never in one place long enough to make a lasting relationship or impression. In romance your naturally flirtatious ways are not always taken so well by your partner. Luck will always seem to strike just when needed and the relationship with the planet Jupiter will have a lot to do with that. One negative side to a Sagittarian Sun is the unintentional arrogance that comes with it. Sometimes you think you and your opinions are bigger and grander than they are. People see this overly inflated attitude and misinterpret is as conceitedness You're never down for long and always see the brighter side of things and can bounce back from adversity faster than most. Possessing bright eyes and high spirits your flamboyance is very contagious, brightening up the day for others. With endless amounts of energy you will find you are happiest when helping others, any enterprises in which you are improving the environment or living conditions are sure to succeed, just make sure not to get too sure of your success before it happens. You can be boastful and arrogant, sometimes you will cross the boundaries of others, not intentionally, just you feel right at home with any one you please.

Sun in Capricorn

Capricorn is a difficult place for the Sun, and it has everything to do with the nature of the sign. Capricorn is the shrewd hearted Ebenezer Scrooge, counting his business earnings despite the cost to others. Deep inside your spirit wants to be left alone to simply tend to your chosen duties. This is a very rigid sign which rarely sways from the standard path once success is discovered. This is the cardinal Earth sign and can be quite obstinate most of the time. They're very similar to their Earth sign cousin Taurus when it comes to hard work and dedication. They may not be the first to show up to practice but that's because they're out running at three AM as a pre-practice warm up. The social side of Capricorn will have as much to do with education as it does with business. Most of your long term friends will be from either work or school. One of the biggest hang-ups with this Sun sign is the passionate desire to get your career noticed but not your personal life. Capricorn is the ultimate lawyer or politician. Remember it's your serious attitude that people can take negatively at times. Ruled by Saturn, Capricorn is a cautious, reserved, calculating sign, which must plan everything precisely. It generally takes you a while to warm up to people, and you don't like strangers just introducing themselves. You enjoy possessions because of the admiration that it draws from others. Much like the other cardinal signs of Aries, Cancer, and Libra, you have a very direct forward approach to your business. Whether it's good endeavors or bad, whatever you set your mind to you usually accomplish. Your failures are due to the repeated actions when solving difficult problems. Capricorn will break their skull ramming the same door in the same manner over and over again.

Sun in Aquarius

Aquarius is considered one of the Sun's dignitaries. Unfortunately, it's the sign of detriment and although it's still an extremely powerful sign there are some unusual difficulties going along with it. Unlike Sun's essence in Leo, this sign craves public recognition but doesn't like attention. Aquarius would rather be the dedicated scientist who hates the public but loves to address the masses about their latest achievement or discovery. This is a very intellectual and opinionated sign. People with their Sun in Aquarius feel everyone must know what they're thinking as if their word is final. Rigidity and inflexibility are often used when describing this sign. It's the fixed air sign whose modern ruler is Uranus but is still considered a ruling sign for Saturn as well. Because of your passionate desire to be different you choose activities that others consider weird. You may be allergic to everything. You may stick to a strict diet or workout regime. You may also dress like a clown and chase drunken foreigners down the street. Much of your success is due to your determination to see things done according to your standards. It's this quality, combined with your genius level innovativeness that propels you higher than the rest. Thomas Edison is a perfect example of an Aquarian Sun. Despite all his opponents disbelief he refused to give up after many of his first inventions failed. Then he invented the light bulb. You're the constant rebel willing to die for the cause. As a child any restrictions were met with possibly violent disagreement. Several times you do something just because someone told you no or that it was impossible. If you can listen to the advice of others you won't end up in those crappy situations. Once you reach the professional level you won't be happy unless you have a definitive role that is superior to those around you. Even if you're not your own employer you will strive for a position of authority and responsibility. Your eccentricity will sometimes push others away. Because you can be such a dominate personality, as you force yourself and your beliefs on others they basically tell you to piss off. You're going to lose friends and business associates because of your inability to cooperate. Take your time and let others warm up to you. Although it will be difficult, pay attention to what others are saying, it might just help you in the long run.

Sun in Pisces

The Sun in Pisces represents unconditional love and ultimate healing at its finest. Possibly the most sensitive sign of the zodiac, you're tender hearted to an uncomfortable extent. This makes you attracted to individuals who seem unstable and in need of help. Their problems unconsciously impact you, and letting them suffer is unbearable. You take on their dysfunctions trying to relate on their level only get sucked into their abyss. Wrong individuals constantly seem to find a way into your life. As the mutable water sign, being ruled by Jupiter and Neptune, if this in houses nine or twelve the compassion is magnified. Deep down you desperately want to make connections on an emotional level. Even when it's just a casual acquaintance, they warm up quickly, and often invade your personal space immediately.

255

You're usually quiet and a wonderful listener because it helps you understand where people are coming from. The fact you're able to help close friends in need provides you with the emotional security. Many times you will want to retreat into the depths somewhere alone but can't because you're too busy with prior commitments. Pisces is one of the most psychic sign and everything in the unconscious realm plays a vital role in your life. You're prone to drugs and alcoholism because they allow you to experience the different perceptions of the universe. Whether you focus on music, art, or theater, you're going to need somewhere to direct your visions.

Moon signs

Moon in Aries

The cardinal fire sign of Aries is a difficult sign for the Moon. This placement makes you emotionally volatile and overly anxious. The natural passiveness of the Moon combined with the fiery passions of Aries creates an uneasy turmoil which is difficult to suppress. You find your emotions are in constant fluctuation and sway dramatically. Unconsciously, you're constantly seeking attention from your peers, and you're not happy being average amongst them. The instantaneous spontaneity buried within your subconscious mind causes you to act hastily. Rash decisions in turn lead to unfortunate situations. Most of your problems are rooted in your conceited emotional needs. You feel deserving of more attention than you get, and when your needs aren't met you act out. Not much can match the emotional over reactivity when positioned here. The condition of the Moon between the Sun, Mars, and your ascendant is indescribably important. Negative afflictions from these will make you an angry bitch. Plain and simple.

Because you take instant action once you decide you want something, people sometimes become offended by your blatant approach to life. Patience will not be your strong suit, and as a child it will be difficult for you to share your toys, along with anything else. Emotions flare up instantly only to die out just as fast. You're full of good ideas once you get into something, but your attention is always diverted elsewhere and distracts you from finishing. In friendships along with romantic relationships you struggle with being tied down or restricted in any fashion. Your fleeting freedom keeps you from attaining any significant relationship.

Moon in Taurus

All of the wonderful, nurturing, and motherly powers of the Moon are exalted in the fixed Earth sign of Taurus. This is a calming influence that hopefully isn't all messed up by other planets. Reason being, you're as bull headed as they come. You get ostentatiously set in your own ways and refuse to listen to anyone. Things get done because you have the desire to work as hard as needed for success. The biggest problem is the direction you focus your passions. You're going to need brain power from somewhere else because Taurus isn't smart. They're represented by a cow for a reason. You carefully calculate your every move and everything must be precisely your way for things to work. In almost everything you do you will find it difficult to compromise with others. Stubborn and bull headed, you will sit with your bottom lip out, pouting until you get your way. Although the Moon is exalted in this sign, Venus is the ruling planet and any aspects between her, along with planets in the second or seventh houses will be prominent in your chart. In romance lunar Taurean's are the most content in a deeply devoted, committed relationship. Be very careful though, you will stay in an unhappy relationship far too long after it should be ended, fearing there is nobody else out there for you. You enjoy sticking with tradition and can't even fathom there could possibly be more excitement elsewhere. If your Sun sign is in an Earth sign this will add to your determination and drive in business. If you have an air Sun sign this will stimulate your drive to think and work for yourself. If your Sun is in a water sign this elevates your creative ability and nurturing senses. If you have a fiery Sun then this Moon placement will add to your physical strength and endurance.

Moon in Gemini

The best way I can describe the Gemini Moon is bltpbltpbltpb. That's me bumbling my tongue against my lips rambling a bunch of nonsense. The Moon in Gemini usually means one thing, completely scatterbrained. Gemini's are known for being quick witted, energetic, high strung, and overly talkative. But the influence of the Moon affects this like none other. The Moon is unstable, and the constant fluctuations are very difficult to handle. Nothing can bounce around from one thing to another faster than Gemini. Picking one thing up, only to put it down thirty seconds later because a butterfly fluttered by. The constant turmoil makes it nearly impossible to identify how you're feeling, and if you can't identify your emotions, the reactions are often wrong. On the brighter side of the Moon you can be brilliantly smart, with an interest in math, science, computers, or technology. Once you focus your attention onto something actual knowledge usually follows. Many times your rise to prominence isn't through hard work, it's through your friends and social connections that success comes about. This is the Mutable air sign and Mercury is the ruler, making your mind constantly active. You're a quick learner and possibly a very talented musician. Foreign language is something you can excel in as well. Conversations with you can get very lively and opinionated. Bouncing around from one random topic to the next you don't always know a lot about something just enough about everything.. Gemini is represented by the twins and there is a duality to your personality. A Gemini Moon is a good start to mental illnesses such as Alzheimer's, dementia, or schizophrenia as well. Any negative aspects from Saturn, Mars, or Neptune can cause this.

Moon in Cancer

As its ruling sign, there is no stronger position for the Moon than Cancer. Whether it be good or bad, emotions run high and there better not be very many harsh alignments from the other planets. The romantic, intuitive nature of Cancer, and the sensuous, receptive qualities of the Moon are in complete harmony and general you tend to be more receptive than active. You don't respond until there's an action from somewhere else. You store away impressions, possessions, and feelings until the end, clinging onto them passionately. You have an extremely retentive memory based on your emotional state. Meaning, you may not always remember what people say or do, but like all water signs, you always remember they made you feel. At heart, you're refined, delicate, and a gentle hearted softy. You may only appear to be aggressive and forceful, especially if the Sun or Mars is in a fire sign.

You tend to let your moods fester. Though you're subject to greater mood swings than any other sign, your ups and downs shouldn't last too long. Provided you don't dwell on them and make anything worse. You need to be left alone for a while in order for the clouds to get out of your head. You're at your best in a deep and committed relationship. Unfortunately, you often have to go through an unhappy love affair before you find the contentment and security you seek. Even though you're strongly motivated by feelings, in a curious way you're also afraid of them. It is your nature to mistrust love, you feel somewhat unworthy of someone else's devotion. You will hold on too long to a relationship that is destructive because you believe deep in your psyche that you will never find another love. You also believe that to be alone is a fate worse than death.

Moon in Leo

With your Moon in Leo the tender, nurturing qualities of the Moon are set ablaze by the fixed fire sign. You have very intense emotions and everything you take in has a distinct dramatic flair to it. You can make mountains out of mole hills easier than anyone, and take offense just as easy. Extravagantly gracious, you will praise your family and friends to an extreme. Leo is the regal king of the zodiac and all the luxuries of life can never fulfill these lions. Being drawn to the finer things, you're a wonderful host and delight in throwing glittering parties. Sometimes overbearing as a parent you cherish your family and the happiness they bring. One or two children will not be enough, you need a large family that remains close by in order to be happy. Be careful not to spoil your kids, Leo's have a tendency to place their children on a pedestal and overlook the faults of their offspring. Be careful not to become an enabler. Make you children work and earn everything you give them. You're expressive and vivacious, and need to choose a profession where you can be surrounded by many people and be the center of attention or power. No amount of attention is ever enough for Leo. You become distraught when things get out of your control the small goldfish becomes a vicious shark. If your graciousness and generosity are not appreciated no sign becomes more offended. Other than Cancer, no other sign can become as depressed as a Leo.

Moon in Virgo

House placement for the Virgo Moon is key because it shows where you're the most organized and nit-picky. No matter what, you always get an A for effort because you go the extra mile making sure your facts are accurate, and neatly presented. Everything has to fit in sensibly and flow into each other. Your shoes must always match your dress, so to speak. When around those who disagree Virgo is less likely to start a fight than most. You can let someone run their mouth being as arrogant as they want. As long as you're not the fool you generally couldn't care less. Until they leave or can't hear you. Then you criticize everything they did wrong and how much of a buffoon they were. It's easy to run your mouth when someone fails, then when you fail it's the equipment's fault. This Moon sign is supposed to be intelligent, analytical, and organized, but like everything else, there are exceptions. The sign of the fair maiden is well kept and abhors uncleanliness. The biggest problem with this is your inability to stop thinking. You analyze everything down the most miniscule detail. Once you take an interest in something you obsess about every little nuance within it. Problem being, so much diverts your attention most projects produce lack luster results, or are abandoned completely. You'll take a three step process and turn it into a ten step fiasco because you feel the work needed in those extra steps makes the project bigger and better.

Everything and everyone has flaws somewhere, and you see all of them. Nothing really lives up to expectations because at the end of the day there's always room for improvement. Virgo's become hoarders because they can see an eventual use for anything. Your flower pots are made out of decorated rain gutters, and wind chimes are hung according to length. Part of your creative style is the ability to see how small cogs drive the big machine. Your biggest downfall is the instant disregard for anyone who doesn't care about your opinion. When someone doesn't care what you think, you lose your mind and completely flip out. Tell them they're wrong when you know they're right and watch the fireworks. Sudden or unexplainable emotional changes are extremely hard for this Moon placement. To defeat a Virgo Moon take them out of their element. The thought of not being in control drives you crazy, which intensifies the emotional instability. Then confused about your confusion the downward spirals continue.

Moon in Libra

As the second of the luminaries the Moon has control of our emotions and habitual reactions stored deep within our subconscious. Ruled by Venus and in love with beauty, this cardinal air sign can make you obsessed with attaining the finer things in life. You're very social and desperately desire everyone's approval. All your personal contacts have a deeper meaning and when things seem to spiral away frantically, you become neurotic and possibly obsessive trying to place them back where they belong. Libra is happiest when in relationships with others, and will probably entice you into several romances until you find your partner. The major malfunction of this is you always see where things are going wrong and need improvement. Whether it be casual or romantic you desire the social contacts provided by your interaction with others. Most times a social butterfly, you get overwhelmed when your distant acquaintances nose too far into your affairs.

This gives you a keen, precise eye for detail, as well as an imagination to go along with it. Unfortunately, this can also make you a space case and extremely neurotic. You surround yourself with comfortable and pleasant objects because you subconsciously absorb the energy of the room. You would love to live in a house filled with flowers and tranquil music playing all the time. Because you enjoy beautiful things you have a tendency to over spend on items for your home. Many times you find that perfect item to go right behind that other thing sitting in the back closet somewhere. The presentation and ritual is just as important as the gift itself whether it is material or not. A Libra moon seeks to balance things out so everyone is treated fairly. You will vocalize any feeling of injustice for others. One negative part of this sign is the aptness to see things for what you want them to be as opposed to what they actually are. You will tolerate a bad relationship longer than most purely for the fact that you can't bear to handle the feelings of loneliness.

Moon in Scorpio

Scorpio is the deepest, darkest, most passionate sign of the zodiac. Because the Moon is so completely entrenched with the human subconscious, only those who experience it can accurately describe the affects. When placed in the intense sign of the scorpion you're extremely secretive and most times obsessive. You're attached to everything you do, and determined to succeed no matter what the costs. Nothing is done half-heartedly. You're always looking to take any advantage available, sometimes resorting to less than ethical tactics in order to succeed. Once something or someone sparks your interest you want to know everything available. Excessively possessive at times, once someone has gained your trust you never let them go. This attachment can cause you to remain in abusive and dysfunctional relationships long past their breaking point. This is a very spiritual placement for the Moon. Whether it be strict dogmatic religion or more modern and progressive spirituality, you intently believe in the higher aspects of the universe and human consciousness. Your vivid dreams are sometime hard to distinguish from reality, and you get caught up in your own fantasies much of your life. Remember spirits and higher beings contact humans through their dreams. Whether you accept it or not you're a spiritual magnet. You attract things and situations that others do not and love every minute of it. Letting people know just what you're up to is out of the questions. You'll criticize everyone else for their shady dealings, but heaven forbid anyone do the same to you. Scorpio truly believes that everything will last forever. They don't realize that everything must either leave, metamorphose, or eventually die. Ultimate emotion is the shortest phrase which can describe this Moon positioning.

Moon in Sagittarius

Of all the fire signs Sagittarius is the easiest for the Moon to handle. Being the mutable of elements, the Jupiter ruled Sagittarius gives you a bouncy, flamboyant, and enthusiastic nature. You're full of optimism and good hopes for the future. Even as the turmoil's of life hit, the brightness of life is always there. Sporadically jumping from one thing to the next, the energy produced here is like none other. In the back of your mind there is always something else to be doing, and somewhere to be going. It's always difficult to settle down, mostly because you constantly live in a wonderful fantasy land. Many astrologer's will agree Sagittarius is the most optimistic and inspirational sign of the zodiac. When the Moon is placed here your connection between nature and the spiritual world is strong. You sense a greater meaning to life, and even when you can't identify it, you still feel the presence. If you choose a path into organized religion, or your own personal journey into the universe, you can attain great enlightenment. If Jupiter is closely involved then expect random luck to cross your path every now and again. Casually playing the lottery or gambling can be lucrative from time to time, but you do possess the tendency to overdo yourself.

You want to help anyone who asks and many times over commit yourself. Sagittarius can take things to extremes whether it be good or bad, and if you aren't careful a woeful tale may end up being a rouse. The most difficult problems caused by this are within your romantic relationships. This sign doesn't want to settle down, and desperately desires to explore the world. Getting bogged down in a committed relationship places restrictions on your wild attitude and you naturally resist. If you can't find someone who accepts your flirtatiousness and outgoing personality there is obviously no hope. Behind Libra then Taurus, this is the third most social sign in the zodiac. This is most definitely not a well grounding place for the Moon. Opposite the schizophrenic Gemini there is a tendency for aloofness.

Moon in Capricorn
When the Moon is in Capricorn you have a disciplined, committed nature which needs to be directed positively. You're extremely rigid in getting your own way, and sometimes when you can't, you just take your ball and go home. The Moon is in a place of discomfort in Capricorn, and her motherly nurture is difficult to feel. Many times this indicates your mother is the greatest cause of tensions in your life, and no one can get under your skin faster and more personally than her. She was probably a harsh disciplinarian or you feel that she ignores you completely. No amount of attention from your mother will ever be enough. Either way, most ill feelings of negativity are simply perpetuated in your own mind. One major pitfall of Capricorn is your repress your agitations to the point of eruption, and won't deal with the problem until it's a significant issue. When you don't care about something you really don't care about it, and won't be affected one bit by it.

You're extremely determined and your single mindedness often turns into obsession. You get all your eggs in one basket and when that basket breaks you are devastated. Napoleon, Adolf Hitler, George Washington, and Abraham Lincoln all had their Moon placed in Capricorn. You have difficulties trusting people, especially if your childhood was less than fortunate. You can be a

264

Grinch like loner, living at the top a cold lonely mountain. You desperately desire companionship yet your compelling habit to retreat to the mountain top overwhelms you. Severe depression and anxiety plague those born with this Moon sign. You find it difficult to warm up to others and when you do it isn't a completely open relationship. If your Sun or ascendant is in Taurus or Virgo advancement in management and places of high authority will naturally find you, even if you have to move around within your profession before you find your place.

Moon in Aquarius

Aquarius is the unconventional fixed air sign, which is ruled by Uranus and also Saturn. This sign turns the Moon unpredictable and completely unstable. For Aquarius, everything must make sense being backed up by facts and evidence, the exact opposite of the Moon. Things only need to feel right for her. The Moon is emotionally volatile and feels it must break away from anything anyone tells you. No matter how much sense someone else is making you still won't learn your lesson until you screw thinks up for yourself. Much like the air cousin Gemini, you'll do something simply because you were told no. When others don't agree with you it feels they are attacking you personally, and you'll argue your point to the death. No other sign spends so much energy just to prove them self wrong. It's this rebellious attitude that can take you very far in life, provided you find a proper outlet. House placement will show the outlet.

You refuse to believe something just because you're told so, and will go to great lengths to discover the truth for yourself. Aquarius is the ultimate scientist who's discovering the latest start galaxy or inventing the newest light bulb. Technological research and development as well as advancements in medicine can prove lucrative professions. Personal independence is very important to you. Aquarius is the rebellious revolutionary who's screaming his beliefs out amongst the masses. The relationship the Moon has with Uranus will indicate how erratic you will be. You enjoy doing things alone and must prove capable of doing them yourself. Every year as the Sun travels through this sign, you will do through a three day period of depression where everything seems to make you sad. This is to force you into seclusion for personal reflection.

Moon in Pisces

Pisces is known as the sign of final undoing, and although there are several wonderful things with a Pisces Moon, some negative characteristics are all too possible. First, you're so compassionate towards others you become a sucker for a sob story. Everyone in need is helped to your fullest capacity leaving you with nothing for yourself. As the mutable water sign, you adapt to your surrounding environment easily. Choosing your friends wisely will be very important. Because your subconscious enjoys the exit from reality they allow, many Piscean Moons have issues with drugs and alcohol. This placement has a deep root system into your inner subconscious. You behave and respond in ways not always clear to you, and many times the reaction is habitual. Another major difficulty with this positioning is that your perception of reality isn't always accurate. You create problems where there aren't any simply because you want to help something. As the Moon approaches Aries the difficulties become more strenuous because you're trying to separate your emotional dependency on others towards independency provided by yourself. Degrees twenty-five through twenty-nine are especially troublesome. Deep inside you're a total romanticist, and at heart you enjoy the warm, comforting security of a home. Your nurturing personality desires a family environment with lots of members, both people and animals alike. Creatively this is one of the strongest signs for the Moon to build upon. Because you can tap deep into the chasms of your imagination if you can manifest them into the real world the results are surprising. Hard physical work is troublesome because the watery nature slows your physical movements. As inspiration strikes you, allow yourself to go into the hypnotic trance of the dream world.

Rising signs

Aries rising

    People born with Aries rising are quite pioneering and adventurous. You enjoy the role of the leader and desire to always voice your opinions, even when it isn't your place. You may be given the reputation as a hard headed troublemaker, and this can be entirely true. The dominant nature of Aries makes it difficult to give up what you want. You make a great employee because you understand the importance of getting things done. You most definitely do not like being told how to do things, but when the deadline is near an Aries is more focused on completing the project on time, even if you don't get your way. Very unwilling to follow rules, authority figures will have to tell you more than once to stop doing something. If you feel the rule is useless you completely ignore it. All too often you find yourself beating your head against the same wall thinking a different result is in store. Be thoughtful about the process in which you handle things, because many times you find more success with an altered plan of action. Those born under the sign of the fire ram are prone to accidents and crashes. Because you're impulsive and all too quick to act without thinking you will find yourself in the hospital for stitches or casts a few times throughout your life. With piercing eyes and a stunning pale complexion you go through many love affairs. You have a fast, fiery pace to your romantic relationships. You can fall in love instantly, and can fall out of love just as fast. Your romantic partner will find you impatient and bossy, and this will be a deterring factor in your love life. Once things have worn out their usefulness they are discarded quickly and sometimes prematurely. Those born with Aries rising are energetic, inventive and flamboyant. You love attention and will never be able to get enough. Aries is the cardinal fire sign and those with this trait in their charts have a fiery and exciting personality.

Taurus rising

There is a slow methodical calm about those born with Taurus rising. Taurus is ruled by the planet Venus and also exalts the Moon, making those two planets powerful in your chart. Nobody has ever called a Taurus rising to be quick and fiery. That was the previous sign of Aries. Taurus likes to be mellow and quiet, in a room filled with beautiful things. Taurus is the sign of material possessions and you identify your self-worth based on whatever cars, houses, or any other physical objects people can see. Other than Libra no sign is more casually passive. No one wants to avoid a fist fight like a Taurus, although strong and physically capable of fighting, they would just rather be on their way. Like the bull which represents it, those with this rising sign take a while to get moving but once they do, watch out! Whether it's anger or love, emotional arousal is slow, just like everything else with this sign. Determination and persistence are two characteristics of this sign. No one will work harder for less than a Taurus. Much like a work bull they can go for long hours of strenuous labor, all the while enjoying every bit of it. Don't expect to be too skinny in your later years, your love of rich and hearty foods won't allow it, especially in females. Exercise and proper diet will be key in maintaining a healthy lifestyle. One major difficulty of this sign is not realizing when something won't work out. Whether a bad relationship or job, Taurus will just continue on taking a beating make sure not to turn into a whipping boy.

Gemini rising

Gemini is the epitome of the phrase "Monkey see, monkey do." They're the pee drinking yahoo's who will do anything for a laugh. Although this childish immaturity is fun at games it doesn't do much for your sense of responsibility. Gemini is the tricky prankster who thinks all his jokes are funny despite what anyone tells him. Those with Gemini rising are talkative, energetic, and very high strung. With this rising sign you tend to jump from one project to another without ever finishing the previous. You may grow up, but do so reluctantly and will never truly lose your childlike sense of humor. Mischief, pranks, and childish humor run rampant in Gemini. They never really grow up, only old. Gemini is represented by the twins and this produces a duality within your personality. Take nothing at face value with a Gemini, for they are the best at hiding their true inner feelings. No one can put on a happy face when things are going bad and do it as convincingly as a Gemini. Mercury is the ruling planet and will play a key role in your chart. Organizing facts, numbers, and computer data are right up your ally.

You possess an abnormal amount of mental energy. Computers and video games are interesting because it keeps your mind busy. You're inclined to several short trips as opposed to long drawn out ones. If you do go on a long vacation make sure to travel from hotel to hotel or place to place. Don't settle down in one place for very long. An uneasy restlessness will plague your brain for your lifetime. The curiosity of Gemini is unmatched and anything that has bells, whistles, or flashing lights instantly gains your attention. Nervous speech impediments will happen because your brain can move faster than your mouth. Success if life is usually through being so adaptable that you find yourself amongst powerful and important people, as opposed to having to go through the grind of getting to the top yourself.

Cancer rising

Kind, generous, and emotional are all frequently used to describe those with Cancer rising. A Cancer ascendant makes you very sensitive to emotional signals from other people. Cancer is a psychic sign and even though you don't realize it, you subconsciously receive the true intentions projected by others. You have an instant response to tense situations which is emotional rather than intellectual. It will be difficult to find a happy medium somewhere in between. Once you learn to control your constant influx of emotions you be able to progress along happily. There's a reserved something about you that's difficult to penetrate, and will take you a while to warm up to people. Once you do the bond will usually last. You're adaptable to different kinds of people although you're not known for making friends instantly.

Cancer rising individuals are usually moody, and others don't always find you in a receptive mind frame. You can be crabbish with a short fuse, and most definitely need to watch what you say to people. You can sometimes exhibit a snappish temper. These qualities will also make you a force to be reckoned with in the professional field. No sign is as devoted to their families; Cancer's want nothing more than to be in a house full of family with lots of children running around. Your home is where you find security; anything threatening it will be instantly eradicated. With Cancer rising the Moon is your ruling planet and will be a significant part your chart. People with Cancer rising tend to be heavy set in the middle and tend to put on weight with age. This can bring on a cycle of and depression as your children grow up and leave home. Candy and sweets will be your worst enemy. Activity and exercise are going to be the best way to combat your love of food.

Leo rising

With Leo rising you're the grandest star out there, and the world is nothing more than stage for you act upon. You're a legend if simply in your own mind, craving attention, praise, or authority. Extremely generous and benevolent, you sing constant praises of your friends and loved ones despite what's really going on. This fixed fire sign is symbolized by the lion and ruled by the Sun. There is certain sense of royalty with Leo rising and many times those with this sign take life too extreme without even noticing it. Men with Leo rising can be late on bill payments, but find a way to buy strangers rounds at the bar. Women think the world is their oyster and the universe revolves around them. In some sense it does. Leo's never like being told what to do and will strike out on their own in order to do so. They love the attention they get when they leave, and then again when they return. If team sports aren't interesting then individual sports like rock climbing and mountain biking should be taken up.

Most people born with this sign rising have an amazing mane of hair and also the beard to go with it. Your charm and flamboyance acquires many friends and acquaintances. Romantic flames come and go as well as well as romantic affairs. With a complete playful love of life extravagance is most likely when finding forms of recreation, no trip too expensive, no adventure too dangerous, or mountain un-climbable. No matter how farfetched an idea you will try to do something simply because someone told you that you couldn't. Having a flair for the dramatic you can make a mountain out of a mole hill, especially if your personal life is affected. Usually more concerned with yourself you will whine and complain if someone else is late for an appointment, but if you're the one who is late, then, "Oh well" is your motto. Leo is an extremely sensitive sign and nothing hurts more than a Leo who doesn't think they have received the attention they need and deserve.

Virgo rising

Those born with Virgo rising possess an analytical mind which needs to dissect everything in life. You enjoy learning how things work in a precise and mechanical way. Because you understand, and many times waste time, with the little intricacies and minute details, this gives you an ability to organize things better than others. Virgos are generally clean and tidy with everything in its specific spot. Although when negatively afflicted this can make you the most disorganized hoarder, refusing to throw away anything. Even though the mischievous planet Mercury is the ruler of Virgo, most born with this rising don't cause too much trouble. They may be smart mouthed and sarcastic, but there is just no sense in causing serious trouble. As the mutable earth sign Virgo's aren't known for being the brash flamboyant leader, rather they chime in when they've found an obscure piece of information that has been casually over looked. Obsessive compulsive disorder is most definitely possible with Virgo. One thing that will drive a Virgo crazy is when others refuse to listen. Organizing facts, toys, clothes, and anything else is what Virgo's live for. Fields of science, philosophy, and music usually spark the interest of Virgo. Virgo is represented by the fair maiden and there is a certain sense of apprehensive femininity within you. Fine works of art and classical music will appeal to you and art dealership is a possible career for you. There will be a fascination with preserving the possessions you have, you want to make you things last as long as they can. Restoration of antiquities and classic automobiles could be interesting hobbies. If science and medicine is more of an interest careers in the fields of surgery, psychology, or even spiritual leadership are likely. It's in a person's best interest to listen to you when you talk. Not one to waste your words, you are direct to the point and usually correct. Most of all, you're probably short. If you aren't it's because you have a stronger planet influencing this point.

Libra rising

People with Libra rising tend to be socially refined and graceful. Represented by the scales, Libra's are usually well balanced and fair, at least in their own mind. Adept in etiquette, you blend into many different social circles, from prince to pauper. Injustice hurts your soul and you will take great strides to bring equality and fairness to others. It will be difficult to do this alone. Although you're well directed and have the best of intentions many times your efforts don't see their full potential. Libra's are easily influenced by others. You can instinctually feel their emotions, and either good or bad, you both will have effects on you. In order for success there will need to be fire from other places in the chart. If your Moon or Sun is in a fire sign, (Aries, Leo or Sagittarius) then this will give you a great motivating drive and almost guarantee success. If you're not careful mindful others may take advantage of you easily. It's difficult to turn away someone in need, even if they don't deserve it. As the cardinal air sign you will be drawn to leadership because it makes you think you are in control. Business enterprises and organization will be two things you excel at. Libra's don't like doing things for themselves and power positions allow you to boss people around with very little physical exertion. If you can use this productively then there will be no limits as to what you can achieve. Venus is your ruling planet and will be important in your chart. Her influence will make you relationship dependent, and needy towards others. Because you're constantly in search of your perfect partner, it will probably take a while for you to find that certain someone you feel comfortable with. Once you do settle down you will be completely blind to the abuses you are forced to endure. You're so in love with being in love that the thought of rejection traumatizes you. Remember to analyze how your actions are affecting your situation and many of your hang ups will be avoided.

Scorpio Rising

Unless you know by experience, Scorpio is the most difficult sign to describe. The reason being it's so intent on remaining secret for only those who possess it. Being a Gemini rising myself I can only do Scorpio mild justice when describing it. One thing can definitely be said, this is an intensely passionate and deeply possessive sign. Those born while it's rising always have a sense of secrecy about them. This is the darkest, deadliest, most sexual sign of the zodiac. It's the fixed water sign, ruled by Mars and Pluto, making both these planets exceptionally strong in your chart. Always referenced with the underworld, death is always an unknown fascination for you. Because you psychically understand how the universe is just a revolving spiral of energy areas of religion, spirituality, and sometimes the extreme occult fascinate you and caution should be used. Stay away from Ouija boards and other forms of witchcraft or black magic. These activities may open portals best left closed.

You plunge yourself into everything you do, and everyone let into your life is always remembered. Although you can't always remember what someone said, you definitely remember how they made you feel. Those born under Scorpio have intense personalities and are usually a dominant force where ever they go. This is an extremely secretive sign which causes you to never allow people to know more about you than you do them. You're represented by the scorpion, and like the tiny avenger you possess a sharp dagger like stinger, dripping poisonous venom. Once attacked you respond with total annihilation. When crossed you'll use every tactic in the book, ethical or unethical can be determined later. In the heat of battle Scorpio must be victorious. Scorpio is basically the ultimate rock star. Drugs, sex, with rock and roll may eventually kill you and alcoholism or addiction to drugs may be your demise. Once again, this sign can be the seediest of seedy. This is why the relationship your ascendant form with the other planets is vitally important.

Sagittarius rising

People with Sagittarius rising have more energy than anybody knows what to do with. You're constantly moving around from one project to another leaving scraps and messes behind. Contrary to its opposite Gemini you complete a finished produce because you love the recognition of your efforts. Awards, medals, and trophies are important to because it shows others what has been accomplished. You don't judge until you've been presented with evidence, but once you cast one, your opinion must be heard. Once the mountain has been climbed now a marathon must be run up it. Your personality has a distinct sparkle unlike any other. The optimism of ruling planet Jupiter possesses an adventurous flamboyance, and not everyone can handle it. Sagittarius is one of the ego inspiring fire signs, and they all must be kept in check. Your belief the failure impossible can put you in situations which are sketchy at best. Life is experienced by filling it with as many experiences as possible. Independence is one of the most important things for Sagittarius, and freedom to do what you want is your primary focus.

The problem with Sagittarius is they're generally self absorbed. You're always eager to debate and express your views forcefully and emphatically. Although you don't spend much time researching your facts you still hold on to them as true. Always on the go, you can expect your life to be filled with quick and sporadic trips and experiences. You have a reputation for frankness and some will consider you rude and inconsiderate with what you say. You prefer a simple life with not too many set in stone commitments or obligations. You have a love of money, but your real appreciation is from the freedom and independence that it brings. Frivolous and child like you never truly grow up, growing old and stingy is one of your worst fears. Marriage is not important to you as you see it as just another thing tying you down, but when you do you are a hopeless romantic. At least once in your life you will get into a dysfunctional relationship or marriage.

Capricorn rising

A Capricorn ascendant tends to turn you into a serious more straight forward individual. By no means does this indicate anything negative, but you won't be known for warming up to strangers quickly. You're cautious in your dealings, and reluctant to make a commitment until obtaining all the facts. Children with this sign are usually more responsible at an earlier age. The biggest problem is your refusal to change your ram headed ways. Like the fire ram Aries, the water ram of Capricorn slams his horns into a problem the same way, over and over, with the same results over, and over. Different than Aries, rather than get angry Capricorn remains cold and leaves for a higher mountain. Late stage Capricorn ascendants are known for having strong personalities with rigid views. Because of the social prominence associated with them fields of business, politics, and law attract many of these individuals. You possess great will power and determination. Status amongst the community is important and having a significant title is just as meaningful as the work you do. It isn't easy for rising Capricorns to show their feelings, some will be put off by this thinking it is arrogance or conceitedness. They couldn't be more wrong, you just want your space in casual settings. Unless there is a specific reason for the meeting you just want to be left to yourself. You tend to fuss over details and can be a worry body if left unchecked. You understand what you achieve in life is up to you, and the effort you're willing to put forth. Saturn, the planet of discipline, ambition, and determination is your ruling planet. Saturn also encourages stubbornness, pessimism, and selfishness. All of these things will be modified within other aspects of the chart. You may change your mind, but you will find it extremely hard to change your habits. Individuals who possess this and are social should maintain a profession dealing with those friends. The only way you can function cooperatively in groups is if you're in charge and everyone is listening to you.

Aquarius rising

Rising signs are one of the three most important points in a natal chart. Aquarius rises at such an accelerated pace it's one of the most infrequent ascendants possible. Despite the numerous possibilities one thing is always true. You're going be difficult to handle and completely inflexible in all your opinions. Everything has to be proven by facts, and if the evidence is too farfetched to believe, it's probably false. This is a strenuous sign to deal with, for as the fixed air sign you never want to change your mind and will go to extremes to prove yourself correct. Uranus is the current ruling planet and Saturn was the previous ruler, making their relationships more important. In fact no sign hates being told what or how to think like an Aquarius. You show brilliance when inventing things, and products you create may just change the world someday. Science, mathematics, or mechanics are three fields you'll be successful in. It's usually best for you to work alone or at least have your own set of certain responsibilities. Aquarius is the Doc Brown mad scientist who discovers time travel while trying to reinvent gunpowder. This is the fixed air sign and most of the characteristics are intellectual. The house placement of ruling planet Saturn will show the best area to direct your career. The most common physical trait is tall and slender, with long arms as well.

Pisces rising

People with a Piscean ascendant are the fuzzy, cuddly, teddy bear of the zodiac. You're generous and caring to an extreme, sometimes too much. You have unfathomable care and sensitivity for others. There will be times when you're drawn to highly unstable people, with hopes that you and only you can help them resolve their issues. Probably chunky and chubby as a child you will never lose all your baby fat, in fact as a water sign you retain water more than most and will find frequent fluctuations in your weight. You have an extremely active imagination and fantasy life. Highly psychic as well, you will probably experience intuition and prophetic dreams. Many times you wake up in the night wondering if you were dreaming or was it in real life. Neptune, the current ruler, and Jupiter the pre-modern ruler will be extremely important in your chart. You're very sentimental and get attached to people and possessions easily. That doesn't mean you don't know how to share, you just really love your teddy bear and the separation is unbearable. When stressed a sensual foot massage will calm you down like none other. Be aware of alcoholism and drug addiction, because these things alter your conscious mind you really enjoy the effects they produce. Be highly cautious with hallucinogens, your imagination is so vivid you may get lost in fantasy too easily and this could bring about serious side effects. You have an artistic talent that must come out at some point in time. Music, theater, and art work are all very good outlets for this creative expression. If the planet mercury is aspecting the ascendant you may have a wonderful singing voice or a talent for mimicry. Negative aspects from other planets can cause confusion, indecisiveness, and self-deception.

Planets in the signs

Aries

Mercury in Aries
        Mercury loves fire signs, and is especially brilliant in the sign of Aries. When Mercury is in cardinal fire you're filled with inspirational ideas, most of which casually flutter by, just like everything else in your head. You're boisterous and outspoken, with a direct approach attracting many friends, as well as driving some away. Foot in mouth disease is commonly associated with an

Arian Mercury. Once you form an opinion on something it takes many facts to derive you from that viewpoint. Different from some signs you're eager to listen to someone even if it's solely to disagree. Your mental agility is quick and keen, and your ability to think on your feet allows you avoid many hazardous situations. Depending on aspects with the Sun this can cause problems as well. If it is too close to the Sun you will make impulsive rash decisions not thinking of the consequences. Your words are spoken quickly and emphatically. Those with Mercury in Aries are usually too smart for their own good.

Venus in Aries
    Venus is the planet who rules femininity and relationships. When she's in Aries the competitive nature of the ram sets your passions on fire and you become fairly volatile. There's at least one thing that sets you off instantly, and you probably have instances of road rage. Lady Venus isn't always ladylike in Aries and the self centered nature of the sign can be quite an instigator within your relationships. Impatience is always associated with fire and you fall in love at first sight only to be disappointed when the flames die down. Relationships start at the blink of an eye and can end just as fast. The biggest problem is you crave the excitement during the first weeks of the attraction and. Then, as the fire dies out you casually stray away. You actively pursue your attraction and become dominate and demanding as the connection develops. Halfway through any long term affairs you start to questions its validity. Sometimes it will endure, other times it will not. You're somewhat of a drama queen, and will pick fights or useless arguments simply for the fun of it. Aries is always looking for the next exciting challenge, while Venus desperately wants to remain steadfast in love. Watch out for Tequila, it will cause many walks of shame, and yes it makes your clothes come off.

Mars in Aries
    Aries is the strongest and most powerful sign for Mars. The red planet in its ruling sign instills you with passion, determination,

and aggressiveness. Planets in your first or eighth houses will be much more potent than the rest. Physically this makes you exceptionally strong and athletics need to be a good part of your life. Following orders is always difficult when you don't agree with the cause. You absolutely refuse when you're told to do something you don't want to do. The selfishness of Mars is highly irritating here in the cardinal fire sign. If anything gets in your way it's either dodged or destroyed completely. Success is found at all costs. Aries looks before he leaps and Mars loves that attitude. House placement is important because it shows where you're going to be the most self driven. The area of your life Mars and Saturn control will show where you can find the most prosperous career.

Jupiter in Aries
　　　When Jupiter is in the cardinal fire sign of Aries, you're assertive, intelligent, and philosophical His sign placement isn't nearly as important as house position and the relationship with other planets. Alone the cardinal air sign instills fire and spirit into the greater benefic. You can be brilliantly smart but without direction your ideas go nowhere. Jupiter is the planet of expansive higher philosophy. Fire only ignites his passions. All and all it's your ability to cooperate with others that will lead you into success. You're always an optimist, and see light where others see darkness. Your inspirational personality is contagious and you have the ability to brighten up the day of others, where ever you may go. Dominating a conversation will get you in trouble. House placement will definitely show where you're the most conceited. Make sure you can stick to your word and live up to your commitments. Many times you over estimate abilities and promise more than you can deliver. Financial troubles will arise when you fail to maintain attention to your spending habits. Over spending on vacations, cars, and beauty products can deplete your monetary resources.

Saturn in Aries

Despite the complete distaste Saturn has for fire signs, the leadership potential during this transit is phenomenal. Self-reliable and determined to control your own destiny, the cardinal fire of Aries runs strong through your veins. Very rarely do you feel less capable than those around you. Because of this you take on more than your share of responsibility in order to see things done properly. Because you're so sure hearted about yourself and your abilities, there will be times of severe strife or discontent when you're not able to admit your faults. Aries is arrogant and selfish, Saturn is cautious and reserved. This combination can cause many hardships within your chart. Saturn's response to this is sometimes much like an ancient slave driver, cracking the whip at every whim. When properly positioned this influence can make you the determined pioneer, set out to conquer whatever the wild may throw at you. This sign placement Saturn isn't nearly as important as it is with the other planets. House placement is just as vital because it shows where you are to focus your responsibility. Aries ignites the passions to learn things on your own. Saturn takes two and a half years to transit each sign. This somewhat generational class will learn much better through their own failures than from studying bookwork. No matter what you teach these individuals they will still just do their own thing.

Uranus in Aries
(1927 – 1934) (2010 – 2018)
As the first of the generational planets Uranus is still a relatively newly discovered planet. Seen first on March 13th 1781, this cosmic entity causes revolutions and uprisings throughout the masses. The unpredictability and instability of Uranus is set on fire and left to burn while in the cardinal fire sign. Those with this influencing their ascendant are original and motivated. They enjoy doing things to the beat of their own drum, and don't care what or who is in the way. With erratic and spontaneous tendencies trouble is never too far away. Patience is most definitely a virtue associated with this positioning, and your temper will get you into precarious situations. Aries wants everything done at lightning

280

speed and to its own liking, Uranus refuses to conform. Thus producing an individual who seeks things beyond the normal realm of society. The technological and medical advances this will produce will be exponential. Because you can't stand being told how to think this rigid set of views, this will allow you to focus on your innovative ideas and creations. House placement shows where you will be the most innovative. Uranus isn't a personal planet, and can't be described as such. It does however, amplify originality and innovation. Because Aries is associated with the spirit and brain one can only assume the consciousness of humans will be considerably different once the current generation matures.

Neptune in Aries
(1861-1874) (2026-2039)
   Imaginative inspiration will be the most basic nature of Neptune transiting Aries. Like Pluto and Uranus it's ridiculous to try and describe Neptune as a personal planet. This mystical magician adds creativity, sensitivity, and dreaminess to our personalities. The cardinal fire ram will produce a generation charged with spiritual revolution on their minds. The inspirations of Aries gives the fragile psyche of Neptune strength and courage to strike out and change society. As seen be the American civil war during the 1860's, Neptune doesn't transit here until over 150 years later in the mid 2020's. This astrologer can only assume this indicates space travel and the return to holistic medicines. Chemicals are destroying the world and eventually humans are going to realize this. Many will be put to sleep by Neptune's transit of Pisces. Whatever medicines and technological advancements occur during progression through water will only be expanded exponentially once Neptune touches spiritual fire. Wars will happen and there will be many innocent causalities in the process but just the effects of war are sometimes necessary for human progression. Unfortunately the delusion caused will create some of the most confused world leaders. Small and radical militias will pop up and cause trouble from time to time.

281

Pluto in Aries
2068--2097
I don't even need to waste my time. I will be in the spiritual realm and you will have to contact me through incense and Velvet Revolver music.

Taurus

Mercury in Taurus

Taurus is not known for speed and Mercury slows down to a definite lull while in this fixed Earth sign. Level headed and fair minded, you stay to the standard normal paths. You enjoy the more traditional and proven means of professional and romantic life. This position is wonderful if your Sun is in Aries or Gemini. If you Sun is in Taurus you're probably not too good at math. You're spear headed towards material possessions and think others will like you because of what you have. This belief drives you into positions of success and authority. Even if your speech and thinking may be slow, you're not necessarily stupid. You just don't process information as fast as others. Complex science concepts may baffle you and you must accept your brain power may be lacking. Taurus is known for motherly compassion and kindness. Consider careers in the health and medical fields. The best asset of this placement is it allows you stay focused at long tedious tasks and if Mars is involved you will be physically stronger than others as well.

Venus in Taurus

Taurus is the strongest most powerful sign for Venus to be placed in. In this sign all the loving, tender qualities of our sister planet can be felt. Beauty, grace, and charm are the enjoyable traits. Snootiness, stubbornness, and obliviousness are the worst. Here, Venus wishes to acquire as many possessions from as many relationships as she can. She clings onto everything and everyone passionately. Then she's completely destroyed when they leave. In love you desire you partner do be demonstrative of their affection towards you. Little surprises mean just as much as the large moments in life. If your partner stops showering you with attention you take your interests elsewhere. You can be very self-indulgent. Later in life you will probably put on more weight than most. This is because of your love of fattening foods and the lack of exercise. Unfortunately this can make you very narrow minded. Venus in Taurus can be snooty and arrogant. If others don't agree with you, or care to follow your every command, you get offended and agitated faster than most. Because it is so difficult for you to break away from your normal routine, when your requests are denied you can sulk and get lost in your own self-pity.

Mars in Taurus

Mars in Taurus is one of the better placements for the red planet. This makes you passionately hardworking and dedicated. While in Earth signs Mars becomes rock solid and extremely tough. Physically and mentally you're stronger than most. Your commitment to a cause is extraordinary, and going beyond the call of duty is your nature. The aggressions of Mars run slower in the fixed Earth sign of Taurus than in most other signs. Loyal to a fault if someone ever betrays your trust you are an atomic bomb. Much like the bull that represents Taurus, you are made for hard work and labor. Preferring routine when it comes to work and your daily life you enjoy a set schedule where everything runs on time with set responsibilities. You can be an obsessive organizer and experience severe migraines when you get over stressed. More reliable and consistent than your peers, superiors see your abilities and put you into authority faster than most. Much of your success because of your ability to work longer hours at physical labor. This increases productivity greatly.

Jupiter in Taurus

Jupiter traveling through Taurus is one of the more prosperous placements for this gentle giant. The basic expansive nature of Jupiter along with the materialistic properties from Taurus generally means lots of possessions. Emotions, philosophies, and ideas can also be considered possessions. House position becomes important because it shows which area of life you're going to be the most confident, arrogant, and possessive. Venus along with the ruling planet of which ever house Jupiter is placed in will dictate good or bad. All alone this is well grounded and Jupiter produces wonderful energy. Judging people by their possessions and not their character is the worst influence this casts. The bullheadedness of Taurus is also a distinguished characteristic from this placement. What it lacks in brain power it makes up for in brawn power and you will definitely think you're smarter than you actually are. Jupiter is definitely not at its intellectual best in any Earth sign. Unless Jupiter is positioned in a fire house, then you can have the best of both worlds. Practical and rational thinking makes it difficult to break from the normal path. It also brings natural responsibility allowing you to accept what needs to be done. Once you're set into a routine you never even think of wavering from those efforts which are tried and tested.

Saturn in Taurus
    If Saturn is in Taurus you're extremely determined to accomplish your goals and acquire possessions here in Earth. Whether it be negative or positive endeavors is up to you. Capricorn is the ruling sign for Saturn, but the fixed Earth sign of Taurus suits him greatly as well. The refined and responsible essence of Saturn loves the hard work and determination provided by the bull. You place significant emphasis on saving up for a rainy day, and when left unchecked you become a hoarder. Everything you do must have an effective purpose and provide something in the future. From the people you associate with, to the activities you partake in, everything you do now is for your benefit later on. The strange and unusual is of no use to Saturn in this sign, but remember, not everyone will have the energies of Saturn prominent in their chart. It will be modified by house placement and the aspects from other planets. Because it naturally moves

284

slowly Earth signs still create difficult tensions for Saturn's restrictive nature. Often it will be very difficult to think outside your box and see the viewpoint of others. To you your way is the only way and you don't want to compromise. You will need to constantly re-evaluate your goals and what you are getting your personal security from. Despite your patience, discipline, and work ethic, when things don't go as smoothly as planned it's tough for you to find alternative paths.

Uranus in Taurus
(1934 – 1941) (2019-2026)
        While Uranus is in Taurus the rigid and stubborn properties of both entities are magnified. Once you make up your mind it's pretty much set into stone and will never be changed, unless sufficient evidence is presented. This is generally a calmer, more reserved placement for Uranus giving an Earthly presence to all your ideas. Taurus is a conventional sign which prefers the worn path of the tried and true, while Uranus is the exact opposite, going off on the wildest adventures. The energy produced by this combination is excellent for bringing the wild ideas of science fiction into the physical world. As the first of the three slow moving generational planets, the aspects forming with other planets, especially your ascendant will determine the influence Uranus. None of the generational planets are best described by sign. While in Aries Uranus was acting about as crazy as possible, and is now calming down. The basic principle while here is to manifest the long range ideas produced by the previous fire sign transit. Aspects towards Venus and the Moon will be very important, as well as the relationship to the ruler of whatever house Uranus is in. Most influential of all will be the alignment between Uranus and your ascendant.

Neptune in Taurus
(1875-1889) (2039-2053)
        Neptune is the second of the Generational planets and the positioning between it and your other planets will be important.

This generation will be charged with bring the spiritual revolutions formed in Aries down to Earth. Until the next passing near 2040 we must see where Neptune is taking us before we can think about where we are going.

Pluto in Taurus
(1852-1883)
Last forming in the middle 19th century the slow moving Pluto won't rise in Taurus again until 2096. This is a long ways a way and I will be in the spirit world bouncing amongst the cosmos by then.

Gemini

Mercury in Gemini
Mercury is right at home in his ruling sign of Gemini. This makes you talkative, versatile, and energetic. As the mutable air sign, this placement allows you to adapt to situations easily. Your excess mental energy can make you high strung, eccentric, and nervous. Your gnat like attention span finds you bouncing from casual idea to the next, rarely completing the first before moving on. You find yourself most efficient and effective when you don't strain yourself for extended periods of time. Energy comes to you in quick, short bursts, and once you hit the wall you're done for. If you can harness your sporadic energy supply you can accomplish twice as much as others. Everything Mercury touches in your chart will be highly charged and any aspects will be very prominent. The childlike qualities of Mercury will enjoy pranks, jokes, and childish games, unfortunately this can make you immature at times. It will be difficult to grow up.Iif you were forced into responsibility early you most likely rebelled. As a child, if something moved, made noise, of flashed lights, you were fascinated. Computers, electronics and communications interest you to the point of obsession sometimes. Finding a career involving once of these fields will prove interesting and satisfying.

Venus in Gemini

When Venus is in Gemini a person's sense of humor, intelligence, and communication skills are just as important as anything else. A wonderful imagination and brain are more attractive than a chiseled physique or large bank account. Your partner must be mentally stimulating and challenging. Understanding that talking and communicating with your partner is essential to a functioning relationship, you must find someone you can open up to. If you try and force something with the wrong person it will crash and burn horribly. Whenever you feel your partner is no longer interested your eye quickly starts to wander. The thrill of falling in love is always on your mind, and all too often you get too caught up in the whirlwind of fun before you realize the relationship is dysfunctional. Venus in Gemini usually indicates a powerful speaking voice or possibly a beautiful singing voice. Extremely flirtatious, charming, and friendly, you're a social butterfly who enjoys meeting new people. Your relationships start instantly and end just as quickly. Desiring to be swept off your feet, you want someone to come around, dazzle you with their charm, and passionately fall in love. It will only be until you accept that there is no perfect partner out there that you will be able to settle down. Poor aspects can make you a nosey gossip, piping up your opinion where it's none of your business.

Mars in Gemini

When Mars is positioned in Gemini you're an energetic and busy socialite. You're always coming from one place only to hurry over to another. If you ever slow down you become easily agitated and angry. Your intellect is sharp and alert, and many times this can cause high anxiety and nervousness. Because you bounce around so quickly you're prone to little mistakes and accidents. Physically quick and agile you're better at short bursts of energy as opposed long durations which require stamina. Games of wit and strategy are intriguing. The competition of battle provides thrills like none other. Gemini is a flighty sign that makes Mars very sporadic. You never know when to fight or when to flee. Many times you will flee just because you know that's the easiest and safest. Those with Mars in Gemini can also be flaky and unreliable when it comes to casual commitments. Your love life will always seem to be out of control. You possess a tendency not to look before you leap into relationship you will suffer heart breaks, along with many other romantic failures. Staying physically active will be the best way for you to relieve your pent up energy. If Mercury is negatively aspecting this you will be verbally aggressive, lashing out at others for unnecessary reasons.

Jupiter in Gemini

Gemini is the mutable air sign which adds intelligence, eccentricity, and energy to those born with this in their charts. Jupiter expands everything, do the math yourself. You can grasp onto difficult concepts with relative ease. Electronics and technology will interest you. Going on short vacations and day trips will be better than extended stay trips. These experiences open your eyes to different cultures, allowing you to see things in different ways than most. It's your philosophic nature that sparks this interest. You see the deeper meanings in life and wish to experience as much as you can in the short amount of time you're on Earth. Mercury is the ruler of Gemini and if Jupiter is aspecting him you will be brilliantly smart, and house placement will direct it. Religion interests you just not in the orthodox manner. You see validity in all the religions throughout the world and desire to understand each one. You never seem to be an expert at one thing, but highly educated about many things. Overly talkative, you should learn to shut your trap more. People will become bored sometimes because of the excessive amount you can gab. Gemini is the sign of schizophrenia and bi-polarity. Jupiter can expand this in an indescribable way. Because it spends about a year in each sign there will be many with this positioning. When it's afflicted by too many things the evidence is in the illnesses you see.

Saturn in Gemini

If your Saturn is in Gemini you enjoy intellectual puzzles, problems, and finding solutions where others don't. Saturn is the slowest moving of the personal planets and takes over two years transiting through each sign. Because of his slow moving speed the relationship formed with your ascendant will be very important. The responsible and cautious properties of Saturn help quell the inconsistent tendencies of Gemini. This positioning can make you studious and organized, spending much of your time placing facts and numbers into order. Your concentration and mental abilities are most definitely suited for research and development in any area. The insatiable curiosity of Gemini is directed onto a more focused path by Saturn allowing you to concentrate on difficult topics for extended durations. One problem associated with Saturn in Gemini is it's extremely difficult to believe things without proof. Scientific fact will always take precedent over faith and it's nearly impossible for your mind to change against the evidence. The sign Saturn is in isn't nearly as important as his relationship with the other planets and house placement. This planet is supposed to be the base structure we build our character around. Any air sign stimulates the intellectual side of society. Space travel will benefit greatly the next time this occurs in the late 2020's and into the early 2030's.

Uranus in Gemini
(1941 – 1948) (2026-2033)
Describing Uranus in Gemini is about as useful and efficient as milking a wild boar hog. Uranus is the epitome of independence and rebellion, while Gemini is an energetic and lively sign which is known for intelligence and curiosity. This is a generation of scientists whose life work is focused on the advancement of technology. This amplifies your innovative thinking and creative ability. Uranus is known for traveling outside the box of normal acceptance within society, and in the naturally bi polar sign of Gemini, this causes a laundry list of effects. Being the first of the generational planets, influences between other planets and your ascendant will determine the intensity you feel. The restlessness of

Gemini and the unpredictability of Uranus will cause you to do things and not really know why. Despite your constant need for everything to make logical sense if it doesn't, you can believe just whatever you choose. If something makes sense to you alone that's good enough. This can cause you to be eccentric and nervous. Speech impediments and psychological breakdowns are likely to occur in your old age. Those with this placement will be charged with the task of great technological advances. As this generation matures the global interest towards gadgets and gizmos will heighten greatly. Mercury is the ruling planet and will inspire brilliance.

Neptune in Gemini
(1888-1902) (2052-2066)
        This happened so long ago that most everyone with this placement has passed into the spirit world. Being a slow moving generational planet, we won't see Neptune travel through Gemini until the middle of the 21st century.

Pluto in Gemini
(1883-1914)
No one alive will have Pluto in Gemini and won't for a significant amount of time. This last occurred during the early 20th century and won't be experienced again for nearly 250 years.

Cancer

Mercury in Cancer
        When Mercury is in the cardinal water sign of Cancer you become connected with your memories because they remind you of the inner securities you had in the past. Your thinking is based more on your emotional reactions as opposed to your logical reasoning. You're interested in the feelings and behaviors of others and will enjoy a profession in which you have social contact with the public. Psychology, counseling, and social work would be good career opportunities. You can be shy when speaking in public, but

in one on one conversation you never shut up. Wonderful at communications, not only can you talk to others on a personal level, but you listen to them on a personal level as well. If Venus is involved you may have a beautiful singing voice, or just belt tunes in the shower. Any aspects from the Moon, Neptune, or Pluto, will produce advanced psychic and intuitive abilities. Although you relate to the people who are having the problems, you don't always solve the issue completely because you become emotionally attached to the people and don't stay focused on the problem at hand.

Venus in Cancer

Cancer is one of the more comfortable signs for Venus, and her affectionate nature is fully able to function. Together they make you an understanding individual who's kind and compassionate. Cancer is the nurturing motherly sign of the zodiac, and its influence on Venus can only be described as wonderful. This allows any soothing powers to comfort the problems caused by harsher aspect elsewhere. At its worst this makes you an over emotional sissy who becomes completely dependent on their partner. If someone is lucky enough to gain your affections they will never be forgotten. When you're depressed you turn to sweet and fattening foods to tend to your sorrows. This in turn leads to you putting on weight causing more depression and insecurity. You have a magnetic personal charm and desire that everyone approves of you. Sometimes you may get caught up with the wrong crowd because it's difficult for you to stand up for yourself when you are in the minority. Any aspects from the Moon or Jupiter will be very influential in your chart. Her snappish side can definitely be brought out by poor relations with the other planets, but all alone this is a great starting point.

Mars in Cancer

Mars does not like the water sign of Cancer, if fact this is the sign of detriment, or worst sign possible, for the red planet. Mars rules our aggression, our assertiveness, and our sexuality. The tender emotions produced by Cancer are of no interest for Mars. Many times you will be overly cautious and let opportunities slip by. Other times you will be aggressive and forceful when you should be more cautious and reserved. Any aspect from the Moon will be especially powerful, adding intensity to your subconscious make up. Due to your passive aggressiveness, instead of confronting someone head, on you make your moves indirectly, attacking from the side. You realize others have a distinct advantage over you because of all the nasty things they're willing to do but you aren't. While in water the energies from Mars becomes consistent. Athletically you can still be inclined but you do get injured easier and bruise faster. Lack of physical strength is one of the biggest insecurities of Mars. Sometimes this over acts and you're obsessed with your fitness.

Jupiter in Cancer

Cancer is the exalting sign for Jupiter intensifying the powers of the greater benefic. This makes you kind, caring and extremely sociable. Desiring a complete Utopia for all, it's easy for someone to take advantage of your generosity and hospitality, especially if the Sun or Moon is in Pisces. Your financial judgment is good, and unless negatively aspected otherwise you will have a positive outlook on life, despite whatever your living situation is. You receive a lot of help from your parents and become extremely attached to your mother. Any traumatic experiences involving her will be monumentally impact on your adult life. This is because of your extensive clinginess to emotions and possessions. The items you pack away and keep aren't always the most expensive of gifts, but the meaning behind them are what you're attached to. This can cause a pack rat like accumulation of boxes and packages in your home, even the ribbon has sentimental value. Chances are your room or home is completely covered in photographs and hand drawn pictures. Jupiter will expand everything it touches and in this case it's you sentiments and emotions. As you reach your later years the delicacies at the dinner table will cause you to gain weight. Pay attention to the sweets and junk food you put into your body.

Saturn in Cancer

Cancer is a very difficult sign for the cold restrictive planet Saturn. This placement causes you to be protective and overbearing, worrying over things far too intensely. When you feel unloved you become moody and snobbish. It's difficult for you to express your true emotions to loved ones. Although your intentions are positive you sometimes come off as uncaring or unemotional. Your relationship with your father is especially strained with this. If Saturn is aspecting your ascendant, especially by conjunction, these tensions are produced because you're just like him. More often than not this indicates you never truly feel loved by him. No amount of attention he gave you was ever enough. Maybe it was directed towards business or siblings. This placement can be especially difficult if you're a middle child. Be very attentive if severe emotional depression arises. When negatively aspected by other planets, especially Uranus, Mars or the Moon, this causes your emotions to spin wildly out of control. Aspects to the sign ruling Moon will be very important. Don't be afraid to consult a professional counselor of psychologist if necessary. As you become aware of your intense mood swings, you will need to find a quiet place where you can be alone for personal reflection and meditation. Be cautious not to become to overly dependent on outside influences such as, drugs, alcohol, or relationships with others. If you fall into a poor or abusive partnership you may cling to them in fear of loneliness. Not everything is negative about this. When you finally can open up to others your caring emotions run deep and true. No matter how bad you are harmed you will forgive, but never forget.

Uranus in Cancer
(1866-1872) (1948 – 1955)

Uranus is the closest of the generational planets and I always start off with the first basic concept. Because it's moves so slowly, the sign Uranus is in will be considerably less important than

293

house placement and its relationship with your ascendant. The alignment formed with your ascendant is important because your ascendant is the physical person you outwardly project. While in Cancer, Uranus takes on the essence of the nurturing mother, wanting to care for all humanity. Until it means actually working. Once labor is involved only close family members get direct affection. House placement is so important because it will indicate the area of life you need the most securely comfortable. The unpredictability of Uranus and moodiness of Cancer don't get along because of the massive emotional fluctuations caused. Logical and rational thinking is neither associated with Uranus, or Cancer. Plus Cancer is clingy and needy, not caring if anything makes sense. As the Moon rules Cancer, Uranus is under a greater dictation of Moon alignments. Generally meaning the Moon has more power and control over Uranus.

Obviously, the relationship between the two are indescribably important. This can be somewhat symbolized by the world healing needed after WW2, and the influence can also be shown during the latter three years when the Korean War began affecting the globe. You will encounter opposing extremes and be forced to find a happy medium. Rather than subject yourself into an unpleasant medium you may just have to face the fact you can't have everything your way. Choose one extreme and be thankful you have an opportunity to choose. Cancer is the fixed water sign and possesses many psychic abilities. Vivid dreams and sometime prophetic visions will sprout from time to time. Learn to trust your natural intuition and gut feeling, many times you will find that it is right.

Neptune in Cancer
(1901-1914) (2064-2078)
Cancer adds sensitivity to the already overly sensitive Neptune. This will be a generation with heightened inclinations to be deceived, worry, and be incredibly spiritual and psychic. The creativity of Neptune and the emotional possessiveness of Cancer will bring out the true art within people. Artist, film makers, and

musicians will imagine some of the greatest works of art ever created. Architecture and engineering will also evolve as the massive creations are brought to life. Being the second of the generational planets the relationship towards your ascendant will provide you with a greater influence from Neptune. So will aspects from Cancer's ruling planet of the Moon.

Pluto in Cancer
1912-1937

Pluto wasn't discovered until 1930 and this was the sign it was in when it was first seen by Clyde Tombaugh. As it takes roughly 240 years for Pluto to complete a cycle through the zodiac it won't be seen again for a while. Those born during this period will have to face great traumas and destructions in their lifetimes. Cancer is gullible and this will induce masses of peoples into believing false lies. Look to the following conflicts during World War 2 and you can see the prime examples. As with all the generational planets, aspects formed with the ascendant and other planets will make this effect more prominent and influential. It will take over 200 years to reach this point, analysis done.

Leo

Mercury in Leo

Those with Mercury in Leo are strongly opinionated and very fixed in their views. When you express yourself you do so dominantly and forcefully. This makes you talkative to an extreme, and you pronounce each word quickly. Mercury functions very well in fire signs making your intelligence keen, with a razor sharp tongue. You're full of imaginative and creative ideas, most of which never leave the boarding station. There's so much going on inside your brain you don't know where to focus. When you do finally figure things out there is much to be accomplished. Mercury only represents a small portion of your chart. Communicating, mental agility, and speed, are all ruled by Mercury. Pay attention to how your words effect the actions of others, you are very powerful with them. When in Leo this makes anything Mercury touches fiery and explosive. Quick on your feet as well as in decision making, you make a great on field general, whether in the actual military or other endeavors. The childlike qualities of Mercury sometimes take longer to mature than others. Immaturity and childish behaviors will come out from time to time. Don't worry you will eventually grow out of it.

Venus in Leo

With Venus in Leo, you're warm hearted, kind, and generous nature is easily. Exceptionally affectionate. A quick temper and dramatic emotions cause you to react instantaneously. When you get worked up you're a tornado of chaos, capable of complete and total destruction. Dramatic theatrics fill your life, like it were a Broadway play. You fall in love deeply and instantly, constantly looking for your hero prince or princess. When poorly afflicted you can be the damsel in distress, freaking out at any strenuous situation. Whether male or female you're highly competitive and demand a partner possessing as many ambitions as you do. Proving your abilities to yourself as well as others is important. Sports and other athletic activities will be great ways to do so. Many times your ego will get to you and your feelings are going to be hurt often. As warm and caring as you are sensitive, once you allow. You lavish your loved ones with affection and gifts, doing anything they ask of you.

Mars in Leo

You're loud, proud, and full of ego when Mars is Leo. Nothing ignites the passions of red planet like fire signs. As fixed fire, the sign of Leo instills you with energy, athleticism, and attitude. You win at all costs and stop at nothing to do so. Taking no prisoners you're, a fierce competitor with a sensitive ego. Your feelings bruise easy especially when harmed by a loved one. Even when you're too proud to show it, which is often, the hurtful and inconsiderate action of others affect you greatly. You always want to be the center of attention and taking a back seat is not an option.

It's important for you to be in the spot light, out in front of the masses, gleaming your cosmic radiance. Because you're direct and straight forward you will get into many fights and arguments, especially when alcohol is involved. If the Moon is negatively aspecting Mars here this shows your mother was probably especially strict, possibly violent. Negative aspects to Saturn indicate issues with you father. The competitor in you will never rest, and you'll fight until the bitter end despite your own personal sufferings. Despite whatever sign it's in, an exact Pluto alignment will make you an exceptional athlete, possibly hall of fame.

Jupiter in Leo

Leo is a wonderful sign for Jupiter to be in. This placement bestows you with kindness, compassion, and several other admirable qualities. Jupiter functions extravagantly while in fire, and no sign is more regal than the Lion. Leo will make you athletic, beautiful, and lucky, especially if positioned in your fifth or ninth houses. Depending on house placement this usually indicates nothing but pleasantries. It will take serious afflictions from Saturn, Uranus, or Mars in order to nullify this. Still then, the awesome powers of Jupiter will not be broken. The most negative difficulty is your tendency to take things to the utter extreme. Depending on aspects you may be completely irresponsible. If your parents were able to provide you with a better off lifestyle chances are you have taken advantage of their assets. If you choose to use their generosity for positive purposes then the sky is the limit for you. Once you learn responsibility and discipline then you can pick your profession and you will advance rapidly. Many times Leo is lazy, and Jupiter magnifies this greatly. Any energy from the Sun will be amplified as well. As this is the most bombastic of planets in the most regal of signs your desire for glitz and glamor is matched for none other. Even if it's not you dressed up yourself you can definitely tell where the line between casual and fancy is.

Saturn in Leo

Of all the fire signs, careless Leo is the most difficult for Saturn handle. Leo likes to play and have fun while Saturn is very restrictive and always being responsible. Saturn is the planet least affected by sign. Although it's placement in the zodiac is important the house positioning and pending aspects from other planet direct Saturn's path. The route Saturn takes is stable, but still reluctantly changes. Chances are you're be a little of both, with house placement showing your tendencies and responsibilities. Only sometimes are you able to go out and have fun, not remembering the responsibilities of tomorrow. When you're consciously aware of how your actions will affect your future the thought of possible consequences prevents you from trying something new. Sometimes when Saturn doesn't know how to react it simply freezes, trying to assess the situation accurately. You always strive to better yourself intellectually because you realize education is important and success in life will require hard work. This can make you an excellent book worm. You can do long tedious tasks better than most. The planet Saturn is planet the affects the relationship that we have with our father. If other planets, especially Mars or the Moon, are negatively aspecting this significant tensions and strife will build up between the two of you. More often than not this indicates you desire public attention for your profession. You aspire for a career more distinguished than most and must prove yourself constantly.

Uranus in Leo
(1872-1878) (1955 – 1961) (2039-2046)

Things will be interesting for those with Uranus traveling through the fixed fire sign of Leo. Uranus takes about seven years to travel through each sign. House placement along with aspects from the other planets will be considerably more important than sign. His influence is generational and can be expressed through several descriptions. Uranus provides us with eccentricity, innovativeness, and independence. Because it's so influenced by the personal planets the aspects formed are highly energized and accentuated. With the combination of the next generational planet,

Uranus is inspired like none other while in fire. Some individuals will be the most athletic and arrogant jackasses you can meet. Technology will eventually make its way into the spirit world, and those with tight aspects to other planets will design the equipment that can do so the holistic all natural healing ways of our ancestors will be rediscovered. As people realize that the chemical drug corporations don't have their best interest in mind, the less harmful yet just effective ways of the natural world will reveal themselves. Human beings are evolving at a very rapid pace, this generation is the start of that acceleration.

Neptune in Leo
(1916-1929)

As Neptune is the second of the generational planets it will take aspects from other planets, especially the ascendant, in order to determine its influence. The aggressiveness of Leo gives the overly timid Neptune some backbone to fight. Those born with this in their charts will have an inspiration to create great and new things. Not many people still alive have this in their charts and it won't happen again for a significant amount of time.

Pluto in Leo
(1938-1958)

The nonconcentric orbit of Pluto around the Sun causes it to be in Leo for and extended amount of time, and it won't return for over 200 years. This distant planet is basically an intensifier which acts as a catalyst for the other planets. Those born with the strong influence of Pluto never break when situations become extreme. The fire of Leo greatly magnifies the obsessive passions and words really can't do this power justice. Over the two decades this transit took, several other planets aligned positively and negatively making it impossible to dictate how this will pan out. Complete obsession, would be the most basic of descriptions. The house placement and other planets will dictate where you focus your strongest opinions. The regenerative powers of this newly discovered planet allow individuals to overcome significant tragedies and atrocities. As seen by the wars throughout the world during that time, one can understand the great effects of this powerful transit. As with all the other generational planets aspects form with the ascendant and others will determine the amount of influence Pluto has in your chart. On a personal level, those with a high Plutonian influence here will take criticism like Tyrannosaur would take an enema.

Virgo

Mercury in Virgo
   Mercury rules in the in mutable Earth of Virgo, giving you an analytical mind which can make you a perfectionist at times. You should possess common sense and tend to develop a specialized skill or technical expertise. If you can use your aptitude for organization to your advantage you will have a head up on most of your professional competition. Random theories, ideas, or knowledge don't interest you unless you can find a practical use for them. When you refuse to accept reality for what it is you believe whatever you want, despite however invalid. Expect hang ups and tensions when you pay too much attention to the minor and insignificant details. When others don't meet your high standards you become overly critical and ignore your own insufficiencies. This intolerance for other people's sloppy thinking will create problems within your workplace. You can make a great scientist, educator, or reporter. This placement of Mercury will make you talkative and energetic, also sometimes immature and unwilling to grow up. Virgo always criticizes until it's their turn to try, then it's the equipment's fault.

Venus in Virgo
   Venus does very well in the mutable Earth sign of Virgo. Quiet, faithful, and devoted to loved ones, it's very easy to get lost in their needs instead of yours. You show your loving feelings towards others by doing things for them. Relatively timid about your true emotions immersing them in work allows you not to deal

300

with them. Being overly critical about yourself and your love ones usually causes those with this influence to marry later in life. This delay is the result of you actually believing there is the perfect partner out there. Good luck finding them. Once you do finally open up and start creating emotional bonds not many influences are as kind, caring, or nurturing. Refined and organized everything has its perfect place. Even if it's a hurricane disaster mess, it will still be an organized blast zone. Your compassion for others may lead you into a profession of servitude. Nursing, social work, or highly advanced degrees in psychology should be considered. Social gatherings and family outings must be planned by you. If you don't they will not be up to your level of acceptance. After voicing your own over inflated opinion fights and arguments begin. It's best if you just do things yourself and have them done right. If you can stay away from being the over cynical nag, you can be friendliest person around. Pay attention to aspects with the ruling planet Mercury. Close aspects with him will likely cause obsessive compulsive disorder or hoarding.

Mars in Virgo

Mars isn't at his strongest in the mutable Earth sign of Virgo. Although this is a very unaggressive sign, you're still an energetic worker who puts in more hours than anyone. This is because you work harder perfecting the fundamentals and refining your technique precisely. A perfectionist at most times, your attention to detail and accuracy is usually spot on. Architecture or structural design may be good career options. You demand a lot out of yourself and others. This makes you irritable and edgy when others don't follow your proven path. You're hardworking and determined to finish what you start. This is a great placement for Mars influencing leadership and authoritative skills. Although Mars doesn't always do to well in Earth signs, the changing abilities of Virgo can ease the tensions. Because of your obsession with perfection, many times if you can't excel at something you just turn your interests elsewhere. Mars is not much of a risk taker here. It would be best to stick to normal physical activities. Action sports are a thrill once in a while, but if you try and make a profession of them you will eventually tire out.

Jupiter in Virgo

There isn't a sign Jupiter doesn't produce wonderful things in. All sign does is adjust what this planet known as the greater benefic is expanding. Here in the analytical and practical Earth sign of Virgo Jupiter tends to calm down, becoming reserved and organized. You have an uncanny ability to decipher fact from fiction, and people don't fool you easily or often. The worst effects are the hyper sensitivity to criticism and disagreements with those who don't accept your ideas. The childlike qualities of ruling planets Mercury usually take a backseat when Jupiter is here. You aren't interested in playing stupid and immature games as you grow older. Reaching your latter years you may turn in into the stingy old miser, yelling at the neighbor kids to stay off your lawn. Common sense is usually associated with Virgo and Jupiter allows you to have a lot of it. This doesn't mean you listen to it every time. If you take an honest reflection on the mistakes you've made in your past you will find every time you knew better and did it anyway. Along with the disregard for criticism, your inability to listen to other will be your biggest downfall.

Saturn in Virgo

Virgo is shy, organized, and studious. Saturn loves all these qualities and does very well in the mutable Earth sign. The perfectionist in Saturn is heightened, causing you to become obsessively focused. Detailed work requiring intense concentration doesn't faze you one bit. Projects involving long tedious hours are enticing and interesting because they intrigue the inner workings of your brain. Despite all the similar properties of these two, there are still significant problems. When negatively afflicted by other planets this turns you more narrow minded and rigid than words can describe. Seemingly cold hearted Saturn makes it impossible to warm up and rarely do you expose your true self. Saturn is economical and responsible, allowing you to see your duties and social obligations. You may suffer from extreme paranoia or hypochondria. It's difficult for both of these cosmic entities to break away from their set ways of thinking. If you can't get over your own ideas and listen to others then those others will take their brilliant ideas elsewhere. Virgo is an organizer, not an inspiration. You will need fire and passions from elsewhere in your chart if you desire to break out on your own. Stick the proven paths to success and you will to just fine. Because of the semi generational influence of Saturn, the house placement is just as important as sign. House placement will show where you're the most obsessively organized.

Uranus in Virgo
(1877-1884) (1961 – 1968)

Uranus in Virgo is a great source of psychological tension, obsessiveness, and extreme nervousness. The overly organized and straight laced qualities of Virgo do not mix well with the eccentricity of Uranus. Being the first in line of the generational planets, house placement and aspects from other planets are key in determining the influence, especially from Mercury. The analytical abilities of Virgo along with the free thinking qualities will make exponential advancements in technology, medicine, and engineering. Not just taking something old and finding a new use for it, Uranus wants to create something different completely. There will be a major revolt in the lifetime of those born under this. The biggest problem for those born during this progression is that the generational planet of Pluto was positioned there as well. Their conjunction is indescribably monumental and can definitely be seen by the space race and beginning of the cold war as well. As the governmental structures created by some of those with this influence are resisted against by those they seek to oppress, the consequences are significant. The social, political, and religious revolutions produced by Uranus are matched by none other. Look to the American and French revolutions during the later seventeen hundreds and the hippie and communist movements during the nineteen sixties to see what Uranus has done in the past.

303

Neptune in Virgo
(1929-1943)

The mystical and magical Neptune is second in line of the generational planets. This means you need an alignment with your ascendant in order to fully feel the powers. When positively aspected your creative abilities produced here are considerable. The Earthly tone of Virgo gives the space headed Neptune a little solid grounding to build upon. Neptune in turn gives dreams and imagination to the sometimes lacking Virgo. The organizational properties of Virgo allow you to take your ideas and manifest them into reality. Generally speaking Neptune doesn't finish what it starts. The other planets or house placement will be needed to give some foundation for Neptune. Allow that to happen. This doesn't mean that everyone in this generation will be successful in every endeavor. Neptune causes confusion and illusions, clouding your better judgment from time to time. It takes Neptune over 150 years to complete a cycle and no one alive today will ever see it in Virgo again.

Pluto in Virgo
(1958-1972)

Being discovered in the sign of Cancer in 1930, not much is known about the most distant and slowest moving planet in our solar system. House placement and aspects to other planets will be very critical. There is a good possibility to be obsessively organized. Hoarding, collections, and personal belongings will have to be meticulously refined to your liking. Negative aspects will make you obsessive and compulsive. Although astrologists don't know much about this, I would assume, Virgo is not a very strong sign for Pluto. Virgo desires to change and improve, but Pluto changes through destruction. Pluto traveling through the mutable Earth sign will intrigue humans into the darker side of the mind and subconscious. Organization of the medical field will improve humanitarian efforts worldwide. It will be the programs started by those of this generation that will rectify the destructions

304

caused by the previous ones. It will be very interesting to see how the connections into the afterlife and spirit world are affected by this. The psychics, mediums, and spirit seers produced by this will spark a revolution of interest into the occult and the magical. It takes over 200 years for Pluto to return to a sign. No one alive will see Pluto transit through Virgo again.

Libra

Mercury in Libra

Libra is the cardinal air sign and while Mercury is traveling through it you become relatively fair minded and balanced, but not always. Represented by the scales, one of your greatest assets is your ability to see thing as they will function most harmoniously. Although if this balance takes away from your stash you may not accept this truth and retreat back into a personal shell. Just because you know the truth doesn't mean you're going to enjoy it. Unless Mars is involved this makes you a patient, tactful debater who loves a vocal competition. Not making judgment until you have sufficient information you allow you opponent to make the first move, rather planning a defense than an attack. All alone this placement makes socializing with unusual characters less interesting. Your opinions usually differ greatly from some people and you'll adamantly argue your point. You would rather sit and listen to others than express your views, this allows you not gain more insight into many different subjects. Easily swayed if someone presents you with enough credible information you can be lopsided and biased towards whichever side has the most amount of evidence. Remember sometimes things go ass backwards with Mercury. At the worst Mercury here makes you think you always have to be in control. When you lose it your psychological breakdowns are worse than others.

Venus in Libra

Libra, along with Taurus, is a ruling sign for Lady Venus. While here her powers of beauty, charm, and social grace, are magnified within your chart. You have a keen eye for beauty and

305

art, desiring the finest amenities of life. As represented by the scales, everything in the realm of Libra must appear fair and equal for all involved. Because you want everyone to like you, this can cause difficulties telling people no, thus leading to others taking advantage of you. Completely desperate to feel loved, you stay in dysfunctional relationships just to avoid the heartbreak. Being alone is a fate worse than death and this may lead you into many failed relationships before you find someone you can grow old with. Generally courteous and considerate, there is definitely a dark side of Venus in this sign. Once in an established partnership you can become ruthless and manipulative in getting what you want. Because you feel you do all you can for your loved ones you expect them to do the same. If you analyze the capacity in what you actually do for others, you may unexpectedly realize you don't do as much as you think. It is also for Venus to just "sweep the problems under the rug," and turn a blind eye to personal issues.

Mars in Libra
With Mars in Libra you can be determined, aggressive, and confrontational. This is the sign of detriment for Mars, meaning this sign is where he feels least comfortable. You fluctuate from being too pushy and insistent on getting your way, into an overly compromising push over. Many times you don't know when to assert yourself or when to back off. Too often you realize you're too aggressive and chase opportunities away or miss out on for being lazy and uninspired. Mars doesn't like things here. You have an idea of how you want things to be, but those things never seem to work out like you had planned. Your personality is generally well balanced and fair minded. Calm and collected until the breaking point, you can be pushed too far then snap violently to prove you're not joking around. In romantic relationships you need to find a partner that sees you as an equal. Decisions must be made together and with the intentions of both people in mind. Ruling planet Venus will have the final say in how Mars will be acting here. Her influence is vitally important.

306

Jupiter in Libra

Libra is the cardinal air sign, and is supposedly well balanced, artistic, and graceful. Focused and down to Earth, unless negatively aspected from other planets you will be very intelligent and articulate. Many famous writers, musicians, and artists come from Jupiter being in Libra. If your Sun is in Gemini, Aquarius, or Sagittarius you can be extremely lucky. Opportunities seem to just fall into your lap and success with them naturally follows. Venus and Saturn will be important in your chart. Negative aspects from them can make you lazy, incompetent, or self-indulgent. You're very charming and make many friends through your numerous social activities. Marriage brings happiness not only for the comfort and security it provides, but the social status from it as well. Most successful when in partnerships, those with a Libran Jupiter should never go into business by themselves. Find a trusted individual to assist you in your endeavors. Financial difficulties occur because of your tendency to overspend when you should be modest. You need to remember that you don't need any more things to put on your shelves and closets.

Saturn in Libra

Libra is one of the most powerful and influential signs Saturn can be in. It's considered the exalting sign, and other than Capricorn, not other sign is better. Of all the planets Saturn is the trickiest to describe because it's the slowest of the personal planets. Retrograde motion along with Saturn's relationship with the other planets is much more important than sign placement alone. The purpose of this planet is to provide a structure. Meaning if the foundation is broken the building can't stand. In my opinion after the Sun, Moon, and ascendant Saturn's conditions is most vital for interpretation. If Saturn is poorly aligned with everything else than it means the other planets are building on unstable ground. Libra is the sign of scales and balance. The responsible characteristics of Saturn can give you considerable amounts dedication. Once you discover focus and where you stand intellectually, you can find a small niche to succeed in. Saturn's house placement becomes extremely important because it will guide you to your career and where you will need to organize yourself most. Remember, there are both positive and negative things being caused by Saturn. It's overly cautious attitude can cause trouble in your love life by delaying marriage until later in life. Whether it's your career, education, or circumstance, it may take a while to settle down.

Uranus in Libra
(1884 – 1890) (1968 – 1974)
Uranus is a slow traveling planet, and while progressing through Libra this will spark your interest to add glamour, style, and fashion in everything you do. You have immense creative abilities and if you ever choose to use and improve them they will take you far. This is a generational planet and the influences are seen through millions of ways. The distinct style of the hippie revolution is known to everyone. Being the first in line of the generational planets Uranus takes about seven years to transit each sign. House placements and aspects from other planets will be very important in assessing the affects or Uranus in your chart. The refined beauty of Venus, the ruler of Libra, will give you an interest in unusual cultural behaviors as well as artwork and jewelry. The generation born under this placement will start a world governmental revolution. The leaders produced under this will strive for complete and total independence from the authority. Horrible atrocities will be committed by those with severely afflicted planets aspecting this. The free spirit of Uranus doesn't always agree with the even balance of Libra. This placement will cause nervous tension, migraines, and other naturopathic diseases.

Neptune in Libra
(1943-1957)
As the second of the generational planets, the forces of Neptune will be intensified for those who have this magical planet aspecting their ascendant. Individuals with the influence of Neptune while traveling through Libra will be susceptible to

delusion and confusion, never knowing who, or what to believe. The easily swayed Neptune naturally goes along with whatever the rest of the chart says. If Neptune and Libra are not prominent within you chart, then the negative influences will be miniscule, but so will the positives. Your delusion allows you to grasp spiritual concepts other generations considered bunk. Libra is the opposite of Aries, it won't be until Neptune reaches the cardinal fire sign in 2026 before the true effects will be distinguishable. This generation understands ultimate compassion. Neptune transits Scorpio next, and that generation is going to screw up the world through death and obsessive possessiveness. Those in this generation will team together with those born while Neptune was in Sagittarius to begin the environmental, governmental, and spiritual clean-up this world so desperately needs. You may travel great distances or you may choose to focus your efforts at home. Either way, you will experience significant personal fulfillment when you do things for others, especially when they are unable to fend for themselves.

Pluto in Libra
(1971-1983)
Pluto is the least known of all the planets. Being discovered in 1930, astrologers are still examining the effects of this distant yet powerful planet. Similar to the other generational planets, house placement and relationship to the ascendant will determine the potency of the distant dwarf. The ruling planet of Venus as well as placement in the second or seventh houses will be significantly powerful. If Pluto is a personal planet you may have jealousy and possessiveness issues. Obsession with sex and drugs, addictions might plague you throughout your life. They may be your own personal demons, or those affecting your loved ones. The powers of Pluto are amazing, many times you find yourself completely desolate or depressed only to make a miraculous turn around, obtaining success. Pluto is the lord of the underworld, compared to Shiva the destroyer, sent to cause total destruction only to rebuild something grander in its place. Fascinations into

spirituality and the occult are influenced by Pluto. If you choose a path into the darker realm of the underworld, make sure you take it easy when dabbling into the. You may unlock secrets you wish you hadn't.

Scorpio

Mercury in Scorpio

Mercury is the closest, fastest moving planet to the Sun. It's from his influence we get our verbal and nonverbal communication skills. When in the sign of Scorpio you're very secretive about yourself, but desire to know as much as you can about others. Your concentration skills are intense and you may become obsessive and possessive. The intellectual ninja of the zodiac, you get in and out quickly. Letting your opponent know more than you is unacceptable. Picking up on the subconscious signals of others you prefer nonverbal forms of expressions and read people well. If you do pursue higher education subjects of medicine, and psychology will likely interest you. If you choose to accept the spiritual powers of this placement, you are completely psychic. Your subconscious is a very deep and seclusive place, in which your understanding is vast. Naturally understanding that there is a greater meaning to life in Earth, you may become very interested in the magical and occult. A close alignment with your ascendant will cause you to speak slowly possibly with a significant mumble or impediment. Communication is most definitely not at its best when positioned in water.

Venus in Scorpio

Scorpio turns Venus into an overly jealous, obsessive control freak. Because Venus is the planet heavily influencing our everyday relationships, whether it be romantic or otherwise, the house this is positioned in is where you will experience the most passion and intensities. The seductive, secretive properties which Scorpio instills are deeply imbedded into your psyche. No matter what the relations are you desire deeply intimate connections with

310

the chosen few of your circle. Emotions run strong and you will have to control them. You're capable of hatred and rage just as much as love and compassion. There is no other sign as sexual as Scorpio. While in retrograde you will have confusion about your sexuality and are probably curious about the same sex. Your fascinated with the mystical and magical, especially the seedy underworld of the occult. You have an interest in the deeper possibly darker side of religion. You feel all relationships are permanent and are deeply disturbed when a loved one leaves. If they part under problematic circumstances remember slashing their tires is a poor choice. No sign can make you more possessive of a lover. Many conflicts in your marriage will be because you still think it's appropriate to socialize with former lovers on a casual level. In turn you partner feel threatened and the problems ensue. Learning to let go will be the most difficult virtue for you to learn, and you probably never will.

Mars in Scorpio
        Placed in Scorpio, Mars is in one of its ruling signs, and is very powerful. Determined and strong willed, you pursue ambitions persistently, refusing defeat in any instance. Scorpio is the darkest, most sinister sign of the zodiac. It can produce obsession, jealousy, and possessiveness. If negatively aspected this can also produce sexual promiscuity and deviousness. Mars will need pleasant aspects from other planets, hopefully Venus or the Moon to produce any positive energy. Any negative aspects will be very powerful and can ruin a chart. This can also produce severe addiction. Drugs, alcohol, and adrenaline can control your life in horrible ways. Never shy in taking what is yours you will tread all over others if given the chance. If there is no one there to stop you, then you will do whatever you want, whenever you want to. Ulcers, high blood pressure, and heart attacks are all associated with this placement as well. Everything involving Mars will be using high octane fuel. Nothing can exactly describe the obsessive nature Mars takes on while in Scorpio. You hate coming last and can be the ultimate competitor at times. House placement will

311

show where you're the most competitive.

Jupiter in Scorpio

When traveling through Scorpio, the philosophically expansive Jupiter takes on a fascination with death, sex, and the seedy underworld. The intellectual properties of Jupiter combined with the secretive tendencies of Scorpio causes you do probe deep into everything you study. You never reveal more about yourself than needed because you see the weakness of your opponent knowing more about you than you do of them. Jupiter will expand everything it touches, and when negatively influenced this can make you deceitful and conniving. If you choose a path of spirituality chances are you will explore the occult and darker side of the universe. It's vital you learn how to remain focused on project not directly needing attention. What happens is you become so focused on a certain few things you forget to tend to something until it's too late. Because you naturally understand that there is more out there than meets the eye, nothing is ever impossible. Your tendencies toward risky speculation must be controlled and checked at all times. The obsessive and possessive qualities of Scorpio can lead you into an overconfident attitude that just get you into trouble. Your best professional choice is somewhere within the medical or psychological fields.

Saturn in Scorpio

Saturn is the slowest moving of the personal planets, taking over two years to transit each sign its powers are easily shifted by house placement. We get determination, perseverance, and as a desire for social status and prominence. The secretive sign of Scorpio combined with the cold, restrictive planet of Saturn will make those with this placement more suspicious of individuals around them. You possess an interest in understanding the deeper more advanced functions of human nature. Saturn is known for creating difficulties in order to teach us the life lessons we need to learn. Emotional pain and strife is caused by Saturn in Scorpio. Those with severely negative aspects from other planets will be monstrous control freaks. In business you may stoop to some of the most unethical and inhumane strategies for advancement. Technological advances into the human psyche will also be invented. We will learn more about the neurological functions of our brains. Our mind is more powerful than we understand. As we evolve as a species we will realize that the universe is a magical and wonderful multi-dimensional plane of existence. When the powers of our subconscious are no longer deniable only then will the world open their eyes towards the light of the cosmos. This is the placement for the ultimate surgeon, psychologist, or criminal.

Uranus in Scorpio
(1890 – 1897, 1974 – 1981)
As the first in line of the generational planets Uranus is usually more analyzed by house placement than sign. Not being discovered until the 1700's it's also the first planet not visible to the naked eye. It's the planet of sudden and unexpected changes, creating strife, anxiety, and eccentricity to all our lives. Those born with it in Scorpio will see wars, natural disasters, and humanitarian atrocities tear the world apart. The addition of a Scorpio influenced Uranus will produce some of the most psychotic and mentally disturbed individuals of all time. The sometimes satanic influence of Scorpio will be brought out, creating destructions all across the globe. In essence Scorpio is the underworld, its deepest, darkest, most deplorable side of humanity. This will be especially difficult for those with this positioned in their eighth house. Horrible, negative things, are not the only things that will come around because of this. Deeper studies into the human psyche and subconscious are also going to under this influence, as well as significant advancements in the way technology, mechanics, and engineering are used in medicine.

Neptune in Scorpio
(1956-1970)
Scorpio is the fixed water sign. Neptune is the ruler of the mutable water sign and is extremely spiritual, emotional, and

obsessive here. The sign of Scorpio represents death, destruction, and complete chaos. Being the second of the generational planets Neptune placed here will continue the evolutionary progress into the spirit world. Scorpio is a very psychic sign, and is considered a portal into the underworld. The negative emotional intensity produced here will bring wars and hostile uprisings with obsessed world leaders committing horrific atrocities against humanity, which is nothing new. Problem being, there are too many agreeing with the perpetuator's of evil. The destruction caused by those who neglect the environment for monetary purposes will come to its spear head. Eventually humans must realize many of our ways will lead to our extinction. New advances in the human consciousness will be produced by this. When influenced by other planets the natural psychic connections to the spirit world will slowly reveal themselves. As our technology advances with our spirituality we will make significant introductions into the realm of the mystical and unknown. As old dogmatic religions slowly wear out their connection to the people, the passion, courage, interest into more personal spirituality will rise in popularity. Shamans and witch doctors may even be back in business sooner then we think.

Pluto in Scorpio
(1984-1995)

In our solar system Pluto is the slowest and most distant planet we know of. Not being discovered until 1930 astrologers are still studying its effects on us Earthlings. Always compared to Shiva the destroyer, Pluto is an intense, secretive, planet. Just like Uranus and Neptune house placement and aspects from other planets will need to be looked at to determine how influential it will be. Those born during this period will see the death and destruction needed for human evolution. In order for something new to be built the old political and social structures will have to be destroyed. Through biblical like plagues, the disease, famine, and wars across the Earth will eventually take its toll on the environment. Many times this is extreme, unanticipated, and totally devastating. As the ruler of the underworld, the calamities

314

Pluto causes are only meant to expand our consciousness and the house Pluto is positioned in will be that pathway. Like the great phoenix rising from the ashes, this Scorpio generation will transform all the atrocities throughout the world and use them to propel the world into a better future. Again, this is the first time we have seen Pluto in Scorpio. It won't pass through this sign again for over 200 years. This is a very powerful psychic and spiritual sign. This can be the darker side of religion, leading you down a path into the occult. Old dogmatic doctrines will no longer be the interest of the masses. The occult and natural aspects of medicine, psychology, and spirituality will see new and innovative breakthroughs.

Sagittarius

Mercury in Sagittarius

Mercury takes on a special spark while in Sagittarius. It especially livens your speech and increases your spunk. Those with Mercury positioned in this sign are quick witted and usually sharp tongued. Although you're open minded and free thinking you're still firm in your opinions. Mercury enjoys fire signs and instills those with this positioning with a passion and spiritual fire. When combined with aspects from other planets this can drive you to great and wonderful things. Helping others will be a key focus on your mind, as you look at things from your own special point of view many times you can find the good where others can't. If Jupiter is involved by any aspects luck in gambling and business can come about at any given time. Your excessive energies cause you to bounce around from one thing to other, usually not completing the previous endeavor. You learn a lot from travel experiences. Many times this signifies education abroad. Experience is the best most efficient teacher and you know that. You desire to have endless life experiences in order to teach you all the knowledge of the universe.

Venus in Sagittarius

    When Venus is in Sagittarius you need to feel connected with your partner spiritually before connecting physically. You idealize love and always think there will be greener pastures elsewhere. This causes you to jump from casual relationship to casual relationship before you settle down completely. When looking for love you're subconsciously drawn those who can help you grow and expand your philosophical beliefs. Attracted to those who are fun loving and playful, adventure with excitement is needed to sustain any significant relationship. Drawn towards someone who is adventurous you may even find love on a vacation or traveling around the world. This may also indicate you marry someone from a completely different background than yours. People from foreign cultures educate you on the living conditions throughout the globe. The beauty of their artwork, religious ceremonies, and theatre enlarges your understanding of the universe. When looking at these magnificent things the in-depth and unseen spirituality will overflow you with emotion. Sometimes you may breakdown and cry for the most insignificant of reasons.

Mars in Sagittarius

    Plain and simple, Mars loves the fire signs. When traveling through mutable fire, the intense passions of Mars are much more spiritual and philosophical. You're bright, energetic, and always seeking to expand your horizons. As you constantly expect to succeed, when others defy your ideas or authority you instantly react, sometimes violently. Despite what you think of yourself your feelings opinions are no more valid or important than those of others. Until you learn humbleness and humility, you will consistently rub others the wrong way. The competitive nature you exude must always be in motion. Athletic and aggressive, physical recreations will be an important aspect of your life. When confined you become restless and irritable. Not knowing where to direct your energy you lash out inappropriately at those who don't deserve it. Sagittarius is a spiritual and philosophical sign, adding inspiration to your personality. This driving force may even propel you into a life of religious and spirituality endeavors. Jupiter is the ruling planet and any aspect with him will make you extremely athletic. Saturn may even provide you with a career in sports.

Jupiter in Sagittarius

Sagittarius is the ruling sign for the planet known as the greater benefic. The optimistic, idealistic, and generous qualities of the planet of expansion are at their strongest and most powerful. Any aspects formed with other planets will be very influential, especially ones in the ninth house. The fiery spirit produced by Jupiter causes you to be expressive and flamboyant. You're a free spirit who must be allowed to roam wherever you please. Jupiter provides us with philosophy and inspiration Gifted with a sense of higher consciousness, if you choose a path into the realm of the spirituality you will experience things not everyone can. The negative side of this placement can be your tendency to overdo everything. To you anything worth doing is worth over doing, and excess can be the only way of life. Whether it be donating your time and money, or spending too much at the bar, an overindulgent lifestyle may lead you into a world of destruction. If you get involved in drugs or alcohol it is very likely that you take it to the extremes. At some point in your life you will have to make a decision, the party life of youth, or the responsible adult life.

Saturn in Sagittarius

Fire signs are difficult for Saturn to handle, as the reserved nature of Saturn doesn't enjoy the spotlight fire signs revel in. Sagittarius is a fun loving sign full of exuberance with the ruling planet of Jupiter providing this flamboyance. The Sagittarian energy is in general confliction with Saturn's conservative philosophies. The mutable fire sign just doesn't want to settle into the routine desired by Saturn. You have a serious mind which finds it difficult to let go of your responsibilities. If negatively afflicted this indicates the complete resistance to your duties in life. Because of Saturn's longer duration in each sign the specific characteristics are difficult to pinpoint. Saturn's attitude in fire makes him arrogant about his career or education. Because you desire to be prominent within your community many times you become so successful you have much to donate to charities. You feel if everyone can work together something great can be accomplished, and you're exactly right. While working in groups with others you stand out amongst your peers. You naturally assume leadership and often step on the toes of your authorities, accepting it where it isn't your place. Saturn is the slowest of the personal planets and its house placement will be equally important as sign. Aspects to Jupiter or the ninth house will be more powerful than others. You can see the valid point of others and wish to get things done correctly and the first time. This leads to more success in the professional world. Success comes after lots of hard work, and you realize this.

Uranus in Sagittarius
(1897 – 1904) (1981 – 1988)
As the first of the generational planets Uranus is looked upon with special consideration. Because it's such a slow moving planet, house placement as well as aspects forming with other planets will be key in determining how influential Uranus will be. The mutable fire of Sagittarius sparks the innovative creativity of this planet greatly. Your thinking skills are quick and clever. Spiritually inspiring, this is going to be the generation instigating the revolution of the religions. All religion throughout the world will go through complete and major overhaul in preparation for the next generation. Wars and conflicts, transitions from one form of government control to the other will face those of this generation. The world is anticipating greatly the doctors, philosophers, and spiritualists that this energy will produce. Rapid innovations in medicine and technology will be abound, creating new advancements for humanity. Eccentric, ingenious and revolutionary, the inspiration of Uranus can cause worldwide

social and political revolutions.

Neptune in Sagittarius
(1807-1820) (1970-1984)

As the second of the generational planets this planet of the mystical and magical, takes on a brilliant shine. While Neptune travels through Sagittarius, those born during this time will be the leading runners into many social and political revolutions. Religion, world policy, and most importantly environmental awareness will be the focus of many uprisings throughout the world. Natural and spiritual healing will rise, as well as holistic form of recuperation. Fields of medicine and psychology will see major advancements as well. Technology will allow us to see things within ourselves in ways have never been conceived. The human brain with its unknown aura and functions will be studied and revolutionized. Those with both Uranus and Neptune will be the generational leaders who begin the movement into the promise land. House placement and any aspects to the ascendant will determine how influential the effects of Neptune will be.

Pluto in Sagittarius
(1995-2008)

Pluto is the most distant known planet in our solar system. As with other generational planets any aspects formed with your ascendant and other planets will alter the effects of Pluto and intensify them in unusual ways. The generation with this positioning will be given the daunting task of completely restructuring the religious belief system throughout the world. Reconditioning humanity into the spiritual beings we once were is going to be a long process in which many lives will be lost. There will be a massive and chaotic mess created by the generations past in which this generation will face all the burdens. As we realize we're destroying our environment, the profits of big business will be forced to take a back seat to sustainable efficiency. Those already alive will begin the revolutionary process. There will be athletes like never before seen. When combined with Mars and

Saturn the natural physical abilities are indescribable. Sagittarius is the most philosophical sign of the zodiac. It hadn't transited here for 200 years and it will be another 200 before it passes here again. One thing is for certain, this will be an extremely volatile base for any of the other planets to build upon. Bad aspects from Saturn and Mars will be extremely difficult and create many tensions throughout your life. House placement is where you will be the most spirituality obsessed and susceptible to jealousy.

Capricorn

Mercury in Capricorn

Mercury in Capricorn turns this naturally talkative and energetic planet quiet and reserved. The timid tendencies make it difficult for you to warm up to strangers, and only until they have gained your trust and respect will you start to open up to them. This is a wonderful placements for parents as it generally makes children grow up early and accept responsibility naturally. Your logic is generally down to Earth, and spending time in useless fantasies doesn't interest you. To you everything passing through your mind needs to be sensible and useful. If it takes a while for you to catch on to advanced topics don't be too worried, Capricorn is a slow and restrictive sign which take a while to learn new concepts. Once locked into a way of thinking it's nearly impossible for you to budge. The rigidity produced here causes you to be very narrow minded and quite abstentious with age. House placement will only influence this a little, and the 1st, 5th, and 9th, fire houses will be the best for adding spirit. Whether for good or bad purposes you focus intently on only a few subjects. Unlike the scatter brained fire or air signs, Earth lulls your intellect into a much more cautious reserve. Remember this only represents a small portion of your personality and doesn't indicate on specific characteristic. If you have calming alignments form other planets you may be shy and reserved. Those with energetic Capricorn Mercury's will be extremely direct and straightforward when they speak. This is definitely a no B.S. sign and you got no time or need for excessive details. Heavy Mars afflictions will make you abstentious and rude. Mercury is a planet very influenced by house placement as well. You will also take on the characteristics of the ruling sign of whichever house he is placed.

Venus in Capricorn

When Venus is in Capricorn you're cautious, quiet, and reserved about your personal relationships. Expressing your affections slowly, you don't care to open to others until forced to. Even when you do you're not very demonstrative towards them. Venus is the most social of planets and Capricorn the most antisocial of the zodiac. Saturn is the ruling planet and the relationship is indescribably important. The social standing of you and your spouse will always play into your decision making. Perhaps you even marry for money or status. In all your relationships you're old fashioned and traditional. Capricorn is the shy, responsible, somewhat restrictive sign making us want to stay on a direct path. Although Capricorn is an Earth sign Venus isn't completely comfortable here. Too often the responsibilities of your work and career will interfere with your personal relationships. This can also make you very demanding around your house. You will not tolerate when things aren't organized in the fashion that you see fit. Your partner will have to be submissive and passive in order for a long term relationship to last.

Mars in Capricorn

Mars is right at home in the sign of Capricorn. Being the exalting sign for the fiery red planet this placement makes you aggressive and physically strong. Determined to finish everything you start, the rigidity of Capricorn can make you a stubborn, ram headed individual most of the time. When not kept in check you can become manipulative and ruthless in your tactics to success. The natural competitiveness of Mars is grounded by cautiousness of the cardinal Earth sign. Your ambition for power makes you unhappy in any situation where your opinion doesn't matter. If you have no authority you simply go off and find something in which you do. Professions in politics, law, or sports medicine can prove as proper outlet for your energy. The controlled and collective thinking by this placement is one of the easier placements for Mars. Despite the eagerness of Mars while it is in Capricorn you enjoy sticking to methods that are tried and true. Your drive is for practical and earthly matters. Never relying on luck or good fortune you understand that your rewards are from your own hard work and efforts. Athletically, no sign is tougher or stronger. Your bones, joints, and muscles can withstand much more than most.

Jupiter in Capricorn

Capricorn is a difficult sign for Jupiter. The outlandish extravagance of Jupiter doesn't like the restricted characteristics of the cardinal Earth sign. The restrictive and materialistic sign of Capricorn bases many of your philosophies. Many of those born with this placement will achieve great things in the business world. As the technologies of the world advance so rapidly, it's hard for the professional world to put them to practical use. It will be the projects and enterprises started by this transit which allows the tech world to merge with the business realm. As the difficulties of this arise many will turn cold and rigid as they enter their middle age years, especially if Saturn is involved. Although unpleasant to deal with, it will be the stingy, shrewd, and stern, old businessman stimulating the world and local economies. Many jobs will ride on the businesses created by these entrepreneurs. It will be your ability to differentiate between personal and professional responsibilities allowing you to succeed.

Saturn in Capricorn

This is the ruling sign for Saturn making its power and influences much stronger. Anything connected to the greater malefic is taken very seriously and the house Saturn is positioned in is where you must be the most responsible in order to feel stable. This planet is only a structure the other planets are meant to build upon. Here it's unbreakably strong and firm. Most are ambitious and hardworking, and realize legitimate effort and work is needed in order to achieve success. If Saturn is aspecting your mid-heaven then a career in politics or law is more than likely. You're patient and disciplined in your work, once you settle down into a career that's usually where you stay. You don't like getting off the beaten path very often, and prefer traditional means when making a living. Saturn is the slowest moving of the personal planets, and house placement will be more influential then with other planets. Because of the strength Saturn receives from Capricorn any aspects with other planets forming negative aspects can be really, really, bad. If there are too many unpleasant influences then you can never be truly happy. You will always see the gloomy downside of everything. Habits formed with drugs, gambling, or sex will be very hard to break if not impossible. Saturn also influences the relationship we all have with our father. If poor aspects are in your chart, chances are that the relationship with your father was tough and strenuous. Maybe he wasn't there, maybe he was strict and stern. Possibly, he was a workaholic and just didn't pay any attention. Harmonious aspects will make your relationship pleasant and wonderful.

Uranus in Capricorn
(1904 – 1912) (1988 – 1995)

Uranus is the fastest moving of the generational planets. On average it spends about seven years in each sign. It's the planet of innovative inspirations. Capricorn is a restrictive responsible sign and Uranus doesn't always handle it well. House placement and aspects from other planets will be more efficient indicators of Uranus' effect in ones chart. This will be especially difficult for those born with Aquarius rising. Innovation in business and engineering will be one of the more global effects from this. New, not always ethical, ways will be developed within our commerce. As Uranus prepares to go into its ruling sign of Aquarius, we will see the technological advance to match this placement. Religious, political and social structure will undergo a radical reform. Those born with this in their twelfth house will eventually experience a mental break down or psychological disorder later in life. The fact Neptune was in Capricorn for the duration as well as Saturn during the early 1990's makes it difficult to describe the solitary effects of this sign placement.

Neptune in Capricorn
(1820-1835) (1985-1998)
Neptune is the second of the generational planets and moves very slowly. It takes about thirteen years to make a pass through each sign, and one full revolution around the Sun takes about 134 years. House placement, especially conjunctions with the ascendant, and aspects from other planets will be very individualizing in your chart. Those of this generation have a difficult task at hand. They will be the ones chosen to bring the mystical and magical powers back from the cosmos and reveal them down on Earth. Advancements in natural, holistic, sometimes even psychic forms healing will take place. Religious and spiritual leaders will rediscover the wonderful, natural powers of not only plants but oils and stones as well. There will be many powerful leaders arise to power in small sections of the globe. Because of the total government reform there will have to be smaller groups of power controlling the public instead of the single few powerhouses. Those small militias will need leadership and organization in order to survive. This transit of Neptune will prove to do just that. Responsibility wise this is a great sign for Neptune. This Cardinal Earth sometimes grounds the dreaminess of Neptune to a screeching halt. Absolutely nothing can be told by the sign Neptune is transiting through. This stimulates creativity in more realms than can be explored. Many will agree the industrial revolution was initiated by this the last time around back in 1920. When Uranus aligned itself during the late 1980's and into the early 1990's things got pretty interesting around the world. The powers of these two aligning like this are indescribable. Watch out for ghosts and space aliens people, this generation is going to time travel.

Pluto in Capricorn
(2009-2024)

Since Pluto wasn't discovered until 1930 astrologists have never been able to analyze its effects here. Because of its nonconcentric orbit it is difficult to even guess when this happened last. It's probably that around the 1770's is when we last felt the effects of a Capricorn Pluto. Those individuals born under a Capricorn Pluto will have to go through complete and total destruction and rejuvenation. Pluto can and will totally destroy one thing and build something entirely new. Since it can take between 13 and 28 years for Pluto to travel through a sign these effects will not be instantaneous. The slow and steady Pluto in the cold and calculating sign of Capricorn will not work fast. To find the individual effects of Pluto in the chart you will need to look to house placement and aspects from other planets. These individuals are going to be extremely hard headed and stingy. This generational planets doesn't provide a distinct characteristic, but it does intensify the planets who do. House placement indicates where you obsess about, and the other planets will amplify it. Any alignments between Mars or Saturn will be especially strong.

Aquarius

Mercury in Aquarius

With an Aquarian Mercury you're an independent thinker who must be allowed to go off on their own. Rigid and stubborn in your views, it's very difficult to change your mind once you believe something to be true. Going to great lengths when proving your correctness, you cling onto your wrong beliefs until there is no other choice but change. This doesn't make you closed minded, you're just a progressive thinker who believes our problems can be solved by logical intelligent thinking. Because you're so open to the free thinking of others you become agitated by those with more conservative and out dated viewpoints. Science, music, and technology will spark you interest. You have an insatiable curiosity and will listen to any one who seems to know what they're talking about. As kind of an oddball you have more unusual interests than most. You may end up possessing an exotic pet, or travel to many parts of the world. Preferably on the leading edge of technology, you will want all the latest gadgets and gizmos. You may even choose a profession in research and development or science exploration. Aspiring to create and invent something entirely new, you may create something that has never been seen.

Venus in Aquarius

Venus in Aquarius makes you flirtatious and charming, desiring personal freedom within all your relationships. Your social wit attracts friends from a wide array of lifestyles. Any clingy, possessive relationships will turn you away. Large groups of friends and acquaintances appeal to you. Whether it be a romantic or casual relationship there must be an intellectual connection. It's imperative you're given proper space by any partner. Pending house placement the independent nature of Aquarius can indicate an extra marital affair and serious hidden secrets. Because you're so prone to taking off and leaving, this can also indicate multiple marriages. The reason for this is it's easy to become emotionally detached from people and situations. You feel this is beneficial because it also allows you to put up a guard protecting yourself from emotional let downs as well. Venus in this sign can also attract you to extremely different individuals. It will be difficult for you to compromise with your partner and still be happy. Even if you do submit your desires deep inside you dwell on the bitterness.

Mars in Aquarius

When Mars is in Aquarius your energy level is high, yet sporadic. You desire to express yourself more divergently than others. Striving to distinguish yourself amongst the crowd, you may go to radical extremes to do so. The rebellious nature you possess drives you to accomplish a great many things. You hate being told how to think and will respond instantaneously when your freedoms are threatened. Because you can think outside the box, areas of technology and science can prove to be interesting outlets for your energy. Your eccentric and inventive ways of thinking will see things were some see nothing. Although it's difficult for your rigid views to get along with others, if you can put your ego aside you become a wonderful asset to any team. The fiery aggressions of Mars function well in air signs, and despite your perceived erraticness you can usually accomplish much. When severely afflicted by other planets this can make you impatient and irritable. Pay attention to the way you communicate with others as quite often you will portray the wrong message.

Jupiter in Aquarius

While Jupiter is in Aquarius the expansion of human knowledge is imminent. When the inventive, innovative qualities of the water bearer are combined with the magnificent powers of Jupiter great things should be expected. Gifted with an ability towards higher learning, you wish to change the belief system of the world. You see the atrocities humanity is perpetuating and it rips at your soul. You want to break free of any old and outdated ways of life, embracing the advancements of the future. Advancements in not only technology but spirituality as well. Ushering a new generation into a new concept of personal spirituality and religion you rebel against the standard rules of old dogmatic religion. This will be a generation fascinated with the research and development into technology. Improvements from cell phones to car technology will then lead into new breakthroughs in medicine. There will be a shift from chemical healing drugs into a more natural, spiritual form of healing. Shaman's and so called witch doctors may even to open their doors.

Saturn in Aquarius

When Saturn is in the fixed air sign of Aquarius, you can be abstentious, narrow minded, and rigid. You possess good common sense and rational thinking. Saturn is a very responsible and restricting planet. Aquarius is the definition of expanding human consciousness. Only individuals with Saturn prominent in their charts really deal with the issues produced by this placement. These people will be very comfortable talking and leading large groups of people about science and improving our minds. Saturn takes about two and a half years to transit through each sign, the longest of the personal planets. Not everyone born with this will be socially responsible. If your focus is into the seedy underbelly of the world then you can be the most cold-hearted criminal out there. If Mercury is positively aspecting this you will be exceptionally smart. Practical thinking and the natural desire to expand and innovate will create breakthroughs and refinements in technology, religion, and medicine. If this placement is in the eleventh house you will be a natural born leader, and success in the public eye is almost guaranteed. Advancements in technology will occur exponentially.

Uranus in Aquarius
(1912 – 1919) (1995 – 2003)
        Aquarius is the ruling sign of Uranus intensifying the powers of this recently discovered planet, first seen in 1781. Aquarius desires to be completely independent, doing whatever it wants, whenever it wants to. Those with Uranus as a personal planet in this sign are abstentious and cantankerous. The rigid thinking makes you very argumentative when you're told you're wrong. Even worse is being proven wrong. Although free thinking and innovative Uranus in this sign cannot tolerate being told how or what to believe. Always needing proof leading towards your opinions, areas of science and technology will expand greatly during these periods. As the first of the generational planets this positioning creates masses of rebellions and social uprisings. The progressive and revolutionary attitude produced will cause the latter generation with this to lead humankind along their path of evolution. As humans discover the divine and spiritual beings we are the energies produced here will propel our intellectual evolution into the universe.

Neptune in Aquarius

(1834-1847) (1997-2011)

Neptune in Aquarius indicates a generation of humanitarianism at its finest. The intelligent and innovative qualities of Aquarius adds character and backbone to the generally passive tendencies of Neptune. As the second of the generational planets this is the sign in which Neptune was discovered in on September 23, 1846. Those born with this mystical and magical planet will be an important generation given the task of improving the social conditions here on Earth. As shown by the American civil war during the 1800's and the new global war on terror in the present, we can see the radically revolutionary essence of this positioning. Aquarius is an extremely rebellious and passionate sign. No sign of the zodiac will go to such lengths just to prove themselves wrong. The intellectual rigidity of this fixed air sign can cause certain individuals to be stingy and rude. Those with Neptune as a personal planet will be spiritually innovative and progressive, propelling the masses into the cosmic world of the magical and divine. Once again the ghosts and space aliens are coming. This generation will be preparing for first contact.

Pluto in Aquarius
(2023-2044)

Pluto wasn't discovered until 1930 while it was in the sign of Cancer, and astrologers haven't been able to analyze the energies of Pluto for very long. While he is in the fixed air sign Aquarius we can only assume the rapid rate that technology develops will only multiply. Chances are this is when humans will develop the ability to contact other universal realms and extra terrestrial life. As it won't enter Aquarius until 2023, we can only assume that this will help advance the subconscious minds of the beings here on Earth. The basic influence of this transit will be the expansion of life into the solar system and outer regions of space. This twenty year progression can't be described in a few words or examples. More or less the human race will become obsessed with technology and advancing knowledge. Spirit and science will slowly integrate themselves, and the undetected spiritual entities will be detected. Meaning we will discover ghosts. House placement is vital as it indicates where you obsess the most. Mostly, Pluto will act as a catalyst amplifying their energies, whether it's positive or negative.

Pisces

Mercury in Pisces

When Mercury is in the mutable water sign of Pisces you communicate in tender, compassionate, and most importantly, psychic methods. The final sign of the zodiac is ruled by Neptune and formerly by Jupiter. Any aspects from those two planets will be especially powerful. Although you're inspired to be creative, many of your projects never get fully completed. You think you need to begin a project with everything that sparks your fancy. Shy away from any work requiring long hours of strenuous labor, it's difficult for you to stay physically active for long durations. Several times throughout your life you will get flashes of psychic intuition; many of these will come through dreams. If you can learn to use these to your advantage, most times you will realize that your initial gut instinct is correct. Your vivid dreams inspire you to pursue the more artistic endeavors of life. As you reach your retirement years hobbies like painting, photography, or expressive writing may interest you. You will need to find an artistic or creative outlet for your imagination.

Venus in Pisces

Pisces is the exalting sign for Venus, and her influence is exceptionally strong here. Ultimate compassion is the general feeling for Lady Venus while in the fish. This is the mutable water sign, and you can adapt yourself into many social circles. You're compassionate and sympathetic, always willing to help someone in need. Quite often others will recognize this and take advantage of you. You're attracted to unstable individuals who always need support, and constantly find yourself in very precarious situations. Be careful not to become dependent in any dysfunctional relationship. You may stay attached long after things turn sour due to your fear of heartbreak. The major malfunction is your diluted perception of the perfect relationship actually being out there. Your imagination is vivid and you will experience very realistic dreams. Use the images produced by your subconscious and turn them into something physical. Your psychic abilities are enhanced by Pisces and you will find your intuitions are usually correct.

Mars in Pisces

If your Mars is in Pisces you tend to be neither combative nor aggressive. Generally a pacifist, fighting anyone or anything displeases you greatly. Staying behind the scenes or confronting the matter by side stepping, you may even resort to surrender before the fight starts. Except Scorpio, Mars doesn't function in water signs very well, and the emotional illusions of Pisces can make you an overly sensitive pansy. Because you're not ego driven you don't seek much personal glorification like others do. Being the best isn't as important as long as you still feel loved and accepted. Winning at the expense of others abhors you and cheating is never tolerated. If your Mars is in the later stages of Pisces you will start to take on the aggressive traits of the following sign Aries, which can add backbone and strength to the softened Mars. If you spend most of your time daydreaming about what my come or what has happened nothing will be accomplished. Your overly sensitive compassions for the world may direct you into a role within humanitarian efforts. As you see the injustices around the world you may feel compelled to take significant action. Volunteer work will provide you with the self-worth and value you so desperately desire.

Jupiter in Pisces

Until Neptune was discovered in the mid 1800's Jupiter was the ruler of Pisces. When positioned here your personal growth is experienced best when you're allowed to help others reach their own personal enlightenment. As you recognize many of the inhumane ways people are treated throughout society, you become compelled to do something about it. Whether it be within your own small community or the expansion of the world, you take an interest in improving the conditions of your environment. If you aren't careful your overly charitable attitude will neglect your own needs and waste limited resources on others. You may possess an interest in the higher philosophies of religion, the occult, or technological advancement. The truth is, you must find this path of ascension on your own. Periodically removing yourself from the hustle of life will be needed for personal relaxation and meditation. Not the most stable sign of the zodiac, Pisces will add significant confusion in your life. Magic and mysticism are imbedded into your subconscious, and despite any denial on your part you are extremely psychic most of the time.

Saturn in Pisces

Pisces is a difficult sign for Saturn. Pisces is the sign of deep inner subconscious and emotions. Saturn doesn't like warming up to emotion. The restrictive nature of Saturn causes you have difficulties setting emotional boundaries. With others as well as yourself. It's almost impossible to separate what your emotional needs are and if they are actually attainable. Everything about your complex emotional make-up is difficult. Your kind, sympathetic nature attracts unstable individuals who don't have your best interest in mind. Pisces a glutton for punishment, and Saturn If Neptune is aspecting Saturn you may find a successful career in music or art. A Piscean Saturn also indicates a very close bond with your father. No matter which sign or house placement Saturn is difficult for us to handle. It is the planet that teaches us responsibility, ethics, hard work, and determination. Serious afflictions mean serious problems.

Uranus in Pisces
(1919 – 1927) (2003 – 2010)

Uranus is the first of the generational planets, and in the final sign of Pisces the idealism, sympathy, and compassions for humanity are intensified. As with the other generational planets,

Neptune and Pluto, the influences of Uranus are stronger when aspected by other planets primarily the ascendant and mid-heaven. House positioning is vital as well causing Uranus to take on the essence of the houses ruling sign. Water signs always have a calming effect on the rather erratic Uranus emotionalizing this rebellious entity. Scientists and doctors will direct their attention more towards all natural or holistic forms of treatment as opposed to chemicals. Artists, musicians, and dreamers will also have unusual inspirations. They will slowly incorporate technology and precision into their crafts. Others will see the horrific atrocities humans have created and begin taking action. The independent desires of Uranus propels individuals to take action and actually do something to help, even if it's all alone. As the generations past have ignored the catastrophic destruction of their ways, those born with a Uranus Pisces are going to be given the task of cleaning it up. The evolution of not only science and technology will be rapid, but the evolution of religion and spirituality as well. Sign placement is only a very small piece of the very complicated Uranus puzzle. This is a building block for the other planets to apply with their energies. It adds sympathy, compassion, and allows the masses to see all as one.

Neptune in Pisces
(1848-1862) (2012-2026)

Neptune is in its ruling sign in Pisces. The generation born with this will end up changing the world. Music, art, theater, will all undergo complete transformations. Psychic abilities will be recognized as well as many other breakthroughs in psychological technology. Individually you're a dreamer and an imaginative creator. When Mercury and Venus are involved you become musically and artistically inclined. If aspected poorly by other planets this can cause great tensions in your inner subconscious. The uneasy insecurities of Neptune can cause you to become recluse with severe isolationist tendencies. You have a humanitarian outlook towards everything. Earth, animals, and humans alike. Many great things are to be expected from this generation in the fields of medicine and spiritual healing. Anyone with this placement is four years old at the time of this writing in 2016. It will be a while before we get to see the creative potentials from these children. Unlike the millennial's who are infatuated with technology, this generation will hopefully get back into side walk chalk and finger paint.

Pluto in Pisces
(2043-2068)

Pluto in Pisces will be so secret I don't even know about it.

Planets in the houses

Description of the houses

First house
 The first house is the most dominate section in your natal chart, and any planet positioned here will be highly distinguished in your character. That's because this house represents the physical being you present to others. This is the house of Aries, co-ruled by planets Mars and Pluto. It's the house of personal identification and how and how you physically appear. Often referred to as the house of self interest, too many planets here will make you intolerably arrogant. Known as the ascendant, whatever sign is on the cusp of the first house becomes extremely important. This is the beginning of the natal chart. The condition of planets in this house will show what you want in life, how you go about attaining your goals, and how easily success will come.

Second house

The second house is the house of independent finances and material possessions. Ruled by Taurus and the planet Venus this is an Earth house which calms down the planets positioned here. Planets positioned in this section of your chart drive your ambitions for materialistic gains, and make you very attached to your possessions. Each planet will add its influence to what you own. No planets in this house can indicate poverty or difficult tensions obtaining money. This section of your chart reveals how easily you acquire money and use the things you own. Financial strengths and difficulties are reflected through the second house.

Third house

Mercury is the ruling planet of the third house and Gemini is the sign in charge. It's your house of communications, intelligence, and everyday surroundings. Brothers, sisters, and cousins are also influenced by this house. It's an air house and planets positioned here will increase your mental aptitude and spark your curiosity. Like the other air houses this is an intellectual section of your chart. Planets positioned here stimulate your curiosity, and inspire you to take short trips where you can come and go in the same day. It also represents siblings and cousins.

Fourth house

The fourth house is first of the emotional houses representing your immediate surrounding home life and early childhood along with the security you seek in your elder years. This house is the domain of the Moon along with the ruling sign of Cancer. Several planets positioned here will make you over bearing and protective. Motherly love and nurturing are embedded in the philosophies of the fourth house.

Fifth house

Your fifth house is the most fun and entertaining part of your chart. Regal king Leo is the sign in charge of this section, and the Sun is the planetary ruler. This is a very creative house including the re-creation of yourself in the form of children. That makes part of this influence sexual in the sense it represents love affairs, new flames, and romantic speculation. Your artistic talent is best expressed through any planets positioned here. This is a house of instant gratifications and what you want directly in front of you.

Sixth house

The Virgo ruled sixth house is the second section the planet Mercury is in charge of in. The astrological cliché is the house of health and service to others. Planets that are poorly aspected usually indicate an injury or illness which will take significant recovery time. Any planets in this house with positive aspects will show your immense desire to help those less fortunate. On a psychological level planets here will indicate a need for over organization and possible neurotic issues and obsessive compulsive disorder. Remember Virgo is the most nitpicky sign in the zodiac and every planet takes on the tone of the fair maiden.

Seventh house

The seventh house is the beginning of the Southern hemisphere of your chart and is dedicated to partnerships and marriage. This is the introductory house distinguishing how you function within your relationships. Here, the beautiful planet Venus and her ruling sign of Libra are in charge of your seventh house. The following eighth house represents the materials you share with your partner this house indicates how you operate within them.

Eighth house

Drugs, sex, and rock and roll is the basic philosophy for the Scorpio ruled eighth house. Mars is the dominant planet along with Pluto and any planet here are extremely important.. As the opposite of the second house the material possessions related here are the ones you share with other people. Following the seventh house of paternership and marriage, these are the items you own together. Bank accounts, cars, houses and other things like that. Like the fourth and twelfth houses this is a very emotional area deeply rooted in the darker side of your subconscious. Poorly aspected planets can show devious behavior which many consider illegal. Remember, Scorpio is the underworld. Unfortunately this is the house of massive transformation and regeneration. Even positively aspected plants can indicate your ability to overcome massive trauma, but the trauma has to occur first. This is the psychological infatuation with sex and death that leads to the physical sex and death.

Ninth house

Along with the tenth house, the ninth house represents higher thinking, education, and is the ego's highest desire of expression. Gigantic Jupiter is the ruling planet with fiery Sagittarius the given sign. This area governs traveling for business, education, and spirituality. It represents foreign countries and individuals from those strange places. Philosophical expansion is the astrological cliché and the creative side of your public image. This house is much closer related to the tenth than the eighth. Long distance travel, both physically and mentally, are also associated with this section of the natal chart. Vacations were you are required to step out of your comfort level are the most eye opening and rewarding. You obtain many of your higher spiritual philosophies through the planets in your ninth house. Unlike the tenth house where standard education is the motif, the ninth house is much more on the spiritual side.

Tenth house

The mid-heaven marks the beginning of your tenth house and it represents your career and what you expose to the public. For some odd reason the generally isolative planet Saturn is ruler and Capricorn is the sign associated with it. Your profession, education, and image are all under this domain. It shows what you want to achieve in life and any planets here will be how you express that desire. Education is ruled by both the ninth and tenth houses. The tenth house recognized knowledge will lead to success, while the ninth house like possessing an expansive knowledge just for show. Defined best as the house of your career and public standing this is a very straight forward house. Planets positioned here make you dedicated to your education and continually receive technical training in your chosen field.

Eleventh house

The eleventh house is ruled by the water bearer and the planets Uranus and Saturn are especially strong here. This is the portion of your chart related to friends, professional groups, and higher aspirations for the future. This is the area of your personality where you think the sky is the limit and possibilities are endless. Too many planets here can make you too optimistic when discerning possible catastrophic fate. Your eleventh house more related to your long term dreams and goals as opposed to instant gratifications like the fifth house. The position you seek amongst the clubs or societies you join can also be seen in the eleventh house. Poorly aspected will show your inability to get along with others and incorporate into society. In the most basic form this is the house of greater idealism and vision.

Twelfth house

The twelfth house is the final section in the natal chart. It represents the innermost psyche of the human make up and it roots tangle deep within your unconscious complexion. Jupiter was the standard ruler until Neptune came along in the 1800's and joined him. Generally speaking this is not a very pleasant house. It somewhat defines your limitations and places significant restrictions to any planets here. This is the house of utter self defeat and sabotage. It rules unknown enemies, accidents, and it's often referred to as the house of karmic prison. Like the fourth and eighth houses this is a very psychic and emotional place in your chart. Unlike the other water houses this house creates travesty through unseen circumstances that are intended for utter transformation. Poorly aspected planets can indicate severe disappointments and place some nasty secret skeletons in your closet.

The Sun in the houses

Sun in 1st House

When the Sun is in your first house you impose your will and desires with forceful aggressiveness. This isn't to say that you're an inconsiderate jerk, but you usually get what you want and don't care how you must go about getting it. You desire to stand out amongst the rest, and possess a flare for attention and personal glorification. Being such a competitor, when you find an area you cannot excel at you simply find something different elsewhere. Aries and Mars greatly affect the Sun in this house. Positioned here the Sun tries to establish dominance everywhere it goes and aspects with other planets will be highly energized. The closer to your ascendant the more energy will be produced, especially if it is within four degrees. Exercise outdoors routinely or else you will become restless and anxious. Nervousness and vivid dreams will keep you awake at night. Reading or writing will be able to settle you down.

Sun in 2nd House

With a second house Sun you have great physical strength and determination. You succeed because you work harder than your competition and simply wear them out. Working many hours at many different things will be simple. If you aren't working like a dog you create imaginary problems for you to go fix. Make sure your objectives are well thought out. Personal possessions are valuable and sometimes you base social status around what someone owns. Taurus the bull is the ruling sign and the stubbornness exudes subtly. You will treasure even the smallest gift when the gesture is sincere, probably keeping it forever in a jewelry box on your dresser. The memory of the event the trinket sparks is what you endear. Because you feel that someone's personal worth is based on their personal wealth you may become snooty and rude to poor people. If there are other planets in this house chance are you will eventually amount vast amounts of wealth, family, or possessions. When it comes to modifying alignments the more planets involved, the more stuff you own.

Sun in 3rd House

A third house Sun makes you quick witted, energetic, and talkative. Aspects to Mercury will be very important and influential. You have and insatiable quest for knowledge, but rarely spend enough time focusing on one thing to become highly educated on any particular subject. The Sun takes on many Gemini traits instilling you with many of its characteristics. You seem to know a little about everything and do a great job making it appear you know more than you do. The high amount of energy you possess enjoys taking short little trips from one place to another. When a friend comes into town you will drag them all over the state, not just the city. Your rise to prominence is through the friendships you develop around your community. Telecommunications, foreign languages, or journalism may provide promising careers. You have a vast array of friends ranging from saints to sinners. Because you're incessantly talkative, you naturally attract those who do so as well. This can also lead to migraines and insomnia when planets are negatively afflicted as they transit through your chart.

Sun in 4th House

When the Sun is positioned in your fourth house you become extremely attached to your home, family life, and early childhood years. It's difficult for you to progress into the future because you feel you're leaving home for good. It may take you a while to move out of your parent's house, and you never want live more than a short drive away. Despite what your own opinions are, the environment you were raised in still plays a major role in your life. This is evident if you were brought up in a sheltered life where your parents controlled your every move. If Mars is aspecting this as well as the Moon you will have a difficult and sometimes violent time dealing with the maternal figure in your life. When disappointed in love you tend to run and hide under the covers. It's good to get away by yourself in order to gather your thoughts and emotions, just make sure your seclusion for too long. Be careful of what you eat when you get depressed. Binging out on chocolate and ice cream will make you fat, leading to more depression. Cancer is the ruling sign and the Moon is the planet in charge. The relationship with Jupiter is very important as well.

Sun in 5th House

The Sun is the most powerful here in its ruling house. The spiritual battery charging your soul is highly energized, and any aspect formed with other planets will significantly more influential than the rest. The negative aspects will be bad, and the positive ones will be grand. Regardless of sign, you take on many of the traits of the ferocious lion, Leo. Over dramatic at times, you revel in attention and your feelings get hurt easily. Fortunately, just as easy as you're hurt, you forgive endlessly as well. Games, competition, and romance are always in your head. Your playful nature will cause you to overindulge in the excessive pleasures. Gambling, alcohol, or drug addictions may plague you throughout your life. Many times your ego and personal ambitions will be your driving force in life. The unconscious forceful nature of your personality can cause unnecessary tensions between you and your associates. Although you don't intend to be rude, you're direct and upfront and your style isn't always taken well by others. When this occurs, make sure to recognize your role in the situation and act appropriately. You're a natural entertainer who loves the spotlight.

Sun in 6th House

When the Sun is in your sixth house you're very refined and disciplined. Although you possess the organizational skill needed for success you're more inclined to work for someone other than yourself. Unless this is a fire sign you need other driving forces from planets to give you the desire to break out on your own. Business management underneath a direct authority will best suit you. If this is an Earth sign you will be driven to achieve social a high social status as well. You will feel others will instinctually

341

respect you for the things that you own and the position in the community you achieve. If positively aspected you are the most loyal of loyal employees, taking less money to remain in the workplace you love. Because you are so attentive to detail others will be agitated when you force them to work harder than they care to. Aspects between Mercury and Mars will produce obsessive compulsive disorder. Migraines are also an issue with this placement. Your best asset should be your organizational skills and your intent on checking facts before you state something as true.

Sun in 7th House

When the Sun is in your seventh house the relationships you develop with others are extremely important, especially your spouse. Venus and the sign of Libra rule this section and their influence will be powerful. You actively pursue relationships and will never be happy until you're settled in a traditional and committed marriage. The social status and position in society is important to you. You desiring a partner you can be proud, and inspires you to be a better person. They will be the one who urges you to break free from your standard path. You're likely to marry someone older and more responsible than yourself. If the Sun is poorly aspected this means you will take a lot of abuse within your relationships. You're naturally attraction to the arrogant, narcissistic, and egotistical individuals who are domineering and controlling. Even though you're likely to be submissive you still demand that you are treated with respect and equality. There are negative aspects to this house position. Even though you demand equality for everyone you may casually place yourself aside, taking a small portion more than others. This can also make you arrogant, thinking you and you alone know what is best for everyone.

Sun in 8th House

When your Sun is placed in your eighth house you have a forceful and dominant personality. You're bold and aggressive, not afraid to make a head first leaps into the unknown. If aspected with Mars you will be athletically inclined, and your natural abilities may even earn you a college scholarship. Despite the intense personality you possess, you don't care to open up to others more than they do you to you. Seeing this as a weakness by giving a possible opponent an upper hand. You probably cried when you found out there was no Santa or Easter bunny. This positioning can indicate an inheritance or large divorce settlement. Because you believe your marriage should be a certain way, when it isn't you may become disinterested and seek love elsewhere. Unfortunately this can also mean you lose your father at an early age. The biggest downfall with an eighth house Sun is you believe everything is forever. Change is not something you accept readily, and once crossed you react instantly. Either through death or divorce you will be separated from your father far sooner than you care to be. This will be a difficult and tragic event and you will need to seek help through your friends or professionals in order to cope with your grief. The relationship the Sun has with Mars is very important, he's the ruler of the eighth house.

Sun in 9th House

A ninth house Sun is a generally great positioning. It takes on the traits of Sagittarius, and the ruling planet Jupiter affects you greatly making you generous, intelligent, and friendly. If the Sun is being aspected by the ruling planet it can also make you extremely lucky. Analyze your chart carefully and you may win big in the lottery or gambling. Outgoing and energetic, you believe you deserve the best of everything, and sometimes feel entitled to it. You always seem to be on the move and must refrain from expending useless energy. Pride is gained through your reputation and status within society or career. The ninth house is the area representing your higher education and may indicate college, if Mars is involved, expect athletics to be involved. Unless athletics is involved, shorter two year or specialized training will probably be more your style. You will need other driving aspects from elsewhere to indicate extensive education. This is also a very spiritual house. You may deny it but you're very religious, and recognize higher philosophies of life. Strict and dogmatic religion might not be for you, but you truly accept there are forces out there greater than human powers. It's easy for you to listen to the views of others because of the knowledge gained from others viewpoints. You may not accept them as your own, but you still give others the respect they have earned.

Sun in 10th House

When the Sun is in your tenth house you're incredibly ambitious, and determined to succeed no matter the consequences. You strive to attain power and authority over others as you establish your dominance. Being recognized and praised for your accomplishments is very important. If you don't get the intended reaction the first time, the next time things will be bigger and better. Your strong motivation allows you to set your responsibilities in order and achieve what you can. The ruling planet of Saturn will be important as well as aspects to planets in the sign of Capricorn. With this placement you're meticulous and precise in all your work. Your career and standing amongst the public is your main driving force. Careers in business, law, or politics should be considered. Family issues will arise if you don't find an equal balance between home life and work life. Although you probably won't be as successful as you would like until later in life. As time goes on three is a good chance that you attain most of your goals.

Sun in 11th House

When the Sun is in your eleventh house you're overly ambitious and many times set goals so high they're unattainable. You have creative and innovative ideas but possess no idea how to use them effectively. This is because so many thoughts go through your head there aren't enough resources to see then through. Once you can figure out how to live within whatever your means are you can finish a few of your sometimes hare brained schemes. For some reason you attain influential friends who allow you to advance your own personal agenda. When working within groups you're a natural leader and actively pursue authority. It's this same

344

desire that causes conflicts with supervisors and authority figures. Until you have gained a position above others you will not be satisfied. You have an open mind are generally accept people for who they are. You basically play the game by your own rules. Until you're finally arrested it doesn't matter what rules you break.

Sun in 12th House

When your Sun is in the twelfth house, there's a desire to serve others in need. You see the injustices or the world and are intent on changing them. No one seeking help is ever turned away. This causes your personal time and resources to be depleted and scarce. Sign and ruling planet of Neptune will be very influential where you direct this energy. The twelfth house is the final and most difficult house in your chart. It controls unseen enemies and realms of the nether world. You may be psychic, clairvoyant, and have visions of previous lives. This may also draw you into deeper forms of spirituality and philosophy. Because of all which is ruled by your twelfth house, this can cause a severe lack of personal self-confidence. Because you can see all your positive qualities you strive to be bigger and better than the rest, yet always come up short. If you follow your passions of working with the needy you will find much of what you are looking for. This also puts really big skeletons in your closet.

The Moon in the houses

Moon in 1st House

The Moon in your first house is difficult for most. Mars and the sign of Aries rule the first house. Any relationship with them will make you more aggressive when you become emotional. This can make you moody, contentious, and disagreeable. An influx of emotion will be a daily occurrence. Happy one minute, angry the next, sad and depressed another. An over insecurity about your looks, you may become obsessive with your personal appearance. You're more sensitive and emotional than most. Extremely receptive within your environment, you unconsciously absorb the

345

emotions of others. Your sub-conscious is very active and many times getting lost in your imagination will cause tensions in your life. This makes you like your mother in more ways than can be listed. Appearance, attitude and maybe even birthday to name a few. She can be your best friend and your worst enemy at the same time, sometimes dictating your actions into your adult years. Her influence and control may last into adult life, and possibly interfere with marriage. As a small child you probably cried a lot, for no particular reason.

Moon in 2nd House

The Moon in the house of Taurus is considerably better than the first. Your feelings and emotions will have a distinct attachment to your material possessions. This can lead to a few difficulties though. It will be hard to throw away things that have any sentimental value. You may clutter your house with useless junk which has been accumulated over the years. Your personal drive to succeed will provide you with the energy to take on any task set before you. The only downside with that is being motivated to do something which doesn't benefit you materialistically. If it doesn't provide direct results your attention will be turned elsewhere. A fluctuation of your savings account occur because you can be thrifty one minute and completely careless the next. Unless negatively aspected you will have an easy time accepting personal responsibility. Professions in which you can make an emotional connection will suit you best. Psychology, medicine, and education are a few. You like your work being admired by the public even if the attention isn't on you. Venus will provide a stabilizing force.

Moon in 3rd House

The third house is an interesting placement for the Moon. You're highly curious and take on many traits of the Gemini Moon. You can excel in music, writing, or science. You're talented in any endeavor which stimulates your mind and keeps you continuously busy. Be careful not to be a motor mouth when discussing personal issues. Although it will be necessary to discuss them with others, your tendency to ramble about significant personal problems gets you in trouble. Emotions run high in this house, especially if Mercury is involved. Migraines and panic attacks are one of the more negative energies produced by this placement. If negatively aspected by Uranus or Neptune a complete psychological break down is imminent, probably later in life. You can be very playful and childlike at times. The third house the home of that tricky little prankster Mercury and responsibility might have to wait and take a back seat to fun and games. Travel appeals to you because it affords new opportunities for learning. You need quick and sporadic experiences in order to stimulate your quick mind. This can also indicate the ability to talk at an early age. Your thoughts can change at a moment's notice and you make the necessary adjustments easily.

Moon in 4th House

The caring and nurturing powers of the Moon are at their strongest in this house. You're very attached to your early home life and probably won't move very far away. Emotions are extremely nostalgic and deeply rooted where you're raised at. Moving from town to town as a child will be extremely traumatic for you. If this house is in a water sign you may bruise easily, emotionally and physically. When you feel shunned an immediate retreat into your personal shell will be your natural reaction, just don't get too comfortable alone here. You desperately need to feel loved by others and the occasional social outing will be important. If you seclude yourself it will only allow negative thoughts to run rampant through your head. You will be fond of older things, restoring collectible cars and antiques would be a good hobby for you. Possessions you acquire throughout your years are strewn about your home. Old photos and crafts decorate your walls. The relationship with your mother will play a profound role in your life, for the good or bad. This can make you nostalgic about your past and very difficult to let go of your traumatic experiences. You may need professional help at times in order to clear your head.

347

Moon in 5th House

Leo is the ruler of the fifth house and the emotional properties of the Moon take on an exceptionally fiery demeanor. You love drawing attention to yourself, and letting others know how you're feeling. If something happens to you everyone must know and acknowledge it. When you feel your need for attention hasn't been met you get violently angry or horribly depressed. The Moon is not very receptive of fire signs, and this can cause extreme emotional anxiety. Especially when negatively aspect by other planets. If several planets occupy this house depression may affect you for your entire life. You love romantic affairs that start off like the fire lion that represents Leo. Many of your relationships begin with a whirlwind but eventually the passion runs out of fuel. Any significant other must be willing to submit to a flurry of rants and raves in order to get along with you. Experiences with children will profoundly comfort you, even if they aren't yours. You can be a true exhibitionist with this placement, especially if the Moon is in a fire sign.

Moon in 6th House

If you have the Moon in your sixth house, you become very compassionate towards the people you work with. You feel co-workers are a form of adoptive family and everyone must get along. This can lead to problems because you're so concerned about someone else that you fail to focus on your own responsibilities. Too often you find you have taken on so many different endeavors there's no time for yourself. You can be a nit-picky organizer who has to have everything their way. Emotional security will come from assisting others, professions which include some form of social work will suit you best. Severe psychological stress will come about when you are placed in an uncomfortable situations. Anything coming along shuffling your emotions or requiring you to think outside the box will make you extremely uncomfortable. It would be best to lay low and relax, helping whoever comes around asking for it. The biggest problem with this is you're refusal to listen to any ideas other than your own. Organization is the key theme with this Moon placement. Even if it's just an organized mess.

Moon in 7th House

A seventh house Moon will increase your desire to be a significant and supportive figure in the lives of others. This is one of the more pleasant placements for Luna and her nurturing compassion is felt throughout all your relationships. You enjoy interjecting into affairs of others thinking you can help where no one else can. There must be several changes in personal relationships in order to find complete balance and harmony. This cycle will continue until you realize happiness and joy are found from within and not by another individual. You desire companionship and recognition from your peer, and are inclined to seek partners who can bring out your sympathetic side and play on your emotions. For men there is often a tendency to seek a "mother figure" and fill emotional voids with relationships. You will seek a partner that is more interested in starting a home and family than traveling the world. Multiple marriages are probable stemming from the desire to find that perfect partner. Escaping the bondage of emotions will be key to making any relationship work. Becoming completely dependent in a marriage is highly likely.

Moon in 8th House

If you have the Moon in your eighth house, you possess an extreme sense of personal insecurity. You have serious issues with self-doubt and must overcome great obstacles in order to feel secure. Psychic abilities can give you a good sense of someone just by being in the same room as them. Fascinations with magic, the occult, and the seedy underbelly of life often go hand in hand with this Moon placement. It takes a while to warm up to people, and you usually never reveal very much. Refusal to talk about your feelings can lead to severe psychological problems. You have a natural tendency to wrap up all emotions, positive or negative, and ball them up in a pit of your subconscious, and never truly experience them. The eighth house is extremely possessive and you may have problems establishing emotional control. Your sense of psychic intuition usually proves to be right. You can become demanding and impatient, wanting everything your way and your way alone. Career wise you will need a professions where you can work alone and at your own pace. This is because you have a natural tendency to seclude away into oblivion. The isolation provides you with a place to focus and reach your inner thoughts. Professions involving medicine or science will be to your liking. You're probably addicted to sex, drugs, and rock'n'roll.

Moon in 9th House

The Moon in your ninth house indicates you have lofty goals and high expectations for life. You enjoy bouncing around from one place to another, never really settling down in one place for too long. Even though you may never switch towns, may move from house to house within a small community. Higher education is likely and you may have to travel long distances to get it. Studying as a foreign exchange student will suit you well. Your biggest problem is you see that greener pastures are always out there and you seek the greenest one. Religion and philosophy provide a psychological support and your spiritual beliefs are very important. You may base your personal value and value of others on their education. This may cause rifts with others as the may think of you as an uptight know it all. There will be a variety of interests in your life, sports, music, and strategy games will spark your energy. Be careful not to overindulge in gambling, and excessive drug and alcohol use. You would make an excellent educator because of your higher than average intelligence and the desire to express that. It may be necessary to obtain an advanced degree in order for you to feel secure about yourself.

Moon in 10th House

The Capricorn ruled tenth house is a cold, responsible, not usually happy house placement for the Moon. It will take you a while to warm up to people, and you won't feel the need to express

350

much about yourself right from the start. The impression others have about you controls your emotions. Being admired by the public will be a driving force in which ever endeavors you choose to participate in. A distinct desire to succeed flows through your veins. A career in politics, military, or law enforcement can suit you well. You crave recognition and public praise. Because of your ability to be resourceful and responsible it will be easier than most to organize large groups of people. A personal charisma attracts people to follow you along your ways. Not only do you desire public recognition you also feel it is your responsibility to establish yourself within a community. As a child you took on responsibility earlier than your peers. Your parents could leave you alone in the house and not worry about it catching fire. Later in life there may be a realization that your entire life has been spent being straight laced and responsible and that you need a sudden, unexplainable change of scenery. A mid-life crisis is highly likely if not recognized and prepared for.

Moon in 11th House

The Moon in your eleventh house can best be described as interesting, very interesting. You're definitely a special kind of spit fire when the Moon in positioned like this. The planetary house ruler Uranus will be a key influence in your chart, and if it's negatively aspected you can be kind of an emotional train wreck. Men with the Moon in this house will go through many love affairs throughout their lives, and women generally find they have more female then male friends. Regardless of your sex, an eleventh house Moon makes you rigid and hardnosed when changing your opinions or beliefs. You feel the need to have large groups of friends and enjoy large social circles. Most women, and occasionally men, with this Moon placement develop more of a friendship with their mother than most. Women with this will have unrepeatable emotional ties to their mother and must contact her frequently. This is the house of ultimate conscious expansion. When heavily influenced you're exceptionally clairvoyant,

351

constantly pick up on the unknown signals others project.

Moon in 12th House
     The Moon in your twelfth house indicates a fascination with the mystical, magical, and sometimes even seedy under belly of society. The difficulties created by the Moon's placement stems from the subconscious nature of both entities. For the Moon it intensifies the way your emotions play on your subconscious. Because the Moon is the luminary controlling your subconscious its powers are naturally intensified here. Chances are you attach yourself immediately. Then, once realizing your mistake, it's impossible to let go. In turn, you go into a shell and become completely impossible to communicate with. The reason for this, is you allow your dysfunction to alter your unconscious habits to the state of your emotions. Easier said, you let your emotions control your thinking. This clouds your judgment many times and you will need significant amount of alone time to detach yourself from everyday stresses. You're extremely sensitive to others, wanting to sulk and hide away from when rejected by a loved one. This will be necessary from time to time in order to get your head on straight, but be careful not to get lost in your own thoughts. Depression will set in if you do not recognize this. Neptune and Jupiter are the ruling planets for this house. You can be a sucker for a good sob story, and will get taken advantage of if you are not careful. At the end of the day your emotions are your worst enemy.

Mercury in the houses

Mercury in 1st House
     When Mercury is in your first house you're curious, clever, high strung, and jittery. If it's close aspect to your ascendant chances are you're small and tiny. Extremely talkative and friendly, you have a childlike nature which never truly goes away. Many times you're self-centered and love talking about what's going on in your life. Because you have such a vast array of

acquaintances it's easy to direct casual conversations towards your personal interests and needs. It's best for you to stay active throughout your day. Pent up energy will make you restless and nervous. If this is positioned within three degrees of your ascendant you will be experience high anxiety and panic attacks. Not waiting around for others, you are usually the first to make a move. It is this direct and up front approach that allows you to get want you want. Your forceful nature can be mistaken by others at times. The aggressive way you confront them is sometimes taken as an attack. When their defenses come up you become defensive as well. This only leads to circles of problems. Try to back off and let others come to you sometimes.

Mercury in 2nd House

When Mercury is in your second house using your intelligence and innovative skills to make money comes easily. This is a great starting point for individuals wishing to run their own business. Many of these people are interested in science, computers, and advanced mechanics or technology. Enjoyment will be found in all those careers. Although you're very smart, unless you're in charge, you don't always stay at one job long enough to rise into significant authority. A wonderful right hand man, you're a jack of all trades and can fit in anywhere in the work place. This may also indicate you have to travel for your job. Sales and distributing may also interest you. If you can find a like-minded group you can accomplish great things. Your associations with friends and acquaintances will prove useful in making money. You and a small social group may start an innovative company and retire early. Left alone this house slows the pace of Mercury and the sign becomes key. Taurus provides a grounding force, and sometimes Mercury rebels completely.

Mercury in 3rd House

Mercury is right at home here in the third house. His rulership adds a special childlike touch all throughout your personality. You're sharp, intelligent, and insatiously curious when positioned. This makes you interested in everything from music to technology. Knowledge is important and you see the power it brings. Video games and other technological devices will probably fascinate you. It isn't enough for you to see them work, you want to know how and why as well. You're friendly and talkative opening up to others freely and expressively. You enjoy conversation and socializing. If Mercury is in a fire or air sign you will be vivaciously flamboyant, and the first to strike up a conversation. If it is an Earth or water sign then you will take a little while to open up, but when you do the flood gates are spread wide. Science, reading, and technology will fascinate you and you will never stop learning. Always remember to stay open minded to everyone, you never know who will teach you something next. Mercury is known for being the little bastard always annoying you. Unless you can out grow your immature habits you developed as a child more adult individuals will be repelled by your behavioral antics.

Mercury in 4th House

     With Mercury in your forth house you become apt to study or be at your creative best in the comfort of your home. Despite your ability to focus at home you still have lots of distractions no matter whatever you do. School work gives you a sense of self-worth, and any personal insecurities are covered up with knowledge. If you can't be dominant physically you will dominate intellectually. You have a sensitive way of talking to others making friends easily because of the tender tone in your voice, and the fact you generally care about their wellbeing. It will be necessary to talk about your emotional hang ups. It's most definitely possible you enjoy getting caught up in the gossip of others. Your subconscious and imagination are both very active and any aspects to the Moon will be very influential. This positioning gives you the desire to talk about your emotional hang ups with others. If Mercury is in a fire sign this will prove to be especially true. This also adds to your psychic and intuitive abilities. It also makes it easier to express your emotions to your mother.

Mercury in 5th House

The fifth house is a great placement for Mercury. The fire of Leo makes you extremely talkative and friendly. The communication skills and mental aptitude of Mercury are bolstered by the ruling Sun. This drives you to prove your intelligence to others, and use those mental abilities to create something prominent. Proving you're smarter than most is important and you strive to do so by the precise way you conduct yourself. When in competition you learn your opponent's strengths and weaknesses, as well as your own. Not relying on your athletic abilities alone you use your in-depth analysis skills to gain an advantage over your adversary. You enjoy talking about what you know and how you feel about it. Wishing to pass your knowledge onto others you may step on toes and cross boundaries when expressing this. Creative, strategic, and competitive, activities in which athletic skill and mental aptitude are used will draw you to them. Most importantly of all you enjoy showing off how smart you are. Sometimes this arrogance leads to poor decisions because you only thought you knew a lot about something. The rash thinking and hasty actions definitely lead to sporadic accidents, like sticking your finger into a light socket.

Mercury in 6th House

The sixth house is the second of Mercury's ruling sections. With this placement you're naturally blessed with great analytical and organizational abilities. You can be a stickler to the rules, finding it difficult to break any habits you've created. Although your attention to detail will allow you to rise into lower positions of authority you're not always comfortable there. This is because you're constantly over analyzing minute details which have little effect on your project. Unusually quiet for Mercury, most times you wait until you have heard the opinions of others before you state your own. Although your thoughts and ideas are good you try listening to others and aren't afraid to change your opinions when someone presents legitimate evidence. Obsessive compulsive disorder and hoarding are entirely possible with this placement. You will experience severe headaches and migraines in your life time. Bad aspects from Mars and Uranus will cause this to occur more frequently and intensely. Bouncing around from job to job is possible as well. You can become very restless if you are forced to stay in one spot for too long.

Mercury in 7th House

With Mercury in your seventh house, this directs much of your focus towards the relationships you have with others. Venus is the ruling planet here and her influence makes you a social butterfly. Whether it be romantic or plutonic you're in constant search for someone new to talk to. You probably get married earlier than your friends and very well may get into several failed relationships or marriages before finally finding your match. If this is a fire sign then you will most definitely go through several difficult break ups before settling down. If this is an Earth sign you will have a great ability in keeping things organized and balanced. High ranks in management and business are in your future if you choose to pursue them. You're a natural born organizer, and a career as a professional's secretary will suit you well. As well as professions in law or politics. Talking to others and stimulating conversation among a group will get you noticed by your supervisors and contribute to your quick rise to prominence in you work place. At its worst this makes you too overly focused into the relationships of others. Consider a career as a marriage counselor.

Mercury in 8th House

The eighth house is a difficult place for Mercury. Many times this indicates you have to deal with someone's death at an early age. Under the worst circumstances possibly even yourself. Because the eighth house rules many of our seedy and shady characteristics this placement can cause you to have a fascination with death, sex, or drugs, and unfortunately at an early age. The dark secretive powers of Mars and Pluto rule this house and their

356

powers will be immensely strong here. You like knowing everyone's secrets but don't dare share yours. When others pry into your personal life as far as you pry into theirs you voice your objection adamantly, failing to see that you do the same. Your artistic and psychic powers can be developed over time. Great success will be found in areas of psychology, surgery, and possibly detective work. Probing far into the business of others fascinates you, and many times you will suffer from foot in mouth disease. Keeping the fat juicy secrets of others is difficult for you. This will cause many rifts between your friends, family, and co-workers. If you choose to, the magical art of holistic and all natural healing can bring a wonderful sense of joy and contentment into your life.

Mercury in 9th House

Mercury in your ninth house makes you quick minded, flexible and adaptable. Ruled by Jupiter and Sagittarius, Mercury will take on the inspirational and exciting traits of those two. Adding to your talkativeness, the sign it is placed in will determine how fast you warm up to others. This makes you very childlike and playful, you will probably never truly grow up. This house rules your higher education, and Mercury positioned here usually means you bounce around from institute to institute before finally completing a degree, if you ever do. It would be better you study abroad and gain appreciation for outside cultures, or find a trade you can learn with shorter technical schooling. You may also shift around from rehab to rehab if drugs or alcohol becomes involved. Combined with your habitual immaturity, your desire to take everything to the extreme will cause you to experience severe consequences. Possibly jail time or an extended hospital visit. Many times this placement indicates many short vacations with your siblings. If you have any brothers or sisters this a good placement. Many of your best memories will be tied to these events. One negative trait is your tendency to over inflate the truth, and can tell some pretty tall tales to go along with it.

Mercury in 10th House

When Mercury is in your tenth house you show great poise and control when speaking in front of others. This placement is great for business, politics, and the military. You know how to get straight to the point and say what you mean in a way that others can understand. Professions which require mental alertness and dexterity will attract you. There is a subconscious desire for authority. Even if you don't have much actual power, an important title is still needed. Greatly influenced by the sign which Mercury is placed in, this is usually a quiet, calming house for Mercury. More frequently than not, you won't introduce yourself to random people, unless a friend already knows them. This isn't because you aren't friendly you just don't care enough to make the first move. Saturn's relationship with Mercury here will be a good indicator of stressful or not stressful. Good alignments will allow you to direct focus onto productive projects, while negative aspects make you irresponsible and lazy.

Mercury in 11th House

Mercury feels right at home in the Uranus ruled eleventh house. Throughout your life you attain many acquaintances but very few close personal friends. This is because your social circle is scattered you're not able to intimately bond and make connections with everyone. It's your unique personality which attracts everyone to you. Overly talkative most of the time, you can start a conversation with about everyone. Not only is your mind quick and agile but your speaking skills are as well. When Mercury is in the Aquarius influenced eleventh house you find it interesting to have conversations with others who have opposing opinions. You do this because being able to see things from many different viewpoints allows you to make a better more educated decision. Understanding that knowledge is infinite makes you curious to learn everything you can about anything you can. One of the problems caused by this placement is your desire to be recognized more than you are. You enjoy thinking your ideas have helped the greater cause.

358

Mercury in 12th House

When Mercury is in your twelfth house this stimulates your desire to probe deeper into a distinctly profound subject. More often than not your thoughts and perceptions are your own worst enemy. When aligned negatively with Venus it can indicate your spouse cheats on you with your sibling. Once you have found enough to fill your interest you point your obsessions elsewhere. The biggest malfunction is your tendency to obsess about something only to waste your time and resources by giving it up a short time later. Unless you have stabilizing forces elsewhere it will be very difficult to complete what you have started. This is because there are so many other experiences out there. Your interest may be into the spiritual or metaphysical world, and the ruling planets of Neptune and Jupiter will be very influential. You possess psychic abilities and have intuitions which are usually correct. It's easy for you to see into the actual person someone is, and not who they just appear to be. Many times your biggest problem is the inability to stop thinking about what is going wrong.

Venus in the houses

Venus in 1st House

When Venus is in your first house you love being part of society and have a distinctly charming attitude. Your magnetic personality will attract as many friends as you choose. You always want to be part of the crowd, and may resort to associating with the wrong people in order to feel accepted. It's difficult for you to be alone, and must surrounded yourself with loved ones at all times. You hate not being in a relationship and will go through many flings before finding your final partner. There is an uncanny ability for you to naturally attract everything you need, and at times you act like a spoiled brat. Chances are you threw fits learning to share and sometimes never do. If negatively afflicted you will use people without even knowing it. This will also cause you to be selfish and arrogant at times. This doesn't mean you are a horrible person, just kind of a priss at times.

Venus in 2nd House

Venus is in one of her two ruling houses in the second house. Generally her positioning here is an indication of acquired wealth and riches through personal relationships. This doesn't in any way mean you will be an instant millionaire nor, does it show you're born into money. However, it does indicate you'll acquire many possessions throughout your life, and keep most things you don't need. The social graces and charm from Venus will attract many friends as well. Because your inner circle is only so large you can't allow everyone as close as they want. This positioning is also a good indicator of your ability to make money off your friends. Not that you use their friendships, but food service or a job which requires social networking can prove prosperous. One downside is you feel the need to please everyone and become a push over. You bend backwards feeling that is the best way to gain approval and attract friends. Hosting parties and social gatherings will allow you to express your social desires. All your possessions must be aesthetically pleasing. You keep your home clean and lovely never knowing when your next guest might arrive. Keeping it decorated with fine works of art will help you unconsciously unwind.

Venus in 3rd House

The third house is your house of communications and Venus here can give you a beautiful singing voice. Even if you can't sing, you probably wail away driving or while taking a shower. No matter what, your kind and compassionate tone entices others to warm up quickly. You enjoy talking about your relationships as well as those of others. You would rather gab and gossip about the affairs of others than yourself. While traveling you must do so with class and style. When you go to a hotel you're willing to spend more for a better room. If you choose to go camping it will hardly be considered roughing it. You need plenty of amenities where ever you settle. This can also indicate you get to travel to many beautiful places. You dislike arguments and will shy away from a vicious verbal confrontation, unless Mars is aspecting Mercury here. Settling differences peacefully is always your preferred option. Many times this indicates a very good relationship with your siblings and cousins.

Venus in 4th House

Venus in your fourth house indicates your strong emotional bond through all your relationships. Simply said, you're a social butterfly who feels nurtured and secure when in close with others. This placement also gives you a desire for a beautiful home and surroundings, but who doesn't? Your house itself doesn't have to be the nicest, newest place in town, but the inside will be decorated with odd works of art in between all the pictures of family. The relationship Venus has with the ruling Moon will influences the relationship with your mother greatly. Their alignment will be a good indicator of how well you and you mother get along. If she was neglectful then the traumas can be overly dramatic. You will never be able to live very far from her, even if there are tensions between the two of you. The fourth house represents your innermost home environment. The social properties of Venus makes you want to develop strong relationships with everyone. Many times this means your family takes advantage of your generosity. If Venus is aligned with Jupiter it usually indicates a large family. All of which live close by.

Venus in 5th House

With Venus positioned in the fifth house you have a fair complexion with bright, beautiful eyes. Leo and the Sun are the rulers of this house and any aspects from them will make you flamboyant and dramatic. You love children and there is a tender place in your heart for all youngsters. Venus does not always function well in the fifth house and her emotions can be thrown into quite a frenzy. You will need aspects from other planets in order to mellow you out. At times you're a drama queen, bringing attention and drama where nothing is needed. You can be very lucky in love, marrying the first person you truly fall in love with.

Like the lion the fifth house represents if Venus is aspecting you ascendant you will have a flowing mane of hair, possibly even bright red if Venus is in a fire sign. Extremely playful you can be irresponsible at times. Partaking in games, sports, and gambling will excite you to the point of excess. Pay attention to your responsibilities and commitments in order to maintain a positive professional career.

Venus in 6th House

When Venus is positioned in your sixth house this makes you fair minded and diplomatic. You can see both sides of a story and usually don't make your decision quickly. You're fond of the Earthly pleasures and can get caught up in the materialistic world easily. Fine works of art, food, and anything else extravagant is towards elegance is to your liking. To you even the finest meal is just ordinary when served on paper plates. But the simplest pizza dinner served on the finest china under a candle light will make you swoon. Sometimes you feel you and you alone can solve the problems of others. Make sure that you don't become too involved in the affairs of others. You eventually get told to butt out if you can't respect personal boundaries. When forming a relationship you will be the one who feels they should make the most concessions. You do so willingly because deep down you would rather have your partner happy than yourself. In its worst form Venus here show your nit-picky criticism of your relationships. You're constantly looking where improvement is needed and not what is already functioning.

Venus in 7th House

The most difficult problem with a seventh house Venus is you constantly seek ultimate fulfillment in all your relationships. Nothing ever lives up to your expectations because you expectations are simply too high. You get a job thinking it will be wonderful and when it isn't, your pissed. You fall in love instantly and for superficial reasons then are surprised when there isn't any structure to the relationship. Venus feels quite at home as this is

362

one of her two ruling houses. Any aspect involving her will have her full attention. This is the house which directly represents your relationships and how you function within them. Her placement here also indicates you put great emotional value in all your relationships. Even with casual acquaintances you wish to create a strong emotional bond. Any profession in which you're allowed to be connected with the public will prove to be satisfying, probably in the customer service industry. You're happiest in when in close relationships with others. If Venus is aligned closely to your ascendant you're going be beautiful and attractive. You have such high idealistic views about how you want your marriage to look and function that you're never completely happy. Afflictions from Mars may indicate a messy and difficult divorce. Unfortunately, this can also sway your interest from fleeting crush to fleeting crush. It may take several failed relationships or marriages until you find a perfect someone.

Venus in 8th House

When Venus is positioned in your eighth house, you enjoy the luxuries and riches of your partner's assets. This doesn't mean you're a lazy individual who leaches off of others, just you'll probably marry someone wealthy. If you're successful independently, this indicates a very material based relationship. It can also indicate after you marry it's your spouse who attains greater success than you. Unfortunately, this can also mean inherited gains through a death or divorce. Lack of self-discipline with your partner's resources will be the number one cause of tensions within the relationship. Pre-occupied with what you can get out of a relationship, you most likely have your first marriage end in divorce. Once you and your spouse reach what you see as the pinnacle of your success, you may go out searching for greener pastures elsewhere. You love of beauty and art take on a darker under tone as well. Unique wooden sculptures, voodoo trinkets, and abstract paintings will decorate your walls before pictures and lace curtains. Mars is the ruler of this house and any aspects with that little red devil will be very important.

Venus in 9th House

    If Venus is positioned in your ninth house you love travel and must do so in style. Nothing is too good while on vacation, and many times you return broke and behind on your bills. You have an interest in foreign cultures. Their art, food, and life style intrigues you to the point of activism. You may move to the other side of the Earth in order to experience this. This indicates an interest in education past high school. You may try a four year university, but probably it isn't for you. Gaining most of your life experiences from travel it may take you twice as long to earn a degree because you have bounced around from school to school for so long. Her relationship with Jupiter and the sign of Sagittarius will be powerful as well, positive aspects like sextiles and trines can possibly mean winnings in gambling. You are extremely concerned about the image you portray towards the public. Make sure not to become too obsessed with what others think. This can also show a relationship with a foreigner or someone from a completely different background.

Venus in 10th House

    When Venus is positioned in your tenth house, the sign of Capricorn and ruling planet Saturn become very important. Your position and status amongst society become so important a career in law, education, or politics is likely. This is because you enjoy being out amongst society, enjoying the casual relationships which come with businesses associated with the public. Part of you gets personal satisfaction from not only authority over others but their envy, and jealousy as well. This isn't to say that you're a self-centered asshole, you just work hard for your success and don't see why others don't. Despite any arrogance, deep down you're very generous to those who truly are in need, but can turn a very cold shoulder to those just looking to free loaf. If Mercury is involved or this is in the sign of Gemini, this placement becomes a favorable for public speaking and activities in the theater arts. If this is in a fire sign you will need to own your own business or at least control your own employment.

Venus in 11th House

Venus in your eleventh house gives her a hint of the Aquarius trait and the relationship with Uranus or Saturn will be important. This house makes you extremely social and friendly, requiring the very most out of your friends. You generally have so many casual acquaintances you don't have time to develop strong bonds with any. You find your circle of friends changes quickly and sporadically. Be careful of who spend significant amounts of time with, as not everyone has your best interest in mind. Many times you get lost in the fantasies about your love life. You desperately desire someone you can develop a strong friendship with along with the romantic relationship. The high expectations you have are only setting you up for emotional let downs and hang ups. If you don't act maturely and responsibly you might become the town floozy. Having many casual sleep over's with random flings. Accept your lovers and casual friends as they are, not what you expect them to be.

Venus in 12th House

The basic nature of this placement makes your romantic relationships your worst enemy. More often than not it indicates a scandalous affair where either you or your spouse ends up cheating. When Venus is in your twelfth house, you enjoy solitude and retreating into your own personal private place away from the hustle of everyday society. Many times your pleasures are kept secret and out of public eye. If you're not careful with your consumption of intoxicants addiction will be your undoing. This Pisces influence gives you compassion for others becoming a sucker for sob stories. All relationships are under the influence of Venus, and when positioned in this area of your chart you're never happy alone. You will need the companionship of someone else in order to feel completely at ease and content. This also makes it difficult to reveal your true feelings towards others. It will take a close, intimate relationship in order for you feel comfortable revealing your true personal feelings. Once you come out of your shell it's only into the open arms of a trusted loved one.

Mars in the houses

Mars in 1st House

     If you have Mars in the first house, you possess an excessive amount of physical energy and determination. You're never hesitant to act, and once you set your mind on something you dive right in. This look before you leap attitude leads you into many unfinished projects. Unless you can focus on an important few, you constantly bit off more than can be accomplished. You know what you want but not always the most cooperative way to achieve it. Sometimes that energy will be misdirected and misguided, resulting with complete failure to meet your expectations. Dominant in nature, you attack things with a head on approach, which isn't always informed. Having a "take no prisoners" mentality, you're shocked when others don't agree with you. Your opinion is just as important as others and you wish for them to know it. Failing to accept the validity of different ideas will also cause you to drive wedges between friends. You're overly assertive and dominant, rarely paying attention to how your actions affect others. You refuse to make concessions and want everything your way. Because of this attitude expect altercations with authorities at work as well as law enforcement. Aspects from other planets can most certainly calm this aggression down, but personal control will need to be learned and executed. Make sure to get enough physical exercise to relieve your pent up frustrations.

Mars in 2nd House

     With Mars in your second house you expend much of your energy into acquiring money and possessions. Your driving ambition for materialistic gains makes you more determined and courageous than most. Mars takes on many of the traits of Taurus the bull while in the second house. Because of your belief that social status is based on what you own, this can make you snobbish and rude to others you see as lazy and unequal. Because you work hard for what you own, you can turn your nose down on those with less drive for possessions. Since you work hard for what you have you expect others to have the same ambition. This is a good positioning for professions in areas of business, politics, or athletics. Your impulsive behavior will get you into trouble throughout your life. If you can't get over your look before you leap tendencies the excessive aggressiveness of Mars will cause over spending, extreme anxiety, and even physical injuries. If aspected by Saturn, Uranus, or Pluto this can make you an obsessed hoarder. The relationship Mars has to the ruling planet of Venus is very important. It shows how easily you share your possessions with your partner.

Mars in 3rd House
　　Mars in your third house makes you intelligent and talkative. The Gemini influence provided here emphasizes your speaking skills and gives you a strong, powerful voice. You may even be a beautiful singer. Your intellect is quick, and this placement can also make you overly nervous and anxious. Because there are so many ideas flowing throughout your brain it's very difficult to focus on one. Many times you start with one plan and the further you go, the farther you deter from the original. The high strung eccentricity you display causes others to become annoyed and irritated. Pay attention to how much you talk and how many questions you ask. A negatively aspected Mars here can indicate severe tensions with your siblings. Things between you and them may even become physical altercations. Communications will be a strong suit for you, and you should consider professions in journalism, radio broad casting, or community politics. If Mars is in a fire sign, this is an excellent source of athleticism.

Mars in 4th House
　　When Mars is in your fourth house you become overly

attached and dependent to your home life and childhood upbringing. If your early childhood was difficult this placement will make things feel worse than they actually are. Because of the Cancer traits Mars projects here the constant emotional fluctuations you experience are considerably more severe than others. On the opposite side, when things are good then they seem better than they are. Your rainbows are brighter and peaches are sweeter. Be careful not to get caught up in your own imagination. One negative effect of this is the inability to leave an abusive relationship. To you being alone is the worst fate one can face. Because of your in ability to let go of you past you may need professional counseling to deal with the enduring traumas. Finding you own personal relaxation place will be necessary to relieve all the pent up stresses. Prayer and meditation can play a positive role in controlling your spiraling emotional world.

Mars in 5th House

Mars in your fifth house makes you naturally athletic and competitive. You're drawn to sports and will never back down from a challenge. Energetic and determined in your own personal projects, many times you can show disinterest in the endeavors of others. At first you agree to assist someone, then once you realize how much work is involved you grow tired and want to go back to your own stuff. You can intimidate others by the forceful way you project yourself. This is the house of recreation and your interest in gambling, drinking, and partying can get you into trouble. Reaction is generally instantaneous, and sometimes hostile. When afflicted severely you may have a hair trigger when it comes to your temper. If the seedy and shady aspect of life interest you that's where you will go. Whether it be towards the negative or positive aspects of live you will succeed at either. Gambling can especially be a problem in your life. Because you get surprisingly lucky from time to time, you start to rely on it and frequently lose your winnings. Mars takes on many of the trait Leo when placed here. The house's ruling planet of the Sun will also be very influential when aspecting this.

368

Mars in 6th House

Mars in your sixth house takes on many of the organizational and analytical traits of the sign Virgo. This Earthly house takes away many of the aggressive and sometimes violent tendencies of Mars, although you become easily irritated and impatient when things are not fashioned to your liking. If you're forced to work in a group organization, being the leader will be the only way you can succeed. It isn't easy for you to take exact directions from your superiors. They must tell you what needs to be done and suggest the best way to achieve it. Then you need to be left on your own to figure out the most efficient way towards completion. Your way isn't always the only way and you have to recognize that. Aspects with ruling planet Mercury will make you talkative and negative aspects make you verbally aggressive. If Saturn is poorly influencing this obsessive compulsive disorder and hoarding will also be in your stars. Be careful not to become overly obsessed with problematic situations. When negatively afflicted this can make you a hypochondriac, or can indicate a massive injury or illness.

Mars in 7th house.

Mars doesn't like the balance Libra induces while positioned in your seventh house. Mars rules the first house, which is the direct opposite. While here you become very demanding in your romantic relationships. If severely afflicted this can indicate significant abuses within that relationship. Either you're the victim or the abuser yourself, this isn't a good spot for Mars. Hopefully you have a trine or sextile with the ruling planet Venus calming things down. If Mars is in a fire sign this most definitely shows your hostilities towards your lover. If you don't handle your aggressions properly then jail time for battery is likely. At its best this makes you completely driven to please your partner. Whether it be romantic, plutonic, or business, you feel you must be in control of all relationships. Don't expect to see a thirtieth wedding anniversary. Chances are you get hitched multiple times. Of all

369

twelve houses this is the most difficult for Mars to handle. Libra seeks balance and equality for everyone and Mars wants everything for himself. Sometimes you will over compensate your selfish desires by immersing yourself into the needs of others.

Mars in 7th House

Mars in your seventh house inspires you to develop relationships with others in a close personal way. Groups and clubs will mean a lot to you because you feel most comfortable within social circles. Although you can be entirely independent on your own, the desire for personal connection is too great. Balance and order in your life are a high priority and you'll go to great lengths in order to preserve your wishes. You have to develop tactfulness and diplomacy in order to get along with others. Many times Mars can't see how his actions are affecting a situation. Although you care how you're influencing someone, quite often you're a complete space case and completely oblivious. Aspects to Venus will be powerful and possible create more tensions to your romantic relationships. You're generally fair minded and reasonable, seeing the inequalities within the ranks of society truly wishing to do something. You're an active go getter who can achieve success in any professional field, although this does not suggest a distinct profession this does give you the driving fire for achievement.

Mars in 8th House

Mars is in one of his ruling houses in the eighth house and this isn't necessarily a good thing. The nickname "the lesser Malefic" wasn't given to him by chance. When negatively influenced you're the most devious of all. Here the aggressive and volatile energies of the red planet are heightened. Obsession, jealousy, and possessiveness are all used to describe the Scorpio sign who rules this house. You're attracted to possessions and the more materialistic aspects of your lover. You're very possessive of them, your money, and your things. You may be the aggressor in the relationship. Even if you're the female many times you get what you want more than your partner. Nothing is ever enough whether it be money, drugs, or sex. Once something sparks your interest you throw yourself into it completely. Psychology and medicine are two professions that will interest you greatly. Your passions run high and you become extremely emotional at times. You get attached to your things and jealous at the smallest slight. This can also make you sexually devious and manipulative in order to rise to the top. The extreme competitor inside you will never just roll over and die. Refusing to accept defeat may eventually lead to your downfall as it uses all your resources and energy.

Mars in 9th House

When Mars is in your ninth house, you're energetic, competitive, and restless. You require constant movement, even if you're just spinning around in circles. Directing your focus and resources will be difficult, and you have so many projects to deal with that several never reach full potential. The planet Jupiter is ruler of this house and his role will be important in the functioning ability of Mars. Social status and professional achievements are how you gain personal security. Unfortunately this can make you shrewd and bitter businessman who steps on the toes of with no problem if it will gain an advantage. Ulcers, high blood pressure, and heart attacks, are also associated with this placement. This is also a good indicator of a career in athletics or a possibly college scholarship. Positive alignments can make you dedicated to continually advancing your education and training level. The arrogance of ruling sign Sagittarius can play both positive and negative roles for Mars. Negatively this placement makes you arrogant and conceited. Athleticism and physical strength are the better assets of Mars in this house.

Mars in 10th House

When Mars is in your tenth house you're ambitious and resourceful, caring very much about the public's perception of you. The sign of Capricorn and ruling planet of Saturn will be very influential with this placement. Success is earned by your own hard work and effort, and this philosophy is imbedded in your brain. This placement adds physical stamina and endurance, also indicating some form of post high school education. Not necessarily a university or college, just some sort of formalized training. One negative effect of this will be a tendency to turn into an obsessive workaholic. You focus so intently on one thing you fail to see how the rest of your environment is being affected. You will suffer many disappointments because of this, romantically and professionally. Being organized and ambitious, most of those born with a tenth house Mars become successful after many years of hard work and dedication. Your public appearance is very important to you. Spending too much on fine cars, clothes, or recreation will happen because you think it makes you fit in with others. If you do have an alignment with Saturn hopefully it the trine or sextile. Anything other than those will add significant psychological tensions and you may want to seek professional help.

Mars in 11th House

When you have Mars in your eleventh house, you desire to be a leader amongst your friends and have high expectations for them. You possess strong leadership abilities and are passionate about living up to them. It's important you socialize with the proper individuals because if you get caught up in the seedy underbelly of life your desire to be the biggest and best can easily land you in jail. When chosen wisely, the friendships you do pursue can turn into many great things. If you can focus your energy into productive enterprises the creative and innovative ideas can turn into wonderful projects. Thinking outside the box is your specialty and if Mars is in a fire sign it can make you brilliantly smart. This positioning gives you the desire to stand out amongst the crowd and be respected for your work. Professions involving politics, law enforcement, or athletics can be valid outlets for your abilities. Jupiter is the ruling planet of this house and if Mars is making an alignment this may turn you into a college or professional athlete.

372

Mars in 12th House

Mars in the twelfth house is a very difficult positioning. This can cause depression, paranoia, and scary secretive desires. The intense emotional reactions provoked by this cause your inner thinking to run around wildly and uncontrollably at times. Without any comforting aspects from other planets this will cause you to be constantly angry, aggressive, and hold grudges until the grave. Many times it will be difficult to forgive those who have harmed you. If the experience is drastically traumatic professional help will be needed to cope. This may also indicate you're subject to false accusations and deceit from others. For some reason others may be jealous of you and don't know how to act appropriately. Your dreams are probably vivid to the point where you have trouble deciphering truth from fantasy. This is one thing astrological psychologist's look for when diagnosing schizophrenia. If you feel alone and lost this is purely natural. Depression and sadness are just as natural as joy and love. Once you realize this, these less fortunate feelings can be used as driving forces behind your projects. Take care not to get lost in the clouds and keep your feet on the ground.

Jupiter in the houses

Jupiter in 1st House

The placement of Jupiter in your first house bestows you with the generous and benevolent qualities the greater benefic is known for. Many times you over spend on payday, buying rounds at the bar after work. If you have Jupiter in a fire sign here you will be highly athletic and competitive. You project yourself forcefully, and your direct approach can intimidate others. Once you get going you don't stop until completion. You're a generally good natured person, and through this energetic attitude you acquire many friends. The confidence you have in your abilities makes you a good leader, although some will take offense to this high level of self-esteem. Some will even think of you as conceded. Chances are they're right. There may be a tendency to take on a larger than life attitude. Unfortunately, this can lead to addictions, over eating, and gambling problems. Although Jupiter rarely produces negative energy, he is known to cause problems by over doing the fun stuff in life "Live in moderation" is the philosophy you will need to learn most.

Jupiter in 2nd House

If you have Jupiter in your second house, financial stability will come through hard work and effort, along with a little luck. Money should come easily through various endeavors as long you can maintain responsibility and sensibleness. If aspected by Uranus work can come through highly unusual means. This can also show you have to travel long distances for your job. Because of all your stuff, a tiny apartment won't suit you and a house or storage space is needed. You inspire trust in others and may benefit from receiving financial assistance from them in order to develop your visionary business ideas. You must guard against self- indulgence and over-extravagance. Weight issues later in life are certain because of your desire for rich, sweet food and desserts. If Jupiter is in Taurus in this house you will identify your self-worth based on your material possessions. The relationship Jupiter has with Venus is the most influential in your second house. Her positioning can indicate how efficiently you use material resources within your relationships.

Jupiter in 3rd House

Jupiter in your house of communications is great for intelligence, curiosity, and aptitude. You're philosophical, optimistic, and probe deeply into every subject which sparks your interest. This positioning expands and broadens your mind, enabling you to learn and understand easily. It can also indicate a large family with lots of cousins or siblings. You should get involved in any occupation requiring large amounts of education. This may take you a while to achieve, but after a few stints at different universities you'll eventually get your certificate. Gemini is the ruling sign and the planet Mercury rules as well, Jupiter's relationship with it will be important. Good aspects will magnify your brilliance, while bad aspects will hinder your intellectual growth. If closely aligned with several other planets nervousness, anxiety and even schizophrenia may be the result. Possibly unbeknownst to you, most of your philosophical beliefs are produced through your vacations and experiences into different cultures. Rather than gain your education completely from texts, what you see around the world changes your views much more than printed words.

Jupiter in 4th House

If you have Jupiter in the fourth House, you're extremely generous and caring, but mostly towards your family. Emotions run high with the giant planet, and if Jupiter is placed in a water sign you become a huge teddy bear. Your love for others will know no bounds, and friends will be accumulated quickly because of this affable nature. Prosperity usually increases in your later years. The powers of Jupiter are slower moving in this house of watery emotions. When things don't pan out as quickly as anticipated you may sulk for a little while, but it will be your eternal optimism that pulls you through. You will feel a deep connection with your home and living partners. Heart break is huge for you. Thing will hit you more emotionally than most. The relationship you have with your mother will play a profound part of your life. With Jupiter well-aspected, you should consider things carefully before moving from home. You will experience severe home sickness when away for an extended time. The relationship Jupiter has with the Moon is Very important while in the fourth house. If there are good aspects then you will experience the happier side of this positioning. If not, you won't.

Jupiter in 5th House

The fifth house is the house of recreations and amusement with Jupiter being quite comfortable here. Sports, games, and gambling will definitely excite you. You're generally a thrill seeker, taking on many Leo traits and sometimes being overly boisterous and arrogant, thinking you simply can't fail. You're affectionate towards children and wish to have as many connections as possible. Because you're so enthusiastic about passing on your knowledge to the younger generation your stories are entertaining and educational at the same time. You would make an excellent teacher. Teaching allows your soul to reconnect with your childhood years. You show children the attention you wish you had gotten as a child. There is an intense desire to make a significant contribution through your creative self-expression. Guard against excessive gambling and speculative investments. This can also indicate a large family of children, not necessarily yours though. Over indulgence with food, gambling, and alcohol definite and must be consumed in moderation.

Jupiter in 6th House

Mercury and Virgo are very influential towards Jupiter in this house. Being the house of health and organization many things are possible with this placement. Any physical problems are usually caused by extravagance and over-indulgence, whether it's food, alcohol, or whatever. Hypochondria and obsessive compulsive disorder are possible as well. You posses a desire to play a major role in your business, and won't settle for second best. If you're not careful you will get too comfortable too soon and wear out your welcome. You may not want to be the boss, but the high ranking superior is right up your ally. This placement allows you to see the limited resources around you. Wasting your money, food, or possessions is ridiculous to you and you may cling to things tightly. You inspire cooperation and good will among your fellow workers and can sometimes try too much. It will be important for to realize that not everyone gets along and you shouldn't try and force it. Some people will consider you a "know it all" because you eagerly tell people how they can better their lives. Teaching, social work, or medicine should be considered as careers. Sometimes this can indicate a catastrophic injury or an illness which is difficult to diagnose and treat.

Jupiter in 7th House

If you have Jupiter in the seventh house, opportunities, wealth, and spirituality may come through marriage. You absolutely hate being alone and only close relationships will ease your mental anxieties. Chances are several relationships will come and go until you finally get married. Because this can make you believe a perfect partner is out there you may suffer multiple divorces as well. You seek a partner who can expand your visions and broaden your horizons. You're generally fair balanced and equal, as well as good at getting all the information before you make a decision. You also think kindly of those less fortunate than you and would be suited for a career as a social worker. Your partner should deepen your faith and strengthen your values. If Jupiter is badly aspected in your natal chart, then your partner may be somewhat lazy, and self-indulgent and you will allow them to rule your life. This may also signify several extravagant marriages. Ending with you gaining large amounts of wealth from a marriage.

Jupiter in 8th House

The house of death and regeneration is one of the less fortunate positions for Jupiter. It usually indicates you must undergo a great spiritual transformation related to the death of a loved one. It may be a parent, a best friend, or possibly a lover. Either way you will be traumatically affected by the passing of someone close. This isn't a chart killer, and you shouldn't be too nervous about this placement, just realize the potential for a catastrophe. Despite this, you're still optimistic and have faith in society. If poorly aspected by Uranus you may die in an unusual fashion. You have an interest in the occult and metaphysical field. Holistic medicines are a good idea for you to study. Your psychic abilities allow you to see through the phoniness of others. You have good judgment of character. If aspected by Neptune you will find great personal satisfaction with a profession in the spiritual realm of society. Unfortunately you may experience more death than most, possible using your experiences and becoming a grief counselor. The passing of a loved one will hit you especially hard. In older age mental illnesses such as Alzheimer's and dementia are possible.

Jupiter in 9th House

Being the fact he and the sign Sagittarius rule this section of your chart, Jupiter in the ninth house is the most wonderful placement for it. As the most comfortable position for this beneficial planet, it usually indicates an interest in higher education. Because you know your success is affected by how much intelligence you possess, you're in constant search of something which can teach you something new. Having the ability to use your resources effectively and efficiently success naturally is one of your greatest assets. Your only failures occur when you over look your actual capabilities and can't follow through. You're highly energetic and feel you can never fail. This positioning sometimes suggests you seek your higher education abroad. ou enjoy taking trips to far exotic places because of the broadened cultural philosophies you develop. Your judgment will be good and your mind open. You never stop education and are highly observant, learning a lot from your friends and social contacts. If Uranus is aspecting Jupiter here you can be insanely lucky, winning at cards, slot machines, and any other speculative endeavor. Play the slots and lottery on your lucky day and you may retire early because of your winnings.

Jupiter in 10th House

Jupiter in your tenth house inspires your desire to be recognized through your career or education. You have a driving force pushing you towards the spotlight and the head of your line. Chances are you eventually succeed at whatever you set your mind to. Not always is this because of hard work and determination as luck will play a role in propelling you forwards. You seem to know just the right people, or be in the right place and the right time. Your magnetic personality draws people towards you, just be careful who you allow into your personal inner circle. Despite all

378

the positive things that are stimulated by Jupiter positioned in your tenth house you may become so obsessed with public recognition that you turn away and alienate your long lasting friends in order to rise into public prominence. At its worst this makes you an obsessed workaholic. If this is close to your mid-heaven then a career in acting or politics is likely. It may also indicate you achieve an extremely prestigious degree from a very prestigious institution.

Jupiter in 11th House

An eleventh house positioning bestows you with the desire to break free from any normal routine and procedures which are placed before you. Any barriers or restrictions will simply be ignored or conquered. You must be allowed to think and act according to your own will and desires. This can prove direly fateful if drugs and alcohol come into your life. You probably have lots of friends who you're willing to do almost anything for you. You're a major player in your circle of friends and love having their attention. Don't get caught up with the wrong crowd. Being drawn to the less fortunate is a way to boost your own ego, but it doesn't do anything productive for your economic status. Amongst your friends you don't enjoy standing idly by. People may find you nosey and there may be a tendency to get too involved in other people's business. Stay away from gossip. You feel that your friends are a reflection of yourself and they are. More often than not this is a wonder placement that give you an extremely optimistic outlook on life. Part of the reason for your success is the gigantic dreams between your ears, despite your inability to follow through. Failure is because you have overestimated your abilities and resources.

Jupiter in 12th House

With Jupiter in the house of sorrow and unseen undoing you have an intense desire to learn about the spiritual world. You're deeply connected to your subconscious mind and understand things which are usually unexplainable. Higher realms of learning and philosophy are imbedded into your brain, and you're extremely inquisitive about all there is to know. Some people don't believe things when they are told, others believe them once they are taught, but you're one of the few who understands naturally. Vivid, sometimes prophetic dreams will fill your sleep causing insomnia and sleep disorders. When you wake up it will be difficult to remember the difference between dream and reality. The compassion and kindness towards others may be your final undoing. Because you see others as the same this can lead you into the wrong crowd of people. Not because you desire to get caught up in their mischief, but because you want to help them towards a better path of life. Stay away from drugs and alcohol as there is a highly addictive tendency with your personality. You have a vast conception of the world, to you there is more to life than meets the eye. With an ability to understand complex philosophies metaphysical an interest in religion, astrology or the occult will stimulate your curiosity.

Saturn in the houses

Saturn in 1st House

     If Saturn is placed in your first house you're hardworking and responsible. You take yourself seriously, and usually need a chill pill. Public recognition for your education or career is very important. Several of your personality traits are similar to your father's, and you may even follow in the same profession. Most times you're slow to warm up, and calculate every move carefully. This ensures your opponent doesn't get an upper hand with more knowledge about you. Your job comes first on your list of responsibilities, and many times you become a workaholic who forgets about commitments to your loved ones. Unless Mars or Uranus is negatively aspecting you will be a law abiding citizen. Following the rules is easy, and wandering from the normal beaten path usually out of the question. Methods which are tried and true are your preferred style. Success is achieved by your own hard work, and you don't expect anyone to give you anything. Depression sets in as you slowly realize nothing is easy. Sometimes the world seems against you. You work day in and day out getting relatively nowhere. Saturn always sees the miniscule inadequacies and makes them into mountains.

Saturn in 2nd House

The house Saturn is placed indicates the area of life you take the most seriously. When it's stationed in the second house this makes your material possessions and home life very important. Feeling a sense of personal security through the admiration of others, you revel in the prominence money brings about. Having social gatherings in your home will be a great way to show your success to others. Although extremely positive house, this still indicates you have to be disciplined and work tirelessly to attain success. Responsibility and determination comes naturally, and this is recognizable by all of your success in your ventures. Friends frequently ask you for help knowing your opinions are educated and honest. You also have a bunch of stuff they want to use. Thinking you can accomplish more than is possible, you take on too much responsibility. Letting others use and lose your stuff is going to happen from time to time. The worst case scenario turns you into a workaholic. Then you become anxious when there's no time for yourself or family. Once you can realize the limitation of your skills there can be a harmonious balance of both work and personal life.

Saturn in 3rd House

The house placement of Saturn is extremely important, as it symbolizes the area of life you need to feel has the most structured foundation. The third house is more good than bad, but Saturn won't have much strength against the other planets. Your third house is an intellectual house which also rules your communication skills. Even though you can be talkative you're choosy as to whom you share deep conversation with. Saturn does a god job organizing your thoughts allowing you to focus on practical projects. Sometimes this can indicate you work with your siblings, or have to travel short distances for work. Ruler Mercury becomes the planet of importance in the third house. Positive aspects with him enhances your aptitude, while negative aspects won't make you dumb, but you won't know how to manifest your good ideas.

Saturn in 4th House

The house Saturn is positioned in indicates the area of our life that you take the most seriously. Here in the fourth house it's your home, family, and emotional structuring. You're usually a conservative traditionalist at heart, and enjoy the proven steadfast ways in romance, work, and friendship. Because you try and live up to picture perfection of what a family should be like, you're a determined and hardworking individual who goes to no end to provide for your family. You may even hold two or three jobs to provide for your loved ones. Accumulating possessions raises your unconscious security by knowing you have something to fall back on. The relationship Saturn is forming with the Moon will be important. Any serious afflictions will cause significant emotional tensions between your parents, especially your father. You often allow your partner to be the dominant force in the relationship. Because the thought of the unknown and unpredictable terrifies you, you feel taking abuse from a loved one is allowable because it will maintain the relationship. Because you're so slow to warm up to others, some will think of you as cold hearted and rude. Pay attention to how you converse with people, you may say something offensive unintentionally. More often than not this will show you're a stickler for family traditions. Like the Hank William's Jr. song, you become what your family molds you to and their influence on you is great, especially the ones who are older.

Saturn in 5th House

The fifth house is a very difficult place for Saturn. This is a house of flamboyance and creativity which Saturn despises. Don't mistake this as entirely bad, but it will take aspects from other planets to ease the tensions. Sometimes the laziness of Leo creeps into your perception of responsibility and you don't take your social duties seriously. Most times you feel underappreciated and unloved, causing severe depression. You take your romantic love affairs seriously and enjoy relationships which are stable and committed as long as you're in charge. Because of your serious attitude towards discipline this can make it difficult for you to relax and have fun. The exuberant Leo like fire produced by the fifth house directly conflicts with Saturn's desires to remain rigid and calculating. This will make you a stern parent and produce unnecessary tensions with your children. Many of these conflicts will be caused because of your inability to express how you're truly feeling towards them. Your personal interests will have a practical purpose in which you may eventually earn a living from. Rather than express your emotions with words and experiences you feel presents and gifts will suffice and take their place. Simply giving material items is no way to truly show someone you care. You will need to realize this in order to maintain a controlled chaos within your life.

Saturn in 6th House
　　　Saturn in the sixth house usually indicates physical limitations or ailments. Your diet needs to be watched, and your exercise routine needs to be regular. Generally this means at some point in your life you're forced to go through an injury or illness which is difficult to diagnose or treat. Whether it be an illness or injury, it will most definitely be significant. This positioning is not negative in all ways. It also instills you with responsibility and more importantly organization, around your workplace. Your supervisors eventually recognize your hard work and efforts, promoting you into roles of leadership and authority. It's your organizational skills that will give you a distinct advantage over your competitors. The knowledge of the little intricacies within the game also gives you an edge. You may also be a workaholic, alienating your friends and family for professional gains. This doesn't mean you don't care about them, just your profession is

very important and you are willing to concede personal relationships for it. If you're not careful you could become extremely paranoid, especially with hypochondria. When positively influenced by the other planets this positioning shows your compassion for others drives you to a profession in medicine or healing. Maybe consider a job in social services or nursing.

Saturn in 7th House

When Saturn is in your seventh house this usually indicates you wish to have a partner who is more responsible and possibly older than you are. This isn't one of the best houses for Saturn because the nit-picky Virgo traits can run rampant with Saturn's need for precision making you an obsessive, compulsive something. Despite your best effort it feels like all your relationships are binding and restrictive. It's the fear of responsibility which causes you to be cautious and reserved when starting a relationship. All too often you feel there is too much duty and hard work on your part. You need to find a partner who is hard working and someone you can be proud of. Once you finally do find someone you enjoy a straight laced and by the books relationship. Even with these unfortunate effects it is still difficult for you to separate from someone once they make a significant impact on you. It will be best to wait until you're older and more settled down before marriage and children. For women this may indicate you marry a "father figure" to fill the void left by yours. One of the most negative effects of this positioning is that poor aspects from other planets can destroy your relationship with your father. Because Saturn represents our father figures and the seventh house is our relationship house this position can be very extreme. It can make you completely detached or attached to your father or someone you look up to as one. Saturn's relationship with Venus will be extremely important. She is ruler here and aspects can make or break your personality.

Saturn in 8th House

The house Saturn is placed is the area of life you take the

most serious and responsibly. The eighth house is the house of marriage, sex, and resources gotten form others. Unless negatively aspected otherwise, you will not be happy until you're in a committed, orthodox relationship. Committed and devoted to your spouse once you're involved romantically. You like things straight laced, traditional, and by the books. This placement causes strain within the relationship to your father. He was never completely in your life as much as you desired and it devastated you. Unfortunately this can also indicate you lose your father early in life to death. It's probably likely that he will not see your children into their adulthood. Despite any unresolved issues between you and him his passing will affect your life tremendously. You may even receive a large inheritance from his estate. Not only does this affect the relationship your marriage and romantic pursuits are influenced as well. You will most likely get married more than once because your first spouse dies on you. The divorces will be bitter and many resentments will have to be resolved. The relationship Saturn has with Mars will be vitally important. Any negative aggressions will result in total sexual chaos.

Saturn in 9th House

Saturn in your ninth house shows an interest in traditional views and gives you a structured set religious principles. If spiritual philosophy isn't a dominant factor in your life then advanced education probably is. You understand knowledge is the key to success and how much you know will determine how far you'll go in life. You take your beliefs seriously and generally don't like to joke around about much of anything. Part of your thirst for intelligence is the admiration of others it can attract. As you establish yourself as a responsible adult you ingrain yourself into the opinions of others. Eventually those in power see your passion for greatness giving you more and more integral duties. Being known for your brain is just as important to you as anything. Because of your rigid opinions, you're relatively intolerant and overly critical of those whose beliefs are substantially different. Getting along with like-minded individuals is very easy, but when approached by those who are unusual the shell you go into is hard to get out of. Despite the flamboyance of ruling planet Jupiter, and the fire of Sagittarius adding a wonderful hint of inspiration, the overly cautious nature of Saturn is usually in direct conflict with these expressive energies. This can be a great indicator long careers in politics, law, or even the military.

Saturn in 10th House

Professional prestige is the simplest philosophy associated with this house placement of Saturn. This planet in your tenth house shows your ability to be self-reliant and the determination to remain that way. Not only is your career important, but the public's perception of it is as well. Because you're so dedicated to your chosen profession you often neglect the emotional and domestic aspects of life. It's vital you find a happy medium between your personal life and professional. Once your job invades your closest personal affairs the psychological stresses are very difficult to talk about. Sometimes you're the professional counselor who needs professional counseling. Saturn is most comfortable in the tenth house and his rulership reigns supreme here. Other planets will be dominated by Saturn and his restrictive characteristics will restrain the powers of which ever planet is associated. Positive alignments will allow you to accept these responsibilities, while poor ones will cause you to reject it completely. Working around the clock prevents you from maintaining contact with your family. Although you feel you're supporting them financially it's the emotional bond that's missing. Part of your rigidity is the environment in which you were raised. Chances are you parents were stricter than others and needed to control your life. Their dominance over you compels you to completely fall in line, or rebel. When you do choose to rebel make sure the bridges you burn aren't completely gone. In time you may want to forgive those who have harmed you and use those bridges again.

Saturn in 11th House

If you have Saturn in the eleventh house you have many acquaintances but only a few close friends, who are probably older. Many of your friendships will be related to work somehow. The relationships you make usually endure for many years and you cherish all of them. You're attracted to groups which have a serious or necessary purpose. Community service projects or even politics can serve as interesting endeavors for you. You feel a strong sense of duty and responsibility to the groups you become involved in. The tasks you do for any groups may receive very little personal recognition and may require hard work. In order to attain your goals and objectives, you have to be patient and willing to work hard. If your lessons are learned, the later part of life will offer greater rewards. You may feel you never fit in with the people or groups around you because of some perceived insecurity. In any case there may be issues regarding feeling different from others. This also gives you great aspiration in your professional career. If you're not careful you may think you are more valuable than you actually are.

Saturn in 12th House

The placement of Saturn in our charts shows the areas of life we take the most seriously, and experience the most restrictions. Because of the subconscious nature of the twelfth house, a Saturn placement here is very difficult to handle. When it's positioned like this it causes your subconscious to be resistant to change. You're extremely cautious and must precisely calculate everything every time. It's nearly impossible for you to realize where your responsibilities start and stop. Sometimes this can indicate accepting too much responsibility, and conversely, this can also make you completely objective to any social requirement. You know you possess a vast array of talents and resources, the problem you experience is you don't know where to direct them. Although you can be brilliantly intelligent, it's difficult to get past your set way of thinking. The creative imagination flowing through your head isn't allowed to project and release itself. Until you find some form of artistic expression you will never be happy. Many times this can indicate successful career in psychology, surgery, or medical research and development. Unfortunately this also shows serious psychological issues during your old age. There is most definitely a total psychological breakdown somewhere in your future, if not as a youngster then as an adult. You're dedicated to responsibility because deep inside you understand the need of planning for the future.

Uranus in the houses

Uranus in 1st House

When planets are positioned in your first house you display many of the qualities of that planet within your personality. Uranus positioned in this house makes you independent, eccentric, and innovative. Your personality is stimulating and exciting, with lots of energy to spare. The rebelliousness of Uranus also leads you down a path of your very own. It's pertinent you're allowed to do what you want and learn from your own mistakes. It's impossible to learn from your elders, and there isn't anything anyone can tell you that you don't already know. The reason for this complete lunacy is that it's very important you prove to yourself you can make it on your own. Being entirely independent is key in your life and you will react significantly if it is threatened. You hate being bound by restrictions and may even intentionally break the law from time to time. The high strung and nervous energy going along with this can make you agitated and restless. This will be especially true if you're forced in one place for too long. Attracting all sorts of people from all walks of life you electric personality can light up a room. The innovativeness provided along with your desire of freedom directs you down a path towards research and development, whether it's in the technological or medical fields.

Uranus in 2nd House

Uranus placed in your second house is one of the better

positioning because the second house represents material possessions, mainly things you own by yourself. Quite often this indicates you have an unusual home which is cluttered by all your random belongings. It may be organized, but there is still a consistent amount of clutter around the house. Sometimes this can indicate you experience a significant and sudden monetary gain or loss. A great effect of Uranus here is your ability to make money in a different fashion. An extremely unique profession is probably in store for you. Maybe you're born into wealth, or spontaneously come into money. It's also possible you work insanely hard and establish wealth all on your own. This particular house placement can make you an extreme hoarder, especially if Saturn or Venus are also in aspect.

Uranus in 3rd House

Uranus in your third house makes you insatiously curious and usually very smart. This is the part of your chart ruled by Mercury and associated with the sign of Gemini. Your restless mind inspires you to take many short trips to most random of places. Ice caverns, wilderness lookout towers, or deep sea diving will probably interest you. Part of your intelligence is the completely scatterbrained mind in between your ears. Because you're only interested in something for a short period you only gain enough knowledge to be moderately informed, then your ability to talk induces others to think you're smarter than you actually are. You can be quite the salesman at times. Whatever surroundings your parents raised you in once you break out on your own the path is completely different. Don't cut off your nose just to spite your face. At the worst this positioning of Uranus can show extreme mental disorders. Gemini is represented by the twins for a reason, and many times that is represented in your psychological makeup.

Uranus in 4th House

If you have Uranus in the fourth House, you experience an unsettled or unusual home or family conditions. If your childhood

389

upbringing was relatively normal then your adulthood home is going to be extremely different. These events usually happen quite unexpectedly, out of the blue. Your family heritage may be eccentric or unusual and family skeletons can appear. This position gives restlessness, perhaps with a desire to move often. Your parent(s) or your relationship with either parent may be unusual, which will affect you emotionally for good or otherwise. There will be many changes in your life, including different localities. You desire to remain free from commitments to either a home or a community. You may be unconventional and not interested in how others view you. More often than not this means your family is bat shit crazy or you have one family member who is completely nuts, usually your mother. If you were raised by a grandparent, aunt, or experienced the unfortunate death of a parent early, check the relationship of this planet to Mars and Saturn. Squares, oppositions, and the bigfoot/sasquatch squad will indicate the harsher effects of this positioning. Remember, Uranus is a generational planet and only acts as a catalyst of crazy and will only instigate the unexpected.

Uranus in 5th House

Few astrologers will argue that Uranus is the most unpredictable of all the planets, and its house placement is where you experience the most sudden changes or unusual experiences. The fifth house is a fire house associated with Leo and ruled by the Sun making this positioning much more volatile than others. You may have unusual children, unusual athleticism, or extraordinary creative abilities. A lot will depend on how the other planets are lining up. Leo is definitely one of the luckier signs and you may have a successful gambling career. Time your numbers right and you just may win the lottery or hit a jackpot at a casino. When tied down into a significant relationship you must have the freedom to pursue friendships elsewhere. Unfortunately this can indicate an extra marital affair once you do start to settle down. Speculation within your love life or your finances will eventually get you into trouble. You might have multiple children from multiple partners.

390

Uranus in 6th House

The sixth is one of the more neutral houses for Uranus. This is a house of organization, health, and work dedicated towards others. As the mutable Earth house, ruling Planet Mercury will play an important role in the condition of Uranus. You can be hyper organized and very nitpicky with minor details. Your attention to the seemingly unimportant nuances can distinguish you above the rest, and drive you crazy as well. One of your biggest pet peeves is when others aren't as organized or don't want to hear your opinion on how things should be done. Despite your erratic tendencies while on the job, you use your mind to effectively improve the conditions and processes whatever you're doing. You prefer work which is fast paced and has a lot of variety. You're a good employee although your energy level comes and goes in erratic spurts. Most times you're extremely impatient, and your hastiness may cause you to be victim of a strange injury occurring at work, this may also suggest that you experience and unusual disease or illness. Catastrophic injuries such as burns or crashes are also likely with this placement. This can also induce nervousness, anxiety, and paranoia. You will need to learn to relax in a quiet place alone to gather your thoughts and energies.

Uranus in 7th House

The seventh house is your house of personal relationships. Uranus is a planet of unexpectedness and eccentricity. The combination of the two is usually an interesting event. If you have Uranus in your seventh house shows you're attracted to people who possess a distinct individuality. Those from different ethnicities or upbringings fascinate you. From your job, to your social circle, to your romance, anything blending into a normal society just isn't for you. Dysfunction occurs in your relationships because you're so attracted to individuals who are completely opposite of you. Part of your desire for such connections is because you value independence and are drawn to those who do as well. Everywhere you go you need as much space and personal freedom as you can get. If your selected partner is overbearing and possessive this will simply not work. If you to try and force the square peg into the round hole you're going to be left broken hearted and down trodden. One of the biggest problems is this indicates that your attraction to others who are already taken, or you possess the flirtatious eye wandering about.

Uranus in 8th House

Uranus placed in your eighth house shows your powerful psychic abilities and your utter refusal to follow the crowd. You're extremely attracted to individuals as unique as you are and have unconventional beliefs about everything. As with all the generational planets the aspects formed with other planets are important, in this case Mars and Pluto. Severely negative afflictions may indicate you or your spouse dies in an unusual fashion, completely unexpectedly, or from a strange illness. Your clothes and possessions are as different as you are. The eighth house represents the underworld and seedier aspects of life. If poorly aligned with Saturn and Mars you may be a career criminal. Uranus positioned here can arouse your interest into the sexual side of human kind. You may have an extremely different sex life than most others, possibly even a porn star or stripper. Areas of sex therapy or marriage counseling will prove to be better outlets for you. You're obsessed about sex and death will serious skeletons in your closet which you will take to the grave. Close Venus alignments, especially when in retrograde, can arouse your interest in the same sex.

Uranus in 9th House

When Uranus is positioned in your ninth house your philosophies, ideas, personalities, are unorthodox and original. You possess a passion for unusual education and will travel to great lengths to get it. You're a highly energized, independent thinker who usually doesn't care what others believe. If this planet is close to your mid-heaven you probably have a job that is extremely unusual compared to most. This can also mean that you

392

have extensive travels around the globe, and possibly you study abroad, or travel for your profession. Uranus feels quite comfortable in the Sagittarius ruled ninth house. When Uranus is positioned like this and is aspected by other planets such as Neptune, Jupiter, or the Moon, will cause vivid and prophetic dreams. There are many portals from Earth into the spirit world and Uranus can easily find one from here. If you have such aspects, especially with the ruling planet of Jupiter, your mind is one of these mystical portals. Every human contains a universe within them. This is especially true for people like you. Your brain is much like the universe, creating sparks of imaginative life everywhere. The innovation skills of those with Uranus in their ninth house will drive us into the future of human existence. This is a very strong and influential placement, and it should not be taken lightly.

Uranus in 10th House

If you have Uranus in your tenth house you're a complete revolutionary who wishes to have nothing to do with a stable and conventional workplace. You're determined to make a name for yourself and mark your own personal stamp onto society. Not a conformer by any means, your desire for total independence definitely means you need to be self-employed. Any routine, uneventful, blue collar job is not for you. Because of your rebellious nature it's difficult for you to do what you are told. Despite what common sense says, you habitually do the opposite, just to do the opposite. Of course, this only leads to mistakes and misunderstandings with your co-workers. Until you can find a career where you can settle down into you experience constant, unexpected changes in your job. This may be from accidents, termination, or other opportunities spontaneously arising. Careers in electronics, teaching, or research and development, are suitable outlets for your needs. It can also indicate a stable position at unusual job, from an equipment manager for a professional sports team, to an aide for the white house there are endless professional possibilities with Uranus here, especially if Saturn is involved as well.

Uranus in 11th House

The house in which Uranus is placed is the area of life you will experience the most amount of sudden changes and unexpected events. When it's positioned in your eleventh house this has to do with your friends, social circles, and wishes for the future. This is the ruling house for Uranus and its influence will be extremely strong. You have a wide array of friends which will range from the craziest of loon bats to the most responsible businessman. Individuals who have a sense of personal uniqueness and rebelliousness appeal to you. A lot of your friends will come and go casually despite any efforts to maintain contact. This will also indicate major disruptions between you and friends from time to time. Any unfortunate terminations are necessary to rid yourself from individuals whose company has grown useless. Most times this will be an immature friend whom repeatedly refuses to refine themselves as they enter adulthood.

Uranus in 12th House

Uranus positioned in your twelfth house is very difficult because of the unconscious rulership the twelfth house posses. The rebelliousness of Uranus is imbedded deeply into your psyche and you must always establish yourself as different from everyone else. Usually this positioning isn't any good at all. Your innermost psychological complexion operates in a fashion others just don't understand. The condition of Uranus becomes vitally important because all alone house placement isn't very powerful. Positive alignments from the other planets will allow you to use your individuality properly, while severely poor aspects can indicate catastrophic consequences. If Uranus is in the sign of Pisces watch out for depression and mental illness. The major conjunction with Neptune during the early to middle 1990's cannot be overlooked when dealing with planet placement. There is a generation of people born with a planetary alignment not seen for centuries. Those born with both planets in this house are special, very, very,

394

special. Innovation and expansion into the holistic, psychic, magical, and mystical will be brought forth by you and your generation.

Neptune in the houses

Neptune in 1st House
   A first house Neptune makes you imaginative and dreamy, often not accepting reality for what it is. You're hypersensitive to the emotional state of the environment and others around you. The subconscious receptors in your brain easily absorb the unseen energies projected by others. Mob mentality will cause you to get carried away from time to time, especially when alcohol is involved. This jaded view of reality will also cause you to get taken advantage of by others. This is because you're so desperate to help those in need. Neptune's ultimate compassion naturally attracts you to unstable individuals. Many of your problems arise because you got too involved with the wrong person. Daydreaming and spending too much time in fantasy land can also be a problem. It's easy for you to avoid your problems by falling into your own happy place, relying on others help too often. The day to day pressures of the world cause severe stress and psychological breakdowns. It is extremely important to pay attention to your mental wellbeing. Take time alone for prayer and meditation. Religion is very important in the realm of Neptune. The house Neptune is placed in is usually the one where we experience the most disappointment and confusion. In the first house it makes it difficult for you to realize who you truly are. If you can't learn to be comfortable with yourself you are doomed to a life of heartbreak and failure. Accept your faults and accentuate your qualities and you will go far in life.

Neptune in 2nd House
   Historically, the house Neptune is placed in indicates the area of life you experience significant confusion and disappointment. When it's stationed in your second house this

gives you false perceptions of what you think you want materialistically. It's nearly impossible to figure out what you want, and obtaining it is just as difficult. After finally making a decision you want your possessions to artistically represent your personality. Consider making your own clothes or jewelry. Neptune has never been associated with sturdiness and this placement is no different. This planet simply adds flair and style to whatever it touches. Negative aspects from other planets make you unsure and insecure while positive influences allow you to express your artistic side naturally. The second house represents what we own and possess. Neptune embeds the vast spirituality of the universe into your brain, and once you get set into a philosophy you don't budge. In some cases this will show you decorate your house with religious artifacts and trinkets. Venus is the ruling planet of the second house making her partnership exceptionally important.

Neptune in 3rd House

Neptune placed in your third house is one of the more interesting positions for this planet. Because this house represents not only communications but sibling relationships there are several energies felt. Neptune is the least stable and is always modified by any other planet. Neptune is fantasy and the unconscious dreamland. Sometimes, this placement makes it difficult to manifest your imagination into reality. It will require stability from other planets for your creative endeavors to materialize and art projects actually finished. Interpersonally, you think you're saying one thing when really the message is jaded and backwards. No matter what, Neptune adds confusion to wherever area of life it's placed. Here, you're going to need to seek the opinion of knowledgeable others to get a broader spectrum. The effects of Neptune are always subtle and accentuate the other aspects. Those who don't have this planet prominent in their chart experience this like a casual summer breeze. Others will become day dreamers getting lost in the wondrous world around them.

Neptune in 4th House

The spiritual planet Neptune in the emotional fourth house can make you frustrated, confused, and insecure with your home and family life. In your mind you have idealize what you want things to look like, not what they actually are. Then you become extremely disappointed when it your high expectations aren't met. The truth is you have no idea what your emotions are, let alone how to identify with them. You don't know what you want, much less how to go about getting it. Neptune's positioning here will attract you towards areas of spirituality, religion, and philosophy, especially when surrounded by family. Perhaps you grew up in an organized church, and have stuck with your beliefs. Possibly, you don't experience personal spirituality until later in your adult life. Either way, until you can establish a meditative connection between your current consciousness and your inner sub consciousness then you will never be happy. If the Moon is involved in any way you will be imaginative, creative, and psychic. Be careful who you choose to let into your home, you are susceptible to deception and fraud.

Neptune in 5th House

When Neptune is in your fifth house you have a natural flair for the dramatic and enjoy being in the spotlight. Loving the role of entertainer and story teller, the attention from others gives you a sense of fulfillment and personal satisfaction. Sporadic and sometimes chaotic love affairs will come and go throughout your years. Your creative abilities are indescribable, and you definitely develop your own sense of style. This fifth house represents creative expression and Neptune loves adding beauty to art. You experience significant confusion in all your romantic affairs. In most matters of love you're a damsel in distress waiting to be swept off your feet. If you don't find an outlet for your imagination you will eventually suffer severe depression or nervous breakdowns. Children are represented by the fifth house and Neptune here may make you children different and artistic. This can also cause mental disorders in the later stages in life.

Alzheimer's and bi polarity will have to be closely monitored. The Sun's relationships to Neptune will be the indicator of how readily you accept your creative self.

Neptune in 6th House

Neptune in your sixth house usually indicates you experience an unusual health issue sometime during your life. Whether it's an abstract illness or something just difficult to diagnose, your health is considerably affected be Neptune's placement here. Sometimes it shows you're careless and lazy when attending to your physical needs. Your compassion for others may lead you into a profession within the health care or social service areas. If you can tolerate the time and effort needed, your natural psychic abilities would make you an excellent psychologist. You absorb the energies of others like a sponge and can see their true inner emotions. Not only are you sensitive to the feelings of others, but yours are hurt easily as well. Slander around the workplace is especially hurtful. Because you feel that everyone in the office should be friends, and when others don't feel the same you're astonished. It's difficult for you to make business decisions on your own because you see all the possible paths you can take and none of the possible pitfalls. Going down one path prevents you from traveling another. Neptune positioned here can cause you to completely change careers much like a mid-life crisis.

Neptune in 7th House

Neptune in your seventh house generally means you have idealistic yet diluted views about marriage and all other relationships. You seek a partner who can help you grow not only emotionally, but spiritually as well. As the house ruler, Venus will have a significant impact on the condition of Neptune. Squares and oppositions will induce you into unfavorable relationships while trines and sextiles indicate you know how to integrate your imagination into your personal connections. Because you psychically detect the inner feelings of your spouse you expect them to do the same. Communication then breaks down due to your inability to fully express your intentions. Neptune is never a planet of strength and courage. This planet cowardly looks the other way simply repeating lies until the thought becomes reality. The balancing scales of Libra cause you to think everything must be equal in all your dealings, and you feel bad when you unfairly receive more than others. Even when you work hard for your accomplishments you still sympathize with those who don't have as many advantages.

Neptune in 8th House

Because of its psychic and sexual nature, the eighth house is one of the more difficult placements for Neptune. You're confused about what you're attracted to and what possessions you wish to acquire throughout life. This is a house representing shared ownership and the material side of all your relationships. Neptune produces imagination and creativity. These are two qualities you place on a pedestal when choosing a partner. Almost always your delusional approach to love causes you to fall for the wrong people, over and over again. Relationships suffer because you can't determine what you want your partner to do for you and what they want you to do for them. When severely afflicted by other planets this can show you put yourself into an abusive relationship hoping to relieve that person of their problems. Neptune is never a personal planet all by itself and its influence is always modified by the other planets. The basic nature of this house placement imbeds the magnificent world of Neptune deep into your psyche. You can be exceptionally artistic and creative because your mind is able to separate itself from reality and receive multiple unseen signals from the universe.

Neptune in 9th House

The ninth house is the fiery spirit house ruled by Jupiter and the sign of Sagittarius. Here, Neptune becomes the very meaning of spiritual inspiration and it definitely has its positive and negative effects. On the good side it provides you with a greater sense of the universe and the expansive philosophies along with it. The difficulty arises when you become so overinflated about your opinions everyone gets tired of you talking about them. If you want to spout out a bunch of religious views go become a preacher. Your idealistic views make you so optimistic you fail to see the upcoming road blocks. It isn't until the problem is directly above your head until your notice something is wrong. Other than Venus, Neptune is the most oblivious planet in the solar system. Here it jades your views on education and religion. The energies of Neptune are very subtle, and if this planet isn't prominent in your chart the energies are rarely noticeable. Traveling to distant lands will provide the most eye opening and life changing experiences. Actually experiencing the cultures of other people allows you to broaden your horizons and sense of spirituality. Deep meditation and reflection will also allow you to experience higher planes of human existence, but once again, the condition of Neptune will determine just how far you can escape into wonderland.

Neptune in 10th House

Neptune positioned in your tenth house is one of the more grounding places it can be. It doesn't do much for your creative abilities, but it does keep your imagination somewhere here on Earth. What this placement does do is allow you the business minded ambitions to use your imagination and creative abilities professionally. This will require other aspects from other planets to indicate a career. All by itself Neptune is out in left field wondering what is going on. The worst problem is your inability to place your finger on what you want to do for a living. Sometimes this means you bounce around from pointless job to pointless job, never attaining an actual career. Because of this you accept positions you're not qualified for and fail despite your best efforts. What you should do is find a job helping others or in the religious sector. Neptune is pure sympathy and the Capricorn ruled tenth house is the meaning of hardened emotion. The obliviousness of Neptune doesn't allow you to clearly see where your social responsibilities are, yet you possess a sense of duty to humanity. Unless there is fire elsewhere you don't have the drive to start a project on your own.

Neptune in 11th House

The house Neptune is positioned in indicates where you're frustrated by the most deception and confusion. When in the eleventh you have spiritual views about how you think life is and how you wish to bring that to your friends. Your desire to inspire others makes you a wonderful counselor, coach, or psychiatrist. The social circle you associate with can run from businessman to homeless man. At its worst this placement makes you think everyone is open to all your spiritual beliefs. It can also confuse you as to who is friend and who is foe. Because of your sincere compassion every time a friend asks for help you say yes, sometimes grudgingly so. You do this so often they eventually assume you're going to agree, when you decide you're not interested they think something is wrong and the drama starts. It's imperative you choose your friends wisely. This already unstable planet is even easier to influence, especially when heavily afflicted by Saturn, Uranus, or Mars. At its worst this distorts your visions of higher aspirations, making you completely confused about what you desire out of life. Quite often Neptune placed here shows you hold and office within your church or religious sect.

Neptune in 12th House

With Neptune in your twelfth house you're psychic to the very meaning of the term. You may not accept or develop your abilities, but you are. Like any muscle in our body the psychic intuition can also be developed, and this intuitive process allows you to read into the emotions and motives of others without them needing to explain. Neptune is in his ruling house and you unconsciously feel the deep expansiveness of the universe. You understand life is nothing but a speck of dust and in the greater scheme of things life is meaningless. These visions of deluded reality cause depression and can turn you into a recluse. Here Neptune becomes the ultimate humanitarian. Deep inside you genuinely want to help everyone in need and will go through personal disparity to help. This routine of abuse dwindles away the resources left for you. If Venus is negatively involved this means an extra marital affair will greatly affect your life.

Pluto in the houses

Pluto in 1st House

Pluto in your first house makes you feel indestructible and unopposable. Nothing is ever allowed to stand in your way, and you have the ability to bounce back from any negative situation. Your personality is obsessive, possessive, and jealous. You think everything lasts forever and are shocked when it doesn't. The deep belief in something greater than yourself will allow faith and spirituality to be significant factors in your life. You're extremely confident and strong willed, you can be a dominate force in anything you do. Pluto, along with any other planets in your first house, project full force into your personality. You wish to break down the systems of old and create something newer and better in its place. With a fascination into the occult, you readily absorb any knowledge you can attain into the dark world. Be careful as how far into it you go. The rabbit hole into the underworld is deep and psychologically destructive. You may not like what you find there. If negatively aspected by other planets this can cause severe trust and self-confidence issues.

Pluto in 2nd House

If Pluto is in your second house aspects to Venus will be very important. The environment in which you live influences your moods intensely. If your surroundings are cluttered and messy, your personal life will reflect it. The reason this is so influencing is because your home is where you must unwind and gather your thoughts. Whether you meditate or not, being alone in your home allows the energies produced by the objects around you to alter your mood and feelings. As Pluto is the slowest moving planet the aspecting distance from your ascendant will be very important. This placement also allows you to earn a living on your own and will stop at nothing to do so. Seeing how your material possessions will benefit your future, you stick all your resources into them. Maybe you become an artist or spiritualist, working for yourself in some odd form of occupation. You stop at nothing to achieve your goals, and must overcome great obstacles in order to achieve them Perhaps you go through a nasty divorce, make a bad investment, or have a catastrophe strike. No matter what is thrown at you nothing can keep you down. Unless poorly aspected by other planets you will conquer whatever mountain you set to climb.

Pluto in 3rd House

Pluto in your third house provides you with an inspired and probing mind. The more intricate workings of technology and science interest you. Once something has your attention you learn as much as you can about it. Psychic and intuitive powers allow you see into people's true motives and you aren't always fooled easy. In conversation you enjoy talking about magical, spiritual, and religious matters. Your mind is quick, sharp, and versatile. Advanced concepts of higher philosophy and spirituality come naturally to you. Deep within your own subconscious you understand the vast emptiness of the universe. The psychic connection you possess with the spirit world allows you to communicate with it easily. Vivid and prophetic dreams are likely. If Mercury is involved these dreams are definite. Talking about your emotional hang ups will be necessary for you to vent pent up frustrations. A close sibling or relative is the one you will confide in, probably a sister. At its worse the bipolar schizophrenic characteristics of Gemini make you mentally unstable and highly volatile. Hopefully you have calming influences from elsewhere.

Pluto in 4th House

Having Pluto in your fourth house intensifies the emotional bond you establish with your childhood and home life along with a maternal figure. It may not have been your mother but there was one female who distinctly sticks out amongst the rest. Whether functional or not, the influence of your parents is strong. If your upbringing was less than fortunate, the traumas endured will seem more painful than they actually are. Don't repress any negative emotions, because this will only cause your temper to become explosive and possibly violent. Jealousy and possessiveness are also traits associated with this alignment. Professional counseling shouldn't be instantaneously rejected. You deeply desire a loving, comfortable, family and will go to great lengths to establish solid roots. The relationship with Venus will show if you're going to be the abuser of the perpetrator. If this means staying in a harmful relationship you will do it just for the sake of saving yourself from heart break. Despite the efforts put forward, the competition for power between you and your spouse cause the most tensions. Your obsession for control makes sharing authority extremely difficult. This can also indicate your mother was very controlling in your early life.

Pluto in 5th House

When Pluto is in your fifth house you're amazingly creative and possess an enhanced imagination. You have an interest in almost everything unusual and provocative, especially games. Taking on the traits of the ruling sign Leo, the relationship Pluto has with the Sun is very important. When negatively afflicted this produces severe psychological turmoil. It will be nearly impossible to forgive those who have harmed you. Responsibility tends to be put aside with this placement as well. This house represents recreation and amusement. If you can divert your attention and talents into tangible endeavors, making a living around the games you love is entirely possible. When you find a legitimate career it's probably in the entertainment field. In romantic affairs you enjoy being the dominant one with most of the control. Afflictions from Mars and Saturn will make you physically violent to your loved ones. If you place too much of your emphasis on the sexual side of your marriage then you will miss out on all the other aspects of the bond. Pluto is a very jealous and possessive planet. The ruling planet of the Sun will also be a good indicator of how you handle Pluto's intensity If Pluto isn't dominant in your chart his energies are only felt through progressions and transits.

Pluto in 6th House

When Pluto is positioned in your sixth house indicates you're going to experience a significant personal transformation in your work place, through an illness, or severe physical injury. Surgeries and hospital visits are to be expected. The situation will be entirely dependent on the relationship between Pluto and the other planets. Psychologically you become obsessed with facts, numbers, and organization. Your dedication to precision is the most beneficial factor with this placement. The Virgo influence makes you very compassionate and perhaps you become involved in large scale charity or social work. You would make a great officer holder, probably the treasurer. The desire to probe deeper into human behavior would make areas of psychology or psychiatry excellent career choices as well. If Pluto is slightly afflicted you may be hypercritical and condescending to others without noticing it. Pluto doesn't really like the refinement Virgo influence, as his nature is very combustible. Severely negative influences will produce deep rooted psychological problems. You may develop obsessive compulsive disorder, possibly even schizophrenia or dementia as you grow older.

Pluto in 7th House

Pluto in your seventh house indicates the desire for control and power within all your relationships. Whether it be a romantic relationship, or a close friendship, you must have most of the authority. Generally attracted to those you can dominate, when someone close finally stands their ground you become astonished they question your authority. Selecting your partner will be difficult. Your inability to give in and cooperate will be the cause of most of your marital issues. Unless you can find someone willing to submit to your demands, the combative atmosphere produced will never last. Instead select someone who will challenge you to realize new personal spirituality and resources. Once you do find that special someone you are passionately

405

committed, and require that they are the same. The elegant style of the ruling sign Libra will give you the desire for a clean living environment. Positive influences will make you charming and socially refined with the desire for large groups of friends and casual acquaintances.

Pluto in 8th House

Pluto feels right at home here in its ruling section and its influences are exceptionally strong when in your eighth house. You naturally realize the universe is a gigantic realm of magic and there are forces out there which are greater than you. Your curious mind wants to know everything about everything. You possess intense moments if intuition and foresight, and many times you will see something happen before it does. The fascination you have with the deeper realms of human nature may propel you into professions involving death, spirituality, or medicine. The compassionate and understanding signals you unconsciously project would make you and excellent psychologist. Despite whatever your beliefs, your psychic abilities allow you to read into others very well. Sometimes this can indicate difficulties over an inheritance or divorce settlement. In business this may show the financial turmoil needed to transform you into something better. Pluto can be an obsessive and jealous planet. You may demand complete control and dominance in your marriage. If you become a power tripping asshole, karma will get you good.

Pluto in 9th House

Due to Pluto being one of the generational planets its house placement is just as important as sign when analyzing his influence. The ruling planet of whichever sign and house placement will be the two most influential planets. The ninth house is ruled by the planet Jupiter and the sign of Sagittarius. Because Jupiter is one of the slower moving personal planets it's alignments with Pluto aren't as frequent as most, making their relationship much more profound. If Jupiter is closely aspecting Pluto here, especially by conjunction, this will make you brilliantly smart, and naturally able to grasp difficult concepts. This house has relations with higher forms of education, philosophy, and religion. Pluto has a way of making you intently obsessed with something, and in this case knowledge may be it. The Sagittarian influence may make you intent on constantly traveling to different lands. It's very difficult for you to stay in one place very long because eventually you become bogged down by what you consider mundane routine. Career wise this is a great starting point for psychologists and doctors. If Saturn is close to your mid-heaven law and politics if Saturn is involved or close to your mid-heaven.

Pluto in 10th House

In the tenth house Pluto is directly influencing your career and higher forms of education. This can give you an interest in religion, medicine, or psychology. You really enjoy working behind the scenes and would rather stay out of the spotlight when it comes to work. Many times those with this in their charts will experience complete and total career changes later in life. You work hard to reach a certain point, but once getting there you realize it wasn't really what you wanted. Then you have a spark of interest into something else and you make the professional swap. If you can get a job in the medical field somewhere it will suit you well for a while. Your final interests will be in the religious or philosophic areas and possibly even the occult. If you do not make this switch it will cause severe psychological anxiety. Aspects to Saturn will have a profound influence on Pluto in this house. The driving ambition caused by Saturn will lead you on a long difficult path into the unknown. At some point in time you will be faced with an unchangeable, life altering decision regarding education. In fact, you may face several. Make sure to take time alone in meditation to set your consciousness straight. This can make you a psychological train wreck if you don't take care of yourself.

Pluto in 11th House

Pluto in your eleventh house shows incredible loyalty to your friends, associates, and the groups you're a part of. You desire

407

intense personal bonds, and can become somewhat of an idealist. Many friends will come and go throughout your life, and you'll discover as you grow and mature so does your circle of friends. Anyone who doesn't have high expectations for themselves has no place around you. Groups and organizations always play a significant role in your life. If you choose to associate yourself with one your desire for power will propel you into a role of leadership. Your passions run high and you can seem obsessive and out of control at times. It will be important for you to divert your attention into other projects. This may also distract you from your normal everyday responsibilities. Negative afflictions from Saturn or Mars will intensify your lust for control and authority. This can also indicate the ruthless tactics you are capable of using in your quest for power. The relationship Pluto has with Uranus and Saturn will be important. His alignment with those two can dictate if your passions are directed towards good or evil.

Pluto in 12th House

Pluto in the twelfth house is one of the most powerful placements for the distant dwarf. The twelfth house represents realms of inner subconscious, hidden enemies, and personal self undoing. This placement gives you intense dreams and powerful psychic abilities. You're able to tap into unknown creative resources deeply locked in your mind. When things get into your psyche they completely destroy you. You truly are your own worst enemy. You're very secretive about yourself, and refuse to give up more information than necessary. However, you do wish to obtain as much knowledge about someone else that you can. This can be anything from casual gossip, to the most personal skeletons in the closet. Heaven forbid anyone talk about what's in your closet. Pluto is the champion of obsession and his powers in this house are ingrained into your habitual reactions. You experience many devastating setbacks because of your lack of ability to see the effects of your behavior on your environment around you. Psychic to the very sense of the word, you're highly intuitive and pick up on the unconscious signals that we all project. The closer to the ascendant this takes place the more powerful the effects will be. Pluto's energies are very possessive and obsessive. The biggest problem with Pluto here is when there are several harsh aspects aligned with it. Any squares or oppositions can be psychological train wreckers. Professional help may be needed.

Bibliography

Hand, Robert. Planets in transit: Life Cycles for Living. Atglen, PA. Schiffer Publishing 1976&2001.

MacArthur study Bible: Nashville TN. Word Publishing 1997

Oken, Alan. Complete Guide to Astrology: Berwick, ME. Micolas-Hays, Inc.

Pelletier, Robert. Planets in aspect: Understanding Your Inner Dynamics. Gloucester, MA. Nimrod press 1974

Schulman, Martin. Karmic Astrology: Samuel Weiser, Inc. York Beach, ME 1975

Woolfolk, Joanna. The only Astrology Book You'll Ever Need: Lanham, MD. Taylor Publishing
1982&2006

Back ground for cover obtained from NASA public domain photos. www.NASA.gov